THE
SEASONS

THE SEASONS

Ten Memorable Years in Baseball,
and in America

• • •

BILL GILBERT

Author of *The Duke of Flatbush*

Foreword by Larry King

CITADEL PRESS
Kensington Publishing Corp.
www.kensingtonbooks.com

CITADEL PRESS BOOKS are published by

Kensington Publishing Corp.
850 Third Avenue
New York, NY 10022

All Kensington titles, imprints, and distributed lines are available at special quantity discounts for bulk purchases for sales promotions, premiums, fund-raising, educational, or institutional use. Special book excerpts or customized printings can also be created to fit specific needs. For details, write or phone the office of the Kensington special sales manager: Kensington Publishing Corp., 850 Third Avenue, New York, NY 10022, attn: Special Sales Department, phone: 1-800-221-2647.

CITADEL PRESS and the Citadel logo are Reg. U.S. Pat. & TM Off.

Designed by Leonard Telesca

First Printing: March 2003
First paperback printing: February 2004

10 9 8 7 6 5 4 3 2 1

Printed in the United States of America

Library of Congress Control Number: 2002113398

ISBN 0-8065-2420-0

To the rest of the Gilbert team—Lillian, Dave, and Katy—for their research assistance and computer services as well as for their interest and support

Whoever wants to know the heart and mind of America had better learn baseball.

—Jacques Barzun, French-born American educator, author, and historian

Contents

Foreword: In Brooklyn and Everywhere by Larry King   xi

Introduction: Baseball and America—History's Partners   xiii

Some Thank-yous   xv

PART ONE: 1945   **1**

   1. The Forgotten Pennant Race   3
   2. "They're Either Too Young or Too Old"   11
   3. A Beginning and an End   20
   4. The Cast of Characters   26
   5. "The Best Thing You Could Do"   34

PART TWO: 1948   **51**

   6. The Good Years   53
   7. The Drama and Babe Ruth   66
   8. Final Scores   78

PART THREE: 1951   **93**

   9. "The Giants Is Dead"   95
   10. Quietly Going Mad   106

PART FOUR: 1961   **123**

   11. Three New Frontiers   125

• Contents •

12. Another International Crisis — 137
13. "I Can't Handle This . . ." — 147
14. When Mirrors Weren't Enough — 156

PART FIVE: 1969 — **161**

15. *Those* Mets? — 163
16. Centennials and the Impossible Dream — 173

PART SIX: 1975 — **189**

17. "The American People Were Not Rejoicing" — 191
18. The Greatest World Series Ever Played? — 201

PART SEVEN: 1980 — **211**

19. Crises — 213
20. Center Stage — 227

PART EIGHT: 1995 — **235**

21. Baseball's Second Savior — 237
22. "The Streak" — 245
23. Two of a Kind — 254

PART NINE: 1998 — **263**

24. Expecting the Unexpected — 265
25. "Like a Fairy Tale" — 274
26. "Para Ti, Mami!" — 283
27. "Get Up, Baby! Get Up! Get Up!" — 294

PART TEN: 2001 — **303**

28. First Confusion, Then War — 305
29. Farewells — 316
30. Shelters, Shadows, and Cheers — 323
31. History's Partners, Again — 335

Bibliography — 349

Index — 351

Foreword

In Brooklyn and Everywhere
• • •

by Larry King

I feel sorry for anyone who isn't a baseball fan. This book shows you why.

I've always wanted to know everything that is going on in the world around me, even when I was a kid in Brooklyn. My world consisted of the Dodgers first—then came other things like school, chores around our apartment, and other activities of lesser importance. Duke Snider, Jackie Robinson, Pee Wee Reese, Roy Campanella, and the rest were the most important people in my life, and not just in mine. Everyone in Brooklyn seemed to feel the same way.

And not just in Brooklyn. All over the country, in major league cities and those with minor league teams, and in towns with no professional teams at all, baseball was an integral part of our lives, interwoven into the American fabric through our daily newspapers and the magic of radio and then television.

Just how much baseball has been a part of life in America is reflected in these pages. Bill Gilbert draws a vivid picture of the unmistakable and unbreakable connection between the two over the past almost sixty years, starting with 1945 and continuing to this day. Almost inevitably, as Bill's book proves, a special year in baseball has been paralleled by a special year in America.

From the first year in this book to the present, baseball and America have gone hand in hand, starting with the grand slam by Hank Greenberg that won the American League pennant for the Detroit Tigers on the final day of the 1945 season in the first days of peace after World War II. It extends to 1998, when the whole world stopped to follow Mark

McGwire's pursuit of Roger Maris, and again only three years later, in 2001, when Barry Bonds topped McGwire with his own storybook season as Americans struggled to cope with the newest threat to our way of life—terrorism.

My only complaint about this book is that Bill insisted on including the 1951 season, when Bobby Thomson hit his "shot heard 'round the world" to defeat my Dodgers for the National League pennant. More than fifty years later, it still hurts, but the full story of 1951—including what else was happening on the home front as we began a new war, the one in Korea—is included because Bill's books, as his readers know, are always complete accounts.

I've been a Bill Gilbert fan for twenty-five years. This book is the latest reason. I love baseball and America as much as he does. That's why I love this book, and it's why you will too.

Introduction

Baseball and America—
History's Partners
• • •

1945 . . . 1948 . . . 1951 . . . 1961 . . . 1969 . . . 1975 . . . 1980 . . . 1995 . . . 1998 . . . 2001.

These years stand out for good reason—because they remain among the most memorable seasons in baseball history, and in American history as well. They didn't necessarily have the greatest teams and maybe some other seasons were even greater, but they were outstanding because the players and their teams in these years wrote history. They did it by putting on some of the most exciting baseball dramas, staging the greatest individual accomplishments, and writing some of the indelible chapters in the history of their sport—heart-pounding pennant races, Bobby Thomson's "shot heard 'round the world," Roger Maris and Mickey Mantle chasing Babe Ruth, and then Mark McGwire and Sammy Sosa chasing them, the "Amazin' Mets," Cal Ripken's streak that was longer than Lou Gehrig's, and Barry Bonds as he broke McGwire's record that people thought would last forever.

In these same years, other people in other endeavors were writing lasting stories of their own in America's history books: victory in World War II, the Berlin Airlift, Harry Truman's upset victory over Thomas Dewey, the war in Korea, the landing on the moon, another war—this one in Vietnam—and heroes responding to the terrorist attacks against the World Trade Center and the Pentagon and in a field in Pennsylvania in 2001.

Americans wrote history in those years, and so did baseball players as the nation and her national pastime became partners in history. This is the story of ten memorable seasons of that partnership—in baseball, and in America.

Some Thank-yous

• • •

Various people deserve special mention for their assistance in the extensive work required in the preparation of this book. Those who rendered valuable help include

Bob Shuman, senior editor at Citadel Press

Jeremie Ruby-Strauss, senior editor at Citadel Press

Pat Kelly, director of the photograph collection at the National Baseball Hall of Fame and Museum in Cooperstown, New York

Bill Burdick, photo services manager at the Baseball Hall of Fame

Russell Wolinsky and Rachael Kepner, research assistants at the Hall of Fame's A. Bartlett Giamatti Research Center

Linda Casey Poepsel, assistant to President George H.W. Bush

Bob Costas of NBC Sports

Kay Reller of Bob Costas's St. Louis office

Greg Schwalenberg, curator of the Babe Ruth Birthplace and Museum in Baltimore

Bill Deane, for fact checking the baseball data in these pages

Marvin Kranz, presidential scholar at the Library of Congress

Carol Petretti of the ABC photography department

Alan Shepard's daughters—Laura S. Churchley, Alice Wackermann, and Juliana S. Jenkins

Lynden Steele, White House photo editor

Wendy Nipper, executive assistant to the director of the White House Office of Media Affairs

Peggy Appleman, photo librarian of the Martin Luther King, Jr., library in Washington, D.C.

Col. Ken Herman and Col. Gail Halvorsen, veterans of the Berlin Airlift

John Correll, editor of *Air Force Magazine*

Gwyn Pitman, administrative assistant in the photo department of the National Aeronautics and Space Administration

Noel J. Francisco, associate counsel to the President

Bryan Reilly, photo editor of Photo File, Inc.

The major league baseball players who have shared their thoughts and experiences with me over the years also deserve special mention, especially Duke Snider, Bob Feller, Dom DiMaggio, Tommy Henrich, Ted Williams, Carl Warwick, Johnny Pesky, Carl Erskine, Brooks Robinson, Bert Shepard, Harmon Killebrew, and Mickey Vernon.

All of them made their own contributions to the seasons described in these pages and to these years in American life. For that, they have my gratitude and my respect.

PART ONE

. . .

1945

1

The Forgotten Pennant Race

One of the most exciting pennant races in the history of baseball has been long overlooked in any discussion of memorable seasons. Maybe that's because it was overshadowed from the start. It happened in 1945, and when spring training started, the biggest stories weren't coming from training camps in Florida and Arizona, for two good reasons:

1. The biggest news of the day was being made not on baseball fields but on battlefields, in Europe and the Pacific in the climactic days of World War II.
2. The baseball teams weren't in Florida and Arizona anyhow. They were restricted to sites close to their cities because of the wartime ban against unnecessary travel.

It was the fourth and final year of America's involvement in World War II, and everything was different. By then, more than five hundred major league baseball players and four thousand minor leaguers were in the armed forces. Baseball was being played by men who were declared 4-F—physically unfit—and those too young or too old for military service.

That baseball was being played at all was thanks to no less than the president of the United States himself—Franklin Roosevelt. The former manager of his prep school team, FDR encouraged baseball to continue with whatever manpower it could assemble during the war. Baseball's first commissioner, Judge Kenesaw Mountain Landis, wrote to Roosevelt in the first weeks after Pearl Harbor and asked for guidance from the White House. He asked Roosevelt, "What do you want it to do? . . . If you feel we ought to continue, we would be delighted to do so. We await your order."

FDR answered promptly on January 15, one month and eight days after Pearl Harbor, saying, "I honestly feel that it would be best for the country to keep baseball going." He encouraged Landis to schedule more night games, still a novelty in those years. "I hope," he wrote, "that night games can be extended because it gives an opportunity to the day shift to see a game occasionally."

Roosevelt made it clear at the same time that professional players, either major leaguers or those in the minors, would not be treated any differently from anyone else when it came to military obligations. "As to the players themselves," he wrote to Landis, "I know you agree with me that

President Franklin Roosevelt, the manager of his prep school baseball team, throws out the first pitch to open the 1937 baseball season at Griffith Stadium in Washington, flanked by owner Clark Griffith of the Washington Senators *(on the president's right)*, and owner-manager Connie Mack of the Philadelphia A's. Next to Mack is the Senators' manager, Bucky Harris. The president did not appear at an opener during World War II. Instead, substitutes performed the honors. (© *The Washington Post.* Courtesy the Washington, D.C., Public Library.)

THE WHITE HOUSE
WASHINGTON

January 15, 1942.

My dear Judge:-

Thank you for yours of January fourteenth. As
you will, of course, realize the final decision about the
baseball season must rest with you and the Baseball Club
owners -- so what I am going to say is solely a personal
and not an official point of view.

I honestly feel that it would be best for the
country to keep baseball going. There will be fewer people
unemployed and everybody will work longer hours and harder
than ever before.

And that means that they ought to have a
chance for recreation and for taking their minds off
their work even more than before.

Baseball provides a recreation which does
not last over two hours or two hours and a half, and
which can be got for very little cost. And, incidentally,
I hope that night games can be extended because it gives
an opportunity to the day shift to see a game occasionally.

As to the players themselves, I know you agree
with me that individual players who are of active military
or naval age should go, without question, into the services.
Even if the actual quality of the teams is lowered by the
greater use of older players, this will not dampen the
popularity of the sport. Of course, if any individual
has some particular aptitude in a trade or profession,
he ought to serve the Government. That, however, is a
matter which I know you can handle with complete justice.

Here is another way of looking at it -- if
300 teams use 5,000 or 6,000 players, these players are
a definite recreational asset to at least 20,000,000
of their fellow citizens -- and that in my judgment is
thoroughly worthwhile.

With every best wish,

Very sincerely yours,

Franklin D Roosevelt

Hon. Kenesaw M. Landis,
333 North Michigan Avenue,
Chicago,
Illinois.

President Roosevelt's "green light letter" to Baseball Commissioner Kenesaw Mountain Landis, giving baseball the go-ahead to continue play during World War II. The letter was written only five weeks after Pearl Harbor. (Courtesy of the National Baseball Hall of Fame Library, Cooperstown, N.Y.)

individual players who are of active military or naval age should go, without question, into the services. Even if the actual quality of the teams is lowered by the greater use of older players, this will not dampen the popularity of the sport."

Historians have called it "the green light letter" that gave baseball the go-ahead to play during the war, even though Roosevelt never used that term in his letter. While so doing, they have credited Judge Landis with saving baseball for "the duration," but the late Shirley Povich of *The Washington Post* insisted in later years that they were wrong.

FDR was a frequent visitor to Washington's Griffith Stadium, and not just on Opening Day. He told Clark Griffith, the owner of the Washington Nats—short for Nationals before they started calling themselves the Senators—that he considered himself the team's mascot because he always seemed to bring them good luck. A friendship developed between the two, and as international tensions grew more severe, Griffith told Povich he simply mentioned to the President that baseball should be allowed to continue if war broke out. He said it would be good for the morale of the people on the home front.

The fan in the White House agreed enthusiastically. Povich, the prize-winning and Hall of Fame columnist for the *Post* for seventy-five years until his death in 1998 and the father of TV's Maury Povich, told me in later years that by the time Landis sent his letter Griffith had already paved the way for the green light.

Besides, Griffith told Povich, Landis couldn't have saved baseball with Roosevelt, and he probably couldn't have saved anything else with him, either. Landis bitterly opposed FDR's decision to run for a third term in 1940. When Roosevelt became the only person to serve more than two terms as president, Landis was not reluctant to voice his opinion of Roosevelt. The President, exceptional politician that he was, had good sources of information—he knew what Landis was saying about him.

For these reasons, Griffith told Povich, "Landis wasn't much more welcome at the White House than the Japanese ambassador."

If Griffith was the man who saved baseball for America in 1942, then what happened in 1945 was a fitting reward for him, one that almost became even more special.

By that time, the fourth year of America's participation in World War II, everything was different. In baseball, such stars as Ted Williams, Joe

The first commissioner of baseball, Kenesaw Mountain Landis, in a typical Opening Day pose. The stern expression on his face was also typical. (Courtesy of the National Baseball Hall of Fame Library, Cooperstown, N.Y.)

DiMaggio, Bob Feller, Johnny Mize, and Stan Musial were serving all over the world. Americans—women as well as men—were still going away to war by the millions. The number reached twelve million before it was all over.

Rationing—the government-imposed limits on all kinds of food, clothing, and other essentials—was still in effect, and anything that wasn't rationed wasn't available anyhow. When you went to the grocery store, you made sure you carried your "ration book" with little stamps that you had to give to the salesclerk if you wanted to buy sugar. That was at the start of the war. By the time 1945 arrived, the list of rationed items had grown to include meat, butter, fats, oils, canned foods, gasoline, even shoes.

Appliances and other products of metal hadn't been seen in America's stores since the start of the war. Plumbing fixtures, flashlights, batteries, garbage cans, even heaters in those days of coal and oil heat almost did not exist. The same was true for toasters, coffee percolators, waffle irons, vacuum cleaners, and irons for pressing clothes. Few of these items could be bought.

The nation's secretaries couldn't look forward to getting new type-writers. The government was getting them. If someone died, the family had to hope it could find a casket. The manufacture of toys was sharply reduced. Hearing aids became scarce, and if you needed a new tube of toothpaste, you had to turn in your old one. Spare parts for automobiles were hard to find. New automobiles were a thing of the past; no new cars were manufactured for four years after the 1942 model. When the 1946 models joined the nation's aging automobile fleet in the first full year of peace, they rolled off the same assembly lines that had been producing tanks, warships, and airplanes during the war years.

Gasoline was rationed. Car owners were limited to four gallons a week, which were later cut to three, but the station attendant still pumped your gas, washed your windshield and checked your oil, all at no charge. In 1942 the government banned all pleasure driving and established a national speed limit of forty miles an hour as America's "victory speed." By December of the same year, the limit was reduced to thirty-five miles an hour. But the milkman still delivered milk to your door—in quart bottles—and the newsboy was able to continue tossing the paper onto your front porch every morning and afternoon because he rode a bike.

Victory gardens sprouted up on every spare piece of ground—back-yards, open fields, the courthouse square—as the government encouraged Americans everywhere to grow their own vegetables so the crops from the farms could go to feed our troops. Polio epidemics every summer were still paralyzing and killing far too many Americans, especially kids.

The sight of American flags that appeared overnight from out of nowhere in the hours following the terrorist attacks against the World Trade Center and the Pentagon in 2001 were replays of the scenes in 1945, when flags flew from buildings of every kind—offices, schools, private homes. Flags of a different design—blue stars against a white background of satin with a red border and gold trim—hung in the windows of millions of American homes, each star representing one family member in the armed forces. If you saw a flag with a gold star instead of a blue one, you knew a member of that family had given his last full measure of devotion. Newspapers were still publishing a "casualty list" on the front page every day with the names of the latest hometown boys who had been reported killed in action, wounded, or missing.

Patriotism was reflected in theaters as well. The one o'clock matinee, the first movie of the day, was always preceded by the playing of our National Anthem, accompanied by a film of a waving American flag on the screen. Everyone stood at attention in the dark.

The Declaration of Independence and the Constitution were secretly moved from their usual display cases in the National Archives on Pennsylvania Avenue in Washington to an undisclosed location. Librarian of Congress Archibald MacLeish transferred the sacred documents to "places of greater security" after the attack on Pearl Harbor, along with the library's copy of the Gutenberg Bible and one of its three copies of the Magna Carta.

Air raid drills were still commonplace, with everyone clearing the streets and taking shelter inside, as practice for that dreaded time when America's cities might be the targets of enemy bombers. After dark each night, when we turned the lights on in our homes, the light was concealed by "blackout curtains," solid shades of dark green that blocked the light in and kept America's cities dark, another measure to guard against an enemy attack by air.

Americans were still singing "God Bless America" in 1945, a big hit throughout the war since Kate Smith, one of the most popular singers of that time, had introduced it with her robust soprano voice in 1938. It had been written by a Russian immigrant, Irving Berlin, for his World War I show, "Yip, Yip, Yaphank," about his life as an Army sergeant at a camp in New Jersey. Berlin, who became one of the most acclaimed composers in American history even though he had no musical training and only two years of schooling, never published his song. He had forgotten about it until Kate Smith asked him for a patriotic song as the war clouds darkened over Europe near the end of the 1930s. The song became a smash hit overnight, just as it did all over again in 2001.

Baseball, as it always seems to do, was a mirror of America in those years of World War II. The wave of patriotism could be seen in the crowds at the ballparks. They formed seas of military uniforms—khakis for the Army, the Air Corps, and the Marines; blues and whites for the Navy, the Coast Guard, and the Merchant Marines. The players took 10 percent of their salaries in war bonds to help pay for the war. And if a player hit a foul ball into the stands, you threw it back onto the field be-cause you knew it would be shipped to military camps for recreational use by "our boys in uniform." Any fan who tried to stuff a foul ball into his pocket would get booed unmercifully.

A growing feeling of optimism prevailed in America as 1944 turned into 1945. In New York, some 750,000 people ignored rain and fog and crowded their way into Times Square, almost as big a crowd as before the war. Thousands more attended church services. A Page One headline in *The New York Times* on January 1, 1945, said: NEW YEAR GREETED WITH HOPE AND JOY BY CITY'S MILLIONS.

The article below it said, "As if anxious to speed the departing mem-ory of another year of war, New York's millions saw 1944 out last night with few backward looks . . ."

Lucy Monroe, a fixture at Yankee Stadium singing the National Anthem before World Series games, "was scarcely audible" above the other 750,000 voices as she sang "The Star-Spangled Banner" from a platform in front of a tall replica of the Statue of Liberty.

The familiar and traditional lighted globe descended ever so slowly from the Times Tower to street level, continuing the tradition begun in 1908 but suspended with the start of the war. The newspaper said the ball was "relighted this year as a measure of confidence that it would remain lighted from now on through victory and peace."

The electronic message that still snakes its way around the Times Building with the headlines of the moment and is so familiar to New Yorkers and tourists alike carried a message this time, instead of head-lines:

Work for victory. It is now twelve o'clock. The New Year is here. Let us make it a year of victory. Let us each pledge ourselves to get on with the job so that those we love may soon be home with us again.

2

"They're Either Too Young or Too Old"

The Page One banner in the newspapers of March 7 told Americans that the Russian army had captured five hundred towns in Germany in one day. On the other side of the world, "heavy fighting" was reported in the bloody battle for the strategically vital island of Iwo Jima, only 775 miles from the Japanese mainland. Baseball and America were linked there too. One of those killed in action was twenty-seven-year-old Harry O'Neill, a catcher for one game with the Philadelphia A's in 1939. Another major leaguer also sacrificed his life in World War II; he was also a twenty-seven-year-old who played in the Major Leagues in 1939. Elmer Gedeon, an outfielder with the Senators for five games, died on a battlefield in France a year earlier, five days after his birthday.

Something else important happened that day, something that gave Americans an escape from the war news: Spring training began. The wartime restriction against all unnecessary travel, in effect since the spring training season of 1943, limited all major league teams to distances declared by Commissioner Landis. He outlined them as "a sharply defined area in which they do their spring training, with the understanding each club would condition at home, or as close as possible, in the interest of curtailing rail travel."

Landis laid out specific boundaries—above the Mason-Dixon Line north of the Potomac and Ohio Rivers and east of the Mississippi, except for the two St. Louis teams, the Browns and the Cardinals. They were baseball's two westernmost teams until 1955, who could choose a location in Missouri, on the west side of the Mississippi. The Browns trained at Cape Girardeau, Missouri, but the Cards stayed east of the Mississippi, at Cairo, Illinois.

The commissioner went even further. He telescoped the season, reducing the number of trips each of the sixteen teams made to the other cities in its league from four a season to three, at the same time retaining the traditional 154-game schedule. He said the complete package would save five million miles of railroad travel.

Landis worked out his program with the director of the government's Office of Defense Transportation, Joseph B. Eastman. Eastman said he was "greatly pleased by the action baseball has taken." He added, "In these circumstances, the action which the Major Leagues have taken on their own initiative is most gratifying. It shows a real and keen appreciation of the very troublesome travel program which our country has under present war conditions, a problem which is bound to grow in difficulty and seriousness."

Instead of the longed-for spring training sojourn to sunny Florida and Arizona, with balmy breezes and swaying palm trees, the teams went to the other extreme. The two Boston teams—the Red Sox and the Braves—stayed in New England, a wartime sacrifice for any player in February and March. The Red Sox trained at Tufts College in Massachusetts, and the Braves went to Choate Prep School in Wallingford, Connecticut. Chicago's Cubs and White Sox went to a resort in French Lick, Indiana.

The New York Yankees trained at Asbury Park, New Jersey, instead of St. Petersburg, Florida. Their intra-city rivals, the Giants, prepared for the '45 season at Lakewood, New Jersey. The Brooklyn Dodgers endured the temperatures at Bear Mountain, New York, near West Point.

Lou Boudreau, the young player-manager of the Cleveland Indians, took his team to Lafayette, Indiana, the home of Purdue University. He got the Indians ready for each of the wartime seasons by putting the Indians through indoor workouts in a field house where the Boilermakers had "beautiful equipment."

As the fiftieth anniversary of the World War II years approached, Boudreau told me, "They dropped a huge net around us so we could practice the fundamentals—pickoff plays, rundowns, and so on. And we could take batting practice and not interfere with their physical education program."

The Washington Senators began spring training a week ahead of all the other teams, with only six players—four pitchers and two catchers. A

United Press story from New York reported that the Major Leagues were "still facing a definitely uncertain manpower outlook" and would begin spring training "with the smallest nucleus of players in modern times." UP said it was "no secret" that the majors would have "extremely tough sledding to survive their fourth wartime season."

One of the two catchers in the Senators camp on that first day of spring training was destined to be one of their unsung heroes that year. Rick Ferrell, a balding thirty-nine-year-old veteran of sixteen seasons in the majors already, with two more in his future, had something the Senators desperately needed in their starting catcher—the ability and the courage to catch baseball's most unpredictable pitch, the knuckleball. It's called "the butterfly pitch" because that's how it behaves, darting here and there on its way to the plate in a way that not even the pitcher who throws it can predict.

The Senators needed a catcher who could handle the knuckleball for four reasons: Dutch Leonard, Roger Wolff, Mickey Haefner, and Johnny Niggeling—four of their starting pitchers that year who were knuckle-ballers. With other catchers refusing to have anything to do with the knuckler because it was too hard to handle, resulting in too many passed balls charged against them, Ferrell was willing to call for the pitch and able to handle it. With that new sense of security, the four knuckleballers combined to account for sixty of Washington's eighty-seven victories in 1945, thanks to Ferrell.

The Senators may have been the most patriotic team of all if patriotism can be measured in miles. They trained in the Washington suburb of College Park, Maryland, the home of the University of Maryland, no more than ten miles out Route 1 from the center of town. At least two enterprising school kids in Washington took full advantage of the situation when the Senators trained in College Park. During Easter vacation—it wasn't called "spring break" then—they rode their bikes up and down the hills of suburban Washington to College Park to watch their heroes and get as many autographs as their books would hold. One of them was a tall, slender kid named Henry Fankhauser, who played first base for our sandlot team. I was the other one, the second baseman.

We were just entering our teens when we pedaled to Byrd Stadium on the University of Maryland campus in those years when kids' bikes didn't have gears. You got where you were going strictly on pedal power. We made the trips all-day excursions, making sure to pack our lunches. For me, it was always two Vienna sausage sandwiches, with plenty of mustard, and a pack of Twinkies. At the campus drugstore on the corner of Route 1 at the entrance to the university, we each bought a bottle of root beer and enjoyed our feast while talking enthusiastically about the Senators' morning workout and what we were looking forward to for that afternoon's fun and excitement.

We did that in 1944 and again in 1945, and in 1945 I scored a major triumph for any kid still only thirteen years old. I walked over to the entrance to the Senators' dressing room at lunchtime and boldly knocked on the door. A short, stocky, and swarthy man chomping on a cigar opened the door and growled, "Yeah? Whadda ya want?"

I answered hesitantly, "You—you—you don't need a batboy, do you?"

He shocked me by answering, again in a growl, "Yeah. Come on in."

Imagine that! I was a batboy—for a major league team! Just like that!

I held that envied position through the rest of the spring training season, for no pay except what we batboys could get by selling foul balls and cracked bats. Our duties included more than just being on the field. We had to shine the shoes of all the players and coaches—more than thirty pairs—every day. And as Opening Day approached, we were taken into town to Griffith Stadium, the field of our dreams, where we were given the privilege of scrubbing down the shower room walls to wash away the grime left from the Washington Redskins 1944 football season which ended four months earlier.

It was at spring training that I met a lefthanded pitcher from Indiana named Bert Shepard, who made baseball history by himself in 1945— and it didn't have anything to do with pitching a no-hitter, or how many games he won, or how many hitters he struck out. He did it by becoming the only man in history to play in the Major Leagues on an artificial leg. A minor league pitcher before the war, he had been shot down in his P-38 over Germany in 1944 and lost his right leg below the knee. He was a prisoner of war for eight months, until being released in the final months of the war.

Shepard was a patient at Walter Reed Hospital in Washington when Under-Secretary of War Robert Patterson came across him during a visit with amputees. When Patterson asked him what he wanted to do after the war, Shepard replied confidently, "I'm going to be a professional baseball player."

Patterson was surprised, so he asked, "You can't do that, can you?"

Shepard replied simply, "Why not? I did before the war."

Patterson telephoned Clark Griffith and asked if he could give Shepard a tryout. Griffith, a staunch patriot who raised funds and donated athletic equipment for America's fighting men in both world wars, readily agreed. With photographers and reporters watching Shepard's every move, he performed well enough—including fielding bunts—that the Senators signed him as a player-coach for the 1945 season.

In the dressing room I would watch as he would strap his artificial leg on before the workout and take it off after and hop on one foot into the shower. The baseball world was to hear more from Shepard in July and August.

As the 1945 season drew near, the manpower shortage gripping America, including baseball, was growing worse. It was the fourth year of America's participation in the war, and the number of able-bodied young men to serve in the armed forces was reflecting the drain. So was baseball, in still another example of how life in baseball so often reflects life in America.

A popular song in that war was the disappointment of a young maiden who complained:

> *They're either too young or too old.*
> *They're either too gray or too grassy green.*

If the manpower shortage was affecting young women that way, imagine what it was doing to businesses and entire industries, including baseball. The sport had a manpower shortage right from the start of the war. The St. Louis Cardinals, World Series champions in 1942 with an upset victory over the mighty Yankees of Joe DiMaggio, operated one of the sport's most successful farm systems until the war started. Before the 1943 season began, they were advertising in *The Sporting News*, which called itself "the baseball bible" in those years. Their ad was a call for minor league players. The Associated Press said it was "probably without precedent in the history of baseball."

The ad described openings on the Cardinals minor league teams. The Cardinals had already lost 265 minor league players to military service. Two minor league teams, the Memphis Chicks of the Southern Association and the Toledo Mud Hens of the International League, placed similar ads in the same paper. The Cardinals' owner, Sam Breadon, had a ready explanation for the ads. In a masterpiece of understatement, he said, "These are unusual times."

Jimmy Byrnes, the director of War Mobilization and Reconstruction and a future Secretary of State, compounded baseball's manpower problem early in 1945 by ordering that all draft deferments for professional athletes be reexamined. He poured oil on the fire by saying, "It is difficult for the public to understand, and certainly it is difficult for me to understand, how these men can be physically unfit for military service and yet be able to compete with the greatest athletes of the nation in games demanding physical fitness."

He said athletes could serve in noncombat positions in the military or work in war plants. Byrnes was obviously unaware that many baseball players were already doing that in the winter and some even in their spare time during the season. Some had been doing it since early in the war.

One of America's staunchest patriots of that time, FBI Director J. Edgar Hoover, disagreed with Byrnes. "If any ball players, or other athletes, were attempting to dodge the service," he said, "it would be our job to look into such cases. But our records show there are few, if any, such cases among the thousands of ball players."

Others who supported the players' position pointed out that many players in various sports had to undergo special treatment every day—massages, whirlpool baths, and heavily taped ankles. Some continued to reinjure key parts of their bodies such as their knees, arms, and shoulders. Lou Boudreau played all through the war on weak ankles aggravated by his career as a basketball star at the University of Illinois. During the war, he broke the same ankle three times. George Kell was born with bad knees and required frequent treatment to continue playing baseball.

Still, the hysteria in some quarters continued. One source was Senator William Langer of North Dakota, nicknamed—some said it was appropriate—"Wild Bill." Langer agreed with Byrnes and even introduced legislation requiring that 10 percent of the players on every major league team be men who had lost one *or more* arms, legs, or hands.

The War Department complied with the orders from Byrnes, and that's where the blatant discrimination came in. The Byrnes directive caused an entire group of young men to be reexamined and, in some cases, drafted, simply because they were professional athletes.

Ron Northey was one of the most shocking examples. He was a twenty-four-year-old outfielder for the Philadelphia Phillies who had been classified 4-F twice, the second time on January 2, 1945, not because he had one physical problem, but because he had three—a punctured eardrum, a heart condition, and high blood pressure.

Northey, who stood five feet ten inches tall and weighed 195 pounds, was coming off the best of his three seasons so far as a major leaguer. In '44 he had hit .288 with 22 home runs and 104 runs batted in. Two weeks after being turned down for the draft a second time, he was ordered to report for his third physical. In between times, he had tried to join the Navy but was turned down because of his punctured eardrum.

Due to the pressure from Byrnes, Langer, and others, Northey received orders to report for his third induction physical on January 29. He was sworn into the Army that same day and before nightfall was on his way to the Army induction center in New Cumberland, Pennsylvania. Fortunately, he lived to tell about it. Northey missed all of the 1945 season but returned in 1946 and was able to complete a twelve-year big-league career in 1957.

Criticism against the positions of Byrnes and Langer built rapidly. Prominent among those leading the opposition was one of Langer's colleagues in the Senate, Happy Chandler of Kentucky. A freshman congressman from Illinois, Melvin Price, also joined the fight against Byrnes and Langer. Price represented the district that included East St. Louis in Illinois, just across the Mississippi River from St. Louis and its Browns and Cardinals.

The Browns had a severe problem. With the 1945 spring training season scheduled to begin in only twelve days, they said they had signed only four players, two of them rookies. An article by the Associated Press reported, "The club's big problem is the national manpower muddle centering around the controversial 'work-or-fight-or-jail' legislation in Congress."

The AP said, "Many of the players are 4-F, but have been working in essential jobs. Some draft boards have warned men in essential industries if they quit they will be drafted regardless of physical condition or Congressional action."

With Senator Chandler, Congressman Price, and others turning up the heat, the War Department suspended its regulation in May. William Mead wrote in *Even the Browns* that the action came just in time to save two of the Senators' starting pitchers on their mostly-knuckleballer staff—Dutch Leonard and Mickey Haefner—plus outfielder Wally Moses of the White Sox and a promising pitcher for the Indians, Allie Reynolds. The good fortune of Leonard and Haefner in being able to continue their baseball careers had a profound effect on the American League pennant race that was beginning. Their teammate, center fielder Stan Spence, wasn't so lucky. After a banner season in 1944, when he hit .316, he was inducted into the service and missed all of 1945.

The Cardinals' poor fortunes continued. Before the War Department directive was canceled, two of their starters, catcher Walker Cooper and left fielder Danny Litwhiler, were also called back to take physical exams again, and this time they were inducted into the military. Cooper hit .318 in 1943 and only one point less in '44. Among the teammates he was leaving behind was his brother, Mort, a right-handed pitcher who had won forty-three games in the previous two seasons. Together, "the Brother Battery" had led the Cardinals to three straight World Series appearances, winning two of them.

An Associated Press story said there was "little doubt" that Walker was a major factor in guiding his team over the 100-victory mark in all three years of the war leading up to the 1945 season. Under Walker Cooper's leadership, the Cardinals won 106 games in 1942 and 105 in both 1943 and 1944, so his departure was a severe blow to the team.

Byrnes and Langer managed to accomplish something in 1945 that the entire National League couldn't—they snapped the Cardinals' streak of winning three straight pennants. They finished second. The big winner after it was over was Senator Chandler. He was named the new commissioner of baseball, succeeding Judge Landis, who had died the previous November.

The manpower shortage accelerated another change that the far-sighted could see coming—the integration of the Major Leagues. Big-league baseball had been a whites-only industry for the entire twentieth century, but the lack of adequate manpower to keep the big-league teams stocked with twenty-five players each was prompting some baseball executives to give more thought to an idea that had surfaced occasionally over the years—signing players from the Negro Leagues.

In 1945, a member of the Boston City Council, Isadore Muchnick, threatened to revoke the law permitting Sunday baseball games in Boston unless the Red Sox held tryouts for black players. He recruited the help of Wendell Smith, a respected writer for a minority paper, the *Pittsburgh Courier*, to line up the best prospects available.

Smith came up with two veteran players from the Negro Leagues—

second baseman Marvin Williams of the Philadelphia Stars and out-fielder Sam Jethroe of the Cleveland Buckeyes. The third player was a young lieutenant who had just been discharged from the Army and was a rookie shortstop with the Kansas City Monarchs in the Negro Leagues, playing for $500 a month. His name was Jackie Robinson.

The three received a tryout with the Red Sox on April 16. They were put through batting and fielding practice plus drills in running and throwing. All three filled out application cards at the request of the Red Sox. None of them ever heard from the team again.

3

A Beginning and an End

When the 1945 baseball season opened, it was against a backdrop of national mourning and national anticipation. President Roosevelt died on April 12, four days before the season was scheduled to start. At the same time, the Allies in Europe, under the command of Gen. Dwight D. Eisenhower, were rolling to what Roosevelt at the beginning of the war had set as the nation's goal—"the inevitable triumph."

Opening Day seemed to reflect the grief over FDR's death. It rained, and the Senators' opener was rained out. The Senators opened their season the next day on the road, in Philadelphia against the A's, the city to be tapped by fate in September. Their traditional home opener was held at Griffith Stadium on April 20 against the Yankees, after Washingtonians read at breakfast that U.S. fighter planes had just shot down 842 German planes in one day. In the Pacific, Americans had just about won the battle for Iwo Jima, but a bloody new one was beginning on another island Americans had never heard of called Okinawa.

President Truman, in office only eight days after succeeding President Roosevelt, wasn't at Griffith Stadium. The tradition of having the president throw out the first ball was still a wartime casualty. It was the fourth straight year that the Senators' opener was not a *presidential* opener. The Speaker of the House, Sam Rayburn of Texas, served as Truman's pinch hitter, flanked by Clark Griffith and the immortal Washington pitcher of earlier years, Walter Johnson.

Irony and symbolism showed up in Rayburn's toss. It was caught by one of Griffith's Cuban players, Sandy Ullrich, a twenty-three-year-old righthanded pitcher from Havana. Griffith was one of the pioneers in signing Latin players beginning as early as the 1930s. With the start of the war, he signed even more, mindful that they were exempt from the military draft. But then things changed, and the Latins were declared eligible for the draft. Many of them decided to stay in their native countries, mostly Cuba, but Ullrich—Carlos Santiago Castello Ullrich—was one of those who decided to take his chances and come north to play in the United States.

That baseball from Sam Rayburn wasn't Ullrich's only reward for coming to America to play baseball in 1945. He also got to win three games that year. He never pitched in the Major Leagues again.

Reporter Al Costello wrote in *The Washington Post* that the atmosphere in Griffith Stadium following Roosevelt's death was "almost eerie." The crowd observed a moment of silence. Then a bugler played "Taps," followed by the National Anthem, performed as always by Goldman's Band.

The Yankees won, 6–3, but Costello revealed a sense of awareness in his reporting of the day. He wrote, "The color of other years was missing . . . but it was baseball and Opening Day despite the lack of pomp and splendor that usually goes with openers. It was baseball despite the lack of the game's big names who are playing a bigger and more important game."

Catcher Mickey Owen, drafted into the armed forces from the Brooklyn Dodgers for most of the 1945 season, told me in later years that Americans weren't afraid of the future by 1945. "People were a little different then," he said. "We had just come out of the Depression and been through some hard knocks, so as far as anything scaring them was concerned, it didn't. Their whole attitude was toughened by the Depression."

The fortunes of war played a decisive role in each wartime season, because how well a team did depended on how it fared in the military draft. The St. Louis Browns finished in sixth place in the eight-team American League in 1943. In 1944, damaged less by the military draft than other teams, they won the only pennant in their history. In 1945, they dropped to third. The Washington Senators finished second in 1943, last in '44, and were contenders for the pennant in '45. Other teams experienced the same yo-yo ups and downs, depending on how hard they were hit by the draft from one season to the next.

The Tigers finished in fifth place in 1943, only two wins above .500, then came within one game of winning the pennant in 1944, losing out to the Browns after finishing twenty-two wins above .500. At the start of the 1945 season, the Tigers had no reason to imagine that they were destined to be the stars of a second straight storybook season. But this time, the Senators, not the Browns, were the co-stars.

As the baseball season was beginning, the war in Europe was ending. With the season less than a month old, V-E Day—Victory in Europe—arrived. General Eisenhower, as supreme commander of all Allied forces in Europe, signed the surrender treaty at his headquarters in Reims, France. Mindful of the battles still being fought against the Japanese in the Pacific, Eisenhower told those around him the score was "one war down, one to go."

President Truman made the dramatic announcement in Washington, simultaneously with a similar announcement in London made by Great Britain's wartime leader, Prime Minister Winston Churchill. The date was May 8, Truman's sixty-first birthday and his twenty-sixth day in office.

On that day, the Chicago White Sox were leading the American League by a half game over the Yankees. By the end of the season, Chicago would be in the World Series—the Chicago *Cubs* in the National League. The New York Giants, led by their player-manager, Mel Ott, were the hottest team in either league. They won twenty-five of their first thirty-two games, the best start in the National League in twenty-five years. On V-E Day, they were leading the Dodgers by two and a half games.

Two weeks after Memorial Day, the first star to rejoin his team during the 1945 season came home—Hank Greenberg of Detroit. His return reversed the question that had affected every team throughout the war. Instead of wondering which teams would be most affected by the military draft, the question became which teams would be helped most by players returning from military duty. Detroit would be helped by Greenberg's return more than anyone could imagine.

Greenberg, a captain in the army, was discharged on June 15 after duty in the China-Burma-India—C-B-I—Theatre of Operations with the 20th Bomber Command. He came home with the Presidential Unit Citation and four battle stars. The writers and broadcasters called him "Hammerin' Hank" and for good reason. He hit 331 home runs in his career and had already led the league in homers three times before the war, including 58 in 1938.

His return to the Tigers in 1945 came just in time. Detroit was in first place, but only by a half game over the Yankees and four games ahead of the Boston Red Sox. The Browns and White Sox were a half game behind Boston. The Senators were in sixth place, five and a half games behind.

Whitney Martin of the Associated Press saw Greenberg as almost an experiment for his fellow players. Martin wrote that Greenberg "will be watched as a symbol of hope to all the other ball players in the service who fear their absence from the game might impair their effectiveness and money-earning capacity. He is in the nature of a test case, the answer to the question: Can the Major League stars in the service come back?"

Greenberg was thirty-four years old by then, but he lost no time in answering Martin's question. On July 1, he made his return in the first game of a doubleheader against the Philadelphia A's. The A's were in last place that year, but the fans showed up at Detroit's Briggs Stadium in impressive numbers—47,729 of them—to welcome and salute their returning hero.

Greenberg went hitless in his first three trips to the plate. In his fourth time up, against a wartime lefthander named Charlie Gassaway, Greenberg hit a home run over the left field wall.

The day after Greenberg's discharge from the Army, the hero of the war in Europe—General Eisenhower—came home too. He was greeted by a mob of a million flag-waving hero-worshipers in Washington, including my mother and me, who got to crowd our way onto the curb in the front row on K Street, then Washington's "Little Wall Street," at its intersection with Fifteenth Street N.W. After his welcome home parade and a visit to the White House, where President Truman awarded him with an oak leaf cluster to his Distinguished Service Medal, a visit to General Pershing, his World War I counterpart and an address to the Congress, Eisenhower went up to New York—and to a baseball game.

Seven million New Yorkers turned out, two million of them at City Hall. Then it was on to one of the real purposes of his visit—a game between the Giants and the Boston Braves at the Polo Grounds. That was no surprise to anyone who knew Eisenhower. He was one of baseball's biggest fans. He had played the sport in a semipro league back home in Kansas and as a freshman at West Point until he injured his knee. In later years, America's thirty-fourth president told a story that reflected his love of baseball and his ambition in his boyhood days:

When I was a boy growing up in Kansas, a friend of mine and I went fishing, and as we sat there in the warmth of a summer afternoon on a riverbank, we talked about what we wanted to do when we grew up. I told him I wanted to be a real Major League baseball player, a genuine professional like Honus Wagner. My friend said he'd like to be president of the United States.

Neither of us got our wish.

While the Tigers were rejoicing over Greenberg's return, the Chicago Cubs had cause for rejoicing too. The Giants were cooling off, and the Cubs were heating up—with one stretch of twenty-six victories in thirty games. Suddenly they were serious contenders for the National League pennant. The year before, they had finished thirty games out of first place. Their drastic improvement in the standings was another reflection of the ups and downs of wartime baseball.

The Cubs were winning despite a drop-off from 1944 by their star slugger, outfielder Bill Nicholson. He was called "Swish" because of his powerful lefthanded swing, and he led the National League in home runs in 1943 with twenty-nine and again in 1944 with thirty-three. On Opening Day of the 1945 season, he gave promise of another league-leading year by hitting the first home run of the major league season, against Ted Wilks of the Cardinals at Wrigley Field.

The rest of the season was just the opposite kind of experience for Nicholson. His batting average dropped 44 points from the year before, to .243, and his home run total plunged to thirteen. Instead, the Cubs offense came from a batting order of five solid hitters, headed by first baseman Phil Cavarretta, who led the league with a .355 average. Third baseman Stan Hack hit .323, and second baseman Don Johnson hit .302. Centerfielder Andy Pafko just missed .300 with a .298 average, and left fielder Peanuts Lowrey hit .282.

Chicago's pitching staff was led by twenty-two-game winner Hank Wyse, followed by Claude Passeau's seventeen victories and sixteen wins from Paul Derringer. The record book shows that righthander Hank Borowy won eleven games for the Cubs that year, but the truth is he was a twenty-one-game winner. The Cubs bought Borowy from the Yankees on July 27 for $97,000. He had won ten games for New York and finished as a twenty-one-game winner overall. His success for the Cubs came as no surprise. He had already won fifteen, fourteen, and seventeen games for the Yankees in the first three years of his big-league career.

The Cubs' fans were taking extra delight in the success of Cavarretta. He was a hometown boy who had been deferred from military service because of a perforated eardrum suffered during an attack of spinal meningitis as a child. During a conversation a few years ago, Cavarretta offered special insights into the 1945 season and what it was like to be playing major league baseball in that last year of the war.

He said success in the big leagues that year wasn't as easy as popular opinion would have people believe. "That wasn't an easy season," he said. "Even though it was during the war, there were a lot of good players still around, and more were coming home from the war."

Travel conditions made playing difficult at times, too, according to Cavarretta. "The travel was harder," he said, "but we weren't complaining. We thought of the guys who were overseas."

The Cubs traveled by bus on some of their trips, such as from Philadelphia to New York, then over to Brooklyn. Players sat up all night on coach cars "quite a few times," he remembered, because Pullman sleepers were unavailable. "It was the least we could do as far as I was concerned," he said, "and a lot of other players felt the same way."

4

The Cast of Characters

The cast of characters who were keeping baseball alive for the American public and our men and women overseas was headed by several players who were characters indeed. One was a colorful pitcher for the Dodgers with one of baseball's most original names—Van Lingle Mungo. He was a six-foot two-inch righthander, the pride of Pageland, South Carolina, who played hard and drank hard. He won 120 games in fourteen big-league seasons, including a 14–7 record in 1945.

He wasn't afraid to voice his opinion. When one of his outfielders, Tom Winsett, missed a fly ball and cost him a win, Mungo trashed the Brooklyn clubhouse. Then he sent a telegram to his wife:

> Pack up your bags and come to Brooklyn, honey. If Winsett can play in the big leagues, it's a cinch you can, too.

His friends and neighbors back home in Pageland named a highway after him, but his biggest tribute may have been in the 1970s, when his name popped up again, this time in a song from a Dave Frishberg record album called *Oklahoma Toad*. The lyrics were simply the names of baseball players from Mungo's baseball career in the 1930s and 1940s. Lingle was his mother's maiden name, and the song was called simply "Van Lingle Mungo." It became a hit.

If Mungo had a temper, and he did, it was matched and maybe topped by Hal Newhouser's. Newhouser was one of the best pitchers in either league in the last two years of World War II and good enough after the war to be elected to the Hall of Fame in 1992. He was called "Prince Hal" because of his regal bearing when he pitched; he was an imposing, erect figure on the mound at six feet two inches and 180 pounds. Joe Falls, the sports editor of *The Detroit News,* described Newhouser as "a man of royalty, a man of high manner and morals." Falls wrote later, "He was leaner and meaner, a tremendous competitor, giving in to no man or team. They say his curveball made noise as it crackled across the plate."

Exempt from military service during the war because of a heart condition, Newhouser had been around since 1939, all that time with Detroit, his hometown, but he never won more than nine games. Then he met a catcher named Paul Richards, who had been traded to Detroit by the Philadelphia A's in 1943. Newhouser lost seventeen games that season, and, to his credit, he approached Richards and asked why he wasn't winning more games. Richards gave it to him straight, telling Newhouser he was "acting like a kid." He told Newhouser his teammates were fed up with his temper and his habit of blaming others for his losses.

Richards wasn't telling Newhouser anything he hadn't heard before. Everyone knew about the Newhouser temper, and he even advertised it with tantrums in the dugout and the clubhouse. Just before his election to the Hall of Fame in 1992, he told me about his habit of knocking out the lights in the tunnel from the Tigers' dugout to their clubhouse if he was lifted from a game.

"That was a ritual with me," he said. "I did it whenever I got knocked out. My teammates could always tell when I reached the clubhouse. They'd count the explosions."

With Richards convincing him to stay calm on the mound, Newhouser jumped his victory total from nine in '43 to twenty-nine in '44, leading both leagues in wins and strikeouts at the age of twenty-three. He topped both leagues again in '45 with twenty-five victories and became the only pitcher in history to win his league's Most Valuable Player award in two straight seasons. In '46, with the prewar stars back from the war, he led both leagues for the third straight season with twenty-six wins.

Newhouser, a lefthander, teamed up with righthander Dizzy Trout, another of the characters in the big leagues that year, to form a powerful one-two, lefty-righty pitching punch for the Tigers. With Newhouser as the explosive one, Trout was the extrovert. The word around the American League was that Trout, whose real first name was Paul, got his nickname from a reliable source—himself. One of several of his versions of how he came up with his nickname came from the days when he was climbing baseball's ladder to the Major Leagues. "I was pitching in the minors," he once said, "and all of a sudden it started to pour. I saw this awning in center field and started to run under it. The only trouble was the awning was painted on the wall. From then on I was Dizzy."

In spring training as a rookie, before he made the Tigers roster, he entertained himself between practices by grabbing a police officer's motorcycle and racing it around the field. As he passed his manager, Mickey Cochrane, Trout had the nerve to holler out, "How'm I doing?"

Cochrane called back, "Just fine. You can keep riding that thing to Toledo, because that's where you'll be this year." Sure enough, Cochrane farmed him out to Toledo.

Character or not, Dizzy Trout was just as solid a pitcher as Newhouser, and just as impressive as a physical specimen. A product of Sandcut, Indiana, Trout was a half inch taller than Newhouser at six two and a half, and 15 pounds heavier at 195. He led the American League with twenty wins in '43, topped that with twenty-seven in '44 and won another eighteen in '45.

The team the Tigers were to duel for the pennant right down to the wire had a character of its own, with a name to match—Bingo Binks. Like Trout, Binks was more than just a character. He could play the game too.

His real name was George Binkowski, and he was from Chicago's Polish neighborhoods. He said he changed his name so it would be easier for writers to remember. When he finally made it to the majors, it was after minor league stops at Monessen, Pennsylvania, and Owensboro, Kentucky, and Tyler, Texas, then Cedar Rapids, Iowa, and Green Bay and Milwaukee in Wisconsin.

When war broke out, Binks left baseball to work as an expert machinist in a converted automobile factory in South Bend, Indiana, manufacturing war materials in 1942 and '43. In 1944, he returned to baseball, with Milwaukee again, as an outfielder-first baseman. He hit .374. That attracted the eyes of the Washington Senators, who bought him for the 1945 season.

When he reported to the Senators' camp in College Park for the 1945 spring training season, he told reporters he started playing baseball for an understandable reason: "to get out of hard work." He started his rookie season with a bang. He broke into the lineup against Buck Newsom and the A's in Philadelphia and rapped out four hits off Newsom and others, followed by three more hits in his next two games. He won the respect of manager Ossie Bluege with his fielding ability as well. Bluege was a superb third baseman for the Senators for eighteen seasons including their glory years when they won three pennants and a World Series. He knew good hands when he saw them. He said, "Binks has the greatest gloved hand I've ever seen on an outfielder. I've never seen him drop a ball that he got his glove on."

So much for his physical ability. When it came to the mental part of the sport, Bluege rated Binks as something less than an all-star. Bluege was from the old school, with its emphasis on fundamentals and the mental part of baseball. Binks drove him nuts, throwing to the wrong bases, hitting when he got the bunt sign and bunting when he got the hit sign and sometimes missing the sign whatever it was.

Binks was able to play baseball during the war because he was classified 4-F in the draft, because he was deaf in his left ear, the result of a childhood mastoid operation. Bluege sympathized with that condition, but he also knew it carried a certain advantage for Binks. "After I bawl him out," the manager said, "he says to me, 'I haven't heard a word you've said.'"

Bluege admitted to reporters, "He's an enigma to me. I've felt like benching him a dozen times for some of the things he does wrong and some of the things he doesn't do at all, but I'm scared to keep him on the bench. It could be the wrong thing to do, because he has a lot of ability."

With Bluege placing that premium on his talent, Binks became one of Washington's most valuable players because he could play both the outfield and first base. He was listed as an outfielder, but he took over as the team's starting first baseman on the Senators' second western swing of the year when starter Joe Kuhel was injured. Binks began to swing a hot bat and led the Senators to sixteen victories in their next twenty-two games. Suddenly, they were pennant contenders—and Binks was soon to be beckoned by fate to be a key figure in the outcome of one of baseball's closest, most dramatic races.

With the end of the war in Europe and the war in the Pacific swinging decidedly in our favor, some of our "boys in uniform" began to be sent home from overseas and be discharged from the armed forces. One of the first was Buddy Lewis, an all-star outfielder-third baseman for the Senators before the war. He had been gone for all of the 1942–44 seasons and half of 1945. He spent those years "flying the hump"—ferrying supplies and equipment over the Himalayas in the C-B-I Theatre of Operations. He flew more than three hundred missions and logged over two thousand hours as the pilot of a twin-engine C-47 cargo plane, the military version of the DC-3 passenger plane still used for various purposes today.

He rejoined the Senators in mid-season and helped his old-new team considerably with a .333 average in sixty-nine games. That average was no fluke because of wartime pitching. In six seasons before the war, Lewis, a lefthander, hit over .300 three times and above .290 in three other seasons.

His first time at bat after his war service was a reflection of the gratitude and admiration Americans felt toward their returning heroes. It happened in Chicago's Comiskey Park against Earl Caldwell of the White Sox.

Caldwell's first two pitches were called balls by Bill McGowan, one of the most respected umpires of his time, even though both pitches seemed to be well inside the strike zone.

"So Caldwell comes down off the mound," Lewis told me, "and walks halfway to the plate and says, 'What in the hell is going on?'

"McGowan tells him, 'This is Buddy's first time at bat after being in the war—and there ain't no way you're going to throw a strike.' "

Lewis walked on four pitches.

The annual All-Star Game would have occurred during the second week of July in 1945, when the best players in the American and National Leagues would have played against each other. Only that year there wasn't any All-Star Game. For the only time since it was begun in 1933, the game was not played. It was another wartime casualty because of the restrictions against unnecessary travel.

Instead, teams played each other in exhibition games, with the proceeds going to war-related charities. In Washington, the Senators played the Brooklyn Dodgers at Griffith Stadium. The gate receipts would go to the War Relief Fund for the families of servicemen killed in action. Washington's starting pitcher: Bert Shepard, the one-legged war hero.

Manager Bluege told Shepard two days before the game that he would be the Senators' starter. When he took the mound on July 10, Shepard was aware that there were skeptics in the stands—and in the dugouts. "I knew there were an awful lot of people who thought I couldn't do it," he told me during the fiftieth anniversary of the World War II seasons. "And there were things that could happen out on the field—if I messed up a bunt or slipped like any other pitcher fielding a ground ball, they'd say it was because of the leg. If that happened to me, it would be lights out."

His nerves showed at the start of the game. Shepard, who once had thrown twenty-seven straight strikes in a batting practice session that season, walked the first two hitters on eight pitches. He had a talk with himself, thinking, "Oh, my God. You've got a house full of people here, and you'd better get this straightened out pretty soon."

His control returned on the third hitter and he got out of the inning without giving up a run. Shepard pitched the first four innings, holding the Dodgers to five singles. He walked only one more hitter, struck out one, and left the game with his team ahead, 3–2.

The Senators had established themselves as Detroit's chief threat by late summer, performing the remarkable feat of playing five doubleheaders in five days and winning nine of the ten games. They began August with forty-five wins and forty-one losses, but by the end of the day on August 5 they were 54–42. On August 1, they swept a doubleheader from the Philadelphia A's, 2–1 and 3–0. On the second, they beat the A's twice again, both times by a score of 2–1. On August 3, they swept the Boston Red Sox, 7–3 and 3–1. On the fourth, they beat the Red Sox again, 4–0, but were shellacked in the second game, 15–4. The next day, August 5, they came back and swept the Red Sox again, this time by scores of 5–4 and 5–1.

That second game on August 4 was when Bert Shepard made baseball history and struck a patriotic chord with every fan at Griffith Stadium. Playing in a major league game on an artificial leg, he accomplished something no one else has ever done before or since. (Monty Stratton, a pitcher with the White Sox in the 1930s, pitched in the minor leagues after losing his leg in a hunting accident, but he never made it back to the majors.)

The Red Sox pounded Washington's pitchers for twelve runs in the fourth inning of the 15–4 loss. With two outs in the inning and the bases loaded, Bluege waved to those in the Senators' bullpen down the right field foul line to send in Shepard. Before 13,035 cheering fans, Shepard walked to the mound. The hitter was George Metkovich—"Catfish"— who was filling in for Boston in center field while Dom DiMaggio was in the navy.

Shepard and Metkovich fought each other to a full count, making

Shepard's situation even more tense. The Red Sox runners took off in full flight as Shepard took his lefthanded windup and landed hard on his artificial right leg and foot as he threw. Metkovich, a lefthanded hitter, swung at Shepard's fastball, above the waist and on the inside half of the plate. He missed.

With the inning over, Shepard, now a full-fledged major league baseball player, walked briskly and confidently to the Washington dugout on the first base side. The fans gave him a standing ovation.

The former POW was sent back to the mound for the fifth inning by Bluege, who was hoping to save any more wear and tear on his pitching staff as his team headed into the dog days of August and its continuing battle with the Detroit Tigers. Bluege also sent Shepard back to the mound for the sixth inning, and the seventh, and the eighth, and the ninth.

The war hero pitched five and one-third innings, holding Boston to one run on three hits. He struck out two men and threw out two hitters on ground balls back to the mound.

The unending pressure of the pennant race forced Bluege to continue using his veteran pitchers in the stretch drive to overtake the Tigers. After five corrective surgeries in the next three years on his war wound, Bert Shepard never pitched in another big-league game. But he can say something the rest of us can't: "I was a major league baseball player."

Another one who could say that was a one-armed outfielder for the St. Louis Browns Pete Gray, who severed his right arm in the spokes of a moving grocery wagon when he was six years old. The arm was amputated above the right elbow, but Gray became a professional player anyhow. As a six-foot lefthanded hitter, he held the bat in his only hand and hit .381 for Three Rivers in the Canadian-American League, leading the league, and then starred for two years in a row for the Memphis Chicks of the Southern Association. When the 1945 season opened, Pete Gray was standing in the outfield at Sportsman's Park in St. Louis as the starting left fielder for the Browns and the second hitter in the batting order behind Don Gutteridge.

Swinging a thirty-five-ounce bat, Gray got a sharp single in his first game—against Hal Newhouser. A sensational catch by Doc Cramer robbed him of a double on another trip to the plate.

All of us who saw him play have our own favorite memories of him. Mine is when he drove one of the Senators outfielders up against the wall in Griffith Stadium to catch his long fly ball in right center field. That was one of his problems—what we now call "warning track power." He had enough power to hit the ball a long way, but not quite far enough.

He was hitting .235 by the end of July, but he slumped to .218 by the end of the year. Skeptics said at the start of the season that he wouldn't be able to hit the big-league fastball, but his low batting average was due to just the opposite—he couldn't hit the other pitches. He could whip his bat around fast enough against a fastball, but off-speed pitches—curveballs and others—got him out.

In one of the laws of hitting, you have to be ready to hit the fastball but able to adjust your timing if it's another kind of a pitch. The reason is that you can't speed up your swing if you're ready for a curveball and it turns out to be a fastball, but you can do the opposite, slow down your swing if you're ready for a fastball and it's a curve—unless you have only one arm.

When the American League pitchers discovered that Gray couldn't control his swing against anything except a fastball, they pitched him accordingly. He was gone from the big leagues after the 1945 season.

I asked him years later if he felt any resentment about being farmed out after getting only one chance to play in the Major Leagues. "No, not at all," he said, "I figured they were going to send me to Toledo, and that's the way it worked out. All I wanted to do was play one game in the big leagues, and that was it."

When I asked him what he might have done with two arms, he answered, "Who knows? Maybe I wouldn't have done as well. I probably wouldn't have tried as hard and practiced as much as I did. And I probably wouldn't have been as determined."

They made a TV movie about Pete Gray later. He liked the title because he said it reflected exactly how he felt about his baseball career. The movie was called *A Winner Never Quits*.

5

"The Best Thing You Could Do"

As July moved into August, the war in the Pacific was nearing a victorious conclusion for America. The United States dropped history's first atomic bomb on Hiroshima on August 6 and another one on Nagasaki three days later. Even before that, Japan had been reeling under relentless air attacks. American planes were bombing Japan every day, including March 9–10, when 334 B-29s turned Tokyo into an inferno overnight with incendiary bombs. One-quarter of Japan's capital city was destroyed that night, and almost eighty-six thousand people were killed—in that one raid five months before Hiroshima. The figure was more than were killed in either Hiroshima or Nagasaki. With the B-29s able to fly at altitudes too high for Japanese fighter planes to stop them, the mission became the most destructive bombing raid in history.

John T. Correll, editor in chief of *Air Force Magazine,* wrote in a lengthy article for his magazine in 1994, "In 1945, the war had finally come home to Japan. B-29s from Guam, Saipan and Tinian were striking the Japanese homeland regularly, systematically destroying the industrial cities on Honshu and Kyushu." Nevertheless, Japanese resistance continued and grew even stiffer. The Japanese cabinet extended the military draft to include men—or boys—from fifteen to sixty, and women from seventeen to forty-five.

President Truman did not learn about the program to develop the atomic bomb until the day he became president, April 12, 1945. In later years he said his decision to approve the use of the bomb was not a difficult one because of the enormous number of lives it would save, both

Americans and Japanese. Winston Churchill, the prime minister of Great Britain, said later he agreed with Truman. Margaret Truman wrote a biography of her father in which she quoted Churchill as saying Truman "saved western civilization" by ordering the use of the bomb to shorten the war.

American casualties were averaging more than nine hundred a day, and things would become far worse if Truman ordered American plans to invade Japan, already on the drawing board, to be put into action. Those plans called for two invasions: "Operation Olympic," a land invasion of Kyushu, Japan's southernmost main island, to be launched on November 1, and "Operation Coronet," an invasion of Honshu, Japan's largest island, which was to begin on March 1, 1946.

The U.S. Joint Chiefs of Staff projected that the invasions would involve five million troops, mostly American. Those planning the dual invasions projected that they would result in five hundred thousand American casualties. President Truman believed strongly that the invasions would produce massive casualties to both sides, including countless Japanese civilians.

In *Truman*, his biography of the president, David McCullough writes that if the bomb been ready in March and dropped then, forcing Japan to surrender, it would have saved the lives of almost fifty thousand American fighting men who were killed in the Pacific after that month, plus the Japanese lives lost during the same period.

The bomb was dropped on Hiroshima at 8:16 A.M. on August 6, from the *Enola Gay*, a B-29 piloted by Colonel Paul W. Tibbets, Jr., and named for his mother. More than half of the city was destroyed in a flash. Estimates are that between seventy thousand and eighty thousand people were killed and an equal number injured.

After four years of stunning news, a time when Americans had grown almost immune to shocking bulletins and dramatic presidential announcements, President Truman delivered the biggest news since Pearl Harbor in an announcement broadcast to the world by radio:

> Sixteen hours ago, an American airplane dropped one bomb on Hiroshima, an important Japanese army base. That bomb had more power than 20,000 tons of TNT. . . . It is an atomic bomb, harnessing the basic power of the universe. . . . What has been done is the greatest achievement of organized science in history. . . . If they [the Japanese] do not now accept our terms, they can ex-

pect a rain of ruin from the air the like of which has never been seen on this earth.

The banner across the top of *The Washington Post* the next morning left no doubt about the sobering significance of what had just happened.

SINGLE ATOMIC BOMB ROCKS JAPANESE ARMY BASE
WITH MIGHTIER FORCE THAN 20,000 TONS OF TNT
TO OPEN NEW ERA OF POWER FOR BENEFIT OF MAN

The second atomic bomb in history was dropped on Nagasaki at 11:02 on the morning of August 9, killing an estimated forty thousand persons. President Truman said, in what must be the most sweeping ultimatum ever issued by the head of a nation, "We are now prepared to obliterate rapidly and completely every productive enterprise the Japanese have above ground in any city."

A week following Hiroshima, Japan surrendered after Emperor Hirohito broke a deadlock on his Supreme War Council and ordered its members to accept the U.S. terms: unconditional surrender. Hirohito said, "I cannot bear to see my innocent people suffer any longer" and overruled his military leaders who were still holding out for continuing the war. The emperor said, "A peaceful end to the war is preferable to seeing Japan annihilated."

He spoke to his people in a recorded radio message broadcast at noon on August 15, Japanese time, and described the frightening potential if more atomic bombs were dropped: " . . . the enemy," he warned, "has begun to employ a new and most cruel bomb, the power of which to do damage is, indeed, incalculable, taking the toll of many innocent lives. Should we continue to fight, not only could it result in an ultimate collapse and obliteration of the Japanese nation, but also it would lead to the total extinction of human civilization." Instead, he said, it was time to "pave the way for a grand peace for all generations to come."

At 7:00 P.M. "Eastern War Time" on August 14, President Truman, dressed in a double-breasted navy blue suit, faced a news conference in the Oval Office. Reading slowly and distinctly from a sheet of paper in his right hand, Truman, in office only four months and two days, said in understated drama, "I have received this afternoon a message from the Japanese government . . . I deem this reply a full acceptance of the Potsdam Declaration, which specifies the unconditional surrender of Japan."

As reporters bolted for the door and the phones outside, the President and his wife, Bess, returned to the living quarters on the second floor of the White House. Outside, ten thousand screaming Americans in Lafayette Park, directly across Pennsylvania Avenue, started a conga line. The cheering grew louder. Church bells rang. Automobile horns blared. The world was at peace again, and the celebrating was unrestrained.

President Truman declared August 14 V-J Day—Victory over Japan. The celebrations all over the world included those American GIs in the Pacific who were training for an invasion of Japan. Among them were Warren Spahn, Bobby Doerr, Pee Wee Reese, and other past, present, and future baseball stars.

As the war was ending, its influence remained, especially in wartime Washington, where the predominance of military uniforms may have been the greatest of any city in America. The city's clothing shops were advertising sailor uniforms—"blues"—for $35. Navy officers could buy blue serge uniforms for $40 at D. J. Kaufman clothing store. At the Hub Furniture and Clothing Store, returning GIs anxious to get married and buy a home could furnish it with a seven-piece eighteenth-century bedroom set for $129.

Those who managed to make it to the sports page of their morning paper the day after reading about this overpowering new bomb saw that the Tigers split a doubleheader with the White Sox the day before and now led Washington by only a half game. In the National League, the Cardinals were rained out of their game with the Pirates in Pittsburgh. The Cubs were idle. They were now leading the Cards by six full games.

On that same day, the Associated Press carried a story by reporter Bus Ham saying that Commissioner Chandler was summoning officials of the Major Leagues and the minors to a special two-day meeting at the Mayflower Hotel in Washington. Purpose: to plan for baseball in the postwar period.

Douglas MacArthur signed the surrender documents on the deck of the USS *Missouri* with Premier Suzuki of Japan on September 2. Six days later, President Truman did something that hadn't been done since President Roosevelt had done it in April 1941—he threw out the first ball at a baseball game. It was September 8, and the Senators were playing the St. Louis Browns. There were 20,310 fans on hand at Griffith Stadium to cheer Truman's arrival, and they were there to cheer someone else's arrival, too—Cecil Travis had come home from the war in Europe, including the Battle of the Bulge. Washington's all-star shortstop, who had hit well over .300 in eight of his nine prewar years, was back. Today he is a trivia answer: the man who finished second in the American League in hitting in 1941, when Ted Williams hit .406 and Joe DiMaggio hit safely in fifty-six straight games. DiMag batted .357 with that remarkable feat, but Travis outhit him by two points and finished at .359.

Truman was accompanied to the ball game that day by his wife, Bess, who kept score every time they went to Griffith Stadium, which was a lot. Both were enthusiastic baseball fans. Truman attended more games— sixteen—than any other president and once remarked, "May the sun never set on American baseball."

Also with the new president and the First Lady in their confidence-

President Harry Truman throws out the first ball before a game between the Washington Senators and the St. Louis Browns on September 8, 1945, the first time a president attended a baseball game at Washington's Griffith Stadium since President Roosevelt performed the honors on Opening Day in 1941. Mrs. Truman is at the president's right. The two managers in baseball uniforms are Ossie Bluege of the Senators (left) and Luke Sewell of the Browns. Both Trumans were enthusiastic baseball fans. (© The Washington Post. Courtesy of the Washington, D.C., Public Library.)

building appearance at the ballpark were Admiral William Leahy, Press Secretary Charlie Ross, Attorney General Tom Clark, Secretary of the Treasury Fred Vinson and three U.S. senators: Alben Barkley of Kentucky, Robert LaFollette of Wisconsin, and Arthur Vandenberg of Michigan.

Truman proved himself a worthy successor to FDR in bringing good luck to the Nats—the Senators. They beat the St. Louis Browns that day, 4–1.

Bob Feller joined Travis, who had received his military draft notice on Christmas Eve in 1941, Buddy Lewis, Hank Greenberg, and other stars from the "prewar" years who were able to come home during the 1945 season. They were qualified through a "points" system established to give priority to those who had served in the armed forces the longest and met other criteria for discharges.

Feller was a genuine hero, although he disclaims the term every time he hears it said about him. He enlisted in the Navy two days after Pearl Harbor, even though he had a deferment from the draft, classified 3-C as the sole support of his dying father, his mother, and his kid sister. He turned twenty-three only the month before, was making the astronomical sum of $35,000 a year and could have stayed home for the duration. He had already won 107 games, the most ever for a pitcher that young.

Instead, Feller volunteered, then asked to be transferred from his assignment as a Navy physical fitness instructor to gunnery school and became the chief of a twenty-four-man gun crew on one of America's biggest warships, the USS *Alabama*. The ship was massive, weighing thirty-five thousand tons. She carried a crew of two thousand nine hundred, six times the population of Feller's hometown of Van Meter, Iowa.

The *Alabama* sailed as an escort in convoys transporting GIs to Europe over the frigid North Atlantic route, hoping to escape detection by German submarines, the dreaded U-boats that stalked the North Atlantic in the winter of 1941–42. Later the *Alabama* was reassigned to the Pacific, where Feller received eight battle stars for participating in eight invasions, including New Guinea, Guam, the Philippines, and Iwo Jima.

When Feller returned to the Indians in August 1945, the Indians telephone operator, Ada Ireland, was so flooded with calls wanting to know when he would pitch that the switchboard broke down. When he made his first postwar start, against Detroit on August 24, 46,477 fans turned out. Before the game, there was a march to the flagpole in center field, followed by the playing and singing of the National Anthem. A group of World War I veterans marched behind Jack Horwitz's band. So did every member of both teams. The Indians gave Feller a Jeep for his farm.

The first hitter he faced after being gone from the big leagues for almost four seasons was Jimmy Outlaw of the Tigers. His first pitch was a fastball for a strike. Then he struck Outlaw out. The Indians won, 4–2, with Feller pitching a four-hitter. He didn't allow Detroit a hit after the third inning. In his return, Feller beat the best—Hal Newhouser.

Another development in baseball, one that has changed the sport all the way into the twenty-first century, occurred in the same month as Feller's dazzling return. Unknown to the rest of the world, the Brooklyn Dodgers negotiated a deal to sign a "Negro," Jackie Robinson, the same infielder who had been given the "don't call us we'll call you" treatment by the Red Sox only four months before. General Manager Branch Rickey met with Robinson in Brooklyn on August 29. Robinson agreed to a bonus of $3,500 and a salary of $600 a month, a raise of $100 over what he was making with the Kansas City Monarchs.

One of baseball's strangest—and most thrilling—seasons entered its climactic stage in late September with the American League championship still up for grabs. It was scheduled to end on September 23—and again on September 30.

That's because Clark Griffith had rented out his stadium to the Washington Redskins for the 1945 football season, as he did every year. The Senators' 1945 season ended a week ahead of the other American League teams to allow the Redskins to open their home season on September 30. With no allowance for the possibility that his team might still be in contention in late September, Griffith had placed manager Ossie Bluege and his players in a position where they would be helpless to do anything for themselves after the twenty-third. Whatever their situation would be on that date, they would have to sit and watch the rest of the American League play another full week, determining the Senators' fate for them.

That's exactly what happened, and with a Hollywood finish that rivals anything in any baseball movie ever produced.

To everyone's surprise, including Griffith's, the Senators had emerged as strong pennant contenders in the last half of the season and were chasing the Tigers throughout August and September. They took on the Tigers in a do-or-die stretch of five games in three days at Griffith Stadium in the next-to-last weekend of their season and won four of them. They were still neck and neck with Detroit when they took the field in Philadelphia on the last day of their season for a doubleheader against the A's.

The Senators knew they needed to win both games to keep as much pressure as possible on the Tigers. A split wouldn't accomplish anything, and after that doubleheader, the Senators wouldn't be able to help themselves, because they wouldn't be able to play any more games, so they needed to win both games on that Sunday, September 23.

The A's, under Griffith's friend, owner-manager Connie Mack, were in last place, but they were threatening to elbow their way into the history books as a decisive factor in the race when they forced the first game into extra innings.

Walter Masterson, back from the Navy in time to pitch in four games that year, was sailing along for the Senators in the twelfth inning after coming on in relief of Dutch Leonard in the eighth. Masterson hadn't allowed a hit, and he was on the verge of getting out of the inning with two outs and nobody on base. The third out looked easy—Ernie Kish, a Washington native playing his only big-league season and hitting .245 with no home runs and only ten runs batted in.

It was one of those days when it's cloudy one minute and sunny the next. When the Senators batted in the top of the twelfth, Philadelphia's center fielder, Sam Chapman, asked for time out and called into the A's dugout for his sunglasses.

When Kish came up in the bottom half of the inning, the sun came out again. In the Senators' dugout, Joe Judge wondered. Judge, a star first baseman with the Senators and a teammate with Ossie Bluege in the Walter Johnson era, was managing the Senators now. Bluege had been thrown out of the game in the eighth inning by umpire Eddie Rommel for arguing a call. As Judge looked out at the sunny outfield, he wondered about the unpredictable Binks in center field: Did he have his sunglasses with him, tucked under the beak of his cap?

Barely moments later, Kish lofted a routine fly ball to straightaway center field, where the talented Binks glided easily into position to make the catch. Suddenly the flaky Binks began to stagger. Judge saw that Binks did not have his sunglasses. Horror of horrors—the ball dropped safely ten feet from Binks. Kish reached second base, the fifth double of his one-year career.

Judge, acting on orders from Bluege, who was still running the team from the runway between the dugout and the dressing room, instructed

Masterson to walk the next batter, first baseman Dick Siebert. The Senators knew Siebert was a serious threat, a .300 hitter twice and a lifetime .282 hitter in eleven seasons. Besides, walking him would set up a force play at any base except home plate. Siebert's run didn't mean anything. If Kish scored, the game would be over anyhow.

The next hitter, future Hall of Famer George Kell, singled to right field. The game was over, and the Senators had been dealt a critical loss.

The Senators came back to win the second game, 4–3, behind Marino Pieretti, called after eight innings because of darkness. Their record at that point was 87 wins and 67 losses, while Detroit was 86–64. The Senators' season was over after the 154-game schedule played by big-league teams in those years. The Tigers had 4 games to play.

A split at any other time in a pennant race that close wouldn't necessarily be disastrous, but coming that late—and with the Senators unable to control their fate from that day on—Washington's loss in that first game in Philadelphia that Sunday was devastating.

Shirley Povich, just back from his duties as a war correspondent, who saw the flag raised on Iwo Jima but then was injured twice on airplanes and again when hit by a half-track, told me later that in the Senators' dressing room between games, "The dead stillness reeked of a morgue." He heard one of Binks's teammates say, "They ought to fine him $4,000," the amount that each player in the World Series might receive.

Nobody said a word to Binks. He sat alone. He hadn't committed either of the two errors made by his teammates that gave the A's three runs in the eighth inning. He was one of the leading reasons for the Senators' success that year, able to play both center field and first base and hit .278 and drive in eighty-one runs. None of that seemed to matter now. As Binks sat on the wooden stool in front of his locker, thinking who knows what, his sunglasses were in his hip pocket. He had gotten them from the bench in the twelfth inning—after Kish's fly ball.

The fly ball that wasn't caught was something of a miracle for the Tigers. They had been struggling and had already lost their game that day to the Browns. If the Senators had swept that doubleheader from the A's, they would have finished the day in a virtual tie with Detroit, whose record was 86–64. Instead, Washington's final record was 87 wins and 67 defeats. Now the Senators could only hope.

In his column from Philadelphia that afternoon, Povich wrote, "Today surely was the blackest day for a Washington team in history . . .

September 23, 1945, is a date to remember, or forget. You can take your choice."

When the Tigers went to St. Louis at the end of that week for the last weekend of the season, they weren't the only ones doing some traveling. Four Washington pitchers—Masterson, Leonard, Mickey Haefner, and Johnny Niggeling—took a train for Detroit that Saturday because Bluege wanted them there and rested in case the Browns knocked Detroit down into a tie with the Senators. In anticipation of that possibility, officials from the two teams had already tossed a coin to see where a one-game playoff would be held. Detroit won the toss. If it happened, it would be the first playoff in big-league history—not a three-game series, or three out of five, but a one-game showdown.

As the Tigers and Browns were taking the field at Sportsman's Park, Washington's fate was in the hands of the Browns. Just like Washington and Philadelphia on the previous Sunday, the Tigers and Browns were playing a doubleheader—and it was a rainy day. If the Browns won both games, the American League season would end in a tie, forcing the play-off. As the moment approached for the start of the first game, Washington's four pitchers checked into the Book-Cadillac Hotel in Detroit, two to a room in adjoining rooms. They turned on the radio in one of the rooms to listen to the broadcast from St. Louis on the Tigers' station.

The start of the game was delayed for forty-five minutes by the rain. It had been raining in St. Louis for three days by then, and that last doubleheader wouldn't have been played at all if it had not been critical to the outcome of the pennant race. Only 6,613 fans braved the weather to see the showdown.

In the ninth inning, the Browns were leading, 3–2. Detroit's manager, Steve O'Neill, sent in a veteran outfielder, Hub Walker, as a pinch hitter to lead off the inning. Walker was additional evidence of the wartime manpower shortage. He had broken in with the Tigers in 1931 but hadn't played in the majors since 1937. He was back now, though, in the last year of the war and playing in twenty-eight games.

Walker singled, and Skeeter Webb, the Tigers shortstop, bunted to sacrifice Walker to second and put him in scoring position so he could score the tying run on a base hit to the outfield. Webb's bunt rolled down the first base line, where it was fielded cleanly by George McQuinn, but his throw to second base to force Walker was late.

O'Neill pushed more buttons. He flashed the bunt sign again, this time to Eddie Mayo, Detroit's veteran second baseman who had been out of the big leagues for five years until the war came along. He returned to the majors in 1943 and was good enough to compete successfully against the returning stars after the war through 1948. Mayo laid down a sacrifice bunt that worked, moving Webb and Walker to second and third. Now the Tigers had both the tying and the winning runs in scoring position, with the heavy part of their batting order coming up and only one out.

The Browns' manager, Luke Sewell, ordered his pitcher, Nelson Potter, to walk Doc Cramer, Detroit's forty-year-old center fielder, for two good reasons: The walk would load the bases, setting up a force play at the plate or a double play. And it would enable Potter to avoid having to pitch to Cramer, who was nearing the end of a twenty-year career in the Major Leagues in which he compiled a .296 lifetime batting average, including eight seasons when he hit .300. If Sewell's strategy worked and the Browns got out of it with a doubleplay or any other kind of play, it would win the game for St. Louis and place extreme pressure on Detroit to win the second game if the Tigers were to avoid a playoff with the Senators. The man who could spoil the Browns' strategy was the hitter, Hank Greenberg.

It was getting dark by then, and still raining. With the bases loaded around him, Potter threw his first pitch to Greenberg. Ball one. Then strike one.

Just before Potter's third pitch, Greenberg spotted something—Potter's grip on the baseball. Screwball. Greenberg knew what was coming.

"Hammerin' Hank" hammered the pitch into the left field bleachers, a few feet inside the foul pole. Third base umpire Cal Hubbard, dashing down the foul line for the best possible view, signaled it was a fair ball—a home run. And not just a home run but a grand slam. The Tigers won the game and the American League pennant. As Greenberg crossed home plate, Eddie Borom, a wartime player for two seasons as a utility infielder with the Tigers, rushed up and kissed him.

In Washington, the Senators had just finished packing. They knew they were going to one of two places: to Detroit for that playoff game if the Browns won both games, or home for the winter if the Browns didn't. They were climbing into cabs at Griffith Stadium when the clubhouse manager, Frankie Baxter, came running out of the ballpark and hollered, "Never mind! It's all over! Greenberg just hit a grand slam!"

Hank Greenberg returned from World War II in time to win the 1945 American League pennant for the Detroit Tigers with a grand slam home run on the last day of the season. (Carl Seid/National Baseball Hall of Fame Library, Cooperstown, N.Y.)

In Detroit, the four Washington pitchers left their hotel rooms and checked out of the Book-Cadillac, only three hours after checking in. Their beds were still made. Meanwhile, the Cubs won the National League pennant by three games over the St. Louis Cardinals.

As America looked forward to its first peacetime World Series since 1941, the influence of the war was still evident in other entertainment, including the movies. At World Series time, Hollywood was offering *Anchors Aweigh*, a musical about Navy life starring Gene Kelly, Frank Sinatra, and Kathryn Grayson, and *Pride of the Marines* with John Garfield.

With the commercial development of television put on hold since before the war, radio was still king. The newspapers carried large display ads promoting the evening's radio programs—comedy shows starring Jack Benny and Blondie, mysteries like *The Shadow* and *The Thin Man* and a popular documentary drama, *We, The People*.

The rosters of both the Tigers and the Cubs were still filled with wartime players, so many observers felt that the World Series still suffered from the same manpower shortage that had affected baseball throughout the war. When Jerry Liska of the Associated Press asked Warren Brown, a prominent Chicago baseball writer, who would win the Series, Brown said, "I can't conceive of either team winning a single game."

But they did. They each won three, and the stage was set for the grand finale to wartime baseball, with its drama and pratfalls and 4-Fs and returning heroes, all topped off by baseball's best autumn showcase, a seven-game World Series. The Tigers just missed winning it all in six games, but their forty-two-year-old outfielder, Chuck Hostetler, tripped trying to score from second with a critical run in the seventh inning and was tagged out as he lay in the base path. The Cubs won the game in twelve innings, 8–7.

That night a friend told Ira Kupcinet, a Chicago newspaper columnist, that he had taken his father to that game. Kupcinet replied, "I know. I saw him fall between third and home."

By the seventh game, both teams' pitchers were exhausted. Manager Charlie Grimm started his ace righthander, Hank Borowy, on only one day's rest. The Tigers weren't in much better shape. Steve O'Neill sent out Hal Newhouser, who had only two days of rest. The strain showed on Borowy immediately. Detroit's first three hitters jumped on him for singles. Grimm brought in another righthanded starter, Paul Derringer, but Paul Richards hit a three-run double and by the time the first half inning of the game was over, the Tigers had a 5–0 lead. They cruised to baseball's last wartime championship with a 9–3 victory. Newhouser went the full nine innings on a ten-hitter.

With the last out of the 1945 World Series, baseball had shown the world that nothing, not even the worst war in the history of the planet, could stop the World Series from being played, a distinction that only a strike by the players could destroy forty-nine years later.

When "our boys in uniform" came marching home again, speculation began to set in. What more would the greats like Ted Williams, Bob Feller, Joe DiMaggio, Johnny Mize, and others have done if there hadn't been a World War II? A computer specialist in Seattle, Ralph Winnie, developed computer projections in 1986 answering that question in his publication, *What If?* Taking a player's last three years before the war and his first three years after it, and barring the unforeseen such as injuries, Winnie projected that Feller would have won another 107 games, giving him 373 victories and making him the third-winningest pitcher in history instead of the twenty-eighth. Winnie's projections show Feller would have pitched five no-hitters instead of three and nineteen one-hitters instead of twelve.

Greenberg, Johnny Mize, and Joe DiMaggio all would have hit more than 500 home runs, but none of them came close. DiMag hit 361, 2 more than Mize and 30 more than Greenberg. Ted Williams, who hit 521 homers, would have hit 743, more than Babe Ruth and anyone else except Hank Aaron, if he hadn't missed three years for World War II and two more as a jet fighter pilot in the Korean War.

The careers of several other stars are persuasive arguments in behalf of electing them to the Baseball Hall of Fame. Cecil Travis is Exhibit A. The Senators' all-star shortstop missed three and a half prime seasons because of his military service in the Army. He hit above .300 in eight of his nine seasons before Pearl Harbor, reaching his peak with that .359 season in 1941 when he topped Joe DiMaggio and his fifty-six-game hitting streak and finished second only to Ted Williams and his .406 average. Travis had other outstanding seasons, including a .344 average in 1937 and .335 in 1938. He was twenty-eight years old, at his physical peak, when he was drafted three weeks after the attack on Pearl Harbor. When he returned, he had lost more than just those three and a half prime years. He had also been slowed by frozen feet, the result of fighting in the Battle of the Bulge.

Dom DiMaggio is another deserving veteran of the armed forces. He broke in with the Red Sox as a star center fielder in 1940 with a .301 batting average. He was his team's leadoff hitter. Dom and shortstop Johnny Pesky, the number-two hitter in the batting order, were Boston's "table setters," charged with the responsibility of getting on base so Ted Williams, hitting third, could drive them in. Dom hit in the .280s in '41 and '42, played in the '41 All-Star Game and drove in his brother Joe from second base, but then missed the next three seasons because of service in the Navy, when he was twenty-six, twenty-seven, and twenty-eight years old .

When Dom returned in 1946, he picked up right where he left off, with a .316 average, fifth highest in the American League. He led the league in times at bat twice, in runs scored twice, and in triples and stolen bases while providing the Red Sox with some of the best outfield play in either league and one of the best throwing arms. He finished his big-league career with a .298 batting average, the same as Mickey Mantle's.

Ralph Winnie's question of *What If?* isn't the only one raised by the military service of these stars like Travis, DiMaggio, and others. Another one is: Shouldn't several of these players, including Travis and DiMaggio, be in the Hall of Fame? Their exclusion raises still another question: Are they being punished not because they *didn't* serve their country during World War II but because they *did?*

The attitude of the baseball players who went away to war and missed those prime years of their careers speaks volumes about the way we were in 1945. Hall of Famer Enos Slaughter of the Cardinals minimized any suggestion that his wartime service cost him anything. During the fiftieth anniversary of World War II, he told me, "Those three years I missed really didn't hurt me that much."

Bob Feller said, "I'm very proud of my war record, just like my baseball record. I would never have been able to face anybody and talk about my baseball record if I hadn't spent time in the service."

Ted Williams, speaking of his time in the Marines during World War II, told me, "The three years that I lost—hell, there were nine billion guys who contributed a lot more than I did."

Rick Ferrell, who was elected to the Baseball Hall of Fame thirty-nine years after being one of the Washington Senators' leaders in 1945, may have spoken for all the players who kept baseball going in that wartime season and the three before it when he told me, "I felt I was making a contribution in my own way. It was the best thing you could do."

The record shows that his fellow Americans agreed with Ferrell, and that President Roosevelt was right when he wrote in his "green light letter" to Commissioner Landis in 1942 that the use of older players, teenagers, and those disqualified as 4-F for physical reasons "will not dampen the popularity of the sport." Attendance at major league ballparks in 1945, the fourth season of wartime baseball, was higher than the last prewar year, 1941, which may have been baseball's most historic season, certainly to that time and maybe even until today. That was the year when Joe DiMaggio hit in fifty-six straight games, Ted Williams hit .406—no player has accomplished either feat since—Lou Gehrig died, and Williams hit what many still consider the most dramatic home run in the history of the All-Star Game. To top it all off, the Yankees beat the Dodgers in the thrilling World Series after New York's Tommy Henrich reached base on what would have been a strikeout to prolong the fourth game, enabling the Yanks to come from behind and win that game and the fifth game the next day for the championship. Two months and one day later, the Japanese attacked Pearl Harbor.

With all those thrills, and the country singing a new hit, "Joltin' Joe DiMaggio," major league attendance in 1941 totaled 9.6 million. In 1945, after four years of watching wartime understudies without losing their enthusiasm for the sport, 10.8 million fans came to big-league games.

PART TWO
· · ·
1948

6

The Good Years

Baseball, and America, were enjoying good years during the second half of the 1940s—exciting and almost too eventful. After that photo finish to the American League season in 1945, the National League staged one of its own in 1946, when the St. Louis Cardinals and Brooklyn Dodgers went down to the wire in history's first tie for a pennant before the Cardinals swept a two-game playoff. The Cards, led by the league's batting champion, Stan Musial, and the winningest pitcher, twenty-one-game winner Howie Pollet, topped that off by defeating the Boston Red Sox of Ted Williams, Dom DiMaggio, and Johnny Pesky in one of the most memorable World Series. That was the year when Enos Slaughter scored from first base on a double by Harry Walker in the eighth inning of the seventh game, giving the Cardinals the championship and left-hander Harry Brecheen his third win of the Series.

The sport continued its grip on Americans' enthusiasm in 1947, the year that Jackie Robinson, ignored by the Red Sox after his tryout with them two years before, broke Major League Baseball's "color barrier" with the Dodgers. The Dodgers and Yankees staged another of their "subway series," with the Yankees winning, as they always did until 1955, in seven games behind the relief pitching of Joe Page and the clutch hitting of Tommy Henrich. The Yankee right fielder drove in the winning run in three of New York's four victories, the kind of performance under pressure that won him the nickname of "Old Reliable" early in his career.

Then came 1948.

The Red Sox were strong contenders again, as they seemed to be every

year, but the Cleveland Indians came from out of nowhere to join the
American League pennant race. While the Boston Braves were winning
the National League pennant by six and a half games over the Cardinals,
the American League was putting on a pennant race so close it became a
season to remember—the first tie in the history of the American League
and the second in the majors in only three years. The stars of the show
were the Indians, the Red Sox, and the Yankees.

Baseball was putting on one of its greatest shows at a time when
America was making plenty of news itself—the eventful times of the first
postwar years. We were singing Dinah Shore's hit, "Buttons and Bows,"
plus Nat King Cole's silky smooth rendition of "Nature Boy," and Bing
Crosby's harmonious "Now Is The Hour." Television was our newest form
of entertainment. We sat in dark living rooms because we thought watching TV with the lights on would hurt our eyes, looking at black-and-
white screens of seven and ten inches, and watched the new shows of
1948—Ed Sullivan's *Toast of the Town,* Milton Berle's *Texaco Star Theater,*
plus *Candid Camera* and one for the kids, *Kukla, Fran & Ollie.* For the
serious-minded, *Meet the Press* was already in its fourth year on the radio.

Berle almost single-handedly led television into a prominent, almost
dominant, presence in American life. At the time of his death on March
27, 2002, it was reported that Berle's ratings in the early days of his show
ran as high as 80 percent. *Variety,* the show business newspaper, said the
volume of business in movie theaters, legitimate theaters, and restaurants dropped sharply on Tuesday nights as Americans flocked to some
place with a TV set to watch the man who became known forever after as
"Uncle Miltie," his nickname for himself.

His show began its first full season on NBC at 8:00 P.M. on September
21, 1948, when there were an estimated four hundred thousand television
sets in the United States. The number jumped to one million in only a
few months and doubled again later in that same year. In only two more
years, the number of television sets in America soared past ten million,
twenty-five times the amount in use when Berle began his weekly show.
NBC agreed with everyone else about Berle's pivotal role in "putting
television on the map" and rewarded him in 1951 with a contract paying
him $200,000 a year for the rest of his life, whether or not he appeared
on TV.

While television was making such deep inroads into American life in
1948, the United States recognized Israel, eleven minutes after Jewish

leaders in Palestine declared their independence from Great Britain and established Israel as a new nation. Inflation, frequently a problem after a war, was one again. New homes that cost $4,440 in 1939 were costing as much as $9,060 in 1948. The cost of food and clothing skyrocketed 129 percent. But there was good news on the inflation front too—the first McDonald's restaurant opened in 1948 in San Bernardino, California. Richard and Maurice McDonald began the chain, selling their hamburgers for fifteen cents. There were no car hops and no options for the burgers. French fries were ten cents. Milk shakes cost twenty-five cents.

The Supreme Court outlawed prayer in public schools. A giant telescope with a twenty-inch lens was dedicated at Mount Palomar in California, able to probe eight times deeper into space than had been possible before. One speaker at the ceremony said,

> Man spends his energies in fighting with his fellow man over issues which a single look through this telescope would show to be utterly inconsequential.

Cortisone and Vitamin B_{12} were discovered. The new Polaroid Land cameras, weighing five pounds, were on sale for $95. Joe Louis retired as the heavyweight champion of the world, in those years when people got excited about boxing champions. Babe Ruth died in the middle of the baseball season. In one of the unfinished items of business left over from World War II, seven Japanese war leaders were hanged in Tokyo. A professor at the University of Indiana, Dr. Alfred C. Kinsey, caused a furor with his report on "Sexual Behavior in the Human Male," which he released after ten years of study and interviews with five thousand men.

Honda motorcycles made their debut that year, plus radial tires, a game called Scrabble, Dial soap, and a new chain of ice cream stores named Baskin-Robbins. And Hollywood's biggest stars were still advertising for cigarettes. Cary Grant, Gregory Peck, and Ethel Barrymore were doing the honors for Chesterfields.

Readers of *The New York Times* woke up to a jolting Page One story on the morning of June 26, 1948.

BERLIN SIEGE
ON AS SOVIET
BLOCKS FOOD

About 2,500,000 Germans in the Western sectors of Berlin came face to face with the grim specter of starvation today as the siege of those two sectors began in earnest.

In the hottest crisis yet of the young Cold War, one fraught with the dreaded possibility of a World War III, the Soviet Union—"the Russians"—had sealed off the residents of West Berlin by blockading Berlin. They threatened to conquer the city's 2.5 million citizens through starvation. The Communist government of East Germany, a puppet regime run by Stalin and his henchmen in the Kremlin, hoped to force the Allies—the United States, England, and France—out of their zones in Berlin and add the entire city to Communist-controlled East Germany.

With World War II barely three years in the past, there were already fears of another world war. Great Britain's wartime leader Winston Churchill said the situation in Europe was "as grave as those we now know were at stake in Munich ten years ago." The American military governor of West Germany, General Lucius D. Clay, warned that the Russians would not be able to force the Allies out of Berlin "by any action short of war."

Overnight, Soviet troops slammed shut all highway and water access to West Berlin in their boldest and scariest move since the end of World War II. A *Times* article by Drew Middleton said the Soviet military administration took the action as part of the Soviet's "calculated policy of starving the people of the Western sectors into the acceptance of the Communist demand for the withdrawal of the Western powers."

The residents of West Berlin, surrounded by Communist territory, were suddenly marooned, deprived not only of their daily shipments of food but also medicine, fuel, clothing, and all other items necessary to sustain human life. An Associated Press dispatch dated June 25 said, "The blockade left the air the only way to get food in to the 2,000,000 inhabitants of the American, British and French sectors. Allied experts said that would prove unworkable in the long run."

Truman ordered the Berlin Airlift immediately. The extent of the tension was illustrated in a stern warning by the American commandant in Berlin, Colonel Frank Howley, who said, "Any joker who thinks the United States, Britain and France are going to be dealt out of Berlin has another guess coming."

Truman signed the Selective Service Act, a bill reinstituting the military draft, the day before the Russians slapped on their blockade. The

An Air Force C-54 cargo plane lands in West Berlin during the Berlin Airlift as the children watch in excitement. (© *The Washington Post.* Courtesy of the Washington, D.C., Public Library.)

bill required all young men between eighteen and twenty-five to register for the draft, with all eligible nineteen-year-olds required to serve twenty-one months if called to duty. Some 200,000 to 250,000 would be called in the first year.

On the first day of the airlift, fifty American C-47s flew in powdered and canned milk for the babies of West Berlin "who can get no fresh milk now that the Russians have stopped the flow from dairies in their zone," the AP reported. The British commander in Berlin called on the Russians to "lift their food blockade at once or take the blame for starving 2,000,000 Germans."

The AP story added, "American experts declared it would be impossible to bring in all the 2,000 to 2,500 tons of food daily needed by West Berlin's population." Still, those men, women, and children living in the Allied zones of West Berlin began looking to the sky at the American and British planes as their pilots flew their precious cargo into the city. For those millions, the skies were now their only avenue of hope.

"The situation was extremely dangerous," David McCullough writes in his book, *Truman*. He continues, "Clearly Stalin was attempting to force the Western Allies to withdraw from the city. Except by air, the Allied sectors were entirely cut off. Nothing could come in or out. Two and a half million people faced starvation. As it was, stocks of food would last no more than a month. Coal supplies would be gone in six weeks."

Truman faced the crisis squarely. In ordering the airlift, one of the twentieth century's most daring acts of sustained heroism, Truman consulted none of the White House staff or any of his political advisers despite "all the political heat and turmoil of the moment," McCullough writes. With the presidential election barely four months away, "There was no talk of how the President's handling of the crisis would make him look or what political advantage was to be gained. And neither did Truman try to bolster the spirits of those around him by claiming the airlift would work. He simply emphasized his intention to stay in Berlin and left no doubt that he meant exactly what he said."

Truman directed the Air Force to begin flying supplies into West Berlin in a massive, in-your-face act of defiance, an around-the-clock operation that lasted fifteen months, always balanced against the menacing presence of the Russians and the threats they bellowed almost daily from East Berlin and Moscow. At the peak of the operation, U.S. and British planes were carrying food, milk, clothing, coal, medicines, and other items essential for sustaining human life. These angels of steel were landing in West Berlin every forty-five seconds.

Despite his public firmness, Truman showed a certain strain in private. In a letter back to Missouri to wife Bess and daughter Margaret in the first months of the airlift that summer, he wrote, "It is hot and humid and lonely. Why in hell does anybody want to be a head of state? Damned if I know."

Once again, baseball played a valuable role in giving Americans something to take their minds off the grim "international situation," with a pennant race that was one for the books. The man who was chiefly responsible was Bill Veeck, a former minor league executive who had earned the nicknames of "the Barnum of the Bushes" and "Baseball's Barnum." His star pitcher, Bob Feller, said, "Bill Veeck deserves much of the credit" for the history that the Indians made in 1948.

Veeck was born into baseball as the son of one of the executives of the Chicago Cubs. He knew baseball, and he knew how to promote it. When

Cleveland Indians owner Bill Veeck, called "the Barnum of the Bushes" for his promotional skills in the minor leagues, put together the Indians' championship team of 1948. Note the picture of Commissioner Landis on the wall. (© *Look* Magazine.)

he bought the Indians in 1946, he immediately captured the imagination of the Cleveland fans and their enthusiasm by staging special nights for the fans, giving orchids to mothers on Mother's Day, putting on fireworks displays, hiring baseball clowns—not the ones in a circus—and putting together a good baseball team.

He took the door to his office off its hinges, saying the fans were always welcome in his office anyhow, so he didn't need a door. In a short-sleeved white sports shirt open at the collar, he sat with them in the bleachers and the unreserved grandstand seats and asked their opinions on what he was doing as the president of the Indians to help their team. He loved the press—what today we call the members of the news media— and they loved him.

He was a veteran of the fighting in the Pacific in the war just ended and had lost a leg. He walked on a wooden leg. He said the only two things in life he was afraid of were fire and termites.

With his flair for promotion, he hired two of baseball's all-time at- tractions, baseball comedians named Max Patkin and Jackie Price, to en- tertain the crowd before games. As the fans sat in Cleveland's Municipal Stadium buying Veeck's hot dogs and cold drinks, and peanuts and pop- corn, Patkin and Price dazzled them and broke them up in laughter. Price would hang upside down by his spikes in the batting cage and spray line drives to every part of the outfield. He would stand at home plate with three baseballs in his throwing hand and fire a strike to each base, all in one throw. For his grand finale, he would catch fly balls from behind the wheel of a Jeep while speeding across the outfield grass.

Price almost met disaster twice while performing his Jeep stunt, but he got away with it both times. In Mexico City and in Denver, while barnstorming with Bob Feller's All-Stars in the off-season, he acciden- tally went right through the outfield fence in his Jeep. He survived by jumping out just in time. He got a standing ovation every time he pulled that trick, and when it backfired on him in those two cities, he received standing ovations again, because the fans thought it was all part of his act.

The Yankees and the Red Sox were established contenders with proven stars for the second half of the 1940s. Ted Williams was back from the Marines. Dom DiMaggio and Johnny Pesky were home from three years in the Navy. Everybody knew at least one thing about those postwar Red Sox teams: they could hit. In 1946, the first postwar season, three of the top five hitters in the American League were on the Red Sox. Williams hit .342 that year, second only to Mickey Vernon's .353. Pesky, the only man in history to get more than two hundred hits in each of his first three years, was right behind him in third place with .335, and Dom DiMaggio was fifth in the league with .316. Williams was second behind Hank Greenberg in both home runs and runs batted in.

The Red Sox kept up their slugging in 1947. Williams won the batting championship with a .343 average, and Pesky finished third with .324.

Williams did more than that—he won baseball's "triple crown" by also leading the league in home runs with thirty-two and runs batted in with 114.

The Yankees were, well, the Yankees. They were coming off a World Series championship year in 1947 and were the team to beat as the clubs reported for spring training in 1948. Behind a new manager, Bucky Harris, the team that had dominated the American League since buying Babe Ruth in 1920, from the Red Sox, boasted a lineup of Joe DiMaggio, Tommy Henrich, Phil Rizzuto, and a rookie catcher-outfielder named Yogi Berra, who played his first seven games in the big leagues in 1946 as a catcher. In 1947 he divided his time between the outfield and behind the plate and hit .280 in eighty-three games. Charlie Keller, a mainstay in left in the same outfield with DiMaggio and Henrich, was slipping, but the Yankees, as always, had enough depth to overcome the drop in Keller's performance. Keller played in only forty-five games in 1947 with an average of only .238, but the Yankees rolled in Johnny Lindell, a six-foot four-and-a-half-inch, 217-pound outfielder who performed adequately with a 1947 average of .275. In the World Series, he led both teams with an even .500 average as the Yankees defeated the Dodgers in seven games.

The Yankees were strong in pitching too, led by their new right-hander, Allie Reynolds, who was obtained from the Indians before the 1947 season in exchange for New York's all-star second baseman, Joe Gordon. Reynolds responded immediately by leading the American League in winning percentage in 1947 and finishing second behind Bob Feller for the most wins with nineteen. Joe Page—"Fireman Joe"—tied Ed Klieman of the Indians in saves with seventeen, and Spud Chandler led the league with the lowest earned run average. Lefthander Eddie Lopat pitched the second most complete games, and Page pitched in the second most games.

That was the formidable opposition facing Bill Veeck's Indians as the 1948 season began. They won seventeen more games in 1948 than in 1947, for several reasons. One was Lou Boudreau. While making all the right moves as manager, he kicked his hitting into high gear and raised his batting average 48 points over 1947, from .307 to .355, second only to Ted Williams. Dale Mitchell's average jumped 20 points, to .336, right behind Boudreau. Bob Lemon, a converted third baseman, and Gene Bearden, a rookie knuckleballer, blossomed into twenty-game winners and finished tied for the second most wins in the league, only one behind

Hal Newhouser. Lemon even added a no-hit, no-run game, 2–0, against Detroit on June 30. Feller was right behind them with nineteen victories, tied with the Yankees' Vic Raschi for fourth best in the league.

Veeck was not only making progress—he was also making history. He integrated the American League in 1947, the same year Branch Rickey did in the National League with Jackie Robinson. Veeck signed a twenty-three-year-old second baseman and future star center fielder from the Newark Eagles of the Negro National League named Larry Doby. In the same year that designer Christian Dior introduced his famous "new look" with hemlines around the ankles, baseball was introducing a new look of its own.

Veeck was enough of a promoter, and an intelligent man who read as many as four books a week on every subject under the sun, to realize that he would be making more than history by integrating the American League. He would be making money too, putting people in his ballpark. And he was confident that Doby was good enough to help his team become successful.

Doby was no instant star. He played in twenty-nine games for the Indians in 1947, mostly as a pinch hitter. He played only six games in the field, four at second base, one at shortstop and one at first. He hit only .156, with no home runs and only two runs batted in. But Boudreau made the move of a genius in 1948, switching Doby to the outfield, where he divided his time between right and center fields. He became a star with a .301 batting average, 14 home runs and 66 runs batted in. In 1949, Boudreau played him only in center field. Doby hit .280 with 24 home runs. He was a star in the Major Leagues for thirteen years, until he retired after the 1959 season.

In mid-season of 1948, Veeck signed a second African American star from the Negro Leagues, who had the combination of ingredients that Veeck used to dream about—talent and showmanship. He was Leroy "Satchel" Paige, and he may have been baseball's greatest pitcher—and its all-time best entertainer.

Even the stories about his nickname are entertaining. There are different versions of how he acquired it, but Satch's own version was that he got it as a seven-year-old porter at the railroad station back in his hometown of Mobile, Alabama.

"I rigged up ropes around my shoulders and waist," he said later. "I carried a satchel in each hand and one under each arm. I carried so many

Satchel Paige, the first African American pitcher in the American League, joined the Cleveland Indians in time to win six games for them in 1948 and help them win the pennant after a career of stardom in the Negro Leagues. (Courtesy of National Baseball Hall of Fame Library, Cooperstown, N.Y.)

satchels that all you could see was satchels. You couldn't see Leroy Paige."

By the time Veeck signed him for the Indians in 1948, Paige had been a dominating star in the Negro Leagues for more than twenty years. He combined a colorful personality with eye-popping performances. In one of his favorite tricks of showmanship, he would call in his outfielders and sit one of them behind each of the three bases, sometimes with the tying run on base—and then strike out the side.

The pregame advertisements during his years in the Negro Leagues promised fans he would strike out the first nine hitters of the game, and he usually did. He frequently warmed up by throwing twenty straight pitches across a chewing gum wrapper on home plate. In Bismarck, North Dakota, Satch set up a matchstick on a stick beside home plate and knocked it off in thirteen of twenty tries. With a white semipro team in Bismarck in the 1930s, Paige won 134 out of 150 games. He pitched the Kansas City Monarchs to four straight pennants in the Negro American League in the late 1930s and early 1940s.

He named his pitches, as part of his psychological one-upmanship. He had his "hesitation pitch," his "jump ball," one called, of all things, his "long ball," and his "bee ball"—because it "be where I want it to be."

When he pitched against the white major leaguers on Bob Feller's All-Star teams during their barnstorming tours in the first years after the war, he won their profound respect. Joe DiMaggio called him "the best and fastest pitcher I've ever faced." Rogers Hornsby, considered the greatest righthanded hitter in history with the second highest lifetime batting average, behind only Ty Cobb, struck out five times against Paige in one game.

Paige became Feller's teammate on those 1948 Cleveland Indians, and there is irony in that. Some historians claim that the publicity accompanying Feller's barnstorming tours—which were always billed as "Bob Feller's All-Stars versus Satchel Paige's All-Stars"—were a key reason that the white executives in the Major Leagues were willing to sign black players. If those black players were good enough to succeed *against* the major league players, so the reasoning went, they were good enough to succeed *with* them.

When Veeck signed him, Paige told reporters he always thought he would be the first black player of the twentieth century to play in the majors, after several played professional ball in the nineteenth century. "Somehow," he said, "I'd always figured it would be me. Maybe it happened too late, and everybody figured I was too old. Maybe that was why it was Jackie and not me."

Paige was a forty-two-year-old rookie in 1948, the oldest rookie in the history of the big leagues. He succeeded immediately. Boudreau called him into a game in relief on July 9, and he pitched two scoreless innings. Only two of his pitches were not strikes. Satch won six games for the Indians that year against only one loss, with a highly respectable earned run average of only 2.48 per nine innings. Late in the season, in that air-tight pennant race with the Red Sox, Boudreau called Paige into a game against the Yankees in relief. It was the ninth inning, and Phil Rizzuto was on third base for the Yanks.

According to one of the many stories surrounding the Satchel Paige folklore, Rizzuto began dancing off the bag as Paige passed him on his way to the pitcher's mound. "Don't get nervous, little man," Paige is said to have told Rizzuto. "You ain't goin' nowhere."

Then Paige struck out the next three hitters—on ten pitches.

When I mentioned to Bob Feller that Paige's record was outstanding for a rookie at that advanced age and considering the pressure he was under both in the pennant race and as the first African-American pitcher in the American League, Feller said, "Any of us barnstormers could have predicted it."

7

The Drama and Babe Ruth

After finishing in sixth place in 1946, the Indians won twelve more games in 1947 and finished fourth. By 1948, they were ready. So, it turned out, were the Red Sox and the Yankees.

The three teams slugged it out toe-to-toe all season long. While the Boston Braves were winning the National League pennant by six and a half games over the Cardinals, the American League was a much different, and much tighter, story, with the Indians, Red Sox, and Yanks finishing with victory totals in the 90s, good enough for any team to win the pennant in most seasons. For the Indians, victory would mean their first pennant in twenty-eight years. For the Red Sox, victory would mean an all-Boston World Series. For the Yankees, victory would mean the same old story. The Yankees always seemed to win.

The Indians were the newcomers to a pennant race. In the end, the two players who seemed to make the difference were Boudreau and Bearden. Boudreau was an all-star shortstop, and in 1948 he was an all-star manager too, making what seemed to be all the right decisions. He was the American League's shortstop in the All-Star Game five times during his career. Some of the writers were comparing him to Honus Wagner as the greatest all-around shortstop of all time.

Boudreau was doing all this while playing on chronically weak ankles, robbed of their strength by his college basketball career, when he ran up and down those hardwood floors for the University of Illinois, where he was an all-American athlete in both basketball and baseball.

He led the American League with a .327 batting average in 1944, the same year he set a league record for highest fielding average for a shortstop. He broke that record only three years later.

Bob Feller remembers Boudreau as "one of the classiest human beings you'd ever want to meet." As evidence Feller points to the action by Boudreau in 1946, when he missed making the starting lineup for the All-Star Game because he voted for someone else instead of for himself, in the years when the players did the voting instead of the fans. That unselfish act prompted Bill Veeck to comment that Boudreau was "the greatest shortstop ever left off the All-Star team."

Bearden, one of the other key factors in the Indians' improvement in '48, was another story, and a unique one. After joining the team briefly in '47, "long enough for a cup of coffee" as the players say, he blossomed into a full-fledged star in '48 after discovering the knuckleball. He used it as what the players call his "out pitch"

Bearden, a lefthander, had people all over the country rooting for him after coming back from injuries received when he was wounded in the Pacific. He mastered control of his knuckleball, something that most pitchers find difficult. Because of its unpredictable directions, the knuckleball is hard to hit. That's also why it's hard to control—the pitcher doesn't have any idea of where it's going. The Indians' catcher that year, Jim Hegan, deserved credit too, for having the courage to call for that pitch and the ability to catch it. Like Rick Ferrell with the 1945 Washington Senators, Hegan was willing to take the risk of having passed balls charged against him because he knew his team's chances of winning with Bearden rested on Hegan's willingness to cope with the knuckler.

With Bearden's ability to throw the knuckleball and Hegan's ability to catch it, the rookie lefthander had a banner year in 1948. He led the league in lowest earned run average, had the second-highest won–lost percentage behind Jack Kramer of the Red Sox and the second most wins with twenty, only one behind Hal Newhouser. He tied Vic Raschi for the second most shutouts with six, four behind Bearden's teammate, Bob Lemon.

Unfortunately, Bearden was a one-year wonder. That rookie year in '48 was his only year of stardom. He developed control problems in '49 and his record fell to 8–8. He never won more than eight games in a season after his sensational year in '48. He was sold to Washington in 1950 and ended his big-league career by pitching for four teams in the next three seasons, never winning more than seven games.

A father holds up his son, wearing his baseball uniform, to see Babe Ruth as he lies in state at Yankee Stadium in 1948. (Courtesy of the Babe Ruth Birthplace and Museum.)

*   *   *

All of baseball, and all of America, received an emotional jolt on August 16. Babe Ruth died. The greatest, most dominating figure in the history of baseball or any other sport—including Michael Jordan in his prime—was gone from American life at the age of fifty-three.

Ruth was a special athlete and a special personality, and Americans knew it. No one else ever hit 714 home runs while also being the best left-handed pitcher in the American League in the first years of his career. And no one else loved the kids of America as much as the Babe, or was loved as much in return.

That's why fans, and some who weren't, turned out in almost shocking numbers to pay their respects. He lay in state at Yankee Stadium, "the House That Ruth Built," in the main lobby only 150 feet from home plate, which he stepped on so many times. He rested in a mahogany casket, a crucifix at his head and candles around him.

The line to view him was five across, and fans filed by him at the pace of a hundred a minute. The line around Yankee Stadium was six blocks long. More than fifty thousand people filed past him the evening he lay there. His funeral was held at St. Patrick's Cathedral on Fifth Avenue.

One American with a special reason to mourn Ruth's death was a future president, the first George Bush. Only a few months before, Bush was the starting first baseman and captain for Yale University's baseball team and had the distinction of being presented a manuscript of Ruth's

Babe Ruth donated the manuscript for his autobiography to Yale University's library in 1948. Accepting the manuscript is George Bush, the future president of the United States, who was Yale's first baseman and team captain. (Courtesy of the Babe Ruth Birthplace and Museum.)

memoirs for the Yale library by the Babe himself in a ceremony before a game against Princeton.

Bush also can claim another baseball distinction—playing in the first College World Series, in 1947 against the University of California, at Yankee Stadium. California won the Series on a home run by future major league all-star Jackie Jensen.

President Bush did not let his disappointment over losing the College World Series lessen his enthusiasm for baseball. As president more than forty years later, he kept his old first baseman's mitt in his desk drawer in the Oval Office and was ready to slip it on for a game of catch on the White House lawn on a moment's notice. It was the old "claw" model popularized by George McQuinn, a smooth-fielding first baseman with the Browns, Athletics, Reds, and Yankees. Bush had a simple explanation for his love of baseball: "It's just got everything."

People everywhere were moved by Ruth's death. In Japan, every baseball game was delayed for one minute of silence out of respect for the Babe, the one the Japanese called "Babu Russu," because he was always so popular after he traveled there with a team of all-stars after the 1934 season. That gesture of respect seemed to be still more proof that World War II was over. In the last stages of the war in the Pacific, with their situation growing more desperate each day, Japanese soldiers were hollering what they considered the supreme insult at the Americans, hoping to anger them out of their foxholes. From their sniper positions on the islands in the Pacific, they yelled, "To hell with Babe Ruth!"

The magical hold that the Babe had on Americans of all ages was reflected in a story told by former President Herbert Hoover when Ruth died. He told reporters that on a visit to Los Angeles while he was president, a boy asked him for three autographs. Hoover said he would be happy to give him an autograph, but why did he need three?

Because, the kid explained respectfully—and with a straight face—he could keep one and trade the other two for one of Babe Ruth.

With the three teams still battling each other as Labor Day weekend arrived and the baseball season headed into its final month, fate intervened in a cruel way against the Indians. One of their starting pitchers the year before, Don Black, was pitching in his eighteenth game after winning ten games for Cleveland in 1947. He was thirty-two years old and in his sixth season in the majors, all with the Indians, when he came to bat against the St. Louis Browns on September 13. Suddenly, he col-

Crowds lined Fifth Avenue in New York as the Babe Ruth funeral procession made its way to St. Patrick's Cathedral. (Courtesy of the Babe Ruth Birthplace and Museum.)

lapsed. He fell unconscious at home plate. Nothing had hit him, no player or ball or anything else. He simply dropped to the ground.

He was rushed to St. Vincent Charity Hospital, where the doctors diagnosed his problem as a brain hemorrhage. For the next several days, as his team and the Yankees and Red Sox fought for the pennant, Don Black fought for his life. He recovered enough to be able to listen to the games on the radio—teams were televising only a few of their home games in those pioneering days of TV. The Indians held a special night for him on September 22 at Municipal Stadium to raise money to defray his medical expenses.

Boudreau tapped Feller, who was in the middle of a hot streak without a loss in the last month, to pitch that night in a crucial game against the Red Sox. A Cleveland victory would create a three-way tie for first place in the American League. Only two years after the Cardinals and Dodgers finished in the first tie in the forty-five-year history of Major

League Baseball, the American League was on the verge of finishing in another one, and maybe a *three-way* tie at that.

With the pressures mounting on all three teams, Joe McCarthy provided even more pressure for himself and his team to overcome. McCarthy was in his first year as the Red Sox manager, after managing the Yankees since 1931 and winning eight pennants and seven World Series with them. A manager with a sparkling record like that could be expected to know what to say in any given situation, and what not to, but McCarthy, for reasons known only to himself, told reporters before the game on "Don Black Night" that he was delighted Feller was pitching for the Indians. He said Boston would "knock his brains out" and called Feller, who was one of the greatest pitchers of that time or any other, "just another pitcher."

Municipal Stadium sits hard by the shores of Lake Erie, and a cold night anywhere else in Ohio is even colder in Municipal Stadium. Feller wore two warm-up jackets in the dugout between innings and took an extra three minutes to warm up before the game.

The Indians scored three runs in the first inning, two on a home run by third baseman Ken Keltner, another star that season with thirty-one home runs, 119 runs batted in, and one of the best gloves of any third baseman in either league. Those three runs were all Feller needed. He pitched a three-hitter, held Ted Williams in check with an 0-for-4 night, and beat the Red Sox, 5–2, before 60,405 fans.

At the end of the night, all three teams had identical records of ninety-one wins and fifty-five losses with eight games to play.

The game raised $40,000 to help pay Black's medical bills. Black improved, but was never able to rejoin his team. He never pitched again. He died eleven years later at his home in Cuyahoga Falls, Ohio, a suburb of Cleveland. He was forty-two years old.

Four days after Don Black Night, Boudreau called on Feller again before 58,919 fans in Detroit. The Indians beat the Tigers, 4–1, behind a five-hitter by Feller and took over sole possession of first place in the American League for the first time in a month, since August 26. Cleveland was now one game ahead of both the Red Sox and the Yankees with five games to play.

Six days later, on October 2, the Red Sox ended the talk about a three-way tie by eliminating the Yankees. Now the race was down to two teams,

Shortstop-Manager Lou Boudreau led the Cleveland Indians to the 1948 pennant and World Series championship after the first tie in the history of the American League. (Carl Seid/National Baseball Hall of Fame Library, Cooperstown, N.Y.)

the Red Sox and the Indians, with the last day of the season at hand and the Indians leading the Red Sox by one game.

Boudreau went with Feller again. If the Indians won the game, they would be the American League champions, for the first time since 1920. When we were writing his autobiography, *Now Pitching—Bob Feller,* he told me he "had nothing when the game started, and nothing when I left it two and a third innings later." He called it "the kind of a day that pitchers dread." Feller gave up five hits and three walks and didn't strike out anyone. The result was a 7–1 loss to the Tigers.

At the same time, the Red Sox were beating the Yankees again, this time 10–5, with the help of two doubles by Ted Williams. Ted was the league's batting champion that year for the fourth time, only two years out of the Marine Corps, with a .369 average, the second highest of his career up to that point. He also hit twenty-five home runs and led the league in slugging average, doubles, and walks. The Red Sox closed the regular season with a three-game winning streak during which Williams had six hits in his last eight times at bat.

The American League had its first tie.

The Red Sox and the Indians were to play off the tie at Boston's Fenway Park on October 4. The selection of Boston as the playoff site was the result of a coin toss in the offices of American League President Will Harridge in Chicago. At the same time, it was also announced that the playoff would be only one game, not the best two of three employed by the National League two years before.

In that historic one-game playoff, Lou Boudreau put his leadership and his baseball ability on display for all the world to see and respect.

As his starting pitcher, Boudreau picked Gene Bearden, the rookie knuckleballer who was bidding to become a twenty-game winner that year. For Bearden, pitching in a history-making, tie-breaking game for the American League pennant and a spot in the World Series was about the last thing he could hope for only five years earlier. At that time, his only hope had been that he could stay alive.

He was a twenty-two-year-old sailor from Lexa, Arkansas, in July 1943 when his ship was torpedoed by a Japanese destroyer near the Solomon Islands in the South Pacific. He was a machinist's mate aboard a cruiser, the USS *Helena,* working in the engine room when it was hit. The "abandon ship" ordered was sounded, and Bearden began to climb a metal ladder leading out of the engine room when a second torpedo struck. The ladder crumbled, and Bearden was thrown to the deck below. His knee was twisted and crushed and he suffered a fractured skull when his head was split open by flying fragments. He was knocked unconscious as the ship began to sink.

Bearden told Harry Jones of *The Cleveland Plain Dealer,* "Somebody pulled me out. I don't know how he did it. The ship went down in about seventeen minutes. All I know is that I came to in the water some time later."

He spent the next two days in semiconscious condition floating on a rubber life raft with several other sailors. But at that, Bearden could count himself among the lucky ones. One-third of the crew of six hundred went down with the ship.

He was rescued by an American destroyer, evacuated to the United States, and transferred to a Navy hospital near Jacksonville, Florida, where surgeons inserted an aluminum plate and screw in his right knee and another plate in the back of his head. Then the doctors told him he would never pitch again.

"I don't know how many doctors told me that," he said in 1948. He was bedridden for a month after the operation and wore a plaster cast for two months. He walked on crutches at first and then with a cane. Seven months after the operation, he was able to walk under his own power again.

A minor leaguer in the Yankee farm system before the war, Bearden resumed his baseball career with their farm team at Binghamton, New York, until he was traded to the Indians in 1947, when he got into one game and pitched one-third of an inning. Through the minor leagues and after he reported to the Indians, Bearden never mentioned his war injury. "Maybe I should have told them about it," he said after winning his first start in 1948, a 6–1 three-hitter over the Senators, "but I didn't want them to get the wrong idea before I had a chance to start. After all, it sounds worse than it really is."

Nobody really believed that, but there he was—five years after being told he would never pitch again, standing on the mound at Fenway Park in Boston in history's first American League playoff game, with those plates in his head and his knee, on the verge of making baseball history and proving what millions of others wounded in the war were proving too—that yes, you can come back.

Bearden would be pitching with only two days of rest. Joe McCarthy, with a tired pitching staff, raised eyebrows all over the country by naming a journeyman righthander, Denny Galehouse, who started the game as an 8–7 pitcher for the season.

Feller told me that Boudreau's choice of Bearden was "a stroke of genius—and a shock to all of us." His reasoning was sound. He explained later that Boudreau thought a knuckleball pitcher could be effective against the powerful Red Sox lineup of Williams, Pesky, and DiMaggio. On the other hand, Boudreau was defying the prevailing wisdom that you don't start a lefthander in Fenway Park because of its short left field wall—"the Green Monster," an inviting target for righthanded long-ball hitters like Ken Keltner, Eddie Robinson, Joe Gordon, and Boudreau, who had eighteen home runs himself that year.

Boudreau took matters into his own hands in the first inning. After Galehouse retired the first two hitters of the game, Dale Mitchell and Allie Clark, Boudreau hit a 2–1 pitch from Galehouse into the screen above the Green Monster in left field and single-handedly put his team in front, 1–0.

The Red Sox tied the game in their half of the first inning, and the score remained 1–1 until the fourth inning. Boudreau took charge again, this time with a single to left. Joe Gordon followed with another hit, giving Cleveland men on first and second with no outs, when Ken Keltner came to the plate.

Now base runner Boudreau had to become manager Boudreau while standing on second base and waiting for Galehouse's first pitch to Keltner. The question facing him was whether to flash the bunt sign to Keltner, hoping to move both Gordon and himself into scoring position with only one out, or give Keltner the green light, remembering his thirty-one home runs that year. Boudreau decided to let Keltner hit away.

The result was a long fly ball over the Green Monster for a three-run homer and a 4–1 Cleveland lead. The Indians were never threatened after that. Boudreau hit another homer and another single for a perfect 4-for-4 day, and Bearden kept the powerful Red Sox weapons silent, going the full nine innings on a five-hitter. He held Williams to a single in four trips to the plate. The Indians won the game and the pennant, 8–3.

For Galehouse, the loss was even more disappointing than for his teammates. He pitched only two innings for the Red Sox the next season

and retired at the age of thirty-seven after fifteen years in the big leagues
and 109 victories.

The Indians had destroyed the possibility of an all-Boston World
Series. Now they were in it themselves, but after such an exhausting pennant race and a playoff, did they have enough gas left in the tank to win
the Series?

The Indians didn't wait to get back to Cleveland for their celebration.
They had a party that night in their Boston hotel, the Kenmore. Early in
the festivities, Boudreau, in the presence of his wife, his players, and the
Indians' executives, walked up to a microphone, raised a glass, and said,
"I offer a toast to someone who right now is in the hospital—Don Black."

Tears were rolling down his cheeks.

For at least one member of the Red Sox, the news was not all bad.
Now Dom DiMaggio would not have to postpone his wedding with Emily
Frederick.

8

Final Scores

While the U.S. Air Force's C-47s and C-54s continued to keep the people of Berlin alive as summer turned into fall, Lou Boudreau was faced with still another challenge, the most formidable of all in baseball—winning the World Series. He was called "the Boy Wonder" manager when the Indians named him to the job in 1942. He was only twenty-four years old, and he was still only thirty-one when the 1948 World Series began. His managerial opponent on the Braves was Billy Southworth, a likeable and respected baseball veteran who already had ten years of experience as a manager in the big leagues, dating back to 1929.

Southworth's Braves had beaten out the St. Louis Cardinals of Stan Musial by six and a half games. The Braves fielded a formidable batting order with four .300 hitters: Eddie Stanky, Alvin Dark, Tommy Holmes, and Mike McCormick. There would have been five, but outfielder Jeff Heath, a former Indian and a .319 hitter that year, broke his ankle sliding into home in September and missed the Series. The Braves had other solid players too, including Bob Elliott and Earl Torgeson.

Their pitching staff was headed by a lefthander, Warren Spahn, and a righthander, Johnny Sain. They were two World War II veterans, with Spahn surviving the Battle of the Bulge and Sain seeing service as a pilot. Both men said their wartime service gave them a new confidence in themselves. On the weekly TV show *Major League Baseball Magazine*, Spahn said, "When I came back, I thought, 'Wow! What a great way to make a living! If I goof up, there's going to be a relief pitcher coming in. Nobody's going to shoot me.'" For his part, Sain said his discovery in

The one-two pitching punch of the Boston Braves in 1948—Warren Spahn *(left)* and Johnny Sain. (Courtesy of National Baseball Hall of Fame Library, Cooperstown, N.Y.)

pilot training that he could fly an airplane gave him the feeling that he was able to do more things than he might have thought possible. He said that confidence stayed with him when the two pitchers returned from the war and rejoined the Braves in 1946.

Spahn was in the early years of a career in which he became the winningest lefthander in history. He won 363 games in his career, 15 of them that year. Sain led the National League with 24 wins and was a 20-game winner, the pitcher's mark of excellence, four times in a career that lasted eleven years and produced 139 victories.

Five other Braves pitchers won only forty-four games among them in 1948, so the running gag in Boston was that Southworth was praying for rain between starts by Spahn and Sain. The fans and the media said it in rhyme:

Spahn and Sain,
And pray for rain.

The drama and the pressure may have been greater for Bob Feller than for anyone else. He was finally getting to pitch in a World Series, at the age of twenty-nine, and he was coming off a letdown after failing to win twenty games for the first time in six full seasons and then losing the Indians' final game of the regular season, three days earlier, when they could have won the pennant without that playoff game against the Red Sox.

The Series opened in Boston on the afternoon of October 6, in the years when the World Series was still played under the sun instead of under the lights. The Braves fans were in a frenzy. Scalpers were getting as much as $50 a ticket. One of the most prominent spectators at Braves Field that day was Boston's mayor, John Fitzgerald—"Honey Fitz," grandfather of future president John Kennedy. He hadn't missed a World Series game by either the Braves or the Red Sox in forty-five years.

When Johnny Sain took the mound for the Braves in the first inning, the two teams were playing the first World Series game to be televised. The city set up a hundred RCA television sets on the Boston Common, for the first ten thousand fans who showed up. The sets were donated by the Gillette Safety Razor Company. The *Boston Post* called it "a vast and unique experiment" and distributed score cards to the viewers. The paper reported, "The action on the baseball field was clearly visible . . ."

Feller's situation was just the opposite of the playoff game. He had what the players call "his good stuff" in his start against the Braves and retired the first eleven hitters in order. He gave up his first hit, a single by Heath's replacement in left field, Marv Rickert, in the fifth inning, then retired the next nine hitters. Through seven innings, Feller was pitching a shutout and a one-hitter. Sain was close to matching him, with a shutout of his own and a four-hitter.

When the Braves came up in the bottom half of the eighth inning, the scoreboard at Braves Field showed fifteen zeroes. Then one of the most controversial plays in World Series history occurred.

Feller committed the pitcher's cardinal sin of walking the leadoff hitter, catcher Bill Salkeld, on a 3–2 pitch in the eighth. Southworth immediately sent in a faster man, the Braves' other catcher, Phil Masi, as a pinch runner. Then he flashed the sign to his next hitter, Mike McCormick, to lay down a sacrifice bunt. McCormick did, advancing Masi to second base—scoring position.

Boudreau then came to the mound and told Feller to walk the next hitter, Eddie Stanky. Feller disagreed with Boudreau's strategy. Boudreau wanted to set up a double play or at least a force play at any base with the pitcher coming up, but Feller was confident he could get Stanky out. Boudreau, however, was remembering what Branch Rickey said of Stanky: "He can't hit, he can't throw, he can't run and he can't field. All he can do is win games."

Feller walked Stanky on orders, bringing up the pitcher. Sain foiled Boudreau's strategy by not hitting the ball on the ground for a force play or a double play. Instead, he got the ball into the air with a fly to short right field. That brought up Boston's right fielder, Tommy Holmes, with runners still on second and third and now two outs. Holmes wasn't the one you would pick to face in a situation like that. He was one of the best hitters in the National League, with the third-highest average in the league that year—.325.

Boudreau was still making managerial decisions. Cleveland had one of the most successful pickoff plays in baseball that year, and Boudreau

Tommy Holmes was the hitter when one of the most controversial plays in World Series history occurred in 1948. Then he drove in the only run of the game. (Courtesy of National Baseball Hall of Fame Library, Cooperstown, N.Y.)

decided this was the time for it. He flashed the sign to home plate, to his catcher, Jim Hegan. The wheels were set in motion for the play the Indians had been practicing for five years. In the press box, Tris Speaker, the retired Cleveland Hall of Famer, knew what was up. He told the reporters around him, "They'll pick him off."

In the Braves dugout, Nelson Potter was thinking the same thing. He had pitched in the American League for ten years before joining the Braves that year, and he knew the Indians—and Boudreau—well. He yelled out to the Braves runners and their coaches on the bases, "They've got a great play at second base! If he gets six feet off there, they'll get him!"

As Feller looked back at second base to make sure Masi wasn't taking any liberties with his lead, he spotted Boudreau's glove. Instead of being folded and resting on his left thigh, it was over his left knee with the fingers extending below his knee—the pickoff sign.

As Feller turned back to face Holmes at the plate, Boudreau flashed a different sign—a raised heel—to Larry Doby in center field. Feller counted silently—"one . . . two . . . three . . . throw!"

At the start of Feller's count, Boudreau bolted toward second base. Doby was dashing in toward second in case Feller made a wild throw. If he did, Boudreau's job was to get tangled up with the runner so he couldn't take third or maybe even score. At the same time, he had to make sure he wouldn't get called by the umpire for interference, which would move the runner to third.

Feller whipped around and threw a strike to second base. The shortstop's responsibility on that play was to make sure he gets to the bag in time. Cleveland's pitchers were told to throw the ball to the bag, not to the shortstop. Feller and Boudreau combined to execute the play perfectly. The ball and Boudreau arrived simultaneously, before Masi could scramble back.

The Indians had caught Masi napping while representing the winning run in the first game of the World Series. A play like that can be a momentum builder that can carry a team to victory in the first game and provide enough of a spark to power it right through to victory in the Series itself.

Boudreau tagged Masi out by two feet. But the Indians also picked off the umpire, Bill Stewart of the National League. He called Masi safe. On the next pitch, Holmes hit a line drive just inside the bag at third as Ken Keltner made a dive for it. The hit scored Masi easily.

Feller finished the game by becoming the tenth man to pitch a two-hitter in the World Series, the first to do it over nine innings and the first to lose one. The Braves won, 1–0, with Sain pitching a four-hitter. Feller told me in later years that the play might not have made any difference anyhow with the way Sain was pitching, too. He said the Indians might not have scored a run if they had played into the night.

The papers the next day ran pictures that clearly showed Masi was out, but Stewart stood his ground. "I was in a perfect position to call the play. I've made millions of those close decisions. Why I've made about a hundred like that this season. Sure I anticipated the play. I anticipate every possible play and the pictures show that I was in a perfect position to call the play."

Ten years later, however, Bill Stewart admitted to Feller that he blew the call. And to this day, more than a half century later, Feller says, "I get asked about that play everywhere I go—and I have never had even one person tell me Masi was safe."

The papers carried another major story that morning, one far more ominous than the outcome of a baseball game, even one in the World Series. On the same front page of *The New York Times* that featured the World Series story from Boston by John Drebinger, an article by Drew Middleton reported that the Soviets—"the Russians"—were massing four hundred thousand men for a civil war in East Germany to stop the growing amount of sabotage.

The Indians won the second game of the Series, 4–1, in a duel by two future Hall of Fame pitchers, Bob Lemon and Warren Spahn. Then it was on to Cleveland, and the next chapter in the Gene Bearden story.

Cleveland was going crazier than ever over the Indians. Some 150,000 fans jammed downtown streets when they won the pennant in that play-off game. Ninety tons of confetti were cleaned up the next day. But in the World Series, the atmosphere was even wilder.

More than twenty thousand fans stood in twenty-two lines during a drizzle to buy the few remaining tickets for the third game. A twenty-four-year-old truck driver named Jim Banyard was one of them. He waited for five hours to buy a $1 ticket for a bleacher seat. Knowing he faced a marathon wait, he came with a homemade oilcloth tent, five boiled eggs, four sandwiches, a piece of pie, a banana, an apple, a quart of milk, an alarm clock, two candles, and a radio.

Three television manufacturers—Philco, Stromberg-Carlson, and

Hammon—donated six big-screen TV sets for use in the Central Armory so fans could see the games free. Not everything was a bargain, however. The price of downtown parking was raised all the way to two dollars.

Bearden continued his heroics with a five-hit shutout as the Indians went ahead in the Series, two games to one, with a 2–0 win. Bearden was doing everything, it seemed. He scored Cleveland's first run after doubling to right. On the mound, he was almost untouchable, retiring sixteen of the last eighteen hitters. In front of 70,306 screaming fans the rookie struck out four, controlled his knuckleball to perfection by not walking a man, and later added a single to his hitting accomplishments. He threw only eighty-four pitches. The game was over in one hour and thirty-six minutes.

But Bearden was not finished with his heroics. The Series stretched out to the sixth game, with the Indians leading, three wins to two. Boston was also the scene for this drama. Boudreau called on his rookie again, this time with three days of rest. Boudreau wheeled Bearden into the game as a relief pitcher with one out in the eighth inning after Bob Lemon got into a jam.

Bearden was not a hero immediately. Phil Masi became a thorn in the Indians' side again, this time with an RBI double off Bearden as a pinch hitter. The blow brought the Red Sox to within one run, 4–3. But Bearden was up to the challenge. He allowed no more hits and saved the game, and the World Series, for the Indians. The rookie with the knuckleball, three years after returning from the war as a wounded veteran, was the pitching hero of the Series. Doby was the Indians' hitting star with a .318 average.

Irony surfaced again in the final out. The Series ended on a fly ball to left field that was caught by the Indians' Bob Kennedy. It was hit by Tommy Holmes, who drove in the only run of the first game.

A crowd of two hundred thousand screaming fans turned out for a victory parade in Cleveland. A Cleveland newspaper quoted Dr. Marguerite Hertz, a clinical psychologist from Western Reserve University, on why fans go nuts when their team wins the World Series or some other sports championship. She said the mobs, the horns blowing, the streams of ticker tape floating down from windows above all are "a healthy release of animal instincts."

Meanwhile, long-playing records were introduced, the Air Force began investigating reports of something called "flying saucers," and Senator Joseph McCarthy of Wisconsin launched investigations into charges of Communism in government, the movie industry, and other segments of American life. His heavy-handed tactics prompted Her block, the editorial cartoonist for *The Washington Post,* to coin the term *McCarthyism.*

The tension between the United States and the Soviet Union over the crisis in Berlin stretched on as the airlift continued to save the lives of the city's citizens while the man who ordered the airlift, President Truman, staged one of the greatest shockers in presidential history by upsetting Thomas E. Dewey, the former governor of New York, in November.

He did it in his hard-hitting, pull-no-punches, "Give 'em hell, Harry" style of campaigning, which is what one voter in a crowd yelled after the campaign got under way in earnest. Truman took on his Republican opponents by calling them "bloodsuckers with offices on Wall Street, princes of privilege, plunderers." The polls were unanimous in predicting that Dewey would unseat the incumbent president, to which Truman responded that the polls were "designed to lull the voter into sleeping on election day. They ought to call them 'sleeping polls.' "

The month before Truman's historic reelection, his eventual successor also became a president. Dwight Eisenhower was named president of Columbia University in New York.

The U.S. and British planes in the Berlin Airlift continued to save those 2.5 million lives, delivering coal from the Ruhr Valley, milk and other dairy products from Denmark, wheat from the United States, coffee from Brazil, and sugar from Cuba. While the airlift was sustaining the people, a *sea*lift was sustaining the *air*lift. Twelve million gallons of airplane fuel were delivered by sea each month to "keep 'em flying," the Air Force slogan of the 1940s.

Halfway around the world, a twenty-five-year-old Air Force pilot from Iowa, Captain Ken Herman, was test-flying new YC-97 Boeing Stratocruisers in California when he suddenly received orders to proceed to Germany in the earliest days of the airlift.

"My orders were to go there for two weeks to pinch-hit for a pilot whose wife was threatening to divorce him," Herman, now a retired colonel living in Arizona, told me in the 1990s. "There were a lot of divorces being threatened as a result of pilots being ordered over there, and some of those marriages collapsed under the pressures caused by the airlift. It was a military crisis that produced marital crises. Many wives felt they had sacrificed enough during World War II, and that they shouldn't have to go through this only three years later. They had a point."

The orders to Captain Herman in California were part of an alert flashed to air force bases around the world from Washington:

PREPARE TO RELEASE ALL AVAILABLE C-54 SKYMASTERS
TO THE UNITED STATES AIR FORCES COMMAND IN EUROPE

The Russians built a practice bombing range near one of the runways used by the American pilots as one of their war-of-nerves tactics. Their Yak fighter planes hassled the Allied pilots. Captain Herman, who flew 190 missions during the airlift, knew that the Russians had more to worry about than just the airlift itself. They didn't have the atomic bomb, and America did.

In the first days of the airlift, Truman dispatched two squadrons of B-29 bombers to England, knowing that everybody in the world remembered B-29s were the planes that dropped the atomic bombs on Hiroshima and Nagasaki.

"Our intelligence in London spread the word that we had a squadron of B-29s based in England, loaded with atomic bombs and ready to take off for Russia on a moment's notice," Herman says today. "They let it be known that if one of those fighter planes hassling us ever really started something, or if one of those bombs from their new bombing range landed somewhere on one of our bases accidentally on purpose, our B-29s would flatten Moscow in a day."

The Americans never worried about getting involved in a nuclear bombing of Moscow over something that might flare up during the airlift. "The Russians didn't know it," Colonel Herman says, "but the English refused to let us keep atomic weapons on British soil." There was something else they didn't know: The B-29s sent to England by Truman had never been modified to carry atomic bombs.

"There never was a squadron of B-29s loaded with atomic bombs," Herman said. "Those Russian fighters never forced any fights with us in the three narrow air corridors that we followed into Berlin—via Hamburg, Frankfurt and Hanover—and they kept their bombs exploding on their territory and not ours. That talk our intelligence people were spreading that those B-29s were loaded with atomic bombs worked. The Russians fell for it."

The danger of war was grave during every day of the airlift. After leaving the presidency, Truman wrote, "There was always the risk that

Russian reaction might lead to war. We had to face the possibility that Russia might deliberately choose to make Berlin the pretext for war . . ."

History shows that in the same month the airlift ended—September 1949—President Truman announced that the Russians had exploded their first atomic bomb.

Captain Herman carried twenty thousand pounds of coal in his C-54 cargo plane on each mission. The operation reached its peak in April 1949, when 1,398 flights in twenty-four hours delivered 12,490 tons of supplies, prompting the men of the airlift to call it "the Easter Parade."

On October 22, Truman authorized the transfer of another twenty-six C-54s to Berlin. General Clay, warned flatly, "The airlift will be continued until the blockade is lifted."

Heroes emerged. One of them was 1st Lt. Royce Stephens, whose C-54 developed a fire in one engine shortly after takeoff. The other four crew members bailed out, but Stephens stayed with his plane. It crashed into an open field, still carrying its load of coal for the people of Berlin. Lieutenant Stephens was killed in the crash. In all, thirty U.S. airmen and one American civilian lost their lives in the airlift.

A hero of a different sort emerged, Gail Halvorsen, who became known as "the Candy Bomber" because he always stashed his own supply of candy on board his plane and "parachuted" his gifts to the children of West Berlin as he came in for his landings. He collected the candy from his fellow pilots and tied pieces to handkerchiefs, forming miniature parachutes. To the German children, the candy was even more delicious than it would have been to children in other countries. Living under Hitler's harsh dictatorship and then under equally harsh Communist rule, this was the first time in their lives that they had tasted chocolate.

The word about the Candy Bomber got out, in a big way, when one of his "parachutes" almost hit a German newspaper reporter on the head. The reporter, of course, asked questions, then wrote a story about Halvorsen's humanitarian operation—and the story went around the world in a flash.

Suddenly, hundreds of pounds of candy, in handkerchiefs, began pouring into Halvorsen's base from America. Military volunteers helped to distribute them to the air crews flying into the Allies' unloading destinations at Tempelhof, Gatow, and Tegel. The candy was dropped in the makeshift parachutes to schools, playgrounds, and other spots all around West Berlin. Another pilot, Captain Eugene Williams, thought of the

Lieutenant Gail Halvorsen "the Candy Bomber," of Garland, Utah, holds one of his miniparachutes that he used to drop candy to the children of West Berlin during the Berlin Airlift in 1948. (Courtesy of the Gail S. Halvorsen Collection.)

Lieutenant Halvorsen reads mail at Rhein-Main Air Base in Frankfurt from Americans who sent him candy to drop to the children of West Berlin. Note the boxes of Hershey bars behind him. (Courtesy of Gail S. Halvorsen Collection.)

kids who couldn't run after the parachutes. He delivered a special load of candy to a hundred children who were patients at a hospital in the American sector of Berlin.

Candy for the kids wasn't the only thing that Americans were sending to Berlin. CARE—the Cooperative for American Remittances to Europe—one of the largest non-sectarian, nongovernment organizations in the world, was sending even more. For $10 a package, Americans were paying for boxes containing meats, margarine, fruit, chocolate, sugar, egg powder, coffee, flour, and soap as well as clothing and medicine. The boxes, with their CARE letters stenciled on the top and the sides, were familiar sights in the movie newsreels, the first TV newscasts, and the daily newspapers. Writer Carolyn Hughes Crowley reported in May 2001 in *Smithsonian* magazine that during the airlift, some two hundred thousand CARE packages were shipped to the people of Berlin from the people of America.

The folks back home remembered the men of the "the Lift"—their sons, husbands, brothers, and boy friends—at Christmas. Bob Hope brought his show to Fassberg with his wife, Delores, plus Irving Berlin,

Jinx Falkenberg, and the Radio City Music Hall Rockettes. *The New York Times* published an editorial saying "We were proud of our Air Force during the war. We're prouder of it today."

The airlift became another victory for Truman and America, with the Russians calling off their blockade the next summer. At its end in 1949, the box score of that challenge read:

> 462 days
> 277,264 flights
> 2,300,000 tons of supplies
> 60,000 flying and administrative personnel

What did all that accomplish? Plenty, according to President Truman, besides saving 2.5 million lives. He said America had stopped Communism in Europe in its tracks in the most serious military confrontation yet between the world's two superpowers in what was being called the "Cold War."

It was the first time an airlift was used as an instrument of policy. The Truman administration adopted the position that it would stop the spread of Communism in Europe, and then applied the airlift as its instrument in putting that policy into effect.

The airlift was also the first major mission of the new United States Air Force, established by President Truman the year before. The airlift's influence is felt even today. It established techniques for airlift operations that are still employed. Airlift practices based on the Berlin experience were part of U.S. military operations in the Korean and Vietnam Wars as well as other U.S. military engagements in Panama, Hungary, the Persian Gulf, and even stateside crises like the nuclear scare at Three Mile Island in Pennsylvania.

As the C-54s flew their final flights during the Berlin Airlift, an American military presence in another of the world's trouble spots ended. On June 29, 1949, the last U.S. forces were withdrawn from South Korea. Only four days short of a year later, North Korean troops, using Russian weapons, ammunition, and equipment, and on signals from Stalin in the Kremlin, stormed across the Thirty-eighth Parallel that divides North and South and started the Korean War.

Like its military applications, the human side of the Berlin Airlift also reaches to today. So grateful were the people of Berlin then, and still today, that they established their own organization, Luftbruckedanke—

"Airlift Thanks"—immediately after the airlift ended. Over the years, it has provided college scholarships, financial assistance to their widows, and funds to airlift veterans experiencing financial troubles.

Just as the organization's help continues to this day, so does the genuine international friendship forged out of that harrowing time in 1948 and 1949. Ken Herman was invited by the organization to visit Berlin in 1994 as president of the Berlin Airlift Veterans Association. The trip was paid for by Luftbruckedanke.

Colonel Herman was thanked literally hundreds of times by Berliners for his role in the airlift. "Everywhere I went," he said, "people couldn't thank me enough, even this many years later."

One man told Herman, "My son was five months old when you began the airlift. You saved his life." As the man spoke, he cried. When Colonel Herman tells the story today, he also cries.

PART THREE
· · ·
1951

9

"The Giants Is Dead"

A half century isn't really that long ago, as history goes, but when you look back at 1951 and the first year or two of that decade, it seems like the dark ages. Americans still had to dial every number on the telephone and wait for the dial to wind its way back to its original position before dialing the next digit because there was no such thing as a push-button phone. If we wanted to call long distance, the operator had to do it for us. Air-conditioned homes and cars equipped with "a/c"? Almost nobody had them. Most secretaries still used manual typewriters, not electric ones.

Color television sets were still a dream for most Americans—millions didn't even have a black-and-white one. Many families still got all their home entertainment from the radio, and from actually talking to each other in the evenings instead of sitting hypnotized in front of a TV set. Many new cars still came without automatic transmissions and with a metal strip dividing the windshield down the middle. And almost all drivers still rolled down their windows and used hand signals because turn indicators were not yet in widespread use.

Still, the good life of the postwar years was continuing. Americans were enjoying two new books that quickly became literary classics, *From Here to Eternity* by James Jones and J. D. Salinger's *The Catcher in the Rye*. On Broadway, music lovers were flocking to see *The King and I*.

All of our dreams of the future were put on hold in June 1950 with the start of the Korean War, only five years after the end of World War II. When the 1951 baseball season started, the United States was in a state of national emergency, formally declared by President Truman. Selective Service was drafting eighty thousand men a month. The whole world kept its fingers crossed. Newspaper columnists started calling our newest conflict "World War Two and a Half."

But there were brighter sides to what *Reader's Digest* used to call "Life in These United States"—television shows that made us laugh, like *Your Show of Shows* with Sid Caesar and Imogene Coca and *Texaco Star Theater* with Milton Berle, who signed a seven-figure, thirty-year contract with NBC that year, and a funny new show starring "America's favorite clown," Red Skelton. A new comic strip—when "the funnies" really were funny—*Dennis The Menace* made its debut in 1951, a year after another national favorite, *Peanuts* with Charlie Brown, entered our lives.

The songs—like "Hello, Young Lovers" from *The King and I*, "Shrimp Boats" by Rosemary Clooney, Nat King Cole's "Unforgettable," and "Because of You" by one of the newest singing stars, Tony Bennett—still had actual melodies and words you could understand. Americans were so prosperous in those post–World War II boom times that we owned 42,700,000 cars, even though the new ones cost $2,000 or more. That was enough cars to justify building the New Jersey Turnpike, which opened that year.

Something else happened in our economy in 1951 that is still in our lives today, for better or for worse: The credit card was introduced, by Franklin National Bank of New York. In 1999, a national survey by the Pew Research Center for the People and the Press showed that 68 percent of Americans felt that widespread use of credit cards was the least beneficial social change of the twentieth century.

New products continued to enter our lives: sugarless chewing gum, Dacron suits, and Chrysler's power steering. The Dow Jones average varied 38 points over the year, from a low of 238 to a high of 276.

Right from the start, the 1951 baseball season was different. On Opening Day at Griffith Stadium in Washington, the president of the United States was booed. The fans middle-aged or older could remember only one other time when a president was booed at a baseball game—Herbert Hoover at the World Series during the depths of the Depression and the national alcohol-free dry spell called Prohibition.

I was there when the fans let Truman have it. I was home on my first leave from the Air Force after completing basic training, and Opening Day was exactly the reason I came home with my Washington buddy,

Jules Loh. We had worked together on the sports staff of *The Washington Post* and when the Korean War started, we decided to enlist together, in January 1951. When April came, we knew where we had to be, and it wasn't on any Air Force base. We had to be at Griffith Stadium doing what we did every April, welcoming the new baseball season.

We were sitting in the upper deck on the third base side when the presidential party arrived in limousines, driving onto the first base side of the field in foul territory in front of the Senators' dugout. The presidential box was adjacent to the dugout. It was April 20, nine days after Truman fired Douglas MacArthur as commander of the United Nations forces in Korea for publicly and repeatedly opposing Truman's policies involving the war.

Truman was a victim of poor timing. Only the day before, MacArthur had rallied millions of Americans to his side of his public fight with Truman in an address before a joint session of Congress with his "Old Soldiers Never Die" speech. In the war that week, the one that Mac-Arthur had predicted would be over by the previous Christmas, American troops were engaged in hand-to-hand combat with the enemy forces of North Korea and Red China, fighting them with their fists and rifle butts.

After his congressional appearance in Washington, MacArthur was hailed as a conquering hero in New York with a parade down Broadway attended by 7.5 million wildly cheering people, twice as many as the number who cheered for Charles Lindbergh in 1927 and Dwight D. Eisenhower in 1945. MacArthur had received the same kind of tumultuous welcome in San Francisco and Washington, and his staff had also received invitations for him to visit Chicago, Philadelphia, Baltimore, and other large cities.

As Truman climbed out of his car at Griffith Stadium, he received the opposite kind of welcome. The booing started and immediately became a loud chorus of protest, raining down on him from behind the presidential box in the lower deck and from above in the upper deck and all around the ballpark. About the only applause came from the presidential party and others near Truman. It was no way to start a new season of America's national pastime, and no time to demonstrate national disunity in front of the rest of the world, especially our enemies in the Soviet Union. The booing remains one of the rudest public greetings ever given to a president, and maybe the worst of all.

Despite the welcomes for MacArthur elsewhere and the rude reception at Griffith Stadium, Truman stood firmly behind his decision to fire MacArthur. With Truman's ability to reduce complicated issues to their simplest dimensions, he explained his dismissal of MacArthur in a letter to Eisenhower, the man who succeeded him in the White House two years later. "I was sorry to reach a parting of the way with the big man in Asia," he wrote, "but he asked for it and I had to give it to him." Eisenhower, who served on MacArthur's staff for nine years, told reporters, "When you put on a uniform, there are certain inhibitions which you accept."

The New York Yankees, in the midst of establishing their record of winning their league's pennant and the World Series five years in a row, their first five seasons under Casey Stengel, started the season buzzing by introducing a "phee-nom," a nineteen-year-old shortstop from Oklahoma named Mickey Mantle. He was being ballyhooed as the man who would replace the aging Joe DiMaggio as the next Yankee superstar. That was enough to worry the incumbent shortstop, Phil Rizzuto, the American League's Most Valuable Player in 1950.

"I read so much about him," Rizzuto told author Bob Allen, "I thought, 'What chance do I have?' Here I was the MVP the year before, and I figured this kid was going to take my job, since he was a shortstop, you know. I read all this stuff about him, and then I saw him."

Rizzuto said he didn't even unpack his bags in St. Petersburg, the Yankees' spring training headquarters, until the team began to play exhibition games. "I watched him field and throw," Rizzuto said. "He had a strong arm, but when he threw, he would clear everybody out of the first base area. They put him in the outfield real quick." Rizzuto shouldn't have been surprised. The year before, while playing for Joplin, Missouri, Mantle set a record for the most errors by a shortstop with fifty-five, many of them on wild throws across the infield past the first baseman.

Stengel assigned the responsibility for converting Mantle into an outfielder to Tommy Henrich, "Old Reliable," the star right fielder in the Yankees' legendary 1940s outfield of DiMaggio, Henrich, and Charlie Keller. Henrich had retired after the 1950 season and was a Yankee coach in 1951. Stengel wanted him to groom Mantle as a center fielder, with an eye toward the rapidly approaching day when DiMaggio would hang up the Yankee pinstripes for the last time. For years, Henrich had been recognized not only as one of the best outfielders in baseball but also one of the smartest. Stengel, an outfielder in the Major Leagues himself for fourteen years, knew Henrich would be the perfect teacher for a young

Manager Casey Stengel guided the New York Yankees to their 1951 World Series victory over the rival Giants in six games. In 1962 he became the first manager of the New York Mets, an expansion team of rejects from other teams. The Mets lost three times as many games as they won, with 40 victories against 120 defeats, as Stengel asked his classic question: "Can't anybody here play this game?" (Carl Kidwiler/National Baseball Hall of Fame Library, Cooperstown, N.Y.)

"can't miss" prospect just up from the minors who wasn't even on the team's roster and whose professional experience totaled only a year and a half in the low minors.

Henrich remembers the unseasoned rookie. "That first year," he said, "he was very shy, and anything I said to him, he believed. He was so quiet. He didn't have that drive in his early years, but he learned. He grew into it. But DiMaggio had that pride from day one."

Mantle became an even greater topic of conversation by putting on a red-hot spring training season. He drove in seven runs in an exhibition game against the University of Southern California, which had just beaten the Pittsburgh Pirates, with a walk, single, triple, and a 430-foot home run. When the Yankees broke camp to head north for the start of the season, Mantle was the starting right fielder, with a .402 spring training batting average and 32 runs batted in.

Stengel told reporters, using his patented—and ungrammatical—"Stengeleese" to express himself, "This is a kid which is going to be tremenjois." DiMaggio joined the chorus of praise for Mantle by calling him "the greatest prospect I can remember." DiMag added, "Maybe he has to learn something about catching a fly ball, but that's all. He can do everything. If he's good enough to take my job, I can always move over to right or left."

Branch Rickey, who had moved from the Brooklyn Dodgers to the Pittsburgh Pirates as their general manager, joined in. Rickey, considered one of the shrewdest judges of talent in baseball history, said, "He's the finest prospect I have ever seen. He has that flawless, level swing, and the fastest break from the plate I have ever seen."

As if he didn't have enough believers already, Mantle closed out his rookie spring training season by going 4-for-4 including a home run against the rival Brooklyn Dodgers in his first game in Yankee Stadium.

With the start of the 1951 American League season, Mantle went into an immediate nosedive. His problems were compounded when the fans became resentful toward him because he was deferred from the military draft with the Korean War still in its first year. The public outcry against him reached such a level that the Yankees asked the draft board's doctors to reexamine their star rookie.

His case went all the way to the Surgeon General, who again declared Mantle unfit for military duty because of osteomyelitis, a bacterial infection of bone and bone marrow causing inflammation that can reduce the blood supply to the bone. Mantle contracted the disease as the result of a vicious hit to his left shin while playing high school football. The doctors at the time thought his leg might have to be amputated, but two weeks of penicillin shots saved it. After two weeks in the hospital, Mantle was healthy again. It was only the first of four flare-ups over the next two years. The young star was in the hospital for two weeks each time. Mantle continued to be plagued periodically by pain from the osteomyelitis throughout his baseball career.

Having been deferred from the military draft again, Mantle returned to the Yankee lineup. The boos from the stands continued, even in New York, and so did his hitting slump. Things seemed to reach bottom when he struck out five times in a row in a doubleheader. Then he was farmed out to the Yankees' minor league team in Kansas City.

His troubles continued there, and it became too much for the kid. In his desperation, the nineteen-year-old put in a call for help to his father back home in Commerce, Oklahoma, thirty miles from Joplin, Missouri, where he had enjoyed such happier times only the summer before. His father, Mutt Mantle, who named his son after the father's favorite player, Mickey Cochrane, took the tough-love approach with Mickey. He told his son if he didn't have the ability and willingness to face adversity, he should come back home and go to work in the mines.

The blunt lecture worked. Mantle became a hot hitter all over again, with eleven home runs and fifty runs batted in only forty games. The Yankees quickly called him back to what major league players call "the big club." Mantle finished his rookie season with a decent average of .267, including 13 home runs and 65 runs batted in. His father had saved Mickey's season, and his career.

While Mantle was beginning his up-and-down-and-up-again rookie season, the Brooklyn Dodgers—"America's team" before the Dallas Cowboys' public relations staff coined the term—jumped off to a fast start in the National League. It was baseball's last decade before expansion, when there were still only eight teams in each league, as compared to almost twice as many today. The Dodgers won eight of their first twelve games, while their crosstown rivals, the New York Giants, were losing twelve of their first fourteen including eleven in a row. The Giants immediately found themselves seven games behind Brooklyn, and it was still only April.

In one of those tricks fate likes to play on us, the Giants were undergoing the same kind of experience with a star rookie outfielder as the Yankees were, and the argument that lingers to this day was about to begin: Who's the best center fielder in New York—Duke Snider, Mickey Mantle, or Willie Mays?

Mays, with a bubbling personality and a nickname to match—"Say Hey!"—reported to the Giants in Philadelphia on May 25, nineteen days after his twentieth birthday and with only the clothes on his back. The Giants, losers of five of their last six games, were delighted to see their bright young prospect after he had starred for two minor league teams.

His first pregame practice before a game against the Phillies fired up the enthusiasm of the team and the reporters covering the Giants, especially Barney Kremenko, a New York sportswriter, who could barely restrain himself in writing about his first sight of Mays.

"Willie, with a mob of reporters looking on," Kremenko wrote, "was a smashing success in the pre-game workout. Wearing uniform number 24, he sent batting practice pitches all over the lot. He whistled line drives in

Rookie Willie Mays hit 20 home runs for the New York Giants in 1951. He was in the on-deck circle when Bobby Thomson hit his immortal "shot.heard 'round the world" that won the 1951 pennant for the Giants in one of the greatest comebacks in major league history. (Courtesy of the National Baseball Hall of Fame Library, Cooperstown, N.Y.)

all directions and ripped screamers into the upper deck of left and center-field."

Kremenko's gushing didn't stop there. "Then he went to the outfield," he wrote, "and started winging the ball in from deep center to third and the plate without a hop. It was a tremendous exhibition and impressed one and all."

However, as they said in baseball in those years, "That was at two o'clock. The game starts at three."

Kremenko duly reported, "When the game began, however, Willie's tightness showed. In his first at-bat, he was called out on strikes. Then in the outfield he let a first inning fly ball by Dick Sisler drop behind him for a triple."

Mays went without a hit in five trips to the plate in his first major league game, a hitless streak that extended to an 0-for-12 stretch in his first three games. After that third game, Giants manager Leo Durocher spotted his rookie crying in front of his locker. Mays claimed he couldn't hit big-league pitching and asked Durocher to send him back to Minneapolis, his last stop before being called up by the Giants.

Durocher would have nothing to do with the kid's plea. He told Mays he was the Giants' center fielder for as long as Durocher managed the Giants. He told the rookie to go home and get a good night's sleep.

When the Giants returned to New York, Mays hit a home run over the left field wall against the Boston Braves in his first time at bat at the Polo Grounds. He didn't hit it off another rookie, either. He did it against no less than Warren Spahn, a twenty-one-game winner in each of the two previous seasons, who was in the first years of his Hall of Fame career. Spahn said in later years, "We might have gotten rid of Willie forever if I'd only struck him out."

However, Mays and Durocher replayed their scene after Mays immediately went into another cold spell, this time going hitless in his next thirteen at bats. Hitting .038 with only that home run in twenty-six times up, he again told Durocher he wanted to be sent back to Minneapolis. Durocher again told him no and stuck with him.

The manager became a father figure to the rookie over the season and beyond. Mays rebounded permanently this time with 20 home runs and a .274 batting average for the year. The momentum from his rookie season propelled Mays to twenty-two years of stardom in the big leagues in which he became the third leading home run hitter of all time with 660, behind only Hank Aaron and Babe Ruth. He was elected to the Hall of Fame in 1979. Durocher, like Mutt Mantle in the same year, had saved a rookie's season, and his Hall of Fame career.

During Mays's hot second half, the manager of the Chicago Cubs, Frankie Frisch, wanted some advice on how to stop Mays. He called his longtime National League friend Charlie Grimm, who had managed against Willie while Mays was playing for Minneapolis the year before.

Frisch put the question to Grimm in simple terms: "How should we pitch to this kid?"

Grimm had a blunt response: "How the hell should I know, Frankie? He hit .580 against us."

Even after the Giants righted their ship, with the help of their rookie outfielder, the Dodgers led the league by thirteen and a half games on August 11 after beating the Boston Braves in the first game of a double-header. A reporter asked Brooklyn's manager, Charlie Dressen, if the

Manager Chuck Dressen of the Brooklyn Dodgers shows how he flashed signs in 1951, the year when he said, "The Giants is dead." Despite his advice to his players to "hang close 'til the seventh inning—I'll think of something," the New York Giants came from thirteen and a half games behind the Dodgers to win the National League pennant. (Courtesy of National Baseball Hall of Fame Library, Cooperstown, N.Y.)

Giants could catch his team. Dressen answered emphatically, "The Giants is dead!" The quote was picked up out of the New York papers and published and broadcast all over the country. Dressen, already famous for his cocky attitude, now became famous for his grammar, too.

For the record, a Columbia University journalism professor came to Dressen's defense, saying he was using "Giants" as a collective noun, like "team," and therefore it took the singular verb—"is." Few others agreed with him, except maybe the Dodgers fans.

The Giants chose that time to take control of their own destiny. They went on a sixteen-game winning streak and cut the Dodgers' lead to five games.

One week later, Bill Veeck made news of his own with his latest team— the last-place St. Louis Browns. As their owner, he signed a new player, Eddie Gaedel, who entered a game against the Tigers on August 19 as a pinch hitter in a Sunday doubleheader before eighteen thousand fans. What's news about that? Gaedel wasn't really a baseball player at all. He was a midget, a professional entertainer only three feet seven inches tall and wearing uniform number 1/8. With Detroit's catcher, Bob Swift, kneeling on the ground behind home plate, the Detroit pitcher, Bob Cain, was laughing so hard he walked Gaedel on four pitches.

10

Quietly Going Mad

The Giants weren't dead in August after all. On the contrary, they were playing at a history-making pace. They finished the season strong by winning twelve of their last thirteen games and thirty-seven of forty-four. The Dodgers struggled in late September, winning only three of their last nine.

But Brooklyn's flair for the dramatic surfaced again in the way "dem Bums" won their final game, after seeing on the scoreboard that the Giants had already won their finale, over the Braves in Boston. What the scoreboard didn't show was an ominous note in the Giants' victory—Bobby Thomson's thirtieth home run of the season.

Brooklyn went into extra innings in Philadelphia. Jackie Robinson, after making a game-saving catch in the twelfth inning on a line drive by Eddie Waitkus with the bases loaded, hit a home run in the fourteenth to win the game and help his team avoid the most embarrassing collapse in baseball history, temporarily.

Five thousand fans greeted the Giants when they arrived at Grand Central Station. Two thousand turned out for the Dodgers at Penn Station, including one Giant fan who told a reporter, "Don't let them kid you. These guys are still bums." But a Brooklyn fan trumped him with a sign that said:

JACKIE ROBINSON FOR BOROUGH PRESIDENT

Giants fans could have been excused if they had nominated their manager, Leo Durocher, for public office too. Durocher was highly controversial, a flamboyant personality with almost a determination to make himself unpopular by his public comments. Branch Rickey, Durocher's boss when Durocher managed the Dodgers and Rickey was their general manager, said, "Leo can take an impossible situation and make it worse."

Despite his personality, Durocher took the Giants' seemingly impossible situation in 1951 and made it work. He made several managerial decisions in the last half of the season that were instrumental in guiding his team to the pennant.

Durocher made three moves with his lineup that enabled his team to come back from the edge of a disappointing season. He switched outfielder Whitey Lockman and first baseman Monte Irvin and moved Bobby Thomson to third base after the regular third baseman, Hank Thompson, suffered a spike injury. Durocher's strategy, plus strong seasons from pitchers Sal Maglie, Larry Jansen, and Jim Hearn, who combined to win sixty-three of the team's ninety-eight victories, brought the Giants back from the brink of disaster and positioned them instead within reach of the pennant.

For Durocher, the 1951 season was becoming one of sweet revenge. He had played shortstop for the Dodgers for six years and been their manager from 1939 until 1947, when Commissioner Happy Chandler, unhappy with the reputations of some of Durocher's friends, suspended him for the entire season for "conduct detrimental to baseball." Durocher returned to the Dodgers in 1948 but shocked the baseball world after seventy-three games by jumping ship and signing to manage the hated Giants.

The Dodger fans were furious, but the Giants fans seemed to be angrier. Some, still filled with their hatred for Durocher after all his years with the Dodgers, vowed never to go to the Polo Grounds again as long as he was the Giants' manager. Some of those who did carried signs proclaiming their objections. Three of them said:

> YOU GOT SAWDUST FOR BRAINS!
> GO BACK TO BROOKLYN!
> SOREHEAD!

Now, three years later, fate was calling the East River rivals to a three-game playoff series beginning on October 1, the day after the end of the regular season in those years when the only "postseason" was the World Series. Reporter Milton Bracker wrote in *The New York Times* that morning:

New York rocked yesterday with the great schism of 1951. As the weary Brooklyn Dodgers squeaked agonizingly into a tie with the New York Giants for first place in the National League, the metropolis went quietly mad trying to figure out which radio station to listen to and which team to root for.

One fan told Bracker, "The Dodgers are like that every year. They always drive everybody crazy."

The front page of the *Times* that morning told its readers that other dramas were unfolding elsewhere, with far more frightening implications. In Rome, the Pope spoke gravely about the growing threat of World War III. Reporter Camille M. Cianfarra described the warning as "one of the most pessimistic Pope Pius XII has made since the end of World War II."

In Korea, United Nations troops captured three positions from the Communist forces. Radio Peiping, with its Chinese army now in the fighting as North Korea's ally despite MacArthur's predictions to the contrary the year before, wanted a "peaceful settlement," something that didn't happen for almost two more years.

In Washington, a report to President Truman from his director of defense mobilization, Charles E. Wilson, said the United States had spent $14 billion in military supplies and equipment for the Korean War since it began a year earlier.

In Gatlinburg, Tennessee, in the Great Smoky Mountains, a majority of Republican governors at their annual conference said they liked Ike— General Eisenhower—over Senator Robert Taft of Ohio as their party's presidential nominee in the coming year.

In New York, the baseball playoff wasn't the only question on people's minds. The president of the Transport Workers Union, Michael J. Quill, threatened to create a transit tie-up in the city if the private bus companies that carried 3.2 million workers to and from their jobs every day did not agree to a forty-hour week.

And baseball, as exciting as it was in New York that year, wasn't the only entertainment in town. There was an all-star lineup of movies in those days when movies were measured by how good they were and not by how much money they made at the box office the week before—*A Streetcar Named Desire* at the Warner, starring Marlon Brando and Vivien Leigh; *David and Bathsheba* at the Rivoli, with Gregory Peck and Susan

Hayward; plus *The Great Caruso,* with Mario Lanza, at the Irvin Plaza; and three stars—Elizabeth Taylor, Montgomery Clift, and Shelley Winters—in *A Place in the Sun* at the Capitol. More than that, an all-time classic was coming to town, *An American in Paris,* with Gene Kelly and Leslie Caron, opening at Radio City Music Hall later in the week.

All that news and those five-star movies were topped by the city's extended baseball drama. After the climax of the regular season on Sunday, America's eyes were on New York.

The Dodgers' center fielder and Hall of Famer, Duke Snider, remembers that his team didn't collapse in the last weeks of the season, despite the opinion that still exists today. Snider, who was beginning a decade in which he led all major leaguers in home runs and runs batted in, told me when we were writing his autobiography, *The Duke of Flatbush,* that the Dodgers did not fall apart. "The idea," he said in the living room of his home near San Diego, "that the Dodgers were psyched out by the Giants in August and September and choked up to lose the pennant just isn't so. We thought we would win it all, right up to the moment Bobby Thomson hit his home run. We were confident, we knew we were good, and we knew we were better than the Giants. There was no reason for us to shake in our boots, so we didn't. Our attitude was, 'Okay, bring on the Giants. Let's have that playoff. Then we can knock off the Yankees for the first time in the World Series.' "

Snider, in fact, didn't worry until the ninth inning of the third game, with the playoff tied at one win each. His team was still winning by three runs, 4–1, when the Giants rallied. They scored one run and had runners on second and third with only one out when Dressen lifted his starting pitcher, Don Newcombe, and brought in another starter, Ralph Branca, to save the game and the pennant.

Snider remembers that Branca seemed confident as he walked onto the field from the bullpen behind the center field fence at the Polo Grounds. Branca's teammates called him "Honker" because of an oversized nose, and Snider called over to him as he walked nearby, "Go get 'em, Honk."

Branca answered, "I will."

As he walked into the infield, Pee Wee Reese and Jackie Robinson also called out words of encouragement. Snider remembers that Branca expected to get the side out and leave the Giants' two base runners stranded.

Pitcher Don Newcombe became a twenty-game winner for the Dodgers for the first time in 1951, as a twenty-five-year-old in his third big-league season. (Courtesy of the National Baseball Hall of Fame Library, Cooperstown, N.Y.)

"I expected him to do it, too," Duke said. "I still was not worried. But then something happened—or didn't happen—and suddenly I was worried."

Dressen didn't wait for a conference on the mound with Branca— when the manager reminds the incoming pitcher what the situation is: the score, how many outs there are, how many runners are on base and where. Then he hands the ball to his new pitcher, pats him on the rear end, and trots back to the dugout.

Snider said, "Dressen didn't do that. When Branca got about five feet from Charlie, Dressen flipped the ball to him and said, 'Get 'em out,' then headed back to our dugout." That left Branca and Brooklyn's backup catcher, Rube Walker, who was filling in because Roy Campanella was injured, by themselves on the mound to discuss how to pitch to the next hitter, Thomson. This was the same man who had hit a home run in the Giants' last game of the regular season to help them tie the Dodgers for the pennant and then hit a two-run homer off Branca when the Giants won the first playoff game.

"I noticed Dressen's absence," Snider said, "and I'm sure some other Dodger players did too, and I thought to myself, 'Oh-oh. Charlie's worried.' That made me worry, too."

Thomson, who already had a single and a double, faced Branca with one out and two men on base. Just before he stepped into the batter's box, Leo Durocher walked down from his spot in the third base coach's box and told him, "If you ever hit one, hit one now."

Thomson thought, "Leo, you're out of your mind."

Instead of worrying about a home run, Thomson was concentrating on one of the fundamental rules of hitting in that kind of a pressure situation—hit the ball hard somewhere. "I kept telling myself to wait and watch, wait and watch, not get overanxious."

Thomson took Branca's first pitch for a called strike, a fastball on the inside corner. Then announcer Russ Hodges gave his now-immortal description of what happened next:

> Branca throws . . . There's a long fly ball . . . It's gonna be, I believe . . . *The Giants win the pennant! The Giants win the pennant! The Giants win the pennant! The Giants win the pennant! Bobby Thomson hits one into the lower deck of the left field stands . . . The Giants win the pennant, and they're going crazy! They're going crazy! Oh . . . oh!*

Brooklyn's left fielder, Andy Pafko, watched helplessly as Thomson's "shot heard 'round the world" cleared the fence 315 feet from home plate. As it did, Thomson said later, "My skin was crawling with excitement." Russ Hodges continued in his uncontrollable excitement:

> I *don't believe it! I don't believe it! I do not believe it! Bobby Thomson hit a line drive into the lower deck of the left field stands, and this whole place is going crazy! The Giants are . . . pennant winners! The Giants win it by a score of five to four, and they're picking Bobby Thomson up and carrying him off the field!*

Nineteen years later, Harold Kaese of *The Boston Globe* wrote emphatically, "It was the most timely, most important, most dramatic home run ever hit."

It is well known among students of the sport that the player in the on-deck circle as the next hitter after Thomson was the rookie Willie Mays. Presumably he was thinking what all great professional athletes think in such a pressure-filled situation: "C'mon. Let me get up there. I can win this pennant for us."

Wrong. Mays was scared stiff. He told Dick Young of the New York *Daily News* ten years later that as he knelt in the on-deck circle that day, he wasn't praying for the chance to win it for his team. Just the opposite. He was praying he wouldn't have to come to bat.

At the end of Mays's career, Young wrote that Mays told him he was saying to himself, "Please, Lord—don't make me get up there. Let him end it right now."

The Lord heard Willie and answered his prayer.

After Thomson's now-legendary home run broke up the game and the season, the Dodgers were on their team bus riding back to Brooklyn when the players began noticing that Branca had been hanged in effigy, with stuffed likenesses of a baseball player dangling from several telephone poles. In every case, the player wore Branca's number—13.

On the morning after Thomson's "Miracle of Coogan's Bluff" cleared the left field wall in front of 34,320 fans as the entire nation listened to the "coast-to-coast" radio broadcast, John Drebinger, the nationally known baseball writer for the *Times*, wrote:

> In an electrifying finish to what long will be remembered as the most thrilling pennant campaign in history, Leo Durocher and his astounding never-say-die Giants wrenched victory from the jaws of defeat at the Polo Grounds yesterday . . .

That was only one of two major news stories on the front page of the *Times* that morning. The other, on the opposite side of the page, shook up most of the free world. Reporter Bill Lawrence wrote that the Russians had exploded "another atomic bomb," their second, according to an announcement by President Truman's press secretary, Joseph Short. The announcement came two years after the Soviet Union detonated its first nuclear bomb, on September 23, 1949.

★ ★ ★

Thomson's blow still hurts TV talk show host Larry King, and it's why he says he still hates one of his boyhood pals in Brooklyn, one Davy Fried. "When I was growing up in Brooklyn during and after World War II," he told me, "the two most hated words in the English language were *the Giants*. The Dodgers, on the other hand, were another word for *heroes*."

The rivalry burned intensely on both sides. When two fans in a New York bar got into a fist fight over whether Snider was better than Willie Mays, someone called the cops. When the cops got there, they found out the two guys slugging each other were father and son.

From the 1946 season, when King was twelve, through 1956, the Dodgers won six pennants and the Giants two. Except for Thomson's home run in 1951 and a loss to the Phillies in the ninth inning of the last game in 1950, the Dodgers would have matched the Yankees' feat of winning five pennants in a row, from 1949 through 1953.

King remembers that only two kids out of the twenty-five in his Brooklyn neighborhood of Bensonhurst weren't Dodger fans. One has been his lifelong friend, Herb Cohen, who later wrote a runaway bestseller, *You Can Negotiate Anything*.

Young Herby rooted for the Yankees just to needle the rest of the members of their club, the Warriors. But Davy really rooted for the Giants, and nobody cared what his reason was. He might as well have rooted for the Germans or the Japanese in World War II.

King remembers that Thomson's home run "sent a knife right through the heart of every Brooklyn fan. No day of my life since has brought me the pain of that day. Even my father's death ten years earlier didn't seem any worse. I was only eight then and I managed to get over it with time. But when you're ten years older and living in Brooklyn and Thomson hits that homer, the pain never goes away—not even in a new century."

After the game, the future TV personality, called "the Mouthpiece" by his pals on the corner of 86th Street and Bay Parkway because of his ability to describe things, especially Dodger games, went outside to walk off his headache, knowing it wouldn't work. The last person on the face of the earth he wanted to run into that afternoon was that Giants fan, Davy Fried.

So who's the first person he sees on the corner? Davy flashed a big ha-ha smile at Larry, then taunted him with delight. "That night," King remembers vividly, "the rest of us stood on the corner and plotted his murder."

King isn't the only one who remembers that moment vividly. Forty-two years later, in 1993, Thomson's home run was chosen as baseball's most memorable moment in a national poll by *Baseball America*. The U.S. Postal Service issued a 33¢ stamp commemorating "the Miracle of Coogan's Bluff" in a series honoring "the most significant people, places, events and trends of each decade of the 20th century." Other subjects in the series included the *I Love Lucy* television show, the Korean War, desegregation, and drive-in movies.

Thomson's home run became a topic of conversation again on January 31, 2001, when *The Wall Street Journal* reported that the Giants were stealing the Dodgers' pitching signals on that day in 1951. Reporter Joshua Harris Prager wrote that twenty-one players on the Giants in 1951 "are at last willing to confirm that they executed an elaborate scheme" to steal the opposing catcher's signs. Prager said the Giants continued their practice "during home games all through the last ten weeks of the 1951 season . . ."

Thomson, however, denied getting any help before hitting his home run. One of the Giants' stars that year, outfielder Monte Irvin, told reporters Adam Miller and Tracy Connor of the *New York Post*, "It wasn't done during that great game. The Giants did use it from time to time, but during that game we didn't use anything. There's nothing to tarnish that great feat of Bobby Thomson."

The Dodgers themselves agreed with Irvin. Duke Snider said, "It doesn't surprise me. Leo Durocher would do almost anything to win a ball game. But it doesn't change anything. Everyone steals signs. It's part of the game. We were stealing signs."

Pitcher Carl Erskine told the *Post*, "There are kids that weren't close to being born when it happened who will be just as fascinated as everyone who lived through it. It's a piece of baseball history that will never go away."

The World Series seemed anticlimactic. The Yankees, in the middle of their record streak of winning the pennant and the World Series five years in a row, defeated the Giants, four games to two. In the final game, won by the Yankees, 4–3, Joe DiMaggio led off the eighth inning with a long double off Larry Jansen between Mays and Thomson in right field. It was the last hit of his major league career. He retired that winter.

As the apostles of the sport often contend, baseball in 1951 seems, on reflection, a metaphor of America herself. Both the national pastime and

The 1951 season was the last for Joe DiMaggio. His home run and single helped to win the fourth game of the World Series for the Yankees over the Giants. (Courtesy of the National Baseball Hall of Fame Library, Cooperstown, N.Y.)

the nation began to change after that year, and by the end of the decade, neither would ever be the same again.

In 1951, the seeds for the only war we ever lost were being sown in Indochina, the region that included Vietnam. Integration of our schools and our society, sparked by baseball and Jackie Robinson in 1947, was accelerated in 1954 by the Supreme Court decision ordering public schools to integrate "with all deliberate speed." The favorite singers of the '40s and early '50s—Bing Crosby, Nat "King" Cole, Rosemary Clooney, Dinah Shore, Eddie Fisher, and others—became casualties of a cultural revolution with the advent of rock 'n' roll music only two and three years after Thomson's homer.

Our American "lingo" was undergoing expansion, with new words and expressions being introduced as a result of the war in Korea, repeating the experiences of World Wars I and II. Wars have a habit of adding to our language. In World War II, "blitz" was added to the American vocabulary, a shortened form of "blitzkrieg," the German word meaning "lightning war" which had been used to describe attacks by Nazi tanks.

"Snafu" was another product of World War II, an abbreviation for "Situation Normal All Fouled Up." Ken Ringle of *The Washington Post* remembered in 2001 that the Korean War gave us "brainwash," a form of psychological torture used by North Korean forces to pry information and confessions out of U.S. prisoners." Back home, Americans were using a word from the new atomic age to describe damage control in the Cold War—"fallout."

Education in America was still in the midst of an enormous expansion thanks to a farsighted legislative advancement, "The Servicemen's Readjustment Act of 1944"—the G.I. Bill of Rights. The bill had been signed into law by President Roosevelt seven years earlier, on June 22, 1944, to provide financial assistance to returning GIs in pursuing a college education or a trade, in buying homes or businesses, and in paying hospitalization costs. The bill caused an explosion in America's education standards. Now it wasn't enough just to be a high school graduate if you wanted to get ahead in a professional field. You needed a college degree.

By 1951, the federal government had provided $14 billion in educational assistance to America's returning service men and women. More than 7,800,000 World War II veterans and more than 2,300,000 veterans of the Korean War were able to attend college or trade schools because of the G.I. Bill. By 1956, when the last World War II veteran graduated from college, the G.I. Bill had provided America with 450,000 engineers, 238,000 teachers, 91,000 scientists, 67,000 doctors, 22,000 dentists, and millions of others who had been able to get a college education.

In *American History* magazine, Michael D. Haydock said, "This landmark legislation helped steer a country geared to winning a globe-spanning war—with roughly eight million citizens in uniform in 1945 and 22 million involved in war production—smoothly back into a peacetime economy, led to lasting changes in America's system of higher education, and turned uncertainty into opportunity . . ."

A luxury called air-conditioning, available mostly in movie theaters and restaurants, was installed in more office buildings and factories, setting off economic booms that transformed sleepy towns, states, and entire regions in the South and Southwest—Atlanta, Miami, New Orleans, Houston, Dallas—into thriving centers of commerce and manufacturing. Even a few private homes and automobiles were being equipped with "a/c."

Pictures of people frying eggs on sidewalks and steps to show just how hot it was were an annual feature in newspapers in the summers before the widespread use of air-conditioning. Two secretaries perform the annual rite on the steps of the U.S. Capitol in 1947. (© *The Washington Post.* Courtesy of the Washington, D.C., Public Library.)

Thanks to the expanding use of air-conditioning, the summer scenes so familiar into the 1950s began to vanish from our lives—workers sent home early because of extreme heat, open car windows on two-lane highways creating such a deafening noise from the rushing wind that passengers in the backseat had trouble hearing those in the front, and newspapers featuring pictures on Page One of somebody frying an egg on a sidewalk to illustrate just how hot the weather was that we were being forced to endure. In Washington, some observers pointed out one disadvantage of air-conditioning: Congress could stay in session all summer.

Weather news of a different, more destructive kind was also made in the summer of 1951 while the pennant races were still going strong. Torrential rains and swirling floods in Illinois, Missouri, Kansas, and Oklahoma caused more than $1 million in damages, an astronomical sum more than fifty years ago.

Americans didn't know it, but McCarthyism, the national fever that was ruining reputations and careers, destroying lives and dividing the nation, was peaking in 1951 and would never be as strong again as the 1950s unfolded. On July 11, as the Dodgers were also peaking, a young mother from suburban Virginia raised her right hand before the House Un-American Activities Committee and stunned the nation with her testimony. Her name was Mrs. Mary Stalcup Markward of Chesterbrook, Virginia, and she didn't look like someone who could deliver blockbuster testimony before a congressional committee on the workings of America's postwar enemy from within, the Communist Party. She was an innocent-looking homemaker only five feet one inch tall with blue eyes and brown hair. She was dressed in a cinnamon-colored suit and straw hat and wore beige stockings and brown-and-white shoes.

The New York Times account of her appearance said she gave her testimony "in a clear voice, easily heard throughout the committee room." Mrs. Markward told the members of the committee that she had posed as a member of the Communist Party for seven years during and after World War II until 1950, all while actually serving as a spy for the FBI. She said she was recruited by the bureau in 1943, shortly after graduating from high school and while she was working as an operator at the Rainbow Beauty Shop in Washington.

The *Times* report said Mrs. Markward was "a calm, composed witness, with a prodigious memory. Without benefit of any notes, she recalled dozens of names of party members, recited their wives' first names, and fixed exact dates for important meetings and developments of five or six years ago."

No one had ever spoken with such deep, firsthand knowledge of the workings of the party, not even Senator McCarthy himself. Mrs. Markward told the committee that her experience inside the Communist Party convinced her that the Communists were conspiring to overthrow the U.S. government, and they would resort to violence if necessary.

When she finished, the audience "applauded loudly and long," according to the *Times*. Congressman Charles E. Potter, a Republican from Michigan who was wounded in World War II, told her she should be awarded a medal for gallantry.

Public concern about the Communist threat grew to such an extent that it took on a sinister-sounding name, "the Red menace." In that same year, a husband and wife, Julius and Ethel Rosenberg, were convicted of conspiracy for leaking classified military documents to the Soviet Union. They were executed two years later.

All of this was happening in 1951, in the midst of the fear of Communism, a fear that bordered on a national paranoia at times, with Senator McCarthy feeding those emotions on a daily basis. Only three years later, in 1954, McCarthy was censured by his colleagues in the Senate for his overpowering, bullying tactics and reckless disregard for the truth and the lives and reputations of people in Hollywood, Washington, and everywhere in between. He died in 1957. The national condition associated with his name—McCarthyism—never again became the feverish epidemic it was in 1951.

Women were entering America's workforce in larger numbers than ever, even including all those who were "Rosie the Riveters" on the assembly lines of factories during World War II. In 1951, the number of women working outside the home reached a new high, a change in American society with shock waves still being felt a half century later.

Consumers had banks and food stores waving come-ons in front of them. Banks gave you a toaster or a radio if you opened a new account. Your friendly neighborhood supermarket "gave" you trading stamps, S&H or Top Value, which could be redeemed for just about anything in their catalogs. The incentives died out later, but at least one company revived the practice in 1999, a mutual fund that offered anyone opening a new account free frequent flyer miles on an airline owned by the fund.

The communications explosion leading to the Internet, cable television, cell phones, and fax machines gathered steam in 1951 with the first transcontinental television broadcast on September 4. As the Dodgers-Giants race grew hotter, President Truman addressed the Japanese Peace Treaty Conference in San Francisco in a telecast carried by ninety-four stations.

Other signs of the coming communications revolution were evident—the first commercial color TV broadcast, on CBS on June 25, and the first cross-country telephone direct-dialing system, on November 10, when the mayor of Englewood, New Jersey, called the mayor of Alameda, California, without an operator doing the dialing for him. Elsewhere, a video camera recorded pictures and sound on magnetic tape.

The computer age took a giant leap forward on June 14, when UNIVAC, the first electronic digital computer built for commercial use, was demonstrated in Philadelphia by its designers. It was manufactured by Remington Rand, which sold the first one to the U.S. Census Bureau.

Baseball, like America, stood on the brink of change. There were rumors that one or more major league teams might actually move to other cities, a development unthinkable since a second major league—the American—was established exactly fifty years earlier, in 1901. After the next season, 1952, the Boston Braves moved to Milwaukee, something unimaginable. Only two seasons later, the unimaginable was repeated when the St. Louis Browns became the Baltimore Orioles. In 1955, the Athletics moved from Philadelphia to Kansas City. Then something even more unthinkable happened—the Dodgers left Brooklyn after the 1957 season, taking the New York Giants with them to California. The two teams became the *Los Angeles* Dodgers and the *San Francisco* Giants.

Then the two leagues expanded, again and again. What used to be sixteen major league teams is now thirty, so many that there is serious talk among the owners at this writing of "contracting" the size of the two leagues by simply abolishing some of the teams. In the meantime, the teams are composed of players making annual salaries in seven figures that are public information, in contrast to the years before when players' salaries were kept confidential between the player and the front office. Players have a union, and so do the umpires. And the game is played on fake grass and under a roof in new stadiums—with air-conditioning.

The French, however, remind us, "The more things change, the more they are the same." It's still America, and it's still baseball. New baseball stars have emerged—home run sluggers like Mark McGwire, Barry Bonds, and Sammy Sosa, and ninety-five-mile-an-hour pitchers like Randy Johnson, Curt Schilling, and Roger Clemens. America has a new high-tech, dot-com society, and even our years sound futuristic—Y2K and 2003. All of which seems to make the baseball season of 1951 even more dramatic and more historic.

And Larry King says, "I still hate Davy Fried."

PART FOUR
· · ·
1961

11

Three New Frontiers

The year 1961 was a time of three New Frontiers. Only two of them are remembered today. Two began in Washington, the third in New York.

Young John Kennedy of Massachusetts, only forty-three years old, was inaugurated president that year after promising to lead his fellow Americans to "a New Frontier." In baseball, another New Frontier was established. The Major Leagues expanded from eight to ten teams in the American League with the transfer of the Washington Senators to Minnesota as the Twins and the establishment of a new Washington Senators team and another team in Los Angeles, the Angels. Two more teams—the New York Mets and the Houston Colt .45s, now the Astros—had already been established to begin play in the National League in 1962. The four were "expansion teams," clubs that had never existed before, as baseball boldly departed from the traditional eight-team leagues and 154-game schedule that baseball had operated under since 1901. The playing schedule was also expanded, to 162 games.

The third New Frontier was about to be slugged out in New York in the brute force of "the M&M Boys"—Roger Maris and Mickey Mantle.

The first New Frontier began on January 20, Inauguration Day, when the new president stood in frigid temperatures on the steps of the United States Capitol building, flanked by banks of snow from a storm the night before, and urged his fellow Americans in words that immediately became classic, "Ask not what your country can do for you; ask what you can do for your country."

The second New Frontier began on April 10, Opening Day of the 1961 season, when President Kennedy arrived at Griffith Stadium and threw out the first ball. For Kennedy, it was a labor of love. He was a lifelong baseball fan, especially rooting for his hometown team, the Boston Red Sox. JFK even kiddingly referred to one of his chief White House staff members, Dave Powers, as his "Under Secretary of Baseball" because it was his job to brief Kennedy every day on the games of the night before and other baseball developments as they took their daily swim in the White House pool.

Another senior presidential aide, Kenny O'Donnell, had been rated a top baseball prospect according to their fellow Bostonian, Ed Doherty, general manager of the new Senators and former public relations director of the Red Sox. Doherty told others that O'Donnell had possessed the potential to make it to the Major Leagues as a third baseman until he decided on a public service career.

To open the 1961 season at Griffith Stadium, the athletic young president, who encouraged his fellow Americans in his New England accent to pursue a life of "vigah," took off his suit coat with the temperatures in the upper forties and uncorked a long throw over the heads of all the members of the Senators and the Chicago White Sox. In so doing, Kennedy was violating the tradition of aiming the throw in the direction of the home team. Instead, a colorful White Sox outfielder, Jim Rivera, dashed back into the infield, running away from the presidential box along the first base line, and retrieved the ball.

Following tradition, Rivera was escorted to the presidential box to get the President's autograph on the ball. After Kennedy signed it and handed it back to him, Rivera, known for his bluntness and controversy, shocked those around the two men. According to a later report by David Condon in the *Chicago Tribune*, Rivera looked at the signature on the baseball and asked bluntly, even disrespectfully, if the professors at Harvard University, Kennedy's alma mater, "don't even teach you to write? What kind of garbage writing is this? What is this garbage autograph? Do you think I can go into any tavern on Chicago's South Side and really say the President of the United States signed this baseball for me? I'd be run off. Take this thing back and give me something besides your garbage autograph."

According to reporter Condon, Kennedy laughed heartily while those around him tried to control their shock, took the ball back, and signed his name more legibly. Then Rivera told him, "You know—you're all right."

The Senators and the Chicago White Sox were making baseball history with the first game ever played by an expansion team. That another Opening Day was taking place in Washington was a story in itself, unknown to the fans. Today, more than forty years later, it is still unknown to most fans, members of the media and those in Major League Baseball's offices on Park Avenue in New York. Shirley Povich was a key figure in the story. He told it to me when we were writing his 1969 autobiography, *All These Mornings.*

Clark Griffith, a star pitcher when the American League was formed in 1901 and who won 237 games in a big-league playing career that lasted twenty years, died in 1955 after owning the Senators for forty-three years. His nephew and adopted son, Calvin Griffith, succeeded him.

The younger Griffith, called simply Calvin by most of the media to distinguish him from Clark, who was accorded the more respectful title of Mr. Griffith, began making noises right from the start about moving the Senators to California. His fellow owners, however, blocked his attempts, saying that having only one team on the West Coast would make travel costs prohibitive. While Calvin was trying to line up supporters, Walter O'Malley of the Brooklyn Dodgers beat him to the punch. He recruited the owner of the New York Giants, Horace Stoneham, and the two moved their teams to California after the 1957 season in a dual move that shook the foundation of Major League Baseball.

Then Calvin began to eye the upper Midwest and the untapped territory of Minnesota. The rumors started spreading that he was playing footsies with the people out there and was going to try to move the Senators at the first opportunity.

Why would a charter team, a member of the American League since the league was formed sixty years earlier, want to move? Money. Calvin owned Griffith Stadium and all the concessions. He also received a rent check from the Washington Redskins every year for playing their games there. But that sweetheart arrangement was coming to an end for the younger Griffith. The federal government was building a new stadium, now Robert F. Kennedy Stadium—"RFK"—and Calvin was going to lose the Redskins as a tenant. Even worse, he was going to be forced to become a tenant himself in the new stadium because nobody would go to the old one—not with its narrow, crowded seats, its view-blocking posts, almost no parking, and its creaky, aging structure in a rundown part of town. The fans wanted to enjoy the gleaming new state-of-the-art stadium with its roomier aisles, unobstructed views, parking for almost ten thousand cars, and the latest luxury in a stadium—a scoreboard with a "Magic Message" screen.

Enter Phil Graham, publisher of *The Washington Post*. He discussed the shaky baseball situation in Washington with Povich from time to time. Finally he asked Povich, one of the most respected sports journalists in American history, "Shirley, what do we have to do to keep our baseball team?"

Povich explained that the key figure was Del Webb, co-owner of the Yankees, because he was chairman of the American League's expansion committee. Graham answered quickly and simply, "Let's play ball with him."

Webb, as owner of the Del Webb Construction Company in Phoenix, built military bases all over the Southwest. Graham and Povich decided that the way to reach him was to tell him it would be in his company's best interests if he saw to it that the Senators stayed in Washington. The three men met over lunch in Washington and mapped out a strategy worthy of Washington intrigue.

Then Graham and Povich went one step further. Through President Eisenhower's press secretary, Jim Hagerty, they arranged for the *Post*'s highly respected White House correspondent, Edward T. Folliard, to ask Eisenhower about his feelings on the matter at one of his weekly news conferences. The story would go all over the country, because Ike had started the practice of allowing television coverage of his news conferences. The fix was in.

At the next news conference, Folliard rose to ask the President a question. Some accounts say it was a reporter for the Scripps-Howard newspaper chain, Andrew F. Tully, who asked the question, but Povich was emphatic that it was Folliard. For Folliard, the role was appropriate. He was a lifelong Washingtonian who, as a boy, had held Walter Johnson's coat when the pitching immortal duplicated George Washington's feat of throwing a silver dollar across the Rappahannock River in nearby Virginia.

Folliard asked Eisenhower how he felt about the possibility that the Senators might be taken out of Washington. Ike, a frequent visitor to Senators games during his military service there and his eight years as president, said he would hate to see baseball leave Washington. That night, it was on the evening news.

Baseball got the message, and the strategy bought Washington fans a few more years of the Senators in Washington, even though they had no idea of all those behind-the-scenes maneuverings. During that period, Calvin wrote a bylined, copyrighted feature article in the *Post* the day before Opening Day one year that began with this simple, flat-out statement:

> "The Washington Senators will not leave Washington in my lifetime."

Graham and Povich stayed in close contact with Webb and were able to keep their finger in the dike and make preparations for the day when Calvin might win the endurance contest. That came in October 1960.

Webb's expansion committee was meeting at the Savoy Plaza Hotel in New York, and Povich was covering it with Burt Hawkins, a respected and veteran baseball writer for the *Washington Star*. They were talking in Povich's room when the phone rang. Del Webb was on the other end. He told Povich, "Calvin says he's going to move for sure this time, and he says he has the votes. I don't think he has, but what would you say if we let him go and put another major league team in Washington?"

Povich answered, "We'd always be wondering when he'd pull the rug out. To hell with him. Let him go."

It was against this background that 26,725 fans sat in Griffith Stadium under cloudy skies and shivering in fifty-degree temperatures on April 10, 1961, for the first game ever played by an expansion team, the day before the California Angels played the second. The result was predictable. The Senators, stocked—or burdened—with rejects from the other teams, lost to the White Sox, 4–3. By the end of the season, the Senators were making history, if you can call losing a hundred games making history.

For President Kennedy, an afternoon at the ballpark was welcome relief from far more critical challenges in the Oval Office. One of the crises on his desk involved an American spy plane, a U-2 piloted by Francis Gary Powers, shot down by the Russians the year before when Powers flew over Russian air space. The Kremlin made political hay out of it with a trial, followed by his conviction and sentence to prison. Early in 1961, President Kennedy negotiated Powers's release.

Exactly one week after Opening Day, with "Under Secretary of Baseball" Dave Powers updating him daily on the first games of the new season, Kennedy suffered the first major defeat of his young presidency. An attempt to invade Cuba and overthrow its new leader, Fidel Castro, who had aligned his island nation with the Soviet Union and had become a Communist puppet of the Kremlin, ended in failure after only two days. Planning for the invasion had begun under Eisenhower, and Kennedy authorized the planning to continue through the Central Intelligence Agency. At the last moment, however, he canceled the aerial attack intended to support the invasion.

On April 17, some one thousand three hundred Cuban refugees, trained under the CIA, landed in Cuba and were wiped out, due at least in part to the lack of air cover. The invasion ended in colossal failure. Ninety members of the invasion party were killed. The rest were captured and held as prisoners until the Kennedy administration negotiated their release more than a year later.

Tension increased in a different location on May 4. A group of civil rights supporters left Washington by bus to demonstrate the need for action to improve the plight of minorities in America's Deep South. The nation was about to enter the first in a string of "long, hot summers" of the 1960s, the decade when civil rights protests and armed resistance against them ignited the South—sometimes literally—dominated the news, and reached their most inflammatory point in 1968 with the assassination of the Rev. Dr. Martin Luther King, Jr.

The Congress of Racial Equality (CORE), under its leader, James Farmer, began a "Freedom Ride" to New Orleans. Its purpose was to call attention to the need for new civil rights legislation. The group's tactic would be to seat white members in the back of the bus and African-American members in the front, a symbolic reversal reminding others that blacks for years had been confined to the back of the bus in local and intercity travel. There was more: At rest stops, whites would use the black rest rooms, and blacks would use those marked "White Only."

To those who complained that the Freedom Riders were violating the law, Farmer had a ready response. He said the riders were "merely doing what the Supreme Court said we had a right to do," referring to the high court's ruling in 1946 that segregated seating in interstate travel was a violation of the Constitution. Farmer and his fellow members of CORE were realistic enough to expect trouble. He said, "When we began the ride, I think all of us were prepared for as much violence as could be thrown at us. We were prepared for the possibility of death."

The Freedom Riders left Washington on May 4 and were scheduled to arrive in New Orleans on May 17, the seventh anniversary of another

Supreme Court decision on civil rights, the historic Brown decision in 1954 that ruled that segregated public schools also violated the Constitution.

Nine days into their journey, the Freedom Riders divided into two groups for the Alabama leg of their journey. The first was confronted by two hundred angry citizens in Anniston who stoned the bus and slashed its tires. The driver managed to get the bus out of the trouble spot, but it was firebombed six miles out of town when the driver stopped the bus to change tires. The second group was also challenged, in Birmingham, where the Freedom Riders were attacked and beaten.

There were no police officers on hand at the Birmingham bus depot to head off any possible violence. Birmingham's Public Safety Commissioner Bull Conner expressed a reason. He said it was a holiday—Mother's Day. The governor of Alabama, John Patterson, had another explanation. "When you go somewhere looking for trouble, you usually find it," he said. "You just can't guarantee the safety of a fool, and that's what these folks are—just fools."

The Freedom Ride appeared to end prematurely in Birmingham when the bus company became concerned about the possibility of losing more buses, and the drivers, all of whom were white, became concerned about their safety. After two days of negotiations, the Freedom Riders, who feared for their own lives, flew on to New Orleans.

A group of students in Nashville decided to pick up the cause. They went to Birmingham and continued the Freedom Ride, but not without incidents and violence. The riders were challenged by a group of angry whites at the bus station in Montgomery. They considered trying to slip out the back of the bus to minimize injuries, but a white rider, Jim Zwerg, stepped out the front door of the bus. He was pummeled by the white mob while the rest of the riders were able to slip out of the bus. In the violence, John Seigenthaler, a member of Attorney General Robert Kennedy's staff, was mobbed and knocked unconscious when he tried to aid the riders. He was left in the street, still unconscious, for almost a half hour.

When Kennedy suggested to Farmer that the riders observe a cooling-off period, Farmer said members of his race had been "cooling off for 350 years." The Freedom Riders tried to continue their journey and made it into Mississippi without incident. However, the group never made it to New Orleans.

At the bus terminal in Jackson, the riders were greeted by police who told them to keep moving. They walked through "the white side" of the terminal and were greeted by patrol wagons on the other side and taken to jail. They were sentenced to sixty days in the state penitentiary. Others arrived to take their place, but they were arrested, too. Before the summer was out, more than three hundred Freedom Riders had been arrested.

Despite not reaching New Orleans, the riders were successful. President Kennedy began to speak out forcefully in support of their cause, and the Interstate Commerce Commission, in response to a request from Robert Kennedy, ruled that segregation in interstate bus travel was illegal, a ruling more specific than the Supreme Court decision on the subject. The ruling took effect in September of that year.

With this abundance of tension at home and abroad, and with every day threatening to bring another crisis, it was no wonder that the Chief Justice of the United States from 1953 to 1969, Earl Warren, told reporters that when he picked up the morning paper, he always turned to the sports page first. He said this was because the sports pages reflected life's fun and triumphs. He said he could turn to the problems of the country and the world later.

The news was better for Kennedy and America on May 5, the day after the Freedom Riders left Washington. The United States scored a major comeback in what was now being called "the space race" after a Russian astronaut named Yuri Gagarin became the first person to enter space several months earlier. An American, Alan Shepard, became the first free person in the free world to do so, flying high above the Atlantic Ocean for 302 miles. It was considered a critical step in playing catch-up with the Russians. They had jumped off to an early lead in the space race by launching "cosmonauts" and the first space satellite, *Sputnik,* in the second half of the 1950s.

Besides the international embarrassments for the United States at the hands of the world's other "superpower," those first spectacular achievements by the Russians carried disturbing implications for military capabilities. The question all across America was that if the Russians can launch men and satellites *into* space, couldn't they use the same equipment and technology to send rockets and satellites *from* space, armed with atomic bombs, over the United States?

The cold war suddenly took on a frightening new dimension, something previously imagined only by the creators of *Buck Rogers* and other

Alan Shepard starts to raise his shield during his descent from his suborbital flight. The photo was taken by a movie camera mounted inside Shepard's *Freedom 7* spacecraft. (Courtesy of NASA.)

comic strips who imagined life in some far-off century. Kennedy recognized this, and so did his vice president, Lyndon Johnson. They were colleagues in the Senate until they defeated two former senators, Richard Nixon and Henry Cabot Lodge, Jr., in the 1960 presidential campaign. In the Senate, Johnson had been one of the leading advocates of a stronger space program for the nation. In 1961, JFK named LBJ the head of a newly accelerated program and declared a national goal of "landing an American on the moon in this decade and returning him safely to earth."

In New York, as the 1961 baseball season unfolded, the "M&M Boys" were making it a historic summer for more positive reasons. They were hitting home runs at a pace not seen since Babe Ruth set the record with sixty in one season thirty-four years earlier, in 1927. In the years that followed Ruth's accomplishment, it had become almost a rite of summer for some slugger to chase his record, only to fade from contention in August

NASA Astronaut Alan Shepard, the first American to travel in space, is recovered by a marine helicopter recovery team after his successful suborbital flight on May 5, 1961. (Courtesy of NASA.)

and September. The two who had come closest were Jimmie Foxx in 1932 and Hank Greenberg in 1938, both with fifty-eight.

Maris and Mantle weren't wilting in the spring and summer heat. They maintained their barrage against Ruth's mark into late summer, to the regret of some fans, reporters, and broadcasters who still loved "The Bambino" and didn't want anyone—Maris, Mantle, or anyone else—to break the record of their beloved Babe.

For Maris, the home run chase was the last thing anyone expected after he started the season with only one hit in his first four games. He didn't hit his first home run until his eleventh game. After hitting 39 homers in 1960 and leading the league in runs batted in, Maris was feeling the pressure of a new star who suddenly found himself anxious to prove that his outstanding season the year before was not a fluke.

The pressure eased somewhat when the Yankees made their first visits to the new cities in the ten-team league, Minneapolis and Los Angeles. Maris hit a home run in each ballpark. The one against the Angels in L.A. was a milestone for him—his one hundredth home run, coming at the age of twenty-six and in his fifth year in the majors. In the middle of May, he hit home runs in four straight games.

Then came a turning point in what became the year when Maris made history. The co-owner of the Yankees, Dan Topping, and his general manager, Roy Hamey, asked Maris to meet with them over lunch. Maris, who had never played two full seasons with the same team, was afraid he was about to be traded again. Just the opposite turned out to be the case.

Topping and Hamey felt Maris had the perfect swing for a lefthanded hitter in Yankee Stadium, with its right field wall only 296 feet down the line from home plate and a low wall in front of the stands. Topping told Maris, "We want you to stop worrying about your batting average. We're not worried, and we don't want you to start pressing. Forget the batting average, and go out and swing for the home runs. We would rather see you hit the long ball and drive in runs than struggle to hit .300."

The appraisal and advice from Topping and Hamey were in stark contrast to what the Chicago Cubs had told Maris after a tryout with them at the beginning of his career. They told him to forget baseball because he was "too small." He stood an even six feet tall and carried 197 pounds over a muscular build.

More relaxed at the plate after his meeting with Topping and Hamey, Maris began hitting more home runs and raised his batting average fifty points. Mantle, the American League home run champion the year before with 40, was also hitting homers. Together, the M&M Boys were rapidly becoming baseball's newest and most feared one-two punch.

Maris began to attract serious attention in June, when he hit 15 homers in the first three weeks. He was making a strong bid to break the record of 18 in one calendar month set by Detroit's Rudy York in August 1937. But then, the monster that all hitters dread—a slump—set in and Maris, with his mind on York's record, didn't hit another home run for the rest of the month.

Maris was still hitting the ball hard, but he just wasn't hitting home runs. Later, in a magazine article with Jim Ogle, Maris talked about the difference between a home run and just another out or a hit that doesn't clear the fence for a home run. He said the difference is what spot on the ball you hit. Maris said, "I really believe the difference between a home run and a single on a hard-hit ball is one-eighth inch. If you hit a ball hard on the under part of it, you have a home run. If your bat hits one-eighth inch higher on the ball, it is a line drive. There is no way a hitter can adjust that one-eighth inch. It just happens."

Despite his cooling-off period in the last week of June, Maris had 27 homers by month's end. Even the All-Star Games in July couldn't generate the excitement that Maris and Mantle were beginning to touch off. In those years the two leagues played two All-Star Games to raise money for the players' pension fund. The first ended in a 1–1 tie in Boston. In the second, a 5–4 win for the National League, the development that received the most publicity was when relief pitcher Stu Miller was blown off the mound by the notorious winds in San Francisco's Candlestick Park. The two teams set an all-star record by committing seven errors.

Maris began to hope for 45 for the season but said he didn't want to think about the possibility of hitting 50. Ford Frick was thinking in those terms, though. He was the commissioner of baseball, a former New York sportswriter who had been Babe Ruth's friend and ghostwriter. He set off a national controversy by announcing in July that if anyone broke Ruth's record, he'd have to do it in 154 games, the length of the seasons before the expansion schedule of 162 games. Frick said if anyone broke Ruth's record in the 155th game or beyond, his mark in the record book would have to be accompanied by "some distinctive mark." New York columnist Dick Young suggested an asterisk.

Frick's announcement did more than touch off a controversy. It also put the national spotlight on Maris and Mantle to a degree even brighter than before. Maris dismissed the Frick pronouncement. "They can put two or three asterisks beside it in the record book," he said, "but it still doesn't matter. Sixty-one is more than sixty any way you look at it."

12

Another International Crisis

When Americans picked up their Sunday papers on the morning of August 13, they were stunned by the day's biggest news, and it didn't have anything to do with baseball. Berlin, always a flash point between East and West in the Cold War, became one again, thirteen years after the Berlin Airlift. President Eisenhower's secretary of state, John Foster Dulles, had told Americans in the 1950s that the world stood "on the brink" of World War III. On August 13, 1961, we were on the brink again.

Berlin was often that brink, the scene of "international incidents" involving showdowns between U.S. and Soviet soldiers and escape attempts by East Germans anxious to follow the beacon of freedom across the border into West Berlin. The locations for these showdowns became household names through the morning paper and the evening news, places like "Checkpoint Charlie" and the Brandenburg Gate.

Beginning in late 1958, Russia's premier, Nikita Khrushchev, demanded frequently that the Allies—the United States, Great Britain, and France—withdraw from Berlin despite the international agreement establishing the four zones of occupation at the end of World War II. In June 1961, Russia renewed its threats. Suddenly more than one thousand East Germans were fleeing from Berlin every day. The government of East Germany tightened its travel restrictions, but the flood of refugees continued and even increased.

The Yankees were in Washington for a four-game series with the Senators. The Senators had snapped the Yankees' nine-game winning streak the day before on Gene Green's grand slam home run in the seventh inning off Luis Arroyo, to the delight of the Washington fans. Something else delighted the fans in Washington during those years: A good box seat in the lower deck, right behind either one of the dugouts, cost $3. Ticket prices in other cities were comparable.

Maris hit his forty-third home run of the season in that game, off Dick Donovan, pulling him to within one homer of Mantle. The Yankees still led the Tigers by three games in the American League pennant race, and the Los Angeles Dodgers led the Cincinnati Reds by two and a half games in the National League.

Maris was in the first stages of a home run binge. He hit two more that Sunday off Bennie Daniels and Marty Kutyna, giving him four homers in the four-game series. Mantle hit one, so the two were tied with 45 home runs each, a hard-to-imagine sixteen games ahead of Babe Ruth's record pace in 1927.

Then the Yankees returned to New York, where Maris hit three more in two games against the White Sox. At that point, Senator Milton Young of North Dakota rose on the floor of the Senate and announced that his constituent from Fargo, Maris, had just hit two home runs off Billy Pierce, one of the best lefthanders in baseball. The torrid streak by Maris broke a major league record with seven home runs in six games, topping the mark of six in six games held by Lou Gehrig, Roy Sievers, and an outfielder for the St. Louis Browns in the 1920s named Ken Williams.

The Yankee players who picked up the *Washington Star* in the lobby of the Shoreham Hotel on Sunday morning, August 13, were greeted by a bold eight-column headline stretching across the entire front page:

COMMUNISTS SHUT BERLIN BORDER

It had rained heavily in Berlin for several days, then the weather turned clear and hot. Through the summer heat, residents going about their business in East Berlin could see construction equipment, including cranes and concrete slabs, on the outskirts of the city.

At midnight Saturday, units of the East German army began operating the cranes and lifting the heavy slabs of concrete into a line on the border between East and West. Along the way, hundreds of soldiers strung out miles of barbed wire fencing. When they had finished, a wall of concrete standing from ten to thirteen feet high snaked its way along the East-West border through Europe's third largest city. Straightened out, the wall would have stretched almost a hundred miles. It was five feet thick. On its eastern side, the wall was smooth and clean, making it hard to climb. Along the top it was rounded off so anyone who was trying to escape would have trouble gripping it.

Those East German soldiers overnight had built one of the world's all-time symbols of a ruthless dictatorship, controlled by the Kremlin, which immediately came to represent all the evil and murderous dictatorships in the history of the world. Its name was as stark as the futures of those Germans behind it—The Berlin Wall. Berliners had a name of their own for it—*Schandmauer.* Translation: "Wall of Shame."

In building "the Wall," the East German soldiers were carrying out an order that had been issued straight from the headquarters of the Soviet government in Moscow. The Soviets were concerned, even alarmed, at the growing number of East Germans who were escaping to freedom in the Western zone of Berlin. The Associated Press reported that the construction of the Wall was in response to "a directive" from the Kremlin to stop the flow of refugees by establishing "a reliable watch and an effective control."

The Wall went up on the same weekend that the largest number of refugees in eight years had already escaped into West Berlin. From 4:00 P.M. Friday to 6:30 P.M. on Sunday, while the Yankees and Senators were playing their four-game series, 2,662 East Berliners had arrived at the Marienfelde reception camp in West Berlin. The AP reported that the refugees "slipped into West Berlin faster than ever today despite all Communist efforts to hold them back by force and propaganda appeals."

For many Americans, the frightening development brought back the chilling warning voiced by President Kennedy to an uncertain world in his inaugural address only seven months before, words that suddenly took on a new and scary importance:

> Let the word go forth, from this time and place, to friend and foe alike, that the torch has been passed to a new generation of Americans—born in this century, tempered by war, disciplined by a hard and bitter peace, proud of our ancient heritage—and unwilling to witness or permit the slow undoing of those human rights to which this nation has always been committed and to which we are committed today, at home and around the world.
>
> Let every nation know, whether it wishes us well or ill, that we shall pay any price, bear any burden, meet any hardship, support

any friend, oppose any foe, to assure the survival and success of liberty.

In that atmosphere of international tension, the federal government was encouraging Americans to be prepared, and state and local governments were sounding the same warnings. Radio and television stations broadcast tests of the nation's EBS warnings every day, and most listeners knew that EBS meant "Emergency Broadcast System." Radios, including those in cars, had the civil defense logo on their dials so citizens could find the spot immediately for emergency information in case of enemy attack. Evacuation routes were laid out and announced to the public and were the subjects of citizen meetings with briefings by government officials, covered widely by the news media.

Private, commercial, and government buildings had black-and-yellow signs on the front—three yellow triangles against a black circle—identifying them as locations where citizens could seek shelter from fallout in the event of an atomic attack. In a lengthy feature article in *The Washington Post* on December 23, 2001, three months after the terrorist attacks on New York and Washington, Libby Copeland reported that Washington's city government had stocked the fallout shelter on Capitol Hill with enough supplies in 1963 to last 35,616 occupants for two weeks. Officials marked thirteen hundred public shelters with a combined capacity for more than a million people, enough to house the entire population of the city with additional space for tourists and employees of the city government.

The shelters in the office buildings and other facilities were not built for that purpose originally. Instead, they were the basements of apartment buildings, schools, churches, and public buildings. They were identified as suitable for double duty as shelters in a massive survey of thousands of buildings in cities all across America. Those that met scientific criteria for protection against fallout were stocked with supplies by local and state governments and the federal Office of Civil Defense.

George Rodericks, Washington's civil defense director in the 1960s, told the *Post*'s Copeland that officials monitored weather conditions daily so they would know where the worst trouble spots would be for radiation from an atomic bomb and how long it would take the radiation to reach Washington from the target of the blast. "We would plot it from the major cities west of us," he said—"how much time we had . . . based on the prevailing winds that day."

It was grim business during grim times.

Governments at every level were encouraging Americans to make sure the gas gauges in their cars never dropped below half. They were told to keep a supply in their homes of canned foods, bottled water, a transistor radio, a flashlight, batteries, blankets, and even reading material in the event of a prolonged stay. The government said to keep these supplies in the basement, below ground, so the earth around the outside walls could serve as protection against fallout.

Better yet, Americans were asked to build fallout shelters in their backyards. For those who were willing to do so and could afford it, the government had plenty of instructional booklets. Schools conducted "duck and cover drills" in which students were shown how to get up from their seats at the first signal of an attack and duck under their desks for cover in case their school might be bombed.

American B-52 jet bombers loaded with atomic bombs circled the globe twenty-four hours a day, seven days a week, ready to drop their payloads on any nation that had launched an attack against America or was considered close to doing so. John Kennedy expressed the awesome dimensions of that aerial guard in frightening terms when he said in his successful 1960 campaign against Richard Nixon that each of those B-52s carried enough power in its atomic cargo "to destroy one-fourth of the world's population—a capability unknown since Cain slew Abel."

With this kind of world situation, one Berlin Wall was cause enough for alarm, but there was a second Berlin Wall a hundred yards into Communist Germany. Between the two walls was a no-man's land patrolled by armed guards and killer dogs. Automatic machine guns, land mines, and 285 watchtowers added to the chilling and deathly setting. Any desperate refugee who was spotted as he—or she—ran from the first wall toward the second never had a chance. Scenes of them as they were gunned down in cold blood appeared on America's television sets during the evening news more than once.

Nevertheless, some determined East Germans were able to escape over the Wall, and some even crashed their way through it. On November 9, 1989, the people of East and West Berlin scaled The Wall and danced along its top and drank champagne toasting the collapse of Communism. Later in the darkness, party-goers from both sides of the Wall produced hammers, chisels, and their own fingernails to begin tearing it down.

The Wall collapsed, just like the system that built it.

* * *

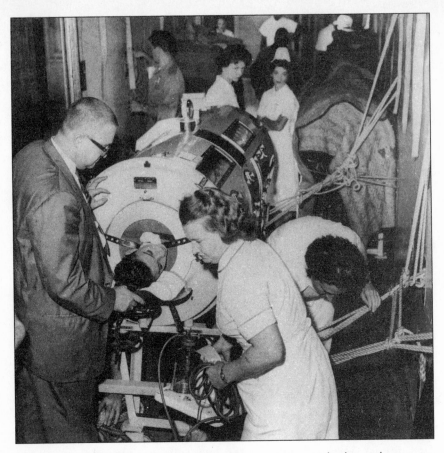

Iron lungs to help polio patients breathe were a common sight during the summer epidemics before the development of the Salk vaccine. This scene is at a hospital in Boston in 1960. (© *The Washington Post.* Courtesy of the Washington, D.C., Public Library.)

One of the scariest parts of summer life in America—polio—was about to disappear. "Polio epidemics" were a part of every summer, with the dreaded, crippling disease striking tens of thousands of Americans every year, most of them children and young adults. Parents warned their children not to go swimming right after becoming overheated because the combination was believed, right or wrong, to be one of the causes of polio. Kids were also warned to stay away from any of their playmates who might have the disease because it was highly contagious.

Its formal name was poliomyelitis, from two Greek words meaning gray and marrow because the disease was caused by tiny virus particles attacking the gray substance in the brain and the spinal column. It was also called infantile paralysis for two reasons, both of them wrong. Members of the medical profession believed in the early years that the disease struck only children and it always caused paralysis. It has been known for years since that it can strike people of any age, and it does not cause paralysis in every case.

In the middle of the twentieth century, polio was one of the leading news items in the papers, on the air, and in the movie newsreels every summer, usually accompanied by photos of children breathing in monster respirator machines called "iron lungs." The feared disease was brought under control in the last half of the 1950s and the early 1960s thanks to the miraculous development of a vaccine by Dr. Jonas Salk of the University of Pittsburgh. Dr. Salk developed his vaccine in 1943 and received government approval for its public use in 1955. Dr. Albert Sabin of the University of Cincinnati later developed an oral form of the vaccine, and kids needed only to pop what looked and tasted like a cube of sugar into their mouths. Both forms of the vaccine were approved for use in the United States in 1961. Between the two, the disease was largely brought until control.

By the time August was over, Maris had 51 home runs to Mantle's 48 and was still two weeks ahead of Ruth in 1927. Bob Cerv had the best view of that home run race between teammates. Cerv, a Yankee outfielder from 1951 through 1956, was traded back to New York by Los Angeles in 1961. With eight home runs that year, he was the only one of the three who wasn't threatening to break Ruth's record.

Cerv roomed with Maris and Mantle that year in an apartment on Long Island. He told *Sport* magazine he was impressed at how the two stars had been able to maintain their friendship while still dueling each other not only for the home run championship but for the historic role of trying to break Ruth's record. "They both admitted many times," Cerv said, "that while they wished the other fellow luck, this was competition for the greatest honor in baseball, and Mickey was rooting for Mickey and Roger was rooting for Roger. But that had nothing to do with the respect they had for one another."

The two power hitters used their apartment in its suburban location as a hideaway, allowing them to escape the unrelenting pressures of the reporters, the fans, and the opportunists who were always anxious to offer tempting business deals. The three teammates took turns cooking breakfast, watched TV, played cards, and went to the movies. They pre-

Roger Maris homers again in 1961 on his way to breaking Babe Ruth's record for the most home runs in one season. (Carl Kidwiler/National Baseball Hall of Fame Library, Cooperstown, N.Y.)

Mickey Mantle hit 54 home runs in 1961 and was in the race with Roger Maris to break Babe Ruth's record until an abscess on his right hip sidelined him late in the season. (Carl Kidwiler/National Baseball Hall of Fame Library, Cooperstown, N.Y.)

ferred westerns, but if they felt like a musical, they could see one of Hollywood's best that year: *Breakfast at Tiffany's*, with its hit song "Moon River."

Mantle, popular with teammates, fans, and the media, was the sentimental favorite over the more reserved Maris, who was playing only his second season as a Yankee after being traded from the Kansas City A's following the 1959 season. Mantle had already established himself as a fan favorite, the outgoing type who loved a good time away from the ballpark and had that rare combination on the field of both power and speed. Maris was the quiet type whose idea of a good time was to spend it at home with his wife and four kids, cooking on the outdoor grill in the backyard.

A former Yankee star, George Selkirk, then an executive with the Kansas City A's, Maris's former team, said, "This is a clean-living kid. He's not interested in bright lights. He prefers country life and barbecue pits. It's like people say, 'You can take the boy out of the country, but you can't take the country out of the boy.' "

While Maris was still not a darling of the Yankee fans, Mantle was. His popularity started as far back as 1953, when he hit baseball's first "tape-measure home run," a 565-foot shot at Griffith Stadium, and followed that with other impressive credentials by leading the American League in homers four times going into 1961. His best year with the long ball was in 1956, when he hit 52 homers. In contrast, Maris, although feared as a hitter, was playing his fifth year without hitting more than 39 home runs.

No one had to tell Maris that the fans, and many of the New York writers and broadcasters, were rooting for Mantle. All Maris had to do was know how to read. His fan mail and articles in the paper made it clear that Mickey was the popular favorite.

After the August trip to Washington, Maris returned with the team to New York to find a high stack of fan mail waiting for him, much of it positive in tone. The rest of it, however, told Maris he was "a lousy hitter" and should never claim to be the new Babe Ruth. Maris denied ever saying that anyhow, and admitted later that such mail "irked me. I had never claimed that I was another Babe Ruth. I was just Roger Maris, a guy trying to do the best he could."

Reporter Lenny Shecter of the *New York Post* wrote an article saying Maris played baseball only for the money. The slur prompted an emphatic response from Maris. "I love baseball," he said. "If I didn't, I'd quit right now." Maris was also being asked if his bumper crop of home runs was because the ball was "juiced"—livelier because of different materials or because the material inside was being wound together tighter than before. "More home runs are being hit," he said, "because more people are swinging for home runs. The old-timers swung for singles. I swing for home runs."

Another reporter asked Maris, "What's a .260 hitter like you doing hitting so many home runs?"

Maris answered simply, "You've got to be a damned idiot."

Still another asked if Maris would rather hit sixty home runs or bat .300. Maris tried to shake him off with, "No comment."

The reporter came back with, "Well, which would you?"

Maris answered the question with a question of his own: "Which would you rather do?"

The reported replied, "I'd rather hit .300."

To which Maris said, "You do what you want, and I'll do what I want."

Joe Trimble of the New York *Daily News* asked him, "Do you think you can break Babe Ruth's record?"

Maris answered, "How the _____ do I know?"

Trimble wrote, "He doesn't take surly pills—he only acts that way."

Some of the fans were just as bad as some of the reporters. Author Peter Golenbock wrote in *Baseball Quarterly* that Maris was the target of abuse from the fans in Yankee Stadium as well as in other ballparks. "At the Stadium" Golenbock said, "he took a frightful booing, and though the people applauding far outnumbered those booing, the ferocity of the minority made a strong impact on Maris."

Remembering how happy he was with his previous team, the Kansas City A's, Maris said, "Give me the Kansas City fans any time. There's no place that can compare with the people there." Maris had justification for his loyalty to the Kansas City fans. During one streak while he was playing for the A's, he hit one of the coldest slumps ever to strike any player—six hits in 110 times at bat. Golenbock writes, "Never once was he booed."

13

"I Can't Handle This . . ."

One of the heroes in the Yankees' two-man home run derby was a pitcher for the Yankees, Spud Murray. He was their batting practice pitcher. He estimated in later years that he gave up 2,000 "home runs" that year to the Yankee sluggers. "I did pretty good against Mickey Mantle and Roger Maris," he told Sandy Grady of the *Philadelphia Bulletin*. "I figure they hit about 350 homers each off me. Shucks, if they let me pitch to Maris every game, he would have broken Ruth's record a half-dozen times."

The record-breaking year by the M&M Boys brought rewards to Murray as well as to the two home run hitters. One reward was an appearance by Murray on one of the most popular network television shows of that time, *I've Got a Secret*. He didn't fool the panel, though. Henry Morgan spotted Murray arriving with one of his teammates, Tony Kubek, but he was stumped by the number on the uniform of the Yankee shirt worn by Murray on the show: 55.

That didn't fool one of the other panelists, Bill Cullen, who guessed that Murray's secret was all those "home runs" he gave up to Maris and Mantle.

The whole country was following the homer race between teammates who were hitting next to each other in their team's batting order. The Yankees' rookie manager, Ralph Houk, in his first year after succeeding Casey Stengel, received mail himself on that subject. Some fans were begging him to switch Maris and Mantle in the batting order, claiming Maris had an unfair advantage over their boy Mantle because he hit in front of Mantle, with Yogi Berra following Mantle.

Mickey Mantle *(left)* and Roger Maris were roommates as well as teammates in 1961, when both chased Babe Ruth's home run record. (Courtesy of Photo File.)

Houk responded firmly, "I have no concern with the home run race. My lineup is the one I think can win the pennant, and that is my job. I have a solid reason for putting Mickey in between Roger and Yogi. That's the way it stays."

Maris went into another slump later in August, with only two hits— one of them a homer—in his next seventeen times at bat. With thirty-nine games to play, he had 49 home runs. "It was natural for me to think that I might have a chance to match Babe Ruth's record," he wrote with Jim Ogle for *Look* magazine. "I felt certain that I would wind up with at least fifty-some homers, and I knew that only eight players had ever reached fifty."

On a trip to Los Angeles, Maris was notified that his wife, Pat, had given birth to their fourth child, a son. That was not a new experience for either mother or father. Maris missed the births of three of their children, all except Roger Jr., because of his baseball schedule. Family and friends decided from the start that they would not tell Roger what was happening back home until Pat delivered the baby.

In the Yankees' first game in Los Angeles, Maris hit his fiftieth home run of the season, becoming the first player to reach that level before the end of August. As September began, the team returned home for a crucial three-game series against their closest contenders for the pennant, the Detroit Tigers of Al Kaline, Norm Cash, Rocky Colavito, Frank Lary, and Jim Bunning.

They swept the Tigers and reeled off thirteen wins in a row and clinched the American League pennant. In the second game of the Detroit series, Maris hit two more home runs. During the third game, Mantle came over to Maris in the dugout and joked, "I just want to warn you that if it's the last day of the season and I'm ahead of you, or we're tied, watch out. If you hit a home run, I'll stand at the plate and, just before you cross, I'll hit you with my bat."

Maris responded in kind. "That's all right, Mick," he said. "If I'm on base and you hit one, then I'll turn and run the wrong way, and you'll pass me on the bases and you won't get your homer either."

As exciting as his baseball exploits were becoming, Maris's life beyond baseball was something less than that to the new star. "I was living the most boring existence imaginable," he told Ogle. "This may sound strange to anyone on the outside. The excitement about the home run race, the publicity and everything else may have seemed glamorous and wonderful. But I had to stay in my room all the time, and I hated it. I like to sit around with friends and shoot the breeze. I like to be free to do anything I want. Now I wasn't free to do anything. The daily press routine at the ballpark was getting monotonous. Going back to the apartment and hiding was getting monotonous. It was as if I were in a trap and couldn't escape."

During their relaxing times in their apartment, Mantle would look up from the daily paper occasionally and say to Maris, "I hate your guts." It was a running gag between the two superstars, stemming from the repeated rumors in the New York news media that Maris and Mantle did not like each other. Maris had the perfect squelch for that rumor. He told reporters, "You don't live with someone you don't like."

As bored as he might have been off the field, Maris became a determined man when he put on the Yankee pinstripes. By mid-September he had 56 home runs, and the M&M Boys had slugged their way into baseball's record books by passing the combined 107 home runs in one season hit by Ruth and Lou Gehrig.

Maris admitted later that by then he was developing a strong determination to break Ruth's record of sixty in one season. He was driven even more by the continued negative talk that he was no Ruth and would make an inadequate successor to the popular Bambino.

With the season nearing its end, the Yankees left for their final trip of the year, to Chicago, Detroit, Baltimore, and Boston. Baltimore was going to be the scene of the 154th game.

Mantle, however, was victimized by his injury jinx again, the plague that followed him during his entire career. Mantle won praise throughout his career for his willingness and ability to play, and perform at the superstar level, on only one good leg. It would be more accurate to say that he played without even one. When first baseman Boog Powell of the Baltimore Orioles was interviewed by Bob Allen for our book *The 500 Home Run Club*, in 1999, he said, "I played one All-Star game with him, and it was just amazing to watch him dress and see how much tape they put on him. His legs were wrapped up from his ankles straight up to his chest."

Fate struck cruelly again late in 1961, when Mantle developed an abscess on his right hip. He landed in the hospital again and was out of the lineup for most of the rest of the season. He missed ten games that year.

★　★　★

As September began, Maris stood at 51 home runs, ten games ahead of Ruth's pace. The pressure on the muscular, crew-cut, shy young man from Fargo, who turned twenty-seven that month, became almost unbearable. Reports on his performance each day or night were on the evening news as the whole nation followed his exploits.

At the start of a four-game series in Baltimore, Maris, mobbed as usual by reporters before the first game, told them, "My daughter, Susan, is four years old, and she's getting to an age where she wants her daddy home. She can't understand why the other kids her age have their daddys home and hers isn't. That's what I'm thinking about. Everybody thinks all I have on my mind are home runs."

The next day, September 20, the date for the Yankees' 154th game of record (they also had one tie), Maris went into the visiting manager's office in Baltimore's Memorial Stadium and told his manager, Ralph Houk, "I can't handle this . . . I need help." He added, "They keep asking the same questions . . . It never lets up."

Then, grabbing his head, he said, "Look at this—my damn hair is falling out." Later, surrounded by a mob of reporters in front of his locker in the visiting team's dressing room, Maris complained, "The only time I'm by myself is when I'm in the john." He buried his head in his hands and cried.

Then he went out and hit his fifty-ninth home run of the season in the third inning, a rising line drive to right field off righthander Milt Pappas of the Orioles. The blow helped the Yankees to clinch the American League pennant—and it made Maris only the second player in baseball history, behind Babe Ruth himself, to hit 59 home runs in one season.

When he came to bat for the last time that day, with two outs in the ninth inning, Maris still needed one more home run to tie Ruth's record of 60 in one season. He was facing Baltimore's superb relief pitcher, knuckleballer Hoyt Wilhelm.

Wilhelm possessed one of the all-time great knuckleball pitches. Hitting a home run against a knuckleballer is harder than against other pitchers because the hitter has to provide almost all of the power himself while also trying to follow the zany flight of the ball. And trying to hit a homer against Wilhlem was harder yet.

Wilhelm, to give Maris a sporting chance to tie Ruth in 154 games, might well have been willing to throw him fastballs, but the manager of the Orioles, Paul Richards, headed off that idea at the pass. Richards, a former catcher and one of the brightest managers of his time, told Wilhelm sternly, "If you throw him anything but a knuckleball, it will cost you $5,000."

Maris saw nothing but knuckleballs. He fouled off the first one. The second pitch, another knuckler, darted and danced its way to the plate. Maris took a half swing in his uncertainty about the ball's movements. The ball bounced ten feet down the first base line. Wilhelm ran over, picked up the grounder and easily tagged Maris out. Ruth remained alone at the top of baseball history as the only player to hit 60 homers in 154 games. The game was over. The Yankees had a 4–2 victory and the American League pennant.

In the dressing room, the Yankees celebrated in what has become a ritual by popping bottles of champagne and thoroughly drenching each other—except Maris. His teammates knew he avoided that kind of activity so they left him alone. Instead of joining in all the fuss, Maris was apologizing to anyone within earshot. "I tried," he said while trying to catch his breath. "I tried," he said a second time. His teammates respectfully shook his hand and congratulated him on his dogged chase of Ruth's record.

Maris continued to feel the pressure. It was compounded when he became suspicious that the Yankee officials themselves were rooting for Mantle. He took strong exception to that, not because they were rooting for Mickey but because they were rooting for either one of them.

"I'm trying to help them win a pennant and not thinking about records," Maris said. "Why should they care which of us gets the most homers? Whether Mickey or I hit a homer that helps win a game should be the same. Am I on this ball club or not?"

The pressure continued, regardless of how he was doing, and it continued to bother the quiet star. "I never wanted all this hoopla," he said. "All I want is to be a good ballplayer, hit 25–35 home runs, drive in around 100 runs, hit .280 and help my club win pennants."

On September 26, in his 158th game, Maris became only the second man to hit 60 home runs in one season. He tied Ruth with a homer off Baltimore's Jack Fisher, a six-foot two-inch, 215-pound righthander, in Yankee Stadium. Now he had four more games in which to break baseball's most cherished record, held by baseball's most popular player.

In his next three games, Maris went homerless twice and sat out the third contest. On October 1, as he stood in the lefthander's side of the batting box at Yankee Stadium—"the House That Ruth Built"—he was still tied with Ruth. It was the Yankees' 163rd game of the season, their last, and Maris had played in all but two of them, compared to Ruth's 151 in 1927. Their opponents were the Boston Red Sox. The pitcher was a six-foot five-inch righthander, a rookie named Tracy Stallard.

Maris missed immortality in the first inning by sending a fly ball to another rookie, Carl Yastrzemski, in left field. In the fourth, before 23,154 fans, Maris, swinging a thirty-five-inch bat that weighed thirty-three ounces, hit a fastball and sent a fly ball toward the right field seats. As Maris watched the flight of the ball during his trot from the batter's box and along the first base line, Mantle watched too. With 54 home runs himself that year, he watched on a TV set in the hospital, still recovering from the abscess on his hip. It was a home run.

In the broadcast booth, Phil Rizzuto, the Yankees Hall of Fame shortstop and then one of their broadcasters, hollered, "Holy cow! Look at the fight for that ball!"

As Maris rounded third base on his home run trot, a young fan bolted out of the stands and rushed to shake his hand. Maris shook it, and also took the hand of the Yankees' third base coach, Frank Crosetti. After he crossed home plate, the whole Yankee team mobbed him. When he returned to the dugout on the first base side, his teammates insisted that he take a curtain call from the screaming fans. When he declined, they pushed him back onto the field anyway—four times.

After the game, reporters in the Red Sox clubhouse asked Stallard how he felt about being the pitcher who gave up the record breaker. He answered, "I'm not going to lose any sleep over it. I'd rather he hit the homer off me than I walk him during the game."

The ball was captured by Sal Durante, a nineteen-year-old from the Coney Island section of Brooklyn. He was wearing a black jacket and white T-shirt, smoking a cigarette, and sitting in box 163D in section 33 with his girlfriend, Rosemarie Calabrese. They were eight rows behind the right field wall in the lower deck, ten feet from the edge of the Yankee bullpen. Sal was in seat 4 and Rosemarie in seat 3.

"As soon as it was hit," he said later, "I knew it was going over my head, so I jumped on my seat and reached as high as I could. I still had the cigarette in my mouth—that's how quick the ball came out to right field. It hit the palm of my hand, like my hand was a magnet. It knocked me over into the next row."

Durante admitted he was "amazed, in shock." He said, "All I could think of was I wanted to give the ball to Roger. I didn't care about anything else. I wanted Roger to have it."

Durante immediately qualified for $5,000, the amount promised by Sam Gordon, a California restaurant owner in Sacramento, for the ball. It would be a nice start for the wedding being planned by the young couple, especially with Durante making only $60 a week in an auto parts store.

But Durante declined. By the time Maris came to bat the next time, in the eighth inning, word had reached him that Durante didn't want the money. He just wanted to give the ball to Maris. Just before stepping into the batter's box, Maris turned to Boston's catcher, Russ Nixon, and said, "What do you think of that kid? The boy is planning to get married and he can use the money, but he still wanted to give the ball back to me for nothing. It shows there's some good people left in this world after all."

Eventually Maris convinced Durante to "make yourself some money." Durante did, plus receiving two season passes to all Yankee home games in 1962 and a free round-trip to the World's Fair in Seattle. Gordon then donated the ball to the Baseball Hall of Fame.

Gordon went beyond the $5,000 for Durante. He also gave Sal and Rosemarie an all-expenses-paid trip to Palm Springs, Reno, and San Francisco. Maris went to California with them. The newlyweds got to meet the Mills Brothers, Louis Armstrong, and Jane Wyman, who asked Sal for his autograph.

The homer set Maris apart from all the other men who had ever played major league baseball—the only player ever to hit 61 home runs in one season, an achievement that seemed safe for the foreseeable future. And it was, for thirty-seven years.

The powerhouse Yankees won the American League pennant by eight games over the Tigers, then polished off the Cincinnati Reds, winners of the National League pennant by four games over the Dodgers, in five games in the World Series. Mantle, still recovering, came to bat only six times and had one hit, a single. Maris hit a home run in the ninth inning to win the third game

The Yankees breezed home with victories of 7–0 and 13–5 to win the next two games and the Series. They won their championship despite being without Mantle and Berra at times and losing their ace lefthander, Whitey Ford, to an ankle injury in the sixth inning of the fourth game.

Before he was forced out of the game, however, Ford set a World Series record by pitching his thirty-second straight shutout inning, breaking the record set by another ace lefthanded pitcher: Babe Ruth.

After the season, Maris was asked about his problems with the news media. He said the problems carried an advantage. "People are usually pleasantly surprised when they actually meet me," he said. "They find out I'm not the monster they've read about."

At a postseason banquet in Milwaukee, Maris was asked what had been the most irritating question during his record-breaking season. "They kept asking me if I thought I could beat Ruth," he answered. "The one that's getting a little irritating right now is, 'Are you going to hit 62 in '62?' "

Looking back on that 1961 season, Maris said, "As a ballplayer, I would be delighted to do it again. As an individual, I doubt if I could possibly go through it again. They even asked for my autograph at Mass." In 1967, his next-to-last season, he said, "I just want to be one of the guys, an average player having a good season. I'd never want to go through another year like 1961."

Mantle, who died of cancer and other ailments in 1995 at sixty-three, was elected to the Baseball Hall of Fame in 1974 in his first year of eligibility. Maris, twice the American League's Most Valuable Player and holder of the home run record for thirty-seven years until Mark McGwire broke it in 1998, died of lymphatic cancer ten years before Mantle at the age of fifty-one and has not been elected to the Hall of Fame.

"It wouldn't change my life any if I got in," the blunt Maris once said, "so what do I care? The record has never achieved the respect it deserves because I set it. I'm just not the hero type."

14

When Mirrors Weren't Enough

The Maris-Mantle dual was only one of two historic baseball seasons in 1961. The new "expansion Senators" in Washington were the other. In stark contrast to the Yankees' season, the Senators' year has been forgotten by baseball's journalists. That story needs to be told, too, in the interest of making the history of that season complete and because it stretches all the way to today.

The Senators, stocked by rejects from the other American League teams, jumped off to a surprisingly successful start by playing .500 ball, winning thirty of their first sixty games by June, to the utter shock of the experts. Manager Mickey Vernon seemed to be doing it with mirrors. Outfielder Gene Woodling, a former Yankee star and a thirty-eight-year-old genius with a bat in his hands, was hitting .290 for Washington. Gene Green, a good-hit, no-field catcher, was doing even better at .325. Willie Tasby, a Baltimore Orioles castoff, was hitting .302. Rookie outfielder Chuck Hinton was showing promise, and pitcher Dick Donovan was headed toward the American League's earned run championship.

Then the Senators went to Boston and ran smack into one of the worst Fenway Park stories of them all.

They dropped out of the exclusive above-.500 neighborhood by blowing a 6–0 lead on a Friday night in the first of a four-game series. On Saturday afternoon, they let a 5–1 lead slip out of their hands and lost again, 6–5. With a chance to pull back up to .500 by sweeping the Red Sox in a Sunday doubleheader, the Senators did just the opposite. They lost both games. And they didn't just lose—they fell apart. They blew a seven-run lead in the ninth inning of the first game, proving that what baseball people say is true—there's no such thing as a safe lead in Fenway Park. The Red Sox scored seven runs with two outs in the ninth. The Senators never got that last out. They lost, 13–12.

In the second game, they lost in thirteen innings.

On their plane ride back to Washington, the atmosphere was like a funeral home. Danny O'Connell, the outgoing third baseman with the Irish tenor voice, wasn't singing his usual "Danny Boy" and Chuck Hinton wasn't conducting his sing-along of "Mathilda."

Mickey Vernon told reporters, "You wouldn't believe it if you hadn't seen it, would you? This is a game I'll never forget . . . I kept thinking of that last out—that never came. I kept thinking, 'This one will pop it up. This one will hit a fly ball which somebody will grab. This one will ground out.' It never happened . . . You go over the ball game and think of a million things you could have done. But it was too late."

The president of the new team, a retired Air Force general and local boy named Pete Quesada, who owned only 10 percent of the franchise, stepped into the crisis by taking immediate action. He announced that he was canceling his team's contract with Eastern Airlines because the flight attendants served sandwiches instead of a meal on the return flight.

The Senators went into free fall. They lost 15 straight games in midsummer, beat the Chicago White Sox in the first game of a twilight-night doubleheader at Griffith Stadium, then lost 9 more in a row—24 losses in 25 games. The team that had been so proud of its 30–30 record in mid-June dropped 31 games below .500 with only 50 wins after 131 games. A Saturday game in September drew only 2,889 fans. A Sunday doubleheader over Labor Day weekend drew only 6,984.

Pressure was everywhere, much of it behind the scenes and away from public view. Quesada, who was known by the media to be interfering in the front office, began to interfere with the team itself too. He looked for his general manager, Ed Doherty, during a night game to get him to phone Vernon in the dugout and tell him to have one of the players lay down a bunt.

As the Senators marketing director that year and into the next, I was an eyewitness to these goings-on. After Quesada tried to find Doherty to order Vernon to flash the bunt sign, the general manager told me, "Bill, if Quesada ever calls you in the press box during a game and wants to know where I am, tell him you don't know, even if I'm sitting right next to you." Doherty was not going to allow himself to get caught in the trap of being told to call Vernon in the dugout and relay one of Quesada's commands.

When the team's nosedive continued, Quesada summoned Vernon and Doherty to report to his office for an all-day, closed-door meeting, then announced that Vernon had decided to bench his three best home run hitters—Green, Tasby, and first baseman Dale Long—for not hustling.

Well, Quesada didn't really announce it himself. He hid behind me. He dictated a cliché-heavy press release to his secretary and told her to give it to me for distribution in the press box before that night's game. When the reporters asked for more information behind the strange release, I told them, "I don't know anything about it. The only thing I know is that I was told to give it to you." When they read it, they saw right though it, not believing for a minute that Vernon had ordered anything. They knew that Quesada's fingerprints were all over those benchings.

The problems continued to mount. The team lost to the Orioles, 9–3, in the first game of a doubleheader on a rainy September Sunday. Quesada wanted to fire his announcers, Dan Daniels and John MacLean, for saying it was raining but was talked out of it by the team's business manager, Joe Burke, who later became the president of the Kansas City Royals. Dick Donovan, leading the league in earned run average, developed a sprained big toe and missed much of September.

The end came on September 22, in a 6–3 loss to, of all teams, the Minnesota Twins, the original Washington Senators for sixty years. Only 1,498 fans showed up for what was the end of the home season and the end of Griffith Stadium. The moment that Calvin Griffith had stubbornly resisted arrived. The team was moving into the new District of Columbia Stadium—now RFK—the following spring. One of the fans who showed up was eighty-five-year-old Nick Altrock, in tinted glasses and walking with the aid of a cane. Altrock had pitched on that same hallowed ground sixty-three years before, in 1898 with Louisville. He was with the Senators when Clark Griffith built his ballpark in 1912. Altrock saw the first game ever played there. Forty-nine years later, he saw the last.

At the end of the 1961 season, the team's record showed 61 wins and 100 losses. Quesada expressed concern publicly that the Senators finished their year a quarter of a million dollars in the red. From Chicago, Bill Veeck, never afraid of spending money to make money, said, "Quesada has every reason to be worried about losing a quarter of a million dollars in his first season. If he were doing his job right, he'd have lost five million."

By the end of the second season, Quesada's nine co-owners bought him out. Seven years after that, in 1969, a businessman named Bob Short, from—that name again—Minnesota, bought the team and ran it into the ground quickly. After three seasons, he was already two years behind in his rent on the still-new stadium. He was feuding with local officials and business executives and was threatening to play his home games on a high school field. He solved his money problems by moving the Senators to Texas and making them the Texas Rangers after only three years as the owner in Washington. After one year in Texas, he sold the team and went back home to Minnesota.

Short was free to leave because Quesada, even with his Washington roots, had been unwilling to sign a lease on the new stadium for more than ten years, which, conveniently for Short, expired after the 1971 season. The Redskins, in contrast, had committed themselves to a thirty-year lease.

What the people in baseball and the fans in Washington began to realize as the 1960s unfolded was that the American League had awarded the expansion franchise to the wrong man in 1961. Several men with far more impressive baseball credentials, experience, and knowledge had entered the bidding for the new team in the fall of 1960, including Bill Veeck and Hank Greenberg. Bob Hope, who had been a part owner of the Cleveland Indians, and the management firm that operated Madison Square Garden were also in the bidding. Quesada got the team because of a heavy emphasis placed by baseball on local ownership in those years.

A friendship with Joe Cronin didn't hurt Quesada's cause, either. Cronin was almost a local boy himself. He married into the Griffith family by wedding Calvin's sister while an all-star shortstop and future Hall of Famer with the Senators. When the American League decided to put an expansion team in Washington for 1961, Cronin was president of the league. By choosing Quesada over the other more qualified candidates, the American League's owners were setting into motion the series of events that led to the departure of major league baseball from Washington in 1971, after eight decades.

The expansion Senators averaged 94 losses a year. They lost one hundred or more games in four of their eleven expansion seasons and finished last five times. Still, the fans remained steadfast in their loyalty, and never mind popular opinion to the contrary. The proof comes from no less a source than the National Baseball Hall of Fame Library in Cooperstown, New York. Figures there show that the Senators drew surprising numbers, even in Short's three-year term and after eight years of repeated ineptitude by Quesada and others. Despite that uninterrupted string of failures and defeats, and with the champion Baltimore Orioles playing their games only forty miles away, Senators fans produced a better attendance record than six of the league's other eleven teams in 1969, only 100,000 short of the league's average. That figures out to a difference of only 1,235 fans per game.

In 1970, attendance in Washington topped four other teams in the league, even though the Senators lost 16 more games than the year before and finished 22 games below .500. They drew almost twice as many fans at home as the White Sox in Comiskey Park. In 1971, Short's third and last year in Washington, while he kept up a season-long filibuster about moving to another city, the Senators won only 63 games, 23 below the total for Short's first year. Still, they drew more than the Cleveland Indians.

Today, more than thirty years later, the White Sox are still in Chicago and the Indians are still in Cleveland, but the national pastime is still missing from the national capital. Baseball is the only major professional team sport not represented there.

PART FIVE

· · ·

1969

15

Those Mets?

In a year when Richard Nixon rose from the political ashes and was inaugurated president, and the first American troops began to withdraw from Vietnam, and three hundred thousand young people sang about peace and did other things at a place near Bethel, New York, called Woodstock, and a human being walked on the moon for the first time in the history of the world, about the only other newsmaking event left would be the New York Mets winning the World Series—and they did. It happened in 1969.

The New York Mets won the World Series? The team that was only in its eighth season? *Those* Mets? The team that set a modern record for futility by losing 120 games in its first year? *Those* Mets? The team that drove its first manager, Casey Stengel, to cry out in frustration, "Can't anybody here play this game?" *Those* Mets?

Yes, *those* Mets. Their championship, in which they staged one of the most shocking upsets in World Series history by defeating the Baltimore Orioles in only five games, topped off one of the most dynamic, convulsive, and dramatic decades in the history of the United States.

It was ten years of headlines, starting with the inauguration of the youngest man ever to be elected president, John F. Kennedy, in 1961, followed in dizzying succession by the invasion at the Bay of Pigs in Cuba, the construction of the Berlin Wall, violence amid civil rights demonstrations by "Freedom Riders" in the Deep South during the "long hot summers" of the '60s, Kennedy's assassination in 1963, the landslide election of Lyndon Johnson in 1964, the explosion of U.S. involvement in

Vietnam into the longest war—and one of the bloodiest—in American history, Johnson's shocking refusal to seek a second full term in 1968, space shots from Cape Canaveral, Florida, the assassinations of Martin Luther King, Jr., and Robert Kennedy only two months apart in 1968, an automobile accident on Cape Cod involving Senator Ted Kennedy and a young woman riding with him who drowned, and Neil Armstrong's walk on the moon in July 1969.

When Armstrong took mankind's first steps on the moon, it was only three months before the Mets produced the final bold headlines of the decade, again illustrating the close relationship between baseball and American life. The last major newsmaker of that explosive decade of network bulletins, Page One banner lines, breaking news, live reports, and national days of mourning was, appropriately enough for America, a baseball story.

★ ★ ★

TOM SEAVER

Tom Seaver—"Tom Terrific"—won 25 games as a twenty-four-year-old pitcher for the 1969 Mets, then beat the Orioles in the fourth game of the World Series on a six-hitter, pitching the entire ten innings. (Courtesy of the National Baseball Hall of Fame Library, Cooperstown, N.Y.)

One of the stars on the Mets that year, a twenty-four-year-old pitcher named Tom Seaver who was destined for the Baseball Hall of Fame, said his team's victory that year over the heavily favored Orioles "was the greatest collective victory by any team in sports."

The impossible dream began nine years before, when the Mets joined the expanded National League. Like any expansion team formed by the rejects from the other teams in its league, the Mets were doomed to failure in their first years. In 1962, they set that record of 120 losses that still stands. They did it with a cast of characters—and they were characters, all right—that included Choo-Choo Coleman, a catcher who used to flash the sign between his legs for the next pitch and then look down to see what he was signaling; and "Marvelous Marv" Throneberry, who once missed *both* first and second bases while running out a triple but became a New York folk hero anyhow as the perfect symbol of his team. The fans loved him, forgave his transgressions, and showed up at the ballpark with signs saying things like:

CRANBERRY, STRAWBERRY, WE LOVE THRONEBERRY

When the New York baseball writers presented him with their "Good Guy Award" at their annual dinner because of his agreeable nature in his dealings with them, Throneberry told the audience, "They told me not to stand up here too long holding the plaque because I might drop it."

And there was Casey Stengel himself. Stengel had been fired by the Yankees after the 1960 World Series for the unforgivable sin of not winning the Series every year. He won it in each of his first five years as the Yankee manager, from 1949 through 1953, and put together a record of seven World Series championships and ten American League pennants in his twelve seasons as their skipper.

When the Yankees fired him, the announced reason was that Casey had reached the age of seventy, which the Yankees, they said, considered retirement age. Stengel told reporters, "I'll never make that mistake again." He was philosophical again when he said, "The only thing a manager can be sure of is that some day he's going to get fired."

Stengel was always the optimist, especially in spring training. He told the writers covering the team, "The Mets are going to be amazin'." He didn't specify the year.

Stengel managed the Mets from their first day in 1962 at the Polo Grounds, where the Giants had played, through ninety-six games of the

1965 season. When they started from scratch in 1962, Stengel told reporters, "You have to start with a catcher, because if you don't you'll have all passed balls." In his book *The Explosive Sixties,* author-historian William B. Mead points out, "The Mets used six catchers in their first season, and still had twenty-six passed balls."

They never won more than 53 games under Stengel, but he never let it get to him, and some of his players didn't, either. Throneberry, a six-foot one-inch outfielder and first baseman from Collierville, Tennessee, was interviewed on a broadcast of a Baltimore Orioles game in the 1990s when he was asked about that record-breaking 120-loss season in 1962. The Orioles broadcaster mentioned that the team must have been awful.

"Oh, we weren't that bad," Throneberry answered. "We just had a lot of tough luck"—leaving the announcer and his listeners to wonder just how much tough luck it takes to lose 120 games in one season.

During that first season, Stengel put in a call to catcher Joe Pignatano in the Mets bullpen and told him, "Warm up Miller."

The Mets had two pitchers named Miller, both of them with the first name of Bob, one of them righthanded and the other a lefty, so Pignatano asked, "Which Miller?"

Stengel said, "Bob Miller."

"Which Bob Miller?"

To which Stengel replied, "Surprise me."

The Mets picked up one of the most popular players in New York history in 1963 with the addition of "the Duke of Flatbush," Duke Snider, a future Hall of Famer who was still an idol in Brooklyn from his career as a star with the Dodgers. Stengel, because of his respect for Duke, turned to him in the dugout during the 1963 season and said, "Hey, kid"—like Babe Ruth, he called many people "kid"—"I'm going to grab a few winks. You're managing the team."

The Mets were losing to the Cincinnati Reds, 3–1, when Stengel dozed off. When he awoke, Duke said, "Casey, I hate to tell you, but now we're losing by a lot more. It's 9–1."

Stengel winked, as he often did when he was enjoying the conversation, and said, "Don't worry about it, kid. It's not your fault. You look over there into the Cincinnati dugout and what do you see? All mahogany. Then you look at our bench and all you see is driftwood."

Jimmy Piersall, one of the most uninhibited players in the sport's history, joined the Mets in 1963. He got on Snider's back when Duke hit his four hundredth home run, off Bob Purkey in Cincinnati. Piersall commented about the lack of publicity for Duke's accomplishment and told him, "I'll get more ink [the ballplayers' word for publicity] when I hit my *one* hundredth than you got with your *four* hundredth."

He was right. He hit it at the Polo Grounds—and rounded the bases backward. He went in the proper order, from first to second and on around to home plate, but he was running with his back to the next base. Then he slid into home plate headfirst. The picture of Piersall's antics appeared in papers and on TV screens all over America. Duke said later, "That's why he knew he'd get more ink than I did. He'd planned the stunt all along."

Duke remembers the time in Chicago when he boarded the team bus for the ride from the Conrad Hilton Hotel to Wrigley Field and Stengel told him, "Sit next to me on the bench today. We'll talk about the '52 Series," when the Yankees defeated the Dodgers. Stengel always enjoyed reliving that string of five straight World Series championships from 1949 through 1953 but always avoided talking about 1955, when Duke's Dodgers finally upset the Yankees and won Brooklyn's only World Series championship.

Snider kidded Stengel, "When are we going to talk about '55?"

Stengel brushed him off with, "Later."

Duke says they never did.

The road to the year of the "Amazin' Mets" of 1969 began on April 11, 1962, in St. Louis, when they lost the first game of their first season to the Cardinals, 11–4. Then they came home to New York and a parade up lower Broadway. Mayor Robert Wagner threw out the first ball just before the Mets played their home opener at the Polo Grounds, vacant since the Dodgers and Giants fled from New York to California before the 1958 season. At that same site in 1962, before 12,447 fans who sat through a steady drizzle, the Mets lost again, this time to the Pittsburgh Pirates, 4–3. It was Friday the thirteenth.

The crowds weren't always that small in that first year. Later in the '62 season, the Mets drew two hundred thousand fans over a five-day stretch against the Dodgers and the Giants—the *Los Angeles* Dodgers and the *San Francisco* Giants. As the Mets stumbled through the agonies and occasional ecstasies of their first season of life, Roger Angell explained the larger crowds by writing in *The New Yorker* magazine, "This was a new recognition that perfection is admirable but a trifle inhuman, that a stumbling kind of semi-success can be so much more warming."

Stengel's Mets won only 40 games in that first season, but they jumped to 51 wins in '63 and 2 more than that in '64. In '65 the team had won only 31 of 95 games when Stengel was fired and replaced by Wes Westrum, who managed the Mets to only 19 more wins for an overall record of 50 wins and 112 losses, dangerously close to their '62 record year.

There had been some reason for optimism on Stengel's part when the '65 season started, because he had added his old favorite, Yogi Berra, to his coaching staff. It's hard to imagine a team headed by an out-and-out character like Casey Stengel and a staff of assistants that included the colorful Yogi, but that was the composition of the Mets' leadership for the '65 season.

The New York writers were aware of Stengel's respect for Berra, who, like Casey himself, was never the bumbling idiot that his public image made him out to be. Stengel was always quick to recognize Berra's intelligence and equally quick to praise him for it in talking to the writers. During their glory times with the Yankees, Stengel used to tell the reporters, "This is Mister Berra which helps me manage the Yankees. He's my lucky fella. I always win when I have him in the lineup. Besides, he's very close to the ownership."

Wes Westrum, a catcher with the Giants for all eleven of his major league seasons from 1947 through 1957, managed the Mets for two full seasons in which they finished in ninth place in 1966 and tenth in 1967. He was fired and replaced by another longtime New York favorite and ex-Brooklyn Dodger, Gil Hodges. Under Hodges, the strong and quiet type, the Mets moved up only one notch in the 1968 National League standings, but they won twelve more games.

Then came 1969, and the Mets made Casey Stengel's prophecy come true—they were amazin'. And they were not going to be one of the doormats of the National League, either. That honor went to two more expansion teams in each league: the San Diego Padres and Montreal Expos in the National League and the Kansas City Royals and Seattle Pilots in the American. Seattle won 64 games and Kansas City 69, but the two new National Leaguers, the Padres and the Expos, duplicated the Mets' experience of 1962. They both finished dead last, with identical records of 52 wins and 110 defeats.

★ ★ ★

Gil Hodges had been a manager for five years, all with the Washington Senators, when he joined the Mets for the 1968 season. The Senators finished last—tenth place—in 1963, when Hodges took the helm from another former first baseman, Mickey Vernon, after forty games. Hodges raised them to ninth in 1964, eighth in 1965 and 1966, and sixth in 1967. His boss in Washington, general manager George Selkirk, the old Yankee, was pleased with his performance, and his future in Washington looked secure. But then the Mets called.

They offered Hodges their manager's job after Westrum's departure. For Hodges, it was a tempting opportunity, but a difficult decision. He felt loyalty to the Senators management, but this was a chance to return to his hometown, where he married a Brooklyn girl, Joan Lombardi, became a folk hero with the Brooklyn Dodgers as their all-star first baseman, and settled there after pulling up his roots from his native Indiana.

Anxious not to disappoint his Brooklyn friends, but confident of his ability to lead, Hodges took the job and elevated his team one step in the National League standings with twelve more wins in 1968. The 1969 season was to be the first year of baseball playoffs, with two divisions in each league. You didn't need the best record in the league to qualify for the World Series as the pennant winner. You could have the second best record, and as long as you won your division's championship, you could still get into the playoffs by beating the champions of the other division, even if they finished your league's season with a better record than your team.

Hodges stood tall in his job in those years, and not just because he was six feet one and a half inches. He was the strong, silent kind of leader, the makeup you might expect to find in a former Marine who won the Bronze Star for bravery during the battle of Okinawa in World War II. He was a religious man who prayed every day but kept his religion to himself.

He stood out among major league managers that year because of the contrast. He was in the same profession with several men completely opposite him in their personalities and conduct. There was the combative, hard-charging, hard-drinking Billy Martin, the once and future Yankee who was the skipper of the Minnesota Twins in '69; Leo Durocher, the always flamboyant manager of the Chicago Cubs and formerly of the Dodgers and Giants; the exuberant and sometimes controversial Ted Williams, a rookie manager that year with Hodges's old team, the Senators; and Earl Weaver, in his second year as the skipper of the Baltimore Orioles, who was destined to meet Hodges in the World Series six months later.

Of that group, only Williams did not stay in the profession. He bailed out after three years of heading the Senators in Washington and their first season as the Texas Rangers. When he left after only four years as a major league manager, Williams said with typical forcefulness, "I wouldn't manage again if you gave me the club and the city it's in."

In contrast, Hodges was enjoying his return to his beloved Brooklyn and his new team. He liked its chances in 1969, predicting in spring training that the Mets would win eighty-five games, enough to establish them as serious contenders for the playoffs, even in a division with at least three other respectable teams, the Cubs, Pirates, and Cardinals.

As the season began, baseball had a new friend in Washington, Richard Nixon, sworn into office only three months before in one of the most surprising political comebacks in the history of American presidential politics. Nixon had been defeated by another baseball fan, John Kennedy, in 1960, and then lost in an effort to be elected governor of his home state of California two years later, prompting his now classic remark to reporters, "You won't have Nixon to kick around anymore."

But they would. He was elected president over Hubert Humphrey in 1968 in the midst of the growing turmoil about America's worsening situation in its war against North Vietnam. On Opening Day of the 1969 season, there was President Richard Nixon throwing out the first ball at Robert F. Kennedy Stadium in Washington, renamed after RFK's assassination the year before, the second Kennedy assassination in less than five years.

For Nixon, that kind of presidential duty was a delight. He was one of the most enthusiastic—and knowledgeable—baseball fans to inhabit the White House. He freely and frequently told reporters of his love for sports in general and baseball in particular. "I like the job I have now," he said, "but if I had my life to live over again, I'd like to have ended up as a sportswriter."

In later years, he told ESPN's Roy Firestone, "If I had a second chance, and could choose to be a politician or go into sportswriting—not playing but writing—I would have taken writing . . . I love the game, love the competition."

Nixon even went to the trouble of composing his own all-time team of baseball stars at the request of Cliff Evans of RKO General Broadcasting. Barely five days after the Watergate break-in of 1972, Evans asked Nixon, "Mr. President, as the nation's number one baseball fan, would you be willing to name your all-time baseball team?" Nixon happily agreed to do so and promptly retreated to Camp David in Maryland's Catoctin Mountains with his son-in-law, David Eisenhower, President Eisenhower's grandson and an equally rabid fan who once worked for the Washington Senators.

William B. Mead and Paul Dickson report in their book, *Baseball: The Presidents' Game,* that as Nixon and Eisenhower "whiled away the hours in the wooded retreat discussing baseball greats, his deputies and advisers back in Washington frantically searched for information about the break-in and worked to contain the political and legal fallout . . . Yet the president was able to turn away from the growing crisis and plunge into this labor of love."

The Nixon-Eisenhower choices as the greatest baseball players of all time as of 1969 were reported by correspondent Evans, the Associated Press, *The New York Times,* and other outlets. The *Times* ran the AP story under Nixon's byline.

The award-winning sports columnist for the *Times,* Red Smith, didn't seem to think much of the selections or of Nixon's frustrated hopes of once wanting to become a sportswriter. "Allowing the cub two or three times as much space as a staff member would get," Smith wrote, "the *Times* published his essay in full Sunday, all 2,800 cliché-ridden words. Frankly, the new boy has a long way to go if he's ever going to cut it in this department."

Nixon followed his 1972 choices with an update in 1992. In his original selections, starting from the time he began following baseball in 1925, he chose Jackie Robinson as baseball's greatest all-around athlete, Ted Williams as the greatest hitter, Joe DiMaggio as the best outfielder, Brooks Robinson as the best infielder, and Sandy Koufax as the best pitcher.

Columnist Dick Young was not surprised at Nixon's knowledge of the sport. In the New York *Daily News,* Young wrote, "This isn't a guy who shows up at season openers to take bows and get his picture in the paper and has to have his secretary of state tell him where first base is. This man knows baseball."

Nixon's frequent salutes to baseball included one particular comment that bears a remarkable application to his own life and career. In their book, Mead and Dickson quote Nixon as saying, "I never leave a game before the last pitch, because in baseball, as in life and especially in politics, you never know what will happen."

16

Centennials and the Impossible Dream

The last half of the twentieth century seemed to be marked by anniversaries that were measured in the hundreds: America's bicentennial in 1976, the two hundredth anniversary of the U.S. Constitution in 1989, the end of the second millennium as the twentieth century expired, and, not to be outdone—and way ahead of every other major sport—professional baseball's own hundredth birthday in 1969.

The Cincinnati Red Stockings became baseball's first professional team in 1869. The players were actually paid to play. In their first game as pros, the Red Stockings defeated the Mansfield Independents, 48–14. They played fifty-two games that season and won fifty-one, with one tie. They didn't lose a game until their second season. They had a record of 130 wins and one tie before finally losing their first game in June of 1870.

The Major Leagues put on a big splash in Washington to mark the sport's centennial, playing the All-Star Game there and staging a red-white-and-blue celebration, including a reception at the White House hosted by President Nixon and honoring stars from the past like Joe DiMaggio, Jackie Robinson, Bob Feller, and others who were voted the greatest living players of the century.

But not even baseball can tell Mother Nature what to do. The All-Star Game, scheduled for the night of July 22, was rained out. Instead, it was played the next afternoon, when the National League defeated the American, 9–3. The game featured five home runs, including two by Willie McCovey of the San Francisco Giants, who became the fourth player in All-Star Game history to do it. One of the other homers was more popular, though—hit by Frank Howard, the gentle giant, the city's other Washington Monument, who stood six feet seven inches tall and was one of the most liked players in either league.

The Mets were beginning to make themselves heard by All-Star time, the traditional halfway point, when the standings in the two leagues begin to take on added significance. According to tradition, the teams in first place at the All-Star break have the best chance of winning the pennants. Now, for the first time, there were four championships to be won, not just two, because there were four divisions instead of only two leagues.

Just before the All-Star break, the Chicago Cubs, holding a slim lead over the Mets, traveled to New York, with their all-star first baseman, Ernie Banks, chanting, "The Cubs are going to shine in '69." The two teams were meeting in a crucial series, the first one in the Mets' seven years. A crowd of 55,096 turned out to enjoy the fun—and the novelty of seeing the Mets in a series that was actually important.

The Mets won the first game in what was a role reversal for the two teams. The Cubs were holding a 3–1 lead as the Mets came up in the bottom half of the ninth inning. Then Don Young, Chicago's center fielder, misplayed two balls, something the fans had come to expect from the Mets in their early years, and New York rallied for three runs and won the game, 4–3, on a two-run double by Cleon Jones and an RBI single by Ed Kranepool. For Kranepool, the season was becoming something even more special than it was to his teammates, because he was the last of the original Mets.

In the second game, Tom Seaver had a perfect game going in the ninth inning, but a rookie, Jimmy Qualls, got to him for a sharp single with one out. Seaver retired the next two hitters and had himself a shutout, 4–0.

The Cubs exercised a certain degree of damage control by winning the final game of the series, but the Mets weren't folding. The two teams met in another three-game series a week later in Chicago, and the Mets again won two. It was late July, and they were only three and a half games out of first place.

The winning Mets—which sounded like an oxymoron—had a team that was no longer the joke of baseball. They had jelled into a solid team under a solid manager. Left fielder Cleon Jones was on his way to a .340 year, the third highest batting average in the league, behind only Pete Rose's .348 and Roberto Clemente's .345. The man next to Jones in the outfield was center fielder Tommie Agee, just like their high school days back home in Alabama. Agee was headed toward a season of twenty-six home runs.

Their pitching, however, was the Mets' strong point because of its balance. In addition to their three biggest winners, six other pitchers won 44 games among them. Tom Seaver, in only his third year in the majors, was destined to lead the league in victories with 25, and Jerry Koosman won 17. Gary Gentry reached double digits with 13 wins. Seaver and Koosman had the fourth- and fifth-best earned run averages in the league respectively, and Koosman had the fourth most shutouts with six. The Mets' hard-throwing twenty-two-year-old righthander, Nolan Ryan, won six games.

Under Leo Durocher, the Cubs were winning with a Hall of Fame hitter and first baseman, Ernie Banks, and a Hall of Fame pitcher, Ferguson Jenkins. Banks was in the process of hitting 23 home runs, driving in 106 runs, and leading the National League's first basemen in fielding with a .997 average. The Cubs were powered by other home run help from Ron Santo, Billy Williams—another future Hall of Famer—and Jim Hickman. Jenkins was winning 21 games, one more than his teammate, Bill Hands. Catcher Randy Hundley was doing more than just handling Jenkins, Hands, and the rest of the pitchers. He also led the National League East catchers by throwing out 79 opposing base runners.

After those two series in New York and Chicago, the two teams weren't finished with each other.

While the Mets were heading toward the history books, so were the newest American heroes, the astronauts, those glamour boys who were following the thrilling achievements of Alan Shepard and John Glenn in the first years of the decade. The newest superstar from NASA—the National Aeronautics and Space Administration—was Neil Armstrong, who accomplished what no other human being had been able to do in the two million years of the world's existence: he walked on the moon.

It happened on July 20.

As the world watched in awe, Armstrong landed the *Eagle* with Edwin "Buzz" Aldrin while the third member of their team, Michael Collins, circled seventy miles above in their spaceship, *Apollo 11*. At the same time, an unmanned Russian spacecraft, *Luna 15*, changed its orbit unexpectedly and without explanation and began to hover close to the surface of the moon. At 4:17 P.M., Eastern daylight time in America, as the world held its breath, Armstrong calmly, in the matter-of-fact manner of a professional, radioed a message back to NASA's Manned Spacecraft Center in Texas which has become an American figure of speech:

"Houston, Tranquility Base here. The Eagle has landed."

From Houston, astronaut Charles Duke answered, "You did a beautiful job. Be advised there's lots of smiling faces down here."

Armstrong said, "There's two of them down here."

From the *Apollo 11* mother ship in lunar orbit above, Collins reminded them, "And don't forget one up here."

Then, later in the summer evening came the moment that produced chills and goose pimples all over the world. Armstrong took his first tentative steps on the surface of the moon and said:

"That's one small step for a man, one giant leap for mankind."

Even veteran space reporters like Walter Cronkite, anchoring the CBS-TV coverage, became emotional on the air over the significance of the accomplishment.

Just as amazing as Armstrong's "moonwalk" was that the whole world was able to watch him live and in color on television, through a small TV camera mounted on the outside of the *Eagle*, piloted by Buzz Aldrin. Half a billion viewers watched in nations around the globe. Not every nation watched, however. In Moscow, Russian television broadcast a movie on the life of an opera singer who had been dead for years. There was no bulletin about the landing. China also ignored the spectacular achievement.

The rest of the world reacted with the enthusiasm the event deserved. The worldwide excitement was typified at the Jodrell Bank Observatory in London. Great Britain's leading astronomer, Sir Bernard Lovell, said, "The moment of touchdown was one of the moments of greatest drama in the history of man."

Walking on the moon wasn't the only Page One story the next morning as 1969 continued to establish itself as one of the biggest news-making years in the last half of the twentieth century.

Israeli and Egyptian jet fighters attacked each other's ground positions across the Suez Canal for the first time since their war two years earlier. The chairman of the joint chiefs of staff, Gen. Earle Wheeler, said a lull in the fighting in Vietnam could not be expected to lead to a de-escalation of the war. He added, however, that after touring Vietnam he left with "a very good feeling about what I have seen." Robert G. Kaiser of *The Washington Post*'s foreign service reported from Saigon that Wheeler, America's highest-ranking military officer, "repeated that the Allies had the upper hand in the war."

Elsewhere on the *Post*'s front page that morning was the news that Sen. Edward M. Kennedy had been cleared of negligence in a fatal automobile accident three days earlier on Chappaquiddick Island in Massachusetts. His car, with Kennedy at the wheel, plunged off a bridge around midnight and landed on its roof in a tidal pond. His only passenger, Mary Jo Kopechne, a twenty-eight-year-old secretary, drowned.

Kennedy was criticized for waiting almost nine hours before reporting the accident to police at Edgartown on nearby Martha's Vineyard. Despite that delay, the chief of police in Edgartown, Dominick Arena, said, "I am firmly convinced there was no negligence involved."

With all the news swirling about them, the Mets were beginning to be taken seriously as a news story themselves. They continued their dogfight with the Cubs but hit a serious slump in early August and dropped nine and a half games behind Chicago, a sizable deficit for that late in the season.

The Mets pulled themselves out of it and closed the gap to four games when Tom Seaver won his twentieth game in front of 40,450 fans. The gap was down to two and a half games when the Mets played the Cubs in a crucial two-game series in New York. They swept the series behind Hands and Koosman, then took over first place all by themselves by sweeping a doubleheader from the Montreal Expos. They put together a ten-game winning streak at the same time that the Cubs were in a tailspin with an eight-game losing streak.

Right fielder Ron Swoboda seemed to be speaking for the whole team in September when he said, "The way we're going, it's hard to keep your feet on the ground. You feel inebriated, high. If they could package us, I don't think we'd be legal."

Jerry Koosman was just as confident as his teammates. While they continued to win, and to shock everyone in baseball, Koosman said with quiet confidence, "We're happy, but we've been happy all year. It isn't a strange idea to us that we should win. We really think we should." Relief pitcher Ron Taylor wasn't surprised at Koosman's success down the stretch. "No matter who is up there at the plate," Taylor said, "Kooz believes he can get them out."

When it was over, the Mets won the National League East championship by the respectable margin of eight games. They beat the spring training prediction by Gil Hodges that they would win 85 games by winning an even 100 instead. They did it by applying the truest formula in sports: win your games and don't worry about the other teams. The Mets won 38 of their final 49 games. Seaver finished with his own private win-

Ace relief pitcher Tug McGraw spent the first nine years of his career with the Mets, then was one of the stars of the 1980 World Series for the Phillies with a win and two saves. (Courtesy of the National Baseball Hall of Fame Library, Cooperstown, N.Y.)

ning streak of ten games and ended the season with a record of 25 wins and only seven losses. Jerry Koosman won eight of his last nine. They were backed up by an effective relief corps headed by a lefty-righty tandem of southpaw Tug McGraw and Taylor, who combined for 25 saves.

While the Mets were achieving a milestone for their team, Willie Mays was achieving one for himself. On September 22 in San Diego, "Say Hey" hit the six hundredth home run of his Hall of Fame career, joining Hank Aaron and Babe Ruth as the only three players to hit six hundred homers. No one joined them in the next thirty-three years.

The hit seemed to symbolize Mays's career. It came with him as a pinch hitter against a rookie righthander, Mike Corkins, and won the game for the Giants. Willie's father figure and manager from their days with the Giants, Leo Durocher, expressed his enthusiasm and admiration for Mays again. "He could pick up a team and carry it on his back," Durocher said of their years together. "Maybe it was a hit, maybe it was a catch, maybe it was the way he ran the bases. Every day he came to play. Every day he'd do the unexpected."

Durocher said the years—Mays turned thirty-eight on May 6 of that season—hadn't slowed him down. "He still can do it all whenever he wants to," Durocher said. "Even today, this minute, he's more exciting than anybody who ever played this game."

Any underdog team has to overcome adversity, and, in the case of the Mets, precedence was something else they had to overcome. The 1969 season was the first year of the playoffs because of the new structure of two divisions in each league. As winners of the National League East championship, they now had to defeat the Atlanta Braves, the best of the National League West, if they were to play in the World Series.

As hot as they were, the Mets were taking on a team that was just as hot. The Braves fielded a power-laden lineup of Hank Aaron, Orlando Cepeda, Felipe Alou, and Rico Carty and a pitching staff headed by Phil Niekro's 23 wins and Ron Reed with 18 victories. They finished their season with a ten-game winning streak, 17 wins in their last twenty games. They won 93 games and finished three games ahead of their closest pursuers, the San Francisco Giants.

The Mets hit a snag with their pitching in the playoffs against the Braves, but their hitting made up for it. Seaver yielded eleven base runners in seven innings in the first game, Koosman was knocked out in the fifth inning of the second, and Gary Gentry couldn't get the side out in the third inning of the third game, but New York's offense offset the pitching by slugging 37 hits and scoring 27 runs. Result: the Mets won the National League pennant in a three-game sweep by scores of 9–5, 11–6, and 7–4.

Then they prepared to meet the American League champions, the Baltimore Orioles, considered by some to be the best team in either league over the last several years or longer. They ran away and hid from the rest of the AL East and finished a dazzling 19 games ahead of the Detroit Tigers, winning 109 games, only 2 less than the American League record at that time. Then they polished off the Minnesota Twins in the first American League Championship Series in three straight, 4–3, 1–0, and 11–2.

Earl Weaver of the Baltimore Orioles did all the managing and hollering he could, but the "Amazin' Mets" were destined to win the 1969 World Series anyhow. (Courtesy of the National Baseball Hall of Fame Library, Cooperstown, N.Y.)

The Orioles were winning with a team that featured four future Hall of Famers: third baseman Brooks Robinson, right fielder Frank Robinson, and pitcher Jim Palmer, plus manager Earl Weaver. Their lineup also included other stars like center fielder Paul Blair, left fielder Don Buford, catcher Ellie Hendricks, and an infield that would make any manager turn green with envy—Boog Powell at first base, Davey Johnson at second, Mark Belanger at shortstop, and Brooks at third.

Palmer didn't even have the most wins among the pitchers, or even the second most. The staff was headed by Mike Cuellar with twenty-three victories. Dave McNally was in second place with twenty. Cuellar's total was the second highest in the American League. McNally tied for third. Frank Robinson and Boog Powell had the fourth- and fifth-highest batting averages.

It was David against Goliath, and they met for the first time on October 11 at Memorial Stadium in Baltimore.

The Series started just about the way most people expected it to end—with a Baltimore victory. The Orioles started on their way as fast as the rules allow, scoring a run with their first hitter of the game. Buford led off the Orioles' first inning with a home run on Seaver's second pitch of the game. Cuellar scattered six hits. The rout was on, or so most people outside New York thought.

The Mets evened things up in the second game, and avoided the possibility of a sweep, with a run in the top of the ninth as Koosman outpitched McNally with relief help from Taylor. The combination produced a 2–1 victory. The underdog Mets had played the mighty Orioles to a 1–1 split in their two games in Baltimore.

New York put on a major league show when the Series moved there for the next three games. The celebrities turned out in force at Shea Stadium, including Jackie Kennedy, her husband, Aristotle Onassis, and her son, John F. Kennedy, Jr., plus New York's top elected officials—Governor Nelson Rockefeller and Mayor John Lindsay. Steve Lawrence sang the National Anthem and Roy Campanella threw out the first ball.

The complexion of the World Series changed decidedly in that third game, thanks to Tommie Agee. The Mets' center fielder hit a home run in the first inning to get his team off to a 1–0 lead, then made two spectacular catches that saved five runs from crossing the plate for the Orioles. That turned out to be exactly the Mets' margin of victory, 5–0, over Jim Palmer.

Agee's first spectacular catch came in the fourth inning when he robbed Ellie Hendricks of an extra base hit with a backhanded catch that saved two runs. In the seventh inning, the Orioles were trailing, 4–0, when Agee made another sensational catch that may have saved the game for the Mets. With the bases loaded and two outs, Paul Blair hit a long line drive to deep right-center field. He said later that as he dashed toward second base, he thought to himself, "If that ball drops, I might have an inside-the-park home run." But it didn't drop, and instead of a home run, it was merely the third out of the inning. Agee made a mad dash for the ball and made a diving catch that is still remembered.

After the game, someone asked Earl Weaver if he believed the Mets were a team of destiny. "No," he answered. "I believe the Mets are a team with some fine defensive outfielders."

As fans arrived at Shea for the fourth game, they were greeted by opponents of America's participation in the war in Vietnam on "Moratorium Day," a nationwide observance when those opposed to the war staged demonstrations in Washington and other cities. At Shea, they handed out pamphlets quoting a statement made by Seaver the week before, when he said, "If the Mets can win the World Series then we can get out of Vietnam."

Seaver went the distance in a ten-inning game and gave the Mets a commanding 3–1 lead in the Series with a 2–1 victory. During one stretch, he retired nineteen of twenty hitters. He told reporters in the dressing room after his victory, "I'm a believer in this club, and I think there are a lot of believers now. Slowly, we're making believers of everybody."

Then Seaver took on the issue of those pamphlets. "I've been used," he said. "I'm not in favor of those pamphlets. I'm an American citizen and have my feelings, but whatever I want to say will come after the World Series is over."

The win wasn't as easy as it sounds. In front of 57,367 Shea faithful, Donn Clendenon homered in the second inning to give the Mets a 1–0 lead, but Frank Robinson singled with one out in the ninth and Boog Powell's single moved him to third, ninety feet from a tie game as the Orioles fought to keep the Mets from taking a 3–1 lead in the Series.

Brooks Robinson tied the score with a line drive to Ron Swoboda in right center. It went into the record book as a sacrifice fly, but it was

Brooks Robinson was robbed of a triple by Ron Swoboda of the New York Mets that could have won the fourth game of the 1969 World Series for the Baltimore Orioles and changed the outcome of the Series. Instead, Swoboda made a spectacular diving catch that saved the game and the Series for the "Amazin' Mets." (Courtesy of the National Baseball Hall of Fame Library, Cooperstown, N.Y.)

much more than that—a sparkling, run-saving, diving, sliding catch that prevented the Orioles from winning the game. Frank Robinson was able to score after the catch to tie the game, but Swoboda, never known for his fielding finesse, had robbed Brooks of at least a double and the Orioles of another run that Powell would have scored. The Mets pushed across a run in the tenth inning, and suddenly they held that 3–1 lead in wins after all, to the utter shock of the baseball world.

"I knew Ron Swoboda would catch the ball," Seaver said later. "The way we've been playing for the last four months . . . the way everything has been going right . . . I felt Ron could catch the ball, and he did."

In 2002, Robinson was talking about the catch and its significance. "It could have changed the outcome of the whole World Series," he said. "We felt that if we won one game in New York, we could come back to Baltimore and win it all. But we started to press and get out of our game plan, and then Swoboda and Agee made those catches."

The Hall of Fame third baseman added that some people were inclined to "short-change the Mets." He said there was a tendency to think of them in terms of their years earlier in the decade instead of remembering that they had become a much better team, with a manager who knew from his own playing experience what it takes to win.

Swoboda said he gambled with Brooks Robinson. "I cheated up about twenty feet on him," he said, "playing shallower so I could throw the runner out at the plate on a short fly. So when he hit it, I was in too close to cut it off. I had to catch it or have it roll to the fence."

Then Swoboda said modestly, "I made a catch like that once before, in high school. A crowd of fifteen people went out of their minds."

Before the fifth game, one of the people drawing attention wasn't even a ballplayer; she was Pearl Bailey. Pearl was a close friend of Gil and Joan Hodges—Joan saw her twenty-eight times in *Hello, Dolly*—and she would have won anyone's best-dressed contest that day. She showed up in sunglasses, wearing a brown pantsuit and matching brimmed hat, and sporting a gold-embroidered walking stick, two diamond rings, and several strands of pearls around her neck. She sang the National Anthem on the field.

She wasn't the only celebrity there during the Series. Louis Armstrong came too, and so did Frank Sinatra, Ed Sullivan, Cary Grant, Mitzi Gaynor, Chief Justice Earl Warren, and former mayor Robert Wagner.

Someone else who was attracting attention was Karl Ehrhardt, a commercial artist who had been preparing signs with various messages that he had been holding up for all to see, especially television viewers, at Mets' home games for five years. But he almost didn't get to that dramatic, climactic final game.

"I was sitting in our art department office at Forty-third and Third and feeling mighty low," he said. Then his boss came up to him, said he couldn't go to the game with Karl stuck in the office, and gave him his own ticket.

The Orioles showed some promise of picking themselves up off the floor when they jumped off to a 3–0 lead in the third inning on home runs by pitcher McNally and Frank Robinson. After Robinson's homer, Ehrhardt raised a card that said: DASTARDLY DEED. Pearl Bailey remained optimistic. "Don't you worry none, darlin'," she said to anyone who might be listening. "I still say they're gonna win, and I haven't been wrong since April."

Clendenon homered again, in the sixth inning, for two runs to narrow the Orioles' lead to 3–2. A home run by Al Weis off McNally tied the game for the Mets in the seventh, another shocker. Weis, who hit only seven home runs in his ten years in the majors, said after the game, "Was I shocked? Hell, yes!"

The Mets won everything by scoring twice in the eighth on doubles by Cleon Jones and Swoboda. Koosman, the winner in the second game, was also the winner in the decisive game.

The last out of 1969 came when Davey Johnson hit a pitch from Jerry Koosman to deep left-center field. Cleon Jones got to it in time and waited for it while saying, "Keep dropping down to me, baby. Keep dropping down."

Back home in Mobile, Mrs. Myrtle Henderson rejoiced as she watched on the new television set that her grandson had bought for her so she could watch the World Series. Her grandson was Cleon Jones.

When Jones made his catch, Ehrhardt held up another sign expressing his message of the moment:

THERE ARE NO WORDS

"Before I pitched the final game," Koosman said, "Pearl Bailey was talking to me and she said, 'Don't worry. I know you're going to win. The only thing I don't know is the score. But I see a number 8.' The final score was 5–3. She had that ESP."

And the baseball world was in a state of shock, along with the rest of America.

Casey Stengel, with special credentials including those five World Series championships with the Yankees and his year as the first manager of the Mets, had a perfectly logical explanation for the Mets' ability to achieve what the whole world considered impossible. Writing in *The Sporting News* in his patented mangled English, Stengel said, "So I gotta say this is terrific for the fans, this World Series, for the ownership and the scouting system which is very good that if it hadn't of been it couldn't have picked up the amazin' players they did."

Gil Hodges, the incumbent manager, had a more coherent reaction. "It was a colossal thing they did," he said. "These young men showed that you can realize the most impossible dream of all."

Cleon Jones had still another explanation. "The key to it all," he said, "was Gil Hodges." The comment was doubly significant coming from Jones, who had once been pulled from left field in front of the fans because Hodges thought he had not hustled on a play. Hodges was firm but fair, and Jones said he appreciated that. "It's the only way to operate," he said. "You must treat them all as men."

In the Mets' dressing room, Tom Seaver was as jubilant as the rest of the mob. He screamed, "It's beautiful! Beautiful! Beautiful! Beautiful! It's the biggest thrill in my life. We played to win. We never quit. We'd come from behind to win. We did it today! Beautiful! Beautiful! Beautiful!"

Each Met received $18,338.18 as his cut of the winners' share. Tug McGraw, a factor in the Mets' success all year with his relief pitching and a bona fide character, said after the Series, when all the hoopla died down, that he used his share to fix up the mobile home he shared with his wife, Phyllis, and their dog, Pucchi. "We got a hot water heater and a Porta-Potti," he said with great pride. "Now I've got it made."

The Mets' third baseman, Ed Charles, was thirty-six years old when the impossible dream came true. After he took off his uniform for the last time, Charles said, "My twenty years in the game were wrapped up in that one season," he said. "It was a miracle."

To put it mildly, the city went nuts. *Newsweek* magazine reported, "A Madison Avenue liquor store had stocked 100 bottles of champagne in anticipation, but sold out in ten minutes. One jubilant bus driver refused to take fares. Cheers broke out in Grand Central Terminal, trees were festooned with toilet paper in United Nations Plaza and auto horns echoed jubilantly through the midtown streets." The weather service revised its forecast to predict, "Cloudy with falling confetti."

Back at Shea Stadium, fans were helping themselves to any souvenir they could grab or pull out of the ground. There were battles for the bases. Clumps of turf were ripped out of the ground. One fan, a man in his late twenties, hugged a clump of sod from the field and said, "I'll put it in my room and water it and it will grow and I'll have it for the rest of my life."

Fans were paying a price for their actions. Thirty-one of them were treated for hyperactivity. Five were taken to Booth Memorial Hospital with possible fractures. One fell from the roof of the dugout. Another was injured while trying to steal home plate.

With all the jubilation and celebration and explanation, Seaver, the one they called "Tom Terrific," may have analyzed the Mets' fairy tale success best and described it most eloquently in only five one-syllable words. Seaver's simple commentary: "God is a Mets fan."

PART SIX
· · ·
1975

17

"The American People Were Not Rejoicing"

America and baseball were both in slumps as 1975 began.

The nation was reeling under the combined impact of the worst economic downturn in thirty years, a frightening unemployment rate of 8.2 percent, the increasingly gloomy outlook concerning the war in Vietnam, and the controversy over the Watergate scandal, climaxed by Richard Nixon's departure in disgrace.

James Reston analyzed the national mood in his article, "Focus on the Nation," in the 1976 edition of *The World Book Year Book*. He acknowledged that Americans were enjoying exceptional times as the nation entered its bicentennial year, with prosperity and peace after our ten-year involvement in the war in Vietnam.

"And yet," he wrote, "at the beginning of their third century, the American people were not rejoicing. . . . Somehow, the problems of the present temporarily overwhelmed the achievements of the past, and clouded the hopes for the future."

One of those problems ended in the first military defeat in American history. The North Vietnamese army, commanded by General Van Tien Dung, captured Saigon, the capital of South Vietnam, on April 30, 1975, after the Ho Chi Minh Campaign, a Communist offensive that lasted fifty-five days and produced what the North Vietnamese called "this great spring victory." After thirty years, the war in Vietnam was over. In a dramatic symbol of their defeat, Americans were airlifted from Saigon by helicopter, standing on the roof of the American embassy and frantically climbing up rope ladders dangling from the planes.

Reston claimed that Americans, their nation led by an appointed president and an appointed vice president for the only time in history, were worried about something more serious and disturbing than inflation, interest rates, and unemployment. What concerned them even more at the beginning of 1975, according to Reston, was "the larger philosophical questions of whether something had gone wrong with the American political and economic systems and with the American spirit of confidence and optimism."

In baseball, the sport was losing ground fast to the other sports. Football was out-marketing baseball under the public relations genius of its commissioner, Pete Rozelle, a former PR man. Basketball was doing the same thing. Hockey was winning increasing popularity because, as some said, it featured two things Americans love—speed and violence. Soccer was gaining ground because every kid could play it as long as he or she could run. Baseball, its doomsayers said, wasn't the national pastime anymore. In fact, some said, it would be gone as a professional sport in ten years. Jim Murray, also writing in *The World Book Year Book,* said baseball's critics were calling it "the dinosaur of sports" as 1975 began, "the sick man of athletics."

In spring training, the Boston Red Sox and their fans would never have predicted such a finish for the sport and for their team. Their All-Star catcher and team leader, Carlton Fisk, had just come off the injured list following surgery on his left knee in June 1974 after colliding at home plate with Cleveland's Leron Lee. It was the latest in a string of setbacks for Fisk that season including a groin injury on a foul tip in spring training that forced him to miss the first 17 games of the season, and then the knee injury after only 52 games that kept him out of action for the rest of 1974.

In an early spring training game in '75, Fisk's right arm—his throwing arm—was broken when he was hit by a pitch from Fred Holdsworth of Detroit. The season hadn't even started, and once again the Red Sox were without one of their most important players, the twenty-seven-year-old star who was the American League Rookie of the Year in '72 and the league's All-Star catcher the next season. For Fisk and his team, the future was just as uncertain as the nation's.

The Boston writers and broadcasters knew just how much Fisk meant to the Red Sox and what his latest absence could do to their hopes for another pennant and maybe even their first World Series championship since the end of World War I in 1918. The morning after he injured his knee, one Boston paper reported the news under a headline that read:

FISK INJURY DOOMS SOX

Columnist Tim Horgan saw the broken arm as the kiss of death for the Red Sox that year. He wrote that the Sox "are going to be hurting precisely as long as Fisk is. He's not only a superior catcher, clearly the best in the American League now that the Yankees' Thurman Munson has arm trouble. He was also slated to be the Red Sox' No. 4 hitter behind Carl Yastrzemski, so his absence will weaken an attack that was no stronger than a swoon last September."

Horgan also put his finger on Fisk's real value to his team. "Perhaps most important of all, however," he wrote, "is that Fisk is a dominant personality on this ball club. His aggressiveness, his hustle, his acknowledged talents plus the fact he doesn't like to lose make him a natural-born leader on a team that suffers a critical shortage of same."

It was hardly the kind of start to the 1975 season that you would expect from the man who, even in defeat, became one of Boston's—and baseball's—biggest heroes six months later.

Fisk returned to the lineup on June 23, playing five innings after receiving a standing ovation in Fenway Park. He told Boston sportswriter Peter Gammons in *The Sporting News*, "It was just like getting married. You plan for it, you know it's coming. And when the day arrives, you're still nervous."

Even with Fisk playing in only 79 games, the Red Sox still managed to win 95 games and beat out the Orioles by four and a half games, then swept the Oakland A's, who had won three straight World Series. Fisk, nicknamed "Pudge," hit a robust .331, tied for the highest average on the team with rookie center fielder Fred Lynn. Another rookie outfielder, Jim Rice, was also a key factor in the Boston attack, with a .309 average and 22 home runs, the most on the team. Lynn and Rice both drove in more than one hundred runs, Lynn with 105 RBIs and Rice with 102. Lynn led the American League in runs scored, doubles, and slugging percentage. For his overall excellence at bat and in center field, Lynn became the first player in big-league history to win his league's Most Valuable Player and Rookie of the Year awards in the same season.

Lynn came from out of nowhere to put together his sensational rookie season. After he starred in college baseball at Southern California, his batting averages in the minor leagues for two seasons gave no hint that he would blossom into a respected hitter in the Major Leagues. He batted only .259 for Bristol in 1973 and .282 for Pawtucket in 1974. When a reporter asked Lynn to explain the reason, he said, "In a way, it's easier to hit in the majors because the pitchers throw the ball over the plate."

The end of Rice's 1975 season wasn't as happy as Lynn's. He broke his left hand when he was hit by a pitch with only one week left in the season and missed the playoffs and the World Series.

Rick Wise, pitching his second year with the Red Sox after nine years in the National League, topped the Boston staff with 19 wins. Luis Tiant, a six-foot righthander from Cuba who would turn thirty-five the month after the World Series, won 18 games with a pitching delivery in which he looked back at center field before turning to look at the hitter. A flaky lefthander (if that's not a redundancy), Bill Lee, called "Spaceman" because of his zaniness, stayed serious long enough and often enough to compile the team's best won-lost percentage with 17 victories and only nine defeats.

Meanwhile, Frank Robinson managed his way into the record books of baseball and America. He became the first African-American manager in the history of baseball when he took over the helm of the Cleveland Indians as their player-manager. In his first time at bat, he hit a home run against the Yankees as 56,204 fans cheered.

One of his fellow managers, Dick Williams, who was managing the California Angels in 1975 and managed in the Major Leagues for twenty-one seasons, said in later years, "I'm glad he got a chance to be the first black manager. He did a hell of a job. He's a great baseball man."

In the National League, the Cincinnati Reds left everyone in the dust. As "the Big Red Machine," the Reds romped to the NL East championship by a whopping 20 games over the Los Angeles Dodgers. Then they swept their own championship series against the Pirates.

"Machine" was the right word to describe Cincinnati. The Reds led the National League in runs scored, stolen bases, fielding average, and saves. Their attack featured second baseman Joe Morgan, the year's Most Valuable Player in the National League, catcher Johnny Bench, first baseman Tony Perez, left fielder George Foster, right fielder Ken Griffey and third baseman Pete Rose, who led both leagues in runs scored and doubles and was second in hits.

Despite their 108 victories, the Reds pitching staff did not include a twenty-game winner. Instead, they did it with balance. Six pitchers were in double figures in wins, including three fifteen-game winners—Gary Nolan, Jack Billingham, and Don Gullett. Fred Norman won 12 games, Pat Darcy 11 and Clay Kirby 10. Among the six men, they accounted for 78 of Cincinnati's wins.

With Fisk healthy for the second half of the season, the playoffs, and the World Series, Cincinnati was able to counter with a catching standout of its own in Bench, a twenty-seven-year-old who was starring in his ninth season in the big leagues. With Bench, success in the big leagues seemed inevitable in the opinion of some, including Ted Williams. After Bench's rookie year, Williams gave him an autographed baseball:

To Johnny Bench, a Hall of Famer for sure.

That kind of statement carried special meaning for Bench, more than just that it came from Williams, one of the greatest of all Hall of Famers himself. Bench always placed special emphasis on being successful. He once remarked, "Failure was the only thing I ever really feared." His record reflects this emphasis, both on the field and in the classroom. He was a straight-A student and the class valedictorian in both junior and senior high school.

On the diamond, he excelled as a catcher from his first days as a Little Leaguer, coached by his father, Ted, whose own dreams of a baseball career were interrupted by two hitches in the armed forces. Johnny was a blossoming catcher, and his throwing arm was so strong that some said he would have found success as a pitcher, too. His father said, "If he had stuck with pitching, he'd have been another Tom Seaver."

And like Babe Ruth's, his bat was too powerful not to have it in the lineup every day. In high school back in Binger, Oklahoma, his hitting earned him the nickname of "the Binger Banger."

His skills both at the plate and behind it prompted the Reds to make him their second-round pick in the 1965 amateur draft, after every team passed him up in the first round and the Mets, Cubs, and Astros passed on him twice. He turned down thirteen college baseball scholarships and four for basketball, then gained success immediately, as the 1966 Player of the Year in baseball's Carolina League. In Buffalo the next year, he was named the Minor League Player of the Year by *The Sporting News* before being called up to the majors by the Reds in time to play in twenty-six games.

When he reported to the Reds for spring training in 1968, Cincin-

Manager Sparky Anderson led Cincinnati's "Big Red Machine" to the World Series championship in 1975. The Series was a thriller, with five of the seven games decided by one run. (Courtesy of the National Baseball Hall of Fame Library, Cooperstown, N.Y.)

nati's manager, Sparky Anderson, said, "They talk about the Messiah coming back. I'm not sure he hasn't returned already in catcher's gear. I mean Johnny Bench." Bench made Anderson look good. In 1975, he hit .283 and was fourth in the National League in slugging average with .519, second in runs batted in with 110, third in doubles with 39 and fourth in home runs with 28.

With a release said to be as quick as Joe Namath's, Bench nevertheless needed improvement behind the plate. Blessed with hands so big he could hold seven baseballs in one hand, he popularized the one-handed style of catching, using a flexible hinged mitt to grasp the ball in his left, gloved hand while protecting his right hand from injuries caused by foul tips and wild pitches that historically plagued catchers. Bench paid a price for his new style of catching, however. He led the league in passed balls with 18 as a rookie while perfecting his new style of catching. Still, his overall performance was good enough to win him the vote as the National League's Rookie of the Year. He also set his first two records—most doubles by a catcher and most games caught by a rookie—154.

By the time the 1975 World Series arrived, Bench was on his way to winning ten straight Gold Glove Awards for his catching while also being elected to the All-Star team thirteen consecutive seasons. He established a National League record by catching one hundred or more games in each of his first thirteen seasons. "Forget his hitting," Anderson said, even though Bench set a record for the most home runs in a career by a catcher and led both leagues in home runs twice and in runs batted in three times. "He could get in [to the Hall of Fame] on defense alone. It was so easy for that man." Anderson also asked a question out loud and provided his own answer: "Is he the greatest catcher who ever caught? This man is in a class of his own."

The kid who practiced his handwriting in the second grade so it would look good when he signed autographs as a big-league baseball player led the major leagues in the 1970s with 1,013 runs batted in as Cincinnati's "Big Red Machine" won six National League West championships, four National League pennants, and two World Series.

That was the team that Carlton Fisk and Company were facing on October 11 as the 1975 World Series began.

America was starving for something as exciting and fun-filled as a good World Series, and its eagerness and enthusiasm for the "Fall Classic" was immediately obvious. Some four thousand fans waited all night outside Fenway Park to buy the few remaining bleacher seats and standing-room tickets. But Doug Madera, twenty-eight years old, and two nineteen-year-old friends, Mr. and Mrs. Robert Mae, topped that with plenty to spare. They started a line at five o'clock Thursday afternoon for tickets that wouldn't go on sale until Tuesday.

America's craving for a good World Series was understandable. The year approaching its end was not one of our happier times. The country was still reeling under the combined blows of Watergate, its cover-up, and the Nixon-Agnew resignations. Nixon resigned after his closest advisers convinced him he was about to be impeached for alleged involvement in an attempt to cover up the Watergate scandal, and Agnew agreed to step down amid charges that he was accepting money in bribes going back to his days as governor of Maryland.

President Ford brought more bad news that year. He told Congress on February 4, "The economy is in a severe recession." Three days later, the Labor Department announced proof of Ford's statement by reporting that unemployment had reached a thirty-three-year high in January, reaching the staggering and worrisome level of 8.2 percent.

On February 21, the grim reminders of Watergate and what Ford had called "our long national nightmare" returned when three of Nixon's top advisers—White House aides Robert Haldeman and John Ehrlichman plus Attorney General John Mitchell—were sentenced to between two and a half and eight years in prison for their roles in the cover-up.

The economy continued to hover over the nation like the dark cloud it was. Unemployment, like a stubborn fever, continued to rise, reaching 8.7 percent in March, the highest level since 1940, and topping that with 9.2 percent in May. President Ford turned thumbs down on a cry for help from New York City and its mayor, Abraham Beame. The city was teetering on the brink of bankruptcy, but Ford rejected Beame's urgent request for $1.5 billion in federal assistance before approving assistance late in the year.

The bad news also came from unexpected sources. On July 31, the family of Jimmy Hoffa, the former international president of the Teamsters Union, reported that he was missing. He had vanished the day before from a Detroit suburb. The speculation immediately was that Hoffa had been kidnapped and killed because he had threatened to reveal that the union's pension funds had been misused and that members of organized crime had infiltrated the union. He has never been found.

That crime merely underlined the overall problem of crime and violence in the United States. As baseball's pennant races were heading toward a climax in September, President Ford was the target of not one but two assassination attempts in California. In the first, on September 5, Ford was walking through a tree-lined park from his hotel to the state capitol in Sacramento shortly after ten o'clock in the morning when a woman pushed her way through the crowd. While Ford was shaking hands with well-wishers, the woman pointed a loaded .45-caliber pistol at him, just as Secret Service Agent Larry Buendorf spotted her and wrested the gun from her. Ford continued on to the capitol to meet with Governor Jerry Brown and address the state legislature.

Ford's press secretary, Ronald Nessen, told reporters Buendorf spotted the hand of the woman in the crowd and saw it come up between two people as she pushed her way toward the president. The woman got the gun to within two feet of Ford but was then grabbed by Buendorf, who seized the gun with his right hand, pulled it away from her, and grabbed her with his left hand. A Sacramento police officer, Gaylin Peterson, rushed to Buendorf's assistance.

The would-be assassin was identified as Lynette "Squeaky" Fromme, nicknamed for her high-pitched voice. She was twenty-seven years old, single, from Sacramento, and a follower of convicted mass murderer Charles Manson who maintained close ties with him while he was in prison. She was charged with an attempted assassination of the president and held on $350,000 bond.

A second attempt on Ford's life occurred only seventeen days later, on September 22, again in California, as Americans wondered in their shock why the nation continued to be rocked by assassinations and attempted ones. It was barely twelve years after the assassination of President Kennedy began a series that included the assassinations of his brother and the Rev. Dr. Martin Luther King, Jr., and the shooting of Governor George Wallace of Alabama. This time the would-be assassin, unlike Squeaky Fromme, was able to fire a bullet at Ford. It happened in San Francisco.

Sara Jane Moore, an activist for social causes and a former FBI informant who was a forty-five-year-old divorcée with a nine-year-old son, fired a shot at Ford with a .38-caliber pistol as he left his hotel. A retired Marine, Oliver Sipple, spotted the gun in Moore's hand and deflected her shot. News accounts reported that Moore's name was not on the computerized list of forty-seven thousand persons who might present a danger to the president.

After the second attempt on his life, Ford vowed he would not allow himself to become "a hostage in the Oval Office."

In both cases, justice was swift and sure. On November 26, Fromme was convicted of attempting to assassinate the president. On December 17, only three and a half months after her attempt, she was sentenced to life in prison. Moore pleaded guilty and was sentenced to life in prison on January 15, 1976, only three months and three weeks after her attempt.

In between these attempts to murder the president, the FBI scored another major victory when it arrested Patty Hearst on September 18, also in San Francisco, nineteen months after she had been kidnapped by members of a radical group called the Symbionese Liberation Army.

Agents arrested Hearst, a member of the prominent Hearst newspaper family, at an apartment in the outer Mission District of San Francisco with an associate, Wendy Yoshimura. Hearst, who reportedly adopted the SLA ideology during her captivity, was charged with twenty-two federal and state counts of bank robbery, kidnapping, assault, and weapons violations. A single woman, twenty-one years old and a resident of Berkeley, she was indicted on charges of robbery, kidnapping, and assault. She was convicted and sentenced to prison. President Jimmy Carter commuted her sentence in 1979, and she was pardoned by President Clinton along with 175 other men and women two hours before he left office on January 20, 2001. In the 1990s, she appeared in several movies. In 1997, she was a voice on an episode of the TV sitcom *Frasier.*

The assassination attempts made Americans worry even more about the spiraling crime rate in 1975. FBI statistics showed that major crime, already a serious and steadily worsening problem in the 1960s and 1970s, increased another 13 percent in the first six months of 1975. Murder was up 4 percent, aggravated assault 9 percent, robbery 17 percent, and rape 4 percent.

Daniel P. Moynihan, the former assistant secretary of labor in the Kennedy administration and the future senator from New York, surveyed the American landscape in 1975 and offered his assessment. He said, "Neither liberty nor democracy would seem to be prospering—or in any event, neither would seem to have a future nearly as auspicious as their past.... Seemingly nothing at present brings forth more gloom than the contemplation of the future...."

James Reston took a more optimistic view of the state of the nation in 1975, saying that "there was in 1975 a pause for reflection in American life, a summing-up of the past, and a practical examination of all political, economic and social institutions. The same sort of thing happened between the Declaration of Independence in 1776 and the writing of the Constitution in 1787, and that earlier period of self-examination proved to be one of the great chapters in American history."

Then the World Series began, and Americans started to smile again.

18

The Greatest World Series
Ever Played?

Baseball has a way of rising to the occasion when America needs it most. It was true during the Depression, when Babe Ruth and other stars took people's minds off their financial worries. It was true during World War II, when a collection of 4-Fs and men either too young or too old for military service made sure that our GIs and the American people themselves had something more than war to think about and cheer about. It was true during the Korean War and the Cold War. And it was true in 1975, when the sport staged what many at that time called "the greatest World Series ever played."

It was a World Series that went the full seven games. Four of them were decided in the ninth inning or in extra innings. The suspense and excitement continued right up to the ninth inning of that last game, with the score still tied, 3–3, when second baseman Joe Morgan of Cincinnati, headed for the Hall of Fame, became the latest in the cast of heroes and drove in the championship run for the Reds.

Even five years later, the glow from that Series still burned brightly in the hearts of baseball fans everywhere. *The Washington Post*'s Shirley Povich captured it best. Povich conceded in *The Sporting News* that baseball had been losing popularity to some of the other sports. "Then," he wrote, "the Reds and Red Sox, as if on signal, put on their 7-game World Series spectacular that recaptured for baseball every fan it ever lost and bred millions more."

Povich trotted out one of his favorite quotes, from his close friend in New York, Red Smith of *The New York Times*, that "baseball is a dull

game only to those with dull minds." To support his claim and his enthusiasm, Povich pointed out that the television ratings for the Series
catapulted NBC from third place in the Nielsen ratings to "a runaway
first" for October.

President Ford, unlike some of his predecessors, didn't make it to any
of the games, but he carried certain baseball credentials of his own anyhow, including one claim to fame not shared by any other president. He
was a frequent spectator at games of the Grand Rapids Chicks in the All-
American Girls Professional Baseball League with his future wife, Betty.
The league was formed during World War II by Phil Wrigley, the chewing gum manufacturer who owned the Chicago Cubs, because of his fear
that the wartime manpower shortage might cause an end to baseball for
the duration of the war. The manpower shortage never caused an inter-
ruption to Major League Baseball, but the league lasted into the 1950s
anyhow. Later it was immortalized in the hit movie *A League of Their
Own.*

The 1975 World Series began in Boston innocently enough, as if setting America up for the dramatics that were to follow. It featured two of
the most overdue teams in baseball. The Reds hadn't won a World Series
in thirty-five years. The Red Sox were still the victims of baseball's famous "Curse of the Bambino," not winning a Series since 1918, the year
before they sold Babe Ruth to the Yankees.

The Red Sox won the first game routinely, 6–0, on a five-hitter by Luis
Tiant, scoring all six runs in the seventh inning. His teammates didn't
have to bother scoring those last five runs. Tiant scored the first one himself after hitting a single, and that was the only run he needed.

Except for the fifth game, when the Reds won comfortably, 6–2, back
home in Cincinnati, that 6–0 win for the Red Sox in the opener was the
only other game that wasn't decided by one run. The scores of the other
games were 3–2, 6–5 in ten innings, 5–4, 7–6 in twelve innings and 4–3.

The Reds evened up the Series by winning the second game, but the
game set the pattern for the rest of the Series by going down to the ninth
inning before the issue was decided. Cincinnati was losing, 2–1, and on
the verge of falling back, two games to none, when Bench doubled off
Boston's starting pitcher, Bill Lee, and scored on shortstop Dave Concepcion's single against reliever Dick Drago. Concepcion, who stole thirty-
three bases that year, then stole second and scored the winning run on a
double by Ken Griffey, the father of one of baseball's stars at the end of
the century and into the next, Ken Griffey, Jr.

That was exciting enough, but the real fun started in the third game when the Series moved to Cincinnati. The two teams hit a record six home runs in that game—by Fisk, Bench, Concepcion, Bernie Carbo, Dwight Evans, and Cesar Geronimo. Evans temporarily saved the Red Sox from defeat with a home run in the ninth inning, but, after so many homers, the Reds won it in the tenth, 6–5, on a bunt. And not just any bunt, either.

The Reds led off the bottom of the tenth with a single by Geronimo. Pinch hitter Ed Armbrister laid down a sacrifice bunt to move Geronimo into scoring position at second base. The ball rolled about three feet in front of the plate as Armbrister hesitated slightly. Fisk jumped out from behind the plate, threw off his mask and darted for the ball, only to run into Armbrister. Fisk pushed Armbrister aside, grabbed the ball, and threw to second in the hope of getting Geronimo on a force-out, but his throw was wild. The runners kept going, with Geronimo reaching third base and Armbrister advancing to second. The Reds had two men in scoring position and nobody out.

The Red Sox argued bitterly that Armbrister should have been called out for interfering with Fisk at the plate. Home plate Umpire Larry Barnett disagreed. After the game he told reporters, "I ruled it was simply a collision. It is interference only when the batter *intentionally* gets in the way of the fielder."

Somebody asked Sparky Anderson what he thought of the play. The Reds manager ducked that one nicely, with his tongue in his cheek. "To be honest with you," he answered, "I don't see all that well."

Tiant, the aging Cuban, got the Red Sox even with the Reds at two wins each in another game decided by one run, 5–4. The Sox reprised their formula from the first game by scoring all their runs in one inning, the fourth. Tiant didn't show his age. He needed 163 pitches, an astronomical number for any age, especially someone only a month away from turning thirty-five, but he survived the endurance test and outlasted four Boston pitchers.

Tony Perez, in an 0-for-15 slump since the Series began, bounced back in robust fashion to lead the Reds to victory, 6–2, in the fifth game. Perez drove in four runs on two homers. His team took a 3–2 lead as the Series headed back to Boston.

Mother Nature stepped in at that point and became the star of the World Series for three days in a row. Game 6 was rained out that many times. The only winners were the merchants of Boston. The president of the Greater Boston Convention and Tourist Bureau estimated that the three days of idleness brought $450,000 into the cash registers of the city's hotels, restaurants, stores, and places of entertainment. When play was finally resumed, no one complained about the wait. The sixth game took four hours and one minute to finish. It needed a pinch-hit home run to tie the game in the eighth inning, plus a sensational catch to save it in the eleventh and a home run for the history books to win it in the twelfth. The two teams used twelve pitchers, eight by Cincinnati. When the game was over, the clocks in the Eastern time zone said it was thirty-three minutes after midnight.

Boston manager Darrell Johnson took advantage of the three off-days from rainouts and sent Tiant to the mound for the third time in the Series. In the stands, extra security was on hand to protect Larry Barnett after his controversial call against the Red Sox in the third game. Barnett had received a threat against himself and his family. The Boston office of the FBI said the threat was contained in a telegram from Cincinnati. Boston police said Barnett and his family were receiving protection around the clock.

Tiant was pitching with six days of rest, and he looked like money in the bank when Fred Lynn hit a three-run homer in the first inning off Gary Nolan, his first home run in five weeks. They seemed to be on their way to tying the Series at three wins each, until the Reds tied the game in the fifth.

Armbrister—that man again—pinch-hit again and drew a walk. Pete Rose lined a 3–2 pitch from Tiant to center field for a base hit, and Griffey lined a 2–2 pitch to the fence in dead center. Lynn made the catch but was injured when he banged into the fence. He was able to stay in the game after a five-minute delay for treatment. Griffey reached third with a triple that drove in Armbrister and Rose.

With the score then 3–2, Joe Morgan popped out, but Bench caught hold of Tiant's first pitch and sent it to the left field wall, Boston's Green Monster, for a single that scored Griffey and tied the game, 3–3.

The Reds threatened to win the game, and the Series, in the seventh inning when Griffey and Morgan singled, giving Cincinnati two men on base with the heart of the order—Bench and Perez—coming up. Tiant gave himself some breathing room temporarily by getting both stars on fly balls. But George Foster sent another drive to dead center for a double

Center fielder Fred Lynn of the Boston Red Sox became the first player to win the Most Valuable Player and Rookie of the Year awards in the same season when he hit .331 in 1975, led the American League in doubles with 47 and runs scored with 103, hit 21 home runs, and drove in 105 runs. The Red Sox won the pennant but lost the World Series to the Cincinnati Reds. (Courtesy of the National Baseball Hall of Fame Library, Cooperstown, N.Y.)

off the wall, scoring two runs, giving the Big Red Machine a 5–3 lead and bringing them to within only three innings of winning the World Series.

Geronimo made the situation even grimmer for the Red Sox and their fans by hitting a home run high into the air past the right field foul pole in the eighth inning, stretching Cincinnati's lead to 6–3 with Boston down to its last six outs of the game, the season, and the Series.

But this game had magic all over it. The Red Sox shocked the Fenway faithful, the nation's television viewers, and the Reds in the bottom of the eighth. Lynn lined a single off the leg of Pedro Borbon and Rico Petrocelli walked, but Dwight Evans struck out and Rick Burleson went out on a soft line drive to left. With two outs, the tying run was at the plate in outfielder Bernie Carbo, who had begun his big-league career six years earlier with the Reds. The Sox could still tie it, 6–6, on a home run, and Carbo had hit a pinch-hit homer in the third game, but now they were down to only four outs.

To the utter shock of everyone everywhere, Carbo, who had hit 15 home runs during the season, did it again. He ripped into a 2–2 pitch and sent it deep into the center field bleachers for a three-run home run and a tie game going into the ninth.

"It was a fastball over the plate," Carbo said after the game. "I was telling myself not to strike out. With four days off because of the rain, I was just trying to put the ball in play someplace."

Carbo's heroics set off wild celebrations in the stands, and the fans got even noisier when Boston loaded the bases with nobody out in the ninth. Then Lynn sent a high fly ball along the left field line that Foster was able to reach. He quickly and alertly fired to home plate, where Bench tagged out Denny Doyle for a double play. The Reds got out of the inning, and as Pete Rose came to bat in the tenth, he turned to Fisk behind the plate, smiled, and said in full view of the national TV audience, "This is some kind of ball game, isn't it?"

With full appreciation of the dramatics around them, Fisk answered, "Yeah, it sure is."

The Reds almost won it in the eleventh. With Griffey on first base, Morgan sent a fly ball toward the seats in right, but there was still plenty of drama left in this World Series. Dwight Evans made a dazzling catch, leaning into the box seats to get the ball, then threw it three hundred feet back into the infield and doubled up Griffey.

Anderson admitted, "It was as good a catch as you'll ever see." Evans's teammate Carl Yastrzemski, agreed. "It was one of the greatest catches I've ever seen."

Evans said, "It would have been a home run. The fans were good. They moved back a little for me, and I was able to make the catch."

The catch set the stage for what was to come in the next inning, the twelfth-inning home run by Carlton Fisk that became an instant monument to World Series drama and remains so to this day.

Fisk stepped into the righthanded hitter's half of the batter's box to lead off the bottom half of the twelfth inning in a 6–6 tie. No one anywhere had any reason to suspect that the high drama that had lasted for more than four hours was to end. Fisk swung on a pitch from Pat Darcy, a twenty-five-year-old righthander, and sent a long, high fly ball down the left field line. As Fisk trotted down the first base line, he never took his eyes off the ball because of his fear it might curve foul. As he half skipped, half trotted toward first base, Fisk waved both arms toward the outfield and away from foul territory. In a few seconds, the night's final stroke of magic touched the Red Sox and Fisk. The ball glanced off the foul pole for a home run. The Red Sox won the game, 7–6, and forced the already dramatic Series to a seventh game, as Americans thrilled to it all—and forgot about inflation, crime, the Watergate cover-up, Vietnam, and attempted assassinations.

"I made sure I touched every one of those sweet white bases," the jubilant Fisk said after the game. "The fans jumped on the field, but I would score even if I had to stiff-arm them." Twenty-four years later, the ball that Fisk hit was sold at an auction in New York. It went for $113,273.

Television viewers across the nation, including the millions in the Eastern time zone who stayed up past midnight because they couldn't bring themselves to turn off their TV sets, were treated to an extended look at Fisk and his reactions as he followed the flight of the ball, thanks to, of all things, a rat. Alan Schwarz reported twenty-five years later in *The New York Times* that an NBC cameraman named Lou Gerard, stationed inside the Green Monster in left field, was told by his producer, Harry Coyle, to follow the ball wherever Fisk might hit it.

Gerard said, "Harry, there's a rat right here next to me the size of a cat, and it's moving closer."

Coyle asked, "What are you going to do?"

"Maybe . . . I ought to just stay on Fisk and see what happens."

"Soon," Schwarz wrote in October 2000, "100 million television viewers were treated to a historic instant replay. Because Gerard had kept his lens fixed on the batter, he caught Fisk as he dropped his bat and frantically motioned for the ball to land fair, bouncing on his toes while throwing his hands to his right, as if directing a jumbo jet on a runway. Never before had a camera captured an athlete's emotions so immediately."

John Filippelli, an associate NBC producer for the game, told Schwarz, "They didn't even know they had that shot at first. It was a wonderful aberration that changed television. No one had ever thought of isolating on an individual."

Even baseball's staunchest supporters admit that their sport cannot always stand prosperity. It happened again shortly after that storybook World Series ended. On December 23, a labor arbitrator, Peter Seitz, ruled that two pitchers, Andy Messersmith of the Dodgers and Dave

McNally, a former star for the Orioles who quit the Expos in mid-season, were free agents and could sign with any team. The year before, Seitz had ruled that Jim "Catfish" Hunter of the A's was also a free agent because, Seitz said, owner Charles O. Finley had breached his contract with Hunter.

An era as old as the Major Leagues themselves ended. Until then, baseball contracts contained a "reserve clause" that bound you to your team for a year after your contract, which was almost always for only one year, expired. Baseball players were in the only profession whose members were not free to change employers. Seitz threw out that clause, saying "one year" meant one year.

The courts upheld his ruling, and today's era of "free agency," with owners bidding against each other in skyscraper numbers for the star players and even for the substitutes, was born. That's why today's stars make millions, and not just a few million. It produced today's age when the rich get richer, with the large market teams able to outbid the teams in smaller cities. And it produced new levels of absurdity each season. From a time when players spent entire careers with one team and signed only one-year contracts with the salary remaining confidential between the player and his team, the sport has moved, for better or worse, to the present age of multiyear contracts in eight figures that are spread all over the sports pages and the evening news. In 2002, the *average* big league salary was $2.38 million.

The new age was symbolized drastically after the 2001 season when a thirty-year-old first baseman, Jason Giambi, left the Oakland A's and signed a seven-year contract with the Yankees for $119 million, an average of $17 million a season. That was stunning enough in itself, but the shock became even greater when fans read on December 13 that Giambi's sky-high salary merely tied him for fifth place on the big-bucks list of the highest salaries in baseball.

It isn't even required anymore for a player to have a good year to earn a good contract. The Baltimore Orioles and one of their pitchers, Sidney Ponson, are proof. The Orioles gave Ponson a raise of $550,000 after the 2001 season, increasing his salary for one season to $2.65 million. The Orioles agreed to the hefty raise even though Ponson was bothered by arm troubles twice in 2001 and won only five games, the worst season of his four years in the Major Leagues.

As if more than $2.5 million for one season isn't enough money to pay a five-game winner, the Orioles also included incentive clauses that would pay him another $125,000 based on how many games he started and how many innings he pitched, plus still another $100,000 if he were chosen as the American League's Comeback Player of the Year. All of this information about Ponson's contract for 2002, which would have been kept confidential by the team and the player before free agency arrived in the mid-1970s, was in the papers and on the air.

George Will, the syndicated columnist and author, once wrote, "Winter begins with the last out of the World Series." True enough—but not after the 1975 season. Not even concern about what free agency could bring was able to dampen the enthusiasm of the fans, the players, the writers, the broadcasters, and everyone else after the 1975 World Series.

That's when Jim Murray was willing to stand up and be counted on the question of baseball versus other sports. He ridiculed baseball's critics in the *World Book Year Book* as people who had given the sport up for dead and wanted to "put baseball in the Smithsonian Institution along with the Lincoln letters and the *Spirit of St. Louis.*" Murray offered a glowing commentary about the 1975 World Series. "Well," he wrote, "a funny thing happened to the corpse of the Grand Old Game on its way to the cemetery. It sat up, sold tickets, and soon had the whole country in a community sing of "Take Me Out to the Ball Game." He argued that the sixth game, with Fisk's home run, "may go down in history as the Game That Saved Baseball."

Columnist Wells Twombly was equally enthusiastic. "After more than two decades of darkness," he said, "baseball is coming back as a popular entertainment attraction. The South will rise again. Richard Nixon will make a political comeback. And baseball will be the national pastime again in one of history's most amazing resurrections."

Pete Rose, the man who knew he was playing in something special when he made his comment to Fisk at home plate in the tenth inning of the sixth game, said, "I tell you this. If the sixth game of this Series didn't turn this country on, there is something wrong. After that show, the Super Bowl had better be up . . . up . . . up. It's going to have to be spectacular to compete with what we did in that game."

Dave Anderson, the Pulitzer Prize–winning columnist of *The New York Times,* said the 1975 World Series showcased the beauty of baseball over other sports. After recounting the remarkable drama and exciting plays that marked the entire Series, Anderson pointed out, "In each case, the solitary artistry was not obscured in a trample of bodies, which occurs in football, or in collisions near the backboards, which occur in basketball, or in a scramble near the goal, which occurs in hockey. The solitary artistry of baseball is there to be seen, not obscured."

After conceding that ranking games as the greatest depends in many cases on which team you might be rooting for, Anderson said, "But the sixth game was a reminder that baseball, when it means something, is the greatest game."

PART SEVEN
· · ·
1980

19

Crises

As 1980 began, America and baseball both faced crises again. The nation itself was reeling from a series of body blows—fifty-two Americans captured by the militant government in Iran and being held as hostages, an economy seeming to be out of control with interest rates approaching the unimaginable height of 20 percent, industrial giants like Chrysler appealing to the federal government for help, and increased tensions between the United States and the Soviet Union after its invasion of Afghanistan in December 1979—all of this compounded by 1980's status as a presidential election year.

America's sports fans, and some who weren't sports fans at all, found excitement in the Winter Olympics at Lake Placid, New York. On national television, the USA hockey team scored one of the most shocking upsets in memory by defeating the heavily favored Soviet Union team, 4–3, in the semifinals on February 23. Some eight thousand five hundred fans saw the Soviets lose their first hockey game in the Olympics since they had lost to Czechoslovakia in 1968.

The captain of the USA team, Mike Eruzione, scored the winning goal against Vladimir Mishkin. As the seconds ticked down to the final buzzer, TV announcer Al Michaels shared the excitement of the crowd and the television audience and uttered one of the immortal lines in the history of sports broadcasting:

"Do you believe in miracles?—*Yes!*"

As the U.S.A. celebrated in the locker room, the players sang "God Bless America."

In baseball, the question at the start of spring training wasn't whether the baseball season would be exciting. Instead, the question was whether there would even be a season. A labor dispute, those things that have plagued baseball and other professional sports periodically since the end of World War II, cast a dark cloud over the sport as spring training began. A four-year contract between the club owners and the Major League Baseball Players Association, which created the free agent system, had expired on December 31, 1979. In negotiations for a new contract, the owners asked for a provision in the new contract that would require teams signing free agents to compensate the former team in each case with established major leaguers. The union responded by saying such a provision would destroy the system.

As spring training neared its conclusion on April 1, no agreement had been reached. The players decided to boycott the remaining exhibition games. They also told the owners they would start playing the regular season eight days later, as scheduled, but would strike if a new contract were not agreed to by May 22. With the deadline imposed by the players less than ten hours away, the two sides reached agreement on all other issues and postponed the free agent issue until January 1981, proving once again the old management philosophy that "no problem is so big or so complicated that it can't be run away from."

Bill Veeck, the always optimistic owner who headed the Chicago White Sox that season, found reason to smile despite baseball's labor unrest. "Dugout to dugout," he said, "the game happily remains unchanged in our changing world. We are an island of stability in an unstable world."

The 1980 baseball season was about to begin.

When the Mariners and Toronto Blue Jays met in Seattle's Kingdome on April 9 to open the American League season, the prime interest rate hit a record high of 20 percent. The Muslim militants in Iran, under the leadership of the world's newest villain, Ayatollah Khomeini, were still holding the American hostages in the U.S. embassy compound in the capital city of Tehran.

Tensions were growing worse rapidly. In a special report to the *Washington Star*, Raji Samghabadi said the militants threatened to kill "all spies instantly if the U.S. engages in the slightest military intervention against Iran." The report said the militants called on Americans back here to "restrain the criminal government of America."

A companion story on Page One by *Star* staff writers Duncan Spencer and Paul Clancy said fifty-one Iranians, including fifteen diplomats and their families, left the United States that day on the last flight available before a deadline for their departure set by President Jimmy Carter.

As the last days of spring training arrived, so did a new television program, born out of the hostage crisis. On the evening of March 24, 1980, the 142nd day of the crisis, Ted Koppel looked into a TV studio camera as an announcer's voice spoke the now-familiar opening words:

> "This is ABC News Nightline. Reporting from Washington, Ted Koppel."

Just as a world war forty years earlier couldn't stop Major League Baseball from being played, the hostage crisis couldn't either. The season opened on schedule, with the Mariners defeating the Blue Jays, 8–6, and

Ted Koppel on the set of *Nightline*. The show started as a feature of ABC News during its coverage of the hostage crisis and began appearing nightly on March 24, 1980. (© ABC Photo Archives.)

the Reds beating the Atlanta Braves, 9–0, in Cincinnati. Alert observers might have detected clues in each game that indicated the possibility that this would be an unusual season.

In Seattle, one of the heroes was Dave Heaverlo, a relief pitcher who got the last four outs of the game for the Mariners. What's unusual about that? Just that he wasn't even a member of the Mariners that morning. He was sold to the Mariners by the Oakland A's earlier the same day and arrived at the Kingdome just in time to save the win for his new team.

The Reds' victory over the Braves was a 1–0 shutout by Frank Pastore, a six-foot two-inch, twenty-two-year-old righthander starting his second season in the big leagues. It was Cincinnati's first shutout on Opening Day since Johnny Vander Meer stopped the St. Louis Cardinals, 1–0, on the first day of the 1943 season.

While the baseball season unfolded, America's most distressing problem suddenly grew worse. As diplomatic attempts to free the fifty-two American hostages from their six months of captivity in Iran met with repeated failure, President Carter authorized the American military forces to attempt a dramatic rescue. The operation, named "Eagle's Claw," involved landing ninety commando troops of the Army and Marines, trained for this specific mission, in the desert and driving them into Tehran to attack the U.S. Embassy.

The attempt began on April 24 but ended in disaster when mechanical failures on five of the eight helicopters forced officials to cancel the operation in the desert at its rendezvous point. In the withdrawal, one of the helicopters collided with a C-130 cargo plane. Eight U.S. military men were killed.

President Carter took full responsibility, but a Pentagon investigative committee criticized the planning for the operation and its execution, pointing to poor communications and lines of authority. The committee also said the attack did not include enough helicopters and that planners of the operation failed to seek review and comment of their plans by senior officials at the Pentagon.

On May 18, a new item was added to the menu of severe problems facing the nation, something virtually unknown to most Americans—an exploding volcano. Mount Saint Helens in Washington State, inactive since 1857, erupted. More than a thousand feet at the top of the volcano were blown away by the force of the explosion, which killed at least thirty-four people and destroyed all life over an area of 155 square miles. Damage was estimated at $2.7 billion. Volcanic ash was scattered over several states, affecting the environment in the northwestern states for years into the future. The explosion was heard 135 miles away and equaled the force of ten million tons of TNT. Scientists estimated its force as five hundred times more powerful than the atomic bomb dropped on Hiroshima.

All of this news about the hostages, the interest rate, inflation, a volcano, and everything else was reported to the American people on a new medium: the Cable News Network—CNN. Ted Turner, a multimillionaire yachting personality and the owner of the National League's Atlanta Braves as well as the Atlanta Hawks basketball team, began his innovation on June 1. CNN provided news twenty-four hours a day by satellite. As the news became an increasing topic of conversation, more American families subscribed to cable systems and began receiving CNN's news coverage as well as the programs offered by other cable channels.

The American and National Leagues were studies in contrast that season. The Kansas City Royals raced away from the rest of the AL West and ran up a lead of twenty full games before finishing fourteen games ahead of the Oakland A's for the divisional championship and a spot in what is now bureaucratically called the "ALCS." The term sounds like a government agency but stands for the American League (or National) Championship Series, as opposed to the term used in the National Football League—and everywhere else—playoffs.

The Yankees won the league's Eastern division by three games over the pennant winners of the year before, the Baltimore Orioles, but it wasn't as close as it sounds. They built a large lead, but public criticisms by owner George Steinbrenner against some of his players and arguments between Steinbrenner and manager Dick Howser took their toll and sliced the Yankees' final margin.

Despite their distance behind the Royals, the A's proved to be the talk of the league in 1980, under their new manager, the old Yankee fireball, Billy Martin. After winning only fifty-four games the year before, the A's jumped to eighty-three victories in 1980 under Martin's innovative leadership and his fiery brand of managing.

He joined Oakland as the A's tenth manager in thirteen seasons, but he made his team—and himself—one of the running stories in 1980 with what became nicknamed "Billy Ball." Martin employed a brand of play that placed great stress on fundamentals: stolen bases, hit-and-run plays, squeeze plays, and the rest, plus a philosophy of pitching that relied on the willingness, and the ability, of his starting pitchers to go the full nine innings.

This method of handling pitchers flew in the face of the growing post-war emphasis on relief pitchers of every kind. Instead of being regarded as second-class citizens, relief pitchers were becoming worth their weight in gold with their own new set of terms: "short relievers," "long relievers," "middle men," and "closers." Whereas it was not unheard of for starting pitchers to record somewhere between 200 and 300 innings a season, or more, some starters were now leading their staffs with under 200 innings. Rick Burris led the Mets' pitchers in 1980 with only 170 innings pitched. The following season, Glenn Abbott was the "workhorse" of the Seattle staff with only 130 innings pitched.

That wasn't the Billy Martin way of handling pitchers. He stuck his starters out there on the mound at the beginning of the game and expected them to go nine innings, or as close to that as humanly possible. In addition to skyrocketing their team to 29 more wins, Martin's pitchers dominated the American League's statistics when it came to working long hours. The top three pitchers in the American League in complete games were all members of the Oakland A's—Rick Langford with 28, Mike Norris with 24, and Matt Keough with 20. Langford and Norris led the league in innings pitched with 290 and 284 respectively.

The National League won the All-Star Game, again, 4–2, at Dodger Stadium in Los Angeles, with Ken Griffey leading the attack for the winners with a single and a home run. It was the National's ninth straight victory and its seventeenth win out of the last eighteen games in the midsummer series.

For American Leaguers, the All-Star Game was becoming a sore point. The American League once led the series, 12 wins to 4, but now the National League led the series with 32 wins to 18 for the American and one tie. American Leaguers, however, could point to their superiority in the true test—the World Series—with 45 championships to 31 for the National League.

The game wasn't the only big story at the midpoint of the season. After announcing in spring training that 1980 would be his last season, Willie McCovey took the field for the final time four days before the All-Star Game and retired after twenty-two years in the big leagues, all but three of them with the San Francisco Giants.

He called it a career on July 6 at Dodger Stadium in Los Angeles after hitting a sacrifice fly in the top of the eighth inning with the score tied,

3–3, and Giants on first and third with one out. Rick Sutcliffe came in to pitch for the Dodgers, and manager Dave Bristol of the Giants sent McCovey up to the plate to pinch-hit for Rennie Stennett. McCovey hit a 1–1 pitch to Rudy Law in left center, scoring Jack Clark. The Giants came rushing out of their dugout, the fans roared even though their team had lost, and McCovey came out of the dugout long enough to take one curtain call. Then he was gone.

McCovey, nicknamed "Stretch" for his ability to reach out and scoop up low throws at first base, followed in the footsteps of Hank Aaron, his hometown hero back in Mobile, Alabama. In his departure, baseball was losing one of its brightest stars, who achieved Hall of Fame status in 1986 despite a career hampered by as many injuries as Mickey Mantle's or anyone else's. He played his way through a serious knee injury, a series of operations on the knee, recurring bouts with arthritis, calcium deposits in his hip, a bad wrist, blurred vision, a dislocated shoulder, a broken arm, jammed wrists, jammed thumbs, and problems with his feet. He still managed to hit 526 home runs, tied at the time with Ted Williams for the sixth most in history, and drew 1,345 bases on balls during his career.

Sparky Anderson, the manager of the Cincinnati Reds and their "Big Red Machine" in those years, once paid him the almost unheard-of compliment of ordering his pitcher to walk McCovey even though first base was already occupied. "He's the best hitter in baseball," Anderson explained. "I'm not going to pitch to him if I don't have to. I'd rather take my chances with someone else. Why let him beat you?"

Walter Alston, then the manager of the Los Angeles Dodgers, went Anderson one better. He ordered McCovey walked intentionally as the leadoff hitter in the ninth inning of a one-run game, violating a centuries-old rule in baseball: never put the winning run on base, intentionally or otherwise, especially in the late innings with nobody out and nobody on base.

Baseball was losing one of its brightest stars, one who at the time of his retirement held the National League records for the most career grand slam home runs—eighteen—the most career home runs by a left-handed hitter, the most homers by a first baseman, the most seasons played by a first baseman, and the most consecutive games in which he received a walk—eleven.

For all this and more, McCovey won the league's Rookie of the Year award in 1959, the National League's Most Valuable Player award in

1969, and the league's Comeback Player of the Year award in 1977. On top of all that, he remains one of only a handful of players who played in the Major Leagues in four different decades—the '50s, '60s, '70s, and '80s.

With all those credentials, maybe the most convincing testimonial to his greatness came from Dick Stuart, the first baseman who was nicknamed "Dr. Strangeglove," a commentary on his fielding ability and a play on the title of a satirical movie about the threat of atomic war. Stuart said that when he was playing for the Pittsburgh Pirates, if Willie Mays reached first base, "he would hide behind me because McCovey was up and he was a strict pull hitter. Every time I would go to move, Mays would take his finger and hook it into my pants and he would hide behind me because I was a lot bigger than him. McCovey would hit a line drive at us, and we'd both fall to the ground at the same time."

Stuart said his manager, Danny Murtaugh, would tell him sternly, "You're supposed to *catch the ball*." Stuart would answer that "Mays had a hold of me and I was trying to get out of the way of the ball. That's how I got my reputation as 'Dr. Strangeglove.' I told Murtaugh I would try to catch the ball if McCovey hit it a little slower."

The most talked-about player in either league that year wasn't a pitcher. He was a third baseman—George Brett—who spent most of July and August threatening to become the first man to hit .400 since Ted Williams had with a .406 average in 1941. He reached .374 on July 16 with two singles, a double, and a triple—and kept right on going. Five days later he was hitting .381, but only for one day before dropping back into the .370s. He reached .381 again on July 29, and stirred more interest by reaching .390 on the last day of July.

On August 17, he climbed to .401 with a 4-for-4 performance against the Toronto Blue Jays and went as high as .408, 2 points higher than Williams in 1941, on August 28. As late as September 19, he was still hitting an even .400

He had his hottest stretch in August, when he hit in thirty straight games, including one streak of hitting safely in seven consecutive times at bat. His teammate, relief pitcher Dan Quisenberry, said, "It's not a question of how to get him out. Right now, it's a question of how to hold him to a single."

Brett was feeling some of the same kind of pressure that Roger Maris felt in 1961. He was being hounded by reporters. "To be honest with you," he told Mike DeArmond of *The Sporting News*, "the lack of privacy bothers me." He said reporters came into his room to talk to him, and he answered phone calls "at three o'clock in the afternoon when you're trying to take a nap. Today I had calls from South Carolina, South Dakota, California, you name it. They always ask if I have a few minutes. I say, 'No. Come to the park and I'll talk to you.' "

Brett stayed with that arrangement until the number of reporters who wanted to interview him at the ballpark before the game reached fifteen and twenty a day. The Royals front office staff later made Brett available to the news media for thirty minutes before each game.

Brett was hitting an even .400 as late as September 19 and finished with a mark of .390, at that point still the highest average in the major leagues since '41, and was voted the American League's Most Valuable Player.

He was doing it the hard way, playing through a succession of injuries and illnesses that would have struck down a lesser man. Although he was only twenty-seven years old, the future Hall of Famer missed 45 games with a torn ligament in his ankle, tendonitis, and, of all things, hemorrhoids, which bothered him increasingly until he underwent surgery after the second game of the World Series. Despite all that, he still managed to hit 24 home runs and drive in 118 runs in addition to topping both leagues in hitting with that .390 average.

As Labor Day arrived and baseball headed toward the home stretch of its regular season, tourists began returning to Mount Saint Helens, then leaving with souvenir packages of ash and bumper stickers that read:

ST. HELENS FORGOT HER EARTH CONTROL PILL

The vacation season was ending. The summer movies were still playing in the theaters—*Coal Miner's Daughter,* the story of country singer Loretta Lynn, played by Sissy Spacek; *Fame,* about the New York High School of Performing Arts; and *Airplane,* a satire on the epidemic of disaster movies. It was an off summer at the box office, but one movie picked up a large part of the slack. That was *The Empire Strikes Back,* a sequel to the special effects hit *Star Wars.* The sequel brought in 25 percent of that summer's box office receipts.

With the arrival of the Labor Day weekend, the traditional start of the final leg in a presidential campaign, America had to choose from not two but three candidates. The Democratic incumbent, Jimmy Carter, and the

Republican opponent, Governor Ronald Reagan of California, were opposed by a third candidate, Independent John Anderson, a Republican congressman from Illinois. The number of entries in the race had changed, but not the issues. The hostages were still being held captive in Iran, the Russians were still in Afghanistan and had boosted their strength to eighty thousand troops, plus tanks, jet airplanes, and helicopter gunships, and the economy remained the number-one issue on the home front.

General Motors raised the prices of its cars $176 in mid-August, then raised them another $238, increasing the price of its new 1981 models to an average of about $9,450. Ford and Chrysler were tapping into the demand for smaller cars. Ford introduced its new models, the Escort and the Lynx, and Chrysler promoted its K cars. Chrysler's chairman, Lee Iacocca, was busy trying to save the company itself. Late in the year he revealed that Chrysler had already received $800 million from a "bailout" of $1.5 billion approved by Congress in 1979, but needed another $400 million.

As the nation returned to work and school, the National League was heading toward two dramatic climaxes to determine its division champions. The Philadelphia Phillies, Montreal Expos, and Pittsburgh Pirates were in a neck-and-neck race for first place in the National League East. The West was just as tight, with the Houston Astros leading the Los Angeles Dodgers by only a half game.

For the Astros, the pennant race was even more of a struggle than for any of the other teams in either league. On July 30, one of their star pitchers, six-foot eight-inch, 230-pound J. R. Richard, winner of 86 games in the previous five seasons, had collapsed during a workout at the Astrodome. A righthander, he had been enjoying another successful season and had ten wins and only four losses at the All-Star break while complaining several times during the season of a "dead arm." Four days before his collapse, he entered Methodist Hospital in Houston for a series of tests lasting three days. Doctors discovered a circulatory problem that affected the flow of blood to his right arm.

After his collapse, he was rushed to the hospital for emergency surgery to remove a blood clot behind his right collarbone that had cut off the flow of blood to his brain and threatened his life. Richard remained in the hospital for six weeks, until September 12. He survived the stroke but was left partially paralyzed on his left side. He underwent surgery again on October 12 at Moffitt Hospital in San Francisco. This time, the operation lasted eighteen hours as vascular surgeons replaced an obstructed artery in his right shoulder and rebuilt his vascular system with arterial grafts and Dacron tubing.

After the surgery, the doctors said Richard might be able to resume his career. He did, but never in the Major Leagues again. He pitched for minor league teams in Daytona Beach, Sarasota, and Tucson and retired as a player in 1983.

It was virtually impossible to have closer races. Both divisions were locked in battles so tight there was no room for error. The suspense continued right up to the last weekend of the regular season.

The Pirates had been eliminated with a week to play, due in part to knee injuries to their two biggest sluggers, Willie Stargell and Dave Parker. That left the Phillies and the Montreal Expos to battle it out for the National League East championship in a crucial three-game series in Montreal.

Mike Schmidt drove in both Philadelphia runs to win the first game. In the second game, the pressure on the teams was increased by a three-hour rain delay. Schmidt ended the suspense and the divisional race by unloading a 425-foot home run with two teammates on base in the eleventh inning to propel the Phillies into the championship series against the Houston Astros. It came the night before the season ended and was Schmidt's fourth home run in four games.

For the Philadelphia star, coming through with the chips on the line was more important than to most other players for one fundamental reason: He was saddled with the criticism that he didn't come through in clutch situations, an allegation that lingered from poor hitting performances in the 1977 and 1978 league championship series.

"You like to think you can handle it," he told one interviewer, "but for me it's hard. Heck, I'm not *trying* to fail. I'm concentrating every second I'm on the field, on doing my best, on doing the right thing. I want it for myself, for my kids, for my wife, for my teammates, for the fans, and for the good Lord. But how do you convince people of that?"

While leading his team to 91 victories in 1980, Schmidt hit 48 home runs, seven more than Reggie Jackson of the Yankees and Ben Oglivie of the Brewers, to lead both leagues. He also led both leagues in total bases. He would have led both leagues in runs batted in too, except that his total of 121 was one less than that of Milwaukee's Cecil Cooper in the

American League. As an infielder who once had trouble fielding his position, Schmidt also led the National League's third baseman that year in assists, double plays, and total chances per game. For all of that, Schmidt was voted the National League's Most Valuable Player, the first of three MVP awards for him.

It was the latest in a series of outstanding seasons for Schmidt, who now was making people wonder just how great he might become. The man who hit .196 in 1973 and struck out 136 times, the low point in his career, had been on an upswing ever since, and three factors explained his dramatic and sustained improvement: God, money, and Pete Rose.

Schmidt had turned to God in the mid-1970s while shooting baskets outside his house on a winter day. He said he had stopped and asked himself, "Why me?" He said it occurred to him that he did not realize why certain things were happening to him, such as that .196 average and those 136 strikeouts. He said later, "I knew there had to be more."

He explained, "The one thing people should realize, and the thing I was beginning to realize, is that if I am out there giving 100 percent, whether I go 4-for-4 or 0-for-4, in Christ's eyes I am a winner." Earlier in his career, Schmidt had been the target of unmerciful booing by the Philadelphia fans, who had a reputation for being willing to boo everybody and anybody, including Santa Claus and the Pope. With his new faith in God and in himself, he said, "I don't care if the whole stadium is booing or cheering. It doesn't matter anymore."

Before the start of the 1977 season, the Phillies rewarded Schmidt's continued improvement by making him the highest-paid player in the history of Major League Baseball until that time. They gave him a contract calling for $3 million for six years. At Schmidt's request, the contract included a no-trade clause for the next four years.

Schmidt anticipated concern by the fans and the reporters that his high salary might affect his performance. He had an answer. He told *The Sporting News,* "I love to play baseball. I never think of the money once I put that uniform on, and I never played a game in my life that I didn't give it 100 percent."

The third turning point in Schmidt's career came when the Phillies signed Pete Rose as a free agent to be their first baseman starting with the 1979 season. Schmidt hit 45 home runs and drove in 114 runs in 1979, then continued with his MVP season in 1980. None of it was coincidence.

Teammate Dick Allen had helped Schmidt to become a better hitter by talking about hitting with Mike at every opportunity. Allen knew what he was talking about. In a fifteen-year career in the big leagues, he hit over .300 seven times and finished with a lifetime batting average of .292.

Rose elevated Schmidt's performance to the next level—greatness. "Pete Rose taught me what I needed to be great," Schmidt said in later years. "He was consumed by the game. I'm not sure I was totally consumed by baseball until I met Pete."

One of the Philadelphia coaches, John Vukovich, agreed with Schmidt. "His approach to the game changed in '78 when Pete came," Vukovich said. "I don't think there's any reason to believe it's a coincidence that Schmitty had his big years when Pete was there. He hit 45 home runs the first year, and he hit 48 the next year."

In the NL West, the Los Angeles Dodgers faced the daunting prospect of having to win three straight games from the Houston Astros just to tie them for first place. They did, only to lose a one-game playoff to the Astros the next day, 7–1, on a six-hitter by Joe Niekro.

What followed were four of the most suspenseful postseason games ever played in one series. The playoffs between the Phillies and the Astros for the National League pennant, and the right to play in the World Series, went the full five games, and the last four went into extra innings.

The Phillies won the first game, 3–1, at their home ballpark, Veterans Stadium, thanks to a two-run homer by Greg Luzinski in the sixth inning. But that game was a runaway compared to the four that followed.

In the second game, the two teams battled to a 3–3 tie after nine innings. The Astros broke things open with a four-run tenth, including a two-run triple by Dave Bergman The two teams flew to Houston to play the next three games in the Astrodome. The third game was an inning longer than the second, but the outcome was the same. The Astros won again, this time 1–0 on a leadoff triple in the eleventh inning by Joe Morgan and a sacrifice fly by Denny Walling. Joe Niekro pitched ten shutout innings for the Astros, but a righthanded relief pitcher, rookie Dave Smith, got the win.

The Phillies and Astros went into extra innings for the third straight time in the fourth game, but this time the outcome was different. The Phils won in ten innings, 5–3, and tied the playoffs at two wins each. Pete Rose set the winning rally in motion with a single, which was followed by doubles by Luzinski and Manny Trillo.

Unbelievably, with the National League pennant and a spot in the World Series hanging in the balance, the two teams played their fourth straight extra-inning game, a ten-inning fight to the finish in which managers Dallas Green of the Phillies and Bill Virdon of the Astros used a total of ten pitchers.

The Phillies looked all but dead when the Astros broke a 2–2 tie with three runs in the bottom of the seventh inning, but they rallied and took the lead, 7–5, going into the bottom of the eighth. In keeping with the whole rest of the playoffs, the Astros staged still another rally, scoring two runs to pull even with the Phillies, 7–7, going into the ninth.

Neither team scored in that inning, and the playoffs, incredible as it may seem, headed into a fourth straight extra-inning game. Garry Maddox put an end to the mounting suspense in the tenth when he doubled to score Del Unser and win the game, 8–7. The victory gave Philadelphia its first National League pennant since the "Whiz Kids" of 1950. By the time the draining suspense was all over, the fans in the Astrodome stood after the final play and applauded both teams for the show they had put on.

In the midst of their dramatic victory and the extended suspense over those four extra-inning games in a row, there was one disturbing note for Phillies fans: Their team may have won the playoffs, but Mike Schmidt hit only .208, with no home runs and only one run batted in. That monkey was still on his back.

The American League Championship Series was just the opposite. The Royals swept their way into the World Series with three straight wins over the Yankees. The most suspenseful moment came on the last play of the second game when New York's Willie Randolph was thrown out at home plate while trying to score the tying run. The Royals won the game, 3–2, after defeating the Yankees, 7–2, at Kansas City in the opener.

The Steinbrenner-Howser feud spilled over into the off-season for the Yankees. In November, either Howser was fired or resigned under pressure, take your pick, with two years left on his contract at $100,000 a season. When reporters asked him about his departure, he answered, "I'm not going to comment on that."

George Brett continued his season-long heroics by hitting a home run in the first game, then winning the playoffs with a three-run homer in the third game after the playoffs moved to New York. Brett's homer came off Goose Gossage in the seventh inning and propelled the Royals to their first pennant in their twelve years of operation.

20

Center Stage

While Americans welcomed the World Series as an escape from the nation's problems, they were finding relief in other television programming as well. *M*A*S*H*, the weekly sitcom-drama about the Korean War, was one of the most popular shows, along with a prime-time weekly soap opera, *Dallas*. Their popularity was proven in dollars. The two shows, plus the CBS Sunday night favorite, *60 Minutes*, charged sponsors in the neighborhood of $150,000 for a thirty-second commercial, and that didn't include the costs of producing the commercials. CBS went even higher than that, charging $200,000 or more for each spot on the November 21 episode of *Dallas*, when viewers hoped to learn the answer to the question sweeping the nation about the show's villain: "Who shot J.R.?"

Baseball, after those National League playoffs and George Brett's attention-getting season and everything else, took over center stage in American entertainment by continuing its dramatics into the World Series. It was the Phillies, who had never won a World Series since their establishment in 1883, versus, the Royals, who had never been in one in their twelve years.

The Phillies took charge immediately, winning the first two games at their home ballpark, Veterans Stadium. In the first, they outlasted the Royals, 7–6, thanks to the slugging of right fielder Bake McBride and the relief pitching of Tug McGraw. McBride hit a three-run homer as the key blow during a five-run rally in the third inning that erased a 4–0 K.C. lead.

McGraw, with 57 appearances and 20 saves during the season, came on to shut out the Royals in the eighth and ninth innings to save the game for his team and record a World Series save for himself. McGraw, an outgoing and outspoken lefthander, had pitched in all five games during the playoffs against Houston. When reporters asked him after the game if he was tired, he said, "What it comes down to, simply, is the ability to do what you're paid to do. The catcher has to throw the ball every day, so do the shortstops. What's so different about me throwing it?"

When a reporter asked him if his secret was mental preparation, he answered, "If that was true, I'd be down in the trainer's room soaking my head in ice. I've never been paid a dime for my brains yet."

In the second game, a 6–4 win for the Phillies, the two stories were Steve Carlton and George Brett. Carlton, a future Hall of Famer, was the dominant pitcher in the National League, leading the league with 24 wins. He led both leagues in innings pitched with 304 and strikeouts with 286. But not this night. Carlton pitched 8 innings and threw 157 pitches. He walked six and gave up 10 hits. When he left the game after the eighth, the Phils were losing to the Royals, 4–2.

The Royals had seemed to be in the driver's seat with their lead when first-year manager Jim Frey wheeled in the American League's best relief pitcher, Dan Quisenberry, to start the seventh. Quisenberry, a six-foot two-inch righthander with 33 saves and the award as the American League's "Fireman of the Year," got the Phillies out in 1-2-3 order. The Royals were three outs away from tying the World Series at one victory for each team. But then came the eighth.

Quisenberry walked the first hitter in the inning—catcher Bob Boone, who scored on a pinch-hit double up the alley in left center by Del Unser. Pete Rose advanced Unser to third with a ground ball to the right side of the infield, putting him in position to tie the game if he could score from there on a fly ball. He scored, not on a fly ball but on a single to right by McBride.

On the next pitch, Schmidt drove in what proved to be the winning run with a screaming shot off the right field wall that scored McBride. Keith Moreland, who hit .314 for the Phils that year while catching 39 games, playing third base for four games and the outfield in two others and pinch-hitting in 17 games, singled in Schmidt. Ron Reed closed things out with a strong ninth inning in relief. The Phillies had their second victory as the teams moved to Kansas City for the third, fourth, and fifth games.

But first, George Brett needed surgery. He left the second game after five pain-racked innings caused by his hemorrhoid condition, then was operated on at St. Luke's Hospital in Kansas City during the day off reserved for travel. Brett was not allowed visitors except for one close friend. After their visit, the friend told reporters, "He was chipper, but in obvious pain. He told me he was definitely going to give it a try."

He was going to be in the lineup for the third game, a testimony both to the surgeon's skills and Brett's ability—and willingness—to play in pain.

Before the third game, Brett predicted, "If we lose, I think everybody is going to feel like they've got hemorrhoids." The Royals' third baseman lost no time in pronouncing his surgery a success. In the first inning, he hit a home run to give K.C. a 1–0 lead.

The Phillies tied the score in the second inning on two singles, a walk, and an infield out, but the Royals jumped back in front, 2–1, with a run in the fourth. That lead lasted only until Mike Schmidt led off the top of the fifth for Philadelphia. He hit a home run that tied the game again, 2–2.

Amos Otis matched Schmidt with a home run in the seventh for K.C., but Larry Bowa beat out an infield hit, stole second, and scored on a single by Rose to tie it again, 3–3, in the middle of the eighth.

Through the whole seesaw game, the Phillies were setting some sort of a record for frustration. They left two runners on base in the first inning, left the bases loaded in the second, left two more on base in the third, one in the fifth, two in the sixth, and two in the eighth—twelve runners left on base in eight innings.

The game, to the surprise of no one who had followed the National League playoffs, went into extra innings, and there the Phils threatened again. Boone singled and was sacrificed into scoring position by Greg Gross. Quisenberry, after snuffing out a rally in the eighth inning, walked Rose intentionally to pitch to Schmidt, who was hitting .400 at that point in the Series.

Remembering his first-pitch success against Quisenberry the last time they faced each other, Schmidt went after the first pitch again and hit it hard again. This one was a low, screaming line drive toward right field. The Royals second baseman, Frank White, flagged it down and turned it into an easy double play by getting Boone off second base to end the inning.

In the bottom of the tenth, U. L. Washington singled off McGraw and Willie Wilson walked. But Boone threw out Washington when he tried to steal, and White struck out, leaving the Phillies and McGraw facing a fast runner, Willie Wilson, on first base with two outs and Brett coming to bat. Everybody in the ballpark knew Wilson, with 79 stolen bases that year and a league-leading 133 runs scored, would be trying to steal second base so he could score from there on a hit to the outfield by Brett.

Sure enough, Wilson broke for second base. Boone's throw was in the dirt, and shortstop Larry Bowa tried to short-hop it but couldn't. Wilson was safe. The Phillies elected to walk Brett and his .390 batting average, bringing up Willie Aikens, who hit .278 that year. The strategy was sound, but Aikens foiled it by hitting a slicing line drive to left center field. Wilson scored, and the Royals had the first World Series victory in their history, 4–3.

In the dressing room after the game, McGraw said, "I got the ball up, and he hit the hell out of it. We've been winning as a team, and tonight we lost as a team. We had an opportunity to blow them out in four or five innings and didn't do it."

Kansas City scored early and often in the fourth game, with four runs in the first inning and an eventual 5–3 victory to tie the Series at two wins each. Aikens picked up where he left off the night before and became the first player in World Series history to have two multiple home run games in the same Series. After hitting two in the first game in Philadelphia, he hit two more in the fourth game.

The real excitement, however, came when George Brett came to the plate with two outs in the bottom half of the fourth inning and the Royals leading, 5–1. The count went to 0–2 quickly when Brett swung and missed the first pitched and fouled off the second. Both pitches were on the outside half of the plate.

The third pitch from Dickie Noles, a six-foot two-inch righthander, came inside, narrowly missing Brett's head and sending him sprawling to the dirt. As he picked himself and brushed himself off, Brett began to laugh. He explained later, "I was laughing because it didn't hit me. I was striding right into it and I was lucky to get out of the way. It was a good hard fastball. I honestly don't know how I got out of the way."

Was Noles throwing at Brett? "If he was," Brett replied, "if he was trying to get me, he's 0-for-1. If he wasn't, it's no big deal."

Brett's manager disagreed vigorously. Jim Frey said later, "I thought it was a knockdown pitch. Any time a team gets off to a big early lead and hits some long balls and a good hitter comes up later and gets knocked down on an 0–2 pitch, I call that a knockdown pitch. I went out and all I said was that I wanted to stop it right away."

Rose said Noles wasn't throwing at Brett. Frey answered, "I said to him that he didn't know if it was or wasn't a knockdown pitch, and I didn't know that it was or wasn't a knockdown pitch. Only the pitcher knows . . ."

Noles gave his side of the story: "You have to use both sides of the plate. You can't throw him a fastball low and away. I'll be in Kansas City Memorial Hospital. The only reason he [Frey] came out is because it's George Brett up there. If Frank White or someone else had been up there, he wouldn't have done a damn thing. And the pitch wasn't that far inside. But he's the manager. He has to fight for his players. If I were the manager, I'd fight for my players."

Frey had the home plate umpire on his side. Don Denkinger went to the mound and delivered a warning to Noles. There were no further incidents.

Some of the principals involved in the fifth game agreed that the outcome was decided, at least in part, by where the third baseman was playing. It happened in the ninth inning with Kansas City ahead, 3–2, and trying to take the lead in the Series before the teams headed back to Philadelphia and the sixth game.

With no outs and the bases empty, Frey moved Brett in close at third base, maybe remembering that Schmidt had attempted to bunt twice earlier in the Series at critical points. In that situation, it was a unique and risky move, especially against the National League's home run champion, who had hit a two-run long homer to dead center field in the fourth inning and homered in the third game of the Series. Schmidt was no singles-and-doubles hitter. He had become one of the most feared sluggers in the big leagues.

With Brett playing in closer than normal, Schmidt sent a shot to Brett's left. The third baseman made a dive for the ball but was able only to deflect it toward shortstop U. L. Washington. Schmidt reached first base. The winning rally was already set in motion.

Brett said candidly, "If I'm playing normally, I make the play."

Schmidt was equally candid. "No way I was going to bunt in that situation. Not one run down in the ninth. My job there is to get a good pitch, try and drive it, try to hit a double, maybe even hit the ball out of the park. No way would I think of trying to get on base with a bunt . . . I didn't really notice how close George was playing me. I just was aware of him guarding the line. If he's back on that ball, I guess he makes a fairly routine play."

With Schmidt on first, Del Unser came through again, this time with a pinch-hit double past Aikens at first base to score Schmidt and tie the score, 3–3. Moreland bunted Unser to third, where he remained after Garry Maddox grounded out.

Manny Trillo sent a scorcher back through the pitcher's box that bounced off Quisenberry's arm and rolled toward Brett at third. Trillo beat it out. Unser scored and the Phillies took the lead and the game, 4–3.

Unser talked about the unique role of a pinch hitter in that pressure situation. "As a pinch hitter," he said, "you've got to come off that bench swinging. There are going to be times when you go up there and it looks like that pitcher is throwing BBs. There will be other times when it looks like he's throwing beach balls. Either way, you've got to swing the bat. You've got to make something happen."

Tug McGraw added to the suspense, which wasn't really necessary, in the ninth inning after entering the game to start the seventh. He loaded the bases, then struck out Jose Cardenal to end the game.

Quisenberry, who obviously followed developments of the Cold War between the U.S. and the Soviet Union in those tension-filled years, described the situation facing the Royals, who were now down, three games to two with the Series moving back to Philadelphia. Kansas City's relief ace said, "Now we're up against the Berlin Wall. The East side of it."

The Phillies won their first World Series championship by scoring the first four runs of the game and relying on the skills of their three stars—Carlton, Schmidt, and McGraw. Carlton, after his shaky performance in the second game, came back strong and limited the Royals to four hits in seven innings. With Schmidt driving in two runs, the Phillies were leading, 4–0, when manager Dallas Green called in McGraw for one more gallant pitching demonstration.

McGraw faced adversity, his constant companion, in both the eighth and ninth innings. "The eighth inning was fun," he told the writers later, "but my arm was so tired in the ninth all I wanted was for the Royals to please hit the ball at one of our guys."

The eighth inning may have been fun for McGraw, but it gave the Phillies fans and players ulcers. The Royals scored a run and loaded the bases, so Green went to the mound and told McGraw, "Hey, Tug—let's not make this S.O.B. as overly exciting as we're trying here." McGraw shut the door. Kansas City didn't score.

In the ninth inning, one of the signs cropped up that makes players believe that their team might be destined to win, that maybe this is their year. It happened on a routine pop fly. With one out and the bases loaded in Kansas City's ninth inning, Frank White hit a pop-up into the air in foul territory in front of the Phillies dugout. Boone dashed over from his catcher's position and camped under it. Rose came in from first base to stand by.

Boone held out his mitt and the ball routinely plopped into it—and then out of it. Horror of horrors for the Phillies fans in the crowd of 65,838! They gasped as they saw the ball in the air again. Rose calmed their nerves by swooping in and snagging the ball himself. Two outs, and the Phillies' fans and players were beginning to think that maybe they were destined to win this World Series after all.

Willie Wilson, the speedster who could get on base with a bunt almost by just wishing for it, was the next hitter. McGraw worked Wilson to a 1–2 count, then struck him out. The Phillies were baseball's world champions.

An exhausted McGraw said, "I don't know what Dallas had in mind, but if I didn't get Wilson I was calling him to the mound because I had nothing left. Nothing."

Then he looked back at the season and the moment. "I think this is the proudest I'll ever be as a baseball player," he said. "It took us a few months under Dallas Green to catch on to what he was saying, but then we got the program together. To me, Dallas is one helluva man. Now, if you'll excuse me, I need to get back to the clubhouse, where there's more champagne."

As Phillies' fans celebrated outside, Wilson hung his head in dejection in the visitors' dressing room. Wilson, who hit .154 in the Series and struck out 12 times in 26 at bats, sat in front of his locker and said, "I'm holding my head down because I let people down. I feel bad about it. All the stories about me not getting on base put extra pressure on me. I tried too hard. You go out there and try to do things that maybe you can't do. You try to hit the ball hard when you don't have to hit the ball hard. I didn't strike out 12 times in six games in I don't know how long . . . I'm a bad loser."

Wilson wasn't the only Kansas City player who cooled off in the World

Series. Frank White hit .545 in the playoffs but only .080 in the Series, with two singles in 25 times at bat. Wilson could have found comfort in his overall statistics for the season. He hit .326, second only to Brett on the Royals, and led the league with 230 hits and 133 runs scored.

Brett, who hit .375 in the Series with nine hits in the six games, including two doubles, a triple, and his postsurgery home run, said, "It's tough to lose in the playoffs because when you lose you don't get to the World Series. I could forget about losing in the playoffs now. Playing in the World Series is something you cherish. When I get old and gray, I'm going to tell my grandchildren that I was in the World Series, not that I lost the championship series."

In the winners' dressing room, Tug McGraw held an ice pack on his left arm and a bottle of champagne in his right hand as he told reporters and broadcasters, "In the eighth inning, I felt in command, but the last inning had me so shook up I can't remember much about it."

Then McGraw talked about Pete Rose's Johnny-on-the-spot catch of White's pop-up after it bounced up out of Boone's mitt. "That made me feel things were going my way," he said. "And that catch saved me a few pitches, too, although I wasn't surprised that Pete caught it. He does things like that."

Two weeks later, an old superstition that the Democrats win the presidential election when the National League wins the World Series and the Republicans move into the White House when the American League wins the Series was exploded. President Carter lost the election in a landslide to Ronald Reagan, the former baseball announcer on Radio Station WHO in Des Moines, Iowa. The superstition had held up in twelve of the previous fifteen presidential elections dating back to World War I and had been true in nine of the previous ten election years before 1980, missing only when Truman upset Dewey in 1948.

PART EIGHT
· · ·
1995

21

Baseball's Second Savior

On the morning of April 1, 1995, Father Bill Metzdorf stood in the pulpit at Our Lady of Mercy church in Potomac, Maryland, with a smile on his face. He told the congregation assembled in front of him on that sunny morning that everyone in the church had two reasons to be especially happy:

1. Dave Gilbert and Katy Christopher were getting married.
2. The baseball strike was about to end.

As my wife, Lillian, and I sat in the front row across the aisle from Katy's parents, Mel and Lou Christopher, many of those in the church knew why Father Bill would begin his homily at a wedding that day by talking about baseball. Dave, our son, has a baseball background as a shortstop, second baseman, and pitcher from the first grade into college. "Father Bill," as coincidence would have it, has one too. His ambition in high school was to become a baseball play-by-play announcer. He worked for the Associated Press during the Baltimore Orioles' World Series appearances in 1969 and 1970 but then decided to become a priest. Father Bill simply was unable to contain his enthusiasm at the news that morning that the most disastrous strike in the history of professional sports, one that stretched all the way back almost eight months to the summer before, was finally ending.

Those who knew the young couple or the priest did not consider it out of place or even unexpected for Father Bill to mention the end of the baseball strike right at the start of his homily. He spoke of the value of baseball as a team sport and told the congregation that the lessons Dave had learned in baseball about the importance of working together with others as a team—in sports, on the job, or at home—helped to bring bright promise to the marriage that he and Katy were beginning.

That nasty business of the most destructive work stoppage in the history of American professional sports, one that was 232 days old that morning, finally ended when baseball's owners agreed to an unconditional offer from the players' union. Since the previous August, the owners had been insisting on a "cap" on players' salaries after seeing wages in the Major Leagues rise to an average of $1.2 million per year in 1994.

Such a level constituted runaway inflation in the minds of the senior owners who were old enough to remember the 1940s, '50s, '60s, and '70s—the years before free agency was established. Those were the decades, along with every decade before, when players considered themselves lucky to be earning $20,000 or $30,000 a year, even less in the '40s and '50s, and were happy to supplement their baseball salaries every off-season by selling cars or working in the post office.

The mere mention of a cap on salaries was always met with stubborn resistance by the players and their union, the Major League Baseball Players Association, and this time was the worst of all. The 1994 season was cut short in mid-August after only 114 games and, for the first time in the history of the sport, the World Series was canceled, something even two world wars couldn't cause.

By April, as the public's patience wore thinner with each passing day and even President Clinton expressed his disappointment, the players said they were willing to start the 1995 season without a new labor agreement with management. They said they would report to spring training in Florida and Arizona two days later so the season could begin on April 24, three weeks later than scheduled. The season would be shortened to 144 games instead of the usual 162.

Owners and players alike were anxious to get back to playing baseball while continuing to negotiate their differences about a new labor-management agreement at the bargaining table. The chief executive officer of the Seattle Mariners, John Ellis, told the Associated Press, "It's what should be done." Mike Ilitch, owner of the Detroit Tigers, said, "It's the right thing for the fans."

Donald Fehr, the head of the Players' Association, expressed optimism that owners and players could agree to a long-term agreement while the 1995 season got under way. "I would like to believe we'll be able to work this out very quickly," he said. "The opportunity is there to begin rebuilding the game now, without waiting. Hopefully, we've learned something from the last seven or eight months."

Ben McDonald, a pitcher for the Orioles, said, "This has been a very frustrating thing for the fans, for us and the owners. I'm just glad it's over so we can get back to doing what we do best—playing baseball."

Three weeks later, on the day before the Florida Marlins played the Los Angeles Dodgers at Joe Robbie Stadium in Miami in the first major league baseball game in eight months, the manager of the Marlins, Rene Lachemann, sounded a blunt warning to those in his sport. "A lot of damage has been done to the fans—a lot of fans aren't going to come back to the game," he said. "We're going to see it in attendance. We have to go back and make an effort to bring the fans back. It's going to take more than signing autographs. Baseball has to go get the young people."

Or, as Yogi Berra put it, "If people don't want to come to the ballpark, there's no way you're going to stop them."

Both parties—the owners and the players—were close to a new labor agreement, but in addition to the lingering question about a salary cap, there was another major issue: what kind of a system should be established to tax the teams in America's major cities and spread the money from such a tax among the teams in the smaller cities. Those in the sport and those in the media were saying the game needed a share-the-wealth arrangement designed to balance the amount of revenue received by each team and remove the advantage enjoyed by teams in the larger cities whose revenue from radio and television and every other source was far greater than the revenue earned by teams in smaller markets.

Public reaction after the strike, and the negotiations that continued, amounted to a wish for a plague on both their houses. Fans and members of the media blamed both management and labor, owners and players, for the conditions that led to the impasse and were still being debated as the 1995 season got under way.

Shirley Povich, who had been covering Major League Baseball for *The Washington Post* for seventy-three years by this time, going all the way back to 1922, seemed to reflect the reaction of the public. He criticized the owners for their twenty-year bidding war against each other since free agency had been established in 1975. He wrote that those bidding practices reached the level of absurdity when the New York Mets signed Bobby Bonilla that year for $7 million "for hitting .300 only sometimes."

Povich continued, "As for the ballplayers, they are offering to return to work under the same conditions they had when they quit last August. After eight months of useless, expensive, boorish bargaining, they have progressed all the way back to square one. Humph."

Luck, or Divine Intervention, was on baseball's side. When the shortened season started, a baseball Moses was waiting in the wings to lead baseball back to the land of milk and honey. If Cal Ripken of the Baltimore Orioles played in his team's first 122 games, he would break one of the most sacred records in baseball. He would scale Lou Gehrig's supposedly insurmountable Mount Everest—playing in 2,130 consecutive games.

By that year, most people in baseball expected Ripken to accomplish the impossible, but few ever dreamed that his feat would have the impact it did. Ripken, we know now, was about to step into the same role in 1995 that Babe Ruth stepped into seventy-five years earlier, in 1920—as baseball's savior.

Fate played tricks with us again, however, with the result that the minds of Americans everywhere were no longer on the baseball strike or on Cal Ripken either, as Opening Day approached. Instead, they were on America's heartland.

On the morning of April 19, with the start of the big-league baseball season only five days away, a terrible blast rocked Oklahoma City just after nine o'clock, destroying the Alfred P. Murrah Federal Building and inflicting heavy damage on six other buildings. Some 168 people were killed, including more than 12 children at a day care center on the second floor of the building. More than 500 persons were injured. Local, state, and federal authorities on the scene immediately identified the explosion as an act of terrorism and said it was the worst such crime in the history of the United States until that time.

The explosion came from a truck bomb and blew out the north side of the nine-story concrete building. Reporter Sue Anne Pressley of *The Washington Post* said it "quickly turned the placid, tree-shaded downtown into a scene more reminiscent of the aftermath of bombings in Beirut or Tel Aviv."

Only ninety minutes later, Timothy McVeigh, an American soldier in the Gulf War five years earlier, was arrested at a routine traffic stop sixty miles away near Billings, Oklahoma, and was charged with a firearms violation. Two days later, McVeigh was charged in the bombing itself, only hours before he was expected to make bail on the firearms charge. On the same day, an army buddy of McVeigh, Terry Nichols, surrendered in Herington, Kansas, after learning that police were looking for him. The two men were indicted by a grand jury on August 10 on charges of murder and conspiracy. Both were convicted. Nichols was sentenced to life in prison after hearing the judge call him "an enemy of the Constitution." McVeigh was sentenced to death.

In an editorial that became a prophecy on September 11, 2001, *The Washington Post* said the day after the Oklahoma City bombing, "If it turns out to have had a political motive as the World Trade Center explosion had [the first one, in 1993], the only effect can be to strengthen Americans' resolve to stand by the allegiances and policies that are under terrorist attack."

Exactly fifty years after the 1945 All-Star Game was canceled while Americans and Japanese fought each other during that final year of World War II, a Japanese man was the starting pitcher for the National League in the 1995 game. From the pitcher's mound at the ballpark of the Texas Rangers in Arlington, Hideo Nomo, a twenty-six-year-old right-hander from Osaka whose first name means "Hero," threw the first pitch. It was 9:30 A.M., Tokyo time, and Japan's national hero was being cheered on by thousands if not millions of his countrymen in public gathering places all over his native land.

They braved a morning rain and stood in public squares across their country looking up at TV screens three stories high to watch the one they called "the Tornado," who was now a rookie star with the Los Angeles Dodgers after completing the journey up the Japanese baseball ladder from his first year with the Kintetsu Buffaloes in Japan's Pacific League. He was the first Japanese baseball player to become such a talked-about celebrity in what the Japanese fans call the "Big League," their term for America's Major Leagues. One other, Masanori Murakami, pitched for the San Francisco Giants in 1964 and 1965. Nomo became a marquee name before the season even started, by receiving a bonus of $2 million for signing with the Dodgers.

His success in the first half of the season had perked up the interest of the fans and the media, even if it didn't show at the gate. Attendance was down 22 percent from 1994, and estimates were already being heard that the twenty-eight teams might lose anywhere from $300 million to $400 million, and that would be on top of $700 million lost in 1994 after the season was canceled in mid-August along with the playoffs and the World Series.

In Japan, where there was no strike, the fans had some of the same reasons that their American counterparts had in turning to baseball that year. Conditions were difficult there, too, and for many of the same reasons—a recession, natural disaster, and terrorism. One of the fans watching in the drizzle in Tokyo, Hideki Nomura, was sitting on a wet patch of pavement. "I can't really say it's comfortable here," he told Reporter T. R. Reid of *The Washington Post,* "but what the heck—there's no way I would miss this game."

The newspapers agreed. One paper that morning published a bold banner reading:

THIS MORNING, THE HISTORY OF AMERICAN BASEBALL WILL CHANGE!

Interest in Nomo's appearance in the All-Star Game was so strong in Japan that the game was televised live on two networks. After his two innings, one Japanese network ended the live portion of its telecast and began running replays of Nomo's performance.

Nomo, who packed 210 pounds on a six-foot two-inch frame, baffled his American League opponents in the game as much as he did his National League foes all season long. He shut them out in his two innings and left with the game tied, 0–0. His National Leaguers won, 3–2, in a game in which fifteen pitchers appeared.

The game did not represent Nomo's peak for the season. He continued his success throughout the second half, finished with a record of thirteen wins and six losses, and led the National League pitchers with 236 strikeouts and three shutouts. Under manager Tommy Lasorda, the Dodgers won the National League West championship but were swept by the Cincinnati Reds in three games in the first round of the playoffs.

In the same city where Hideo Nomo had caused so much excitement the month before, Mickey Mantle died on August 13. He succumbed to a lengthy series of illnesses including liver cancer, hepatitis C, and cancer of the lungs. The manager of Mantle's old team, Buck Showalter of the

Yankees, told the team's radio announcers in a pregame interview, "It's almost like a part of your childhood has been taken away. I don't care if you're from the south, the north, the east or the west, kids grew up wanting to be a switch-hitting outfielder for the New York Yankees. I know I did." He said he used to stand in front of the family TV set in Florida when he was six years old in 1962 and imitate Mantle's swing.

One of Showalter's players, first baseman Don Mattingly, etched the number 7—Mantle's number—on the back of his cap. Flags flew at half-staff at Yankee Stadium for the game that day.

Fans, writers, and broadcasters all were able to marvel at Mantle's accomplishments over eighteen seasons with the Yankees as their successor to Joe DiMaggio—536 home runs, 1,509 runs batted in, 1,677 runs scored, 2,415 hits, and three times the American League's Most Valuable Player, in '56, '57, and '62.

"The Mick" led the American League in home runs four times, hit more than fifty home runs twice, played in the second most World Series games, has the second most Series hits, and holds the records for the most World Series home runs, runs scored, runs batted in, and walks. And then there's this, the mark of a winner: he led the Yankees to twelve pennants and seven World Series championships

Americans everywhere had watched Mantle's final struggle, because of his superstar status and because he was, well, because he was Mickey Mantle. He had always been one of the most popular figures in baseball while also being one of its greatest players.

It was the tragedy of "the Mick" that an athlete who could conquer heights undreamed of by mere mortals could not conquer alcohol. By his own admission, he drank too much during his playing days, and when he retired and discovered how much he missed the camaraderie of his teammates and opponents, in the clubhouse and the dugout, at home and on the road, he drank even more.

Most of those in baseball were not surprised. His former teammate, outfielder Hank Bauer, told Bob Allen in an interview for our book, *The 500 Home Run Club,* that Mantle was "a lonely man. He was well known throughout the world, and anywhere he went he got bothered. As a result, a lot of times, Mickey didn't go anywhere. He'd stay in his room and evidently the four walls closed in on him and the outcome was the bottle."

Mantle tried to save himself from himself by enrolling in a twenty-eight-day program at the Betty Ford Center at Rancho Mirage, California, in early 1994 after his doctors told him his next drink might be his last. When he completed the program, he taped television public service announcements urging heavy drinkers to stop before it was too late. In what amounted to a deathbed confession, Mantle said, "God gave me a great body to play with, and I didn't take care of it. And I blame a lot of it on alcohol."

At a press conference only weeks before he died at Baylor University Hospital, Mantle pleaded, "Don't be like me."

22

"The Streak"

As August turned into September and the vacation season neared its end with the approach of Labor Day weekend, baseball, despite all of its problems, was becoming one of America's favorite topics of conversation again, thanks to Cal Ripken, Jr., the six-foot four-inch shortstop of the Baltimore Orioles.

The Orioles weren't going anywhere in 1995. They finished in third place in the American League East, two games under .500 with 71 wins and 73 losses. Ripken, as usual, was the heart of the team. He hit 17 home runs and led the league's shortstops in fielding and in turning in the most double plays.

By September Ripken had played in more than 2,100 consecutive games and was only a few days away from breaking one of the supposedly unbreakable records of his sport, Lou Gehrig's "Iron Man" achievement of playing in 2,130 straight games. There had been talk off and on beginning several years before that he just might do the impossible. Now he was a cinch to do it, but only after a last-minute complication that could have prevented him from reaching Gehrig's number. The complication was that same villain: the strike.

If the owners had decided to start the 1995 season on time with replacement players while the labor impasse dragged on, Cal's streak would have been snapped at 2,009 games. It was suggested that nobody would hold it against Cal if he played despite the strike, but Ripken responded by saying he would go along with the players union even if it meant ending his streak. The decision to start the season made it possible for

Ripken to continue his streak and then break Gehrig's record, the achievement that saved the sport for owners and players alike, almost in spite of themselves.

Every newspaper in the country was writing about *The Streak.* Every sportscast was covering it. The Orioles hung an enormous banner on the facing of the warehouse-style building which housed their offices just beyond the right field wall at Camden Yards, on the same ground where Babe Ruth romped as a kid. In numbers that seemed a mile high, the banner had no words on it, just the number of consecutive games for Ripken as of that night. On Labor Day, September 5, the banner proclaimed simply but eloquently:

2,130

VIPs from every walk of life were going to be on hand at Oriole Park at Camden Yards the next night to witness the historic moment, everyone from the president of the United States himself to Gehrig's teammate who knew something about breaking records himself, Joe DiMaggio. America was talking baseball again.

The streak had begun thirteen years earlier, on May 30, 1982. John Hinckley's trial for shooting President Reagan was being conducted in Washington. Computers were just beginning to show up as part of the facilities in American homes, and they weren't cheap. A new Apple III cost $2,999—with a green monitor. Marc Fisher remembered in *The Washington Post* that CDs were still only something you bought at the bank. Videocassette recorders—they weren't called VCRs yet—cost $700 or more.

The Orioles had won 22 games and lost 23 after splitting a doubleheader with the Toronto Blue Jays on Saturday, May 29, and then losing their Sunday game with Ripken playing third base, his position in the minor leagues. Baltimore's manager, Earl Weaver, rested his young infielder in the second game of the Saturday doubleheader but inserted him back into the lineup on Sunday. He went hitless in two trips to the plate as the Orioles lost, 6–0. What was to become the most acclaimed streak in the history of American sports was born.

Comedian Woody Allen once remarked that success comes mostly from just showing up, and Ripken from the start compiled a set of numbers that made him qualify for any award for showing up. He played in

160 games as a rookie that year and came to bat 598 times, but even from the start of his streak, Ripken was doing more than merely showing up. In that rookie season, he hit .264, hit 28 home runs, drove in 93 runs and scored 90. He was the solid choice for the American League's Rookie of the Year award, finishing ahead of such future stars as Wade Boggs and Kent Hrbek in the voting.

He topped himself in his second year, the season when outstanding rookies often fall victim to what baseball people call the "sophomore jinx" as the league's pitchers and fielders make adjustments against a rookie from the year before because of what they learned about his habits during his first season.

Ripken did just the opposite in his sophomore season. He raised his batting average 54 points to .318, hit 27 home runs, and drove in nine more runs, raising his total to 102 RBIs. In the field, playing exclusively at shortstop instead of dividing his time between short and third, Ripken led the league's shortstops in assists, total chances, chances without an error, and double plays.

It came as no surprise, then, that he was selected as the league's Most Valuable Player, the first man to win the Rookie of the Year and MVP awards back-to-back. He was named to the American League All-Star team. By season's end he led both leagues with 211 hits and 47 doubles. And he was fast becoming one of the leaders on a championship team. The Orioles won the pennant that year, then became baseball's world champions by defeating the Philadelphia Phillies in the World Series in five games. Ripken caught a line drive at shortstop for the out that ended the Series.

During part of his streak, Ripken had the pleasure and the distinction of playing for his father, Cal Ripken, Sr., who became the Orioles' skipper in 1987. The team became a family affair on July 11, 1987, when Cal Jr.'s younger brother Bill joined the Orioles and became the team's second baseman. When the brothers played next to each other in the middle of the Baltimore infield, they made Cal Sr. the first father in major league history to manage two sons on the same team during the regular season.

Bill was able to handle the pressure of being the superstar's little brother nicely. Having a credible career in the big leagues helped him. He played for the Orioles for six years as one of thirty second basemen who played next to Cal during his streak and also played for the Texas Rangers, Cleveland Indians, and Detroit Tigers. He laughed off the big brother question by saying, "Sometimes somebody in the stands will yell, 'You'll never be as good as your brother!' I just smile and think, 'You got me there! Who is?' "

Brother Bill was reflecting the loyalty and respect he always felt toward his big brother, going back to their days as kids. "When we were growing up," he said as Cal was approaching Gehrig's record, "he'd beat me up. But the great thing about Cal was that he wouldn't allow anyone else to—he was the *only* one who could beat me up."

Seeing three Ripkens in Orioles uniforms was almost predictable. The Ripkens were a baseball family to the very core, starting with Cal Sr.'s lifelong career in the Orioles organization. The family revolved around his years in the minor leagues, his years as Baltimore's third base coach, and his years as the manager of the Orioles, with his sons playing for him on both sides of the second base bag.

The family was steeped in Dad's way, because he was steeped in the Orioles' way—the right way in those years—of doing everything. Cal Sr.'s values and attitudes always seemed to be expressed in what he told his players at the ballpark, the same things he told his family at home: "Practice doesn't make perfect. *Perfect* practice makes perfect." And he held his family and his players to the same high standards. It wasn't good enough to make a nice stop, only to throw the ball past the first baseman. Senior used to tell his sons and his other players, "Don't make half of a great play."

The family grew up in Aberdeen, Maryland, only a few miles from Baltimore. Besides Cal and Bill, the Ripken household included a third son, Fred, and a daughter, Ellen. Their mother, Vi, still marvels that none of the three boys suffered any broken bones when they were children. "I don't know how they got away with it," she said, "because they weren't little bookworms. They all read, don't get me wrong, but they were very, very active kids."

Cal Jr. started playing baseball at the age of eight, partly to please his father. "Everything I seemed to do for a while seemed to be to make him proud of me," he told *USA Weekend*. "I wasn't playing for myself. I knew deep down inside he wanted me to play. I could tell by the look on his face."

Cal Jr. became a star baseball player for Aberdeen High School with a future in professional baseball as either a shortstop or a pitcher. Many said he was good enough to make it all the way to the Major Leagues. The Orioles sized up his potential the same way. They chose him as the forty-eighth pick of the 1978 player draft and assigned him to their farm team in Bluefield, West Virginia.

He progressed to the Orioles' top farm team, in Rochester, New York, and made it all the way to the top—the Orioles—on August 10, 1981, as a third baseman. The next year, Earl Weaver moved Ripken to shortstop, and the streak began.

One of the worst bumps in the road for Cal during his streak, and for brother Bill too, came when the Orioles got off to a miserable start in 1988 and set a record by losing their first 21 games. Cal Sr. was fired after six games, the low point in Junior's career, and Junior went 0-for-29 in April, before pulling himself out of his nosedive by hitting safely in 16 of his next 17 games.

Cal was able to play through his deep disappointment and resume his starring ways, always while never missing a game. In 1990, he set eight major league fielding records including fewest errors by a shortstop when he made only three errors in 161 games. On June 12, he started people talking more seriously than ever about his streak when he passed Everett Scott, Gehrig's predecessor as captain of the Yankees, by playing in his 1,308th straight game.

In 1991, he won the home run hitting contest before the All-Star Game with 12 "homers" in 22 swings, then won the game itself with a three-run shot off his old teammate on the Orioles, Dennis Martinez of the Montreal Expos. He was voted the American League's MVP for the second time and was also chosen as the Major League Player of the Year by *The Sporting News, Baseball Digest,* and the Associated Press. He joined Maury Wills of the Dodgers as the only two players to win those awards plus being chosen as the MVP in the All-Star Game and the winner of the Gold Glove Award as the best fielder at his position, all in the same season.

In '92, Ripken won his second Gold Glove Award, led all players in both leagues with the most votes for the All-Star Game, and continued his streak even though he twisted his right ankle while running out a double against the Milwaukee Brewers. It was his 1,713th straight game, and he played again the next day.

Two other awards that year say even more about Cal, the man. He received the Roberto Clemente Award as the player who most closely reflected Clemente's sportsmanship, community work, and contributions to his team and to baseball. Clemente, a Hall of Fame outfielder with the

Pittsburgh Pirates, was killed in a plane crash in December 1972 while flying to the aid of the people of Nicaragua after that nation was struck by a devastating earthquake.

In what may be the most appropriate award Ripken has ever received, Phi Delta Theta fraternity honored him with its Lou Gehrig Memorial Award as the major league player who best reflected Gehrig's image and character. Gehrig was known, respected, and loved throughout his playing career as a gentleman and a modest, clean-living athlete, the kind who today would be called a "role model." The term didn't exist in Gehrig's time—the 1920s and 1930s—but he qualified for the title as much as anyone could today. In that sense, Ripken and Gehrig were cut from the same mold.

Interrupted by occasional hitting slumps, Ripken nevertheless continued to show up every day, and continued to put together a stellar career. On July 15, 1993, he broke the record for the most home runs by a big-league shortstop, set by Ernie Banks of the Chicago Cubs. In the 1,790th game of his streak, he twisted his right knee when he caught his spikes in the infield grass during a fight between the Orioles and the Seattle Mariners. He stayed in the game but admitted later, "It was the closest I've come to not playing."

When the strike paralyzed the sport in 1994 after 112 Orioles games, Cal was having the best season of his career since his MVP year three years earlier. When the rest of the season was canceled in the middle of August, he was hitting .315, had slugged the three hundredth home run of his career, and led the league in games played, double plays, and fielding percentage for a shortstop.

As the attention on him grew greater through 1994, with the accompanying increase in the demands on him, Ripken continued to win fans for himself and for his sport. He signed autographs before the games and for an hour or more after, until the last fan had been accommodated. He posed for pictures. And he didn't do these things in a mechanical, quiet way. Instead, he engaged the fans in conversation, asking little boys what position they played, asking elementary school girls who their favorite player was, and always looking at them and chatting with them in a friendly manner that went far beyond merely signing something without ever looking up.

As if to make the picture complete, there was even a death threat. A man who said he was Lou Gehrig, Jr., called the Kingdome in Seattle and threatened to kill Ripken if he played in a game there against the

Mariners in August. When the authorities told Cal after the game about the threat, he shrugged it off. "I try to accept it for what it is," he said. "I don't try to deal with it or give it much thought."

When he broke Gehrig's record on September 6, 1995, all America seemed to be there, but what mattered most to family man Cal was that his family was there, even his father, who had not visited the Orioles ballpark since his firing in 1988. The streak could have stopped right there, seven years before Cal broke Gehrig's record, because of Cal's bitter disappointment that his dad was fired. But like everything else during the streak and his entire career, he played through that tough time, too, and the streak went on.

A look back at what happened in America and in the world during the sixteen years of the streak emphasizes both its length and the monumental dimensions of Ripken's accomplishment. It began in the second year of Ronald Reagan's eight years as president, the year when seven people in Chicago died from taking Tylenol pills laced with cyanide. Over the years of the streak that followed, astronaut Sally Ride became the first woman to fly in space; the United States invaded Grenada; the baseball players went on strike for two days in 1985 in opposition to the owners' proposal for a salary cap; the *Challenger* space shuttle exploded only minutes after it was launched, killing all seven crew members; the Branch Davidian compound in Waco, Texas, was raided by FBI agents and later burned down, killing at least 75 persons; race riots erupted in Los Angeles; the Soviet Union collapsed; America fought and won a war against Iraq; Pete Rose was banned from baseball for gambling; O.J. Simpson was arrested for the murder of his former wife and a friend; and three presidents were elected.

Then it was *the* night, his 2,131st straight game. President Clinton was there, and for him the occasion amounted to a night out with the boys, bringing him relief from everything that was going on in Washington, Europe, China, and elsewhere. First Lady Hillary Rodham Clinton was addressing an international women's forum in China and criticizing the Chinese government for denying women their human rights. Her appearance almost caused an international incident. President Clinton's secretary of health and human services, Donna Shalala, had to push her way through a line of Chinese guards to get inside a theater to hear the First Lady speak.

A Senate subcommittee in Washington was investigating the killing of a woman during an FBI raid in Ruby Ridge, Idaho, in 1992. NATO warplanes bombed targets in central Bosnia. The Senate Ethics Committee voted unanimously to recommend that the chairman of the Finance Committee, Bob Packwood, a popular and respected Republican from Oregon, be expelled from the Senate for sexual and official misconduct. In Los Angeles, Detective Mark Fuhrman refused to answer when he was asked in the O.J. Simpson murder trial if he had planted any evidence against Simpson. Instead, Fuhrman invoked his rights under the Fifth Amendment.

A night at the ballpark seemed to be just what American needed. Joe DiMaggio was there. So was Brooks Robinson, the Orioles Hall of Fame third baseman and, like Ripken, one of the most popular players ever to play the game anywhere. Earl Weaver, their Hall of Fame manager who guided the Orioles to four American League pennants and a World Series championship, was there too. Branford Marsalis and Bruce Hornsby played a duet of the National Anthem. The whole Ripken fam-

With the number of his consecutive games showing on the wall behind the right field fence, Cal Ripken celebrated by hitting a home run on the night he broke Lou Gehrig's record for playing in the most games in a row. It happened on September 6, 1995. (© Richard Lasner Photo.)

ily was on hand—Cal's parents; his wife, Kelly; their kids, Rachel, their five-year-old daughter, and Ryan, their two-year-old son; and Cal's brothers and sister.

It was a night that had everything, including a home run by Cal on a 3–0 pitch when his manager, Phil Regan, flashed the hit sign. The game, the home run, and the Streak entered the history books in indelible ink at 9:20 P.M. when the second baseman for the Orioles, Manny Alexander, caught a pop-up by Damion Easley of the California Angels in short right field to end the Angels' fifth inning. The crowd began cheering while the ball was still in the air. When it settled into Easley's glove, the game became official, meeting the rule book's stipulation that a game is official when four and a half innings have been completed and the home team is leading. The numbers on the banner on the warehouse wall were changed to tell the story in simple, dramatic terms:

2,131

At that moment, a message was flashed by the Associated Press to news rooms all over America:

BULLETIN
By Ben Walker
AP Baseball Writer

BALTIMORE—Cal Ripken broke Lou Gehrig's unbreakable record Wednesday night when he played his 2,131st consecutive game, becoming the most dependable, most durable athlete in the history of America's oldest sport.

23

Two of a Kind

The reaction of the sellout crowd of 46,272 fans was immediate and prolonged. The applause lasted twenty-two minutes and fifteen seconds. Fireworks exploded. The game was halted. The pitchers and catchers in the Orioles' bullpen dashed onto the infield. The Angels stood in their dugout and on the field and joined in the applause. The announcers for the national telecast on ESPN, Chris Berman and Buck Martinez, did what good announcers do—they let the picture tell the story. They remained silent for the entire twenty-two minutes. Berman then called it "a moment that will live for 2,131 years."

Another ESPN commentator, Peter Gammons, immediately recognized the enormous value in goodwill that Ripken was restoring to baseball that night. "This is one of the major parts of the road back," he said. "Bud Selig and Don Fehr [the acting commissioner of baseball and the head of the players' union] are here. Maybe they'll announce an agreement at home plate."

Selig was willing to admit the significance of Ripken's achievement in helping to save baseball after the disastrous strike. "The recovery was much more difficult than we thought it was going to be," he said. "Baseball is forever grateful to Cal Ripken, because that moment played an enormous role in our recovery. We really needed something historical and positive. September 6 was the event that did it."

The president of the American League, Gene Budig, echoed Selig's sentiments, saying, "He gave the game life during its darkest hour."

Caught up in the magic of the moment, Ripken didn't seem to know exactly what to do, an understandable reaction since no one had ever been in that position before. He went back to the Baltimore dugout on the first base side of Oriole Park after the Angels' fifth inning, but then his teammates shoved him back onto the field to take a curtain call. The roar continued, so they shoved him back there seven more times.

In between curtain calls, Cal walked over to the seats behind home plate and shared the moment with Kelly and their kids. He gave Kelly a kiss, and gave his cap to Rachel and his uniform shirt to Ryan. It wasn't the kids' first moment in the spotlight that night. Before the game, they threw out the ceremonial first pitch—with Dad as their catcher. Cal looked up to the highest point in the ballpark, to the box where his parents were watching, and gave Dad the thumbs-up sign. Then he returned to the Orioles' dugout—or tried to.

His teammates wouldn't hear of it. First baseman Rafael Palmeiro and infielder-outfielder Bobby Bonilla pushed him back up the steps and onto the field in the foul territory near first base and told Ripken to run a victory lap along the edge of the stands around the infield and outfield. Ripken explained after the game, "They said 'We'll never get this game started [again] unless you run around the field.' "

Ripken told reporters at his postgame news conference, "I said I didn't have the energy to make it. They said, 'You can walk.' " So he walked, and trotted, stopping many times along the way to chat, shake hands, even take time to sign a few autographs. There was an electricity in the air between player and fans, a feeling that seemed to transmit itself to the crowd and even to the radio and television audiences at home.

Ripken described the experience as more than a victory lap. He called it "intimate" and "very spontaneous." He said seeing the enthusiasm firsthand was "very meaningful." Always one to do more than just the minimum in his dealings with his fans, he shook hands not just with fans but with members of the ground crew, police officers, and others. He made sure to touch hands with his longtime pal, Ellie Hendricks, the Orioles' veteran bullpen coach, who had seen every game of the streak. He also shook hands with the California players and coaches who had left their dugout on the third base side and instead were lined up in front of it. He ended his victory lap where you might expect, back with his family. Then he went back to the Orioles dugout, but only for a moment. The crowd coaxed him into one final curtain call.

★   ★   ★

There was a ceremony after the game, when Cal's teammates from his first year with the Orioles were introduced: Ken Singleton, Rick Dempsey, Rich Dauer, and Dan Ford. Ripken and members of his family received a variety of gifts, including a mahogany pool table from his current teammates and a lawn stone etched with the numbers "2131." The owner of the Orioles, Peter Angelos, gave his star an engraved piece of Waterford crystal, plus a Chevy Tahoe.

Brooks Robinson, the Orioles' Hall of Fame third baseman, said to the crowd, "I played baseball here in Baltimore for over twenty years, and they called me 'Mr. Oriole.' But now, Cal Ripken, you're 'Mr. Oriole.'"

Joe DiMaggio told the crowd, "Wherever my former teammate, Lou Gehrig, is today, I'm sure he's tipping his cap to you, Cal Ripken."

The praise was showered down on Ripken from every corner. President Clinton said, "I admire him not only for his talent, but for his constant determination day in and day out. He's been loyal to his team, his fans, the community and professional sports every phase of his career. His determination and talent have been great for baseball and America." Proving that presidents are fans, too, Clinton told Jon Miller, the Orioles' radio announcer who now broadcasts the Sunday night baseball games on ESPN, "I'm not ashamed to say I asked him for an autograph."

NBC sportscaster Bob Costas said that Ripken and Gehrig "are both so extraordinary that I can't say enough good things about either one of them." Then he made a telling point: "A lot of fans seem to fret that by Cal's setting this record, he will somehow obscure Gehrig's place in history, which I disagree with. History matters more in baseball than in any other sport, and Cal's approaching this record enabled a new generation of fans to learn more about Gehrig than they may possibly otherwise ever have."

Cal's fellow players were unabashed in expressing their admiration. Brother Bill said, "I hope he goes two more years after that day [when he breaks the streak], and plays every game. He's not going to go one day over and say, 'Now I need a day off.' That's just not his style. He's going to go as many days as he can to help the ball club win. I hope he goes two or three years past the mark, and keeps on going."

Ozzie Smith, the star shortstop for the St. Louis Cardinals and one of the newest members of the Hall of Fame, said, "To play shortstop every day is not an easy task for anybody, and it actually becomes tougher as you get older. Things break down a little easier . . . You can still do it, but you don't do it as often. That's why, as you get older, you take a few more days off."

Hank Aaron, the home run king who broke Babe Ruth's record with 755 home runs in his career, said, "I've always said that record, along with the Babe Ruth record, are the hardest records I know of to break—those two, and Joe DiMaggio's consecutive-game hitting streak... You've got to be blessed to do what he's done. And, hell, he's been great."

The Orioles' pitching coach that year, Mike Flanagan, Ripken's former teammate, explained Ripken's determination to play every day. "He loves to play," Flanagan said. "He loves to compete. And you can't compete from the dugout."

Ripken himself explained the streak—as well as anyone could—when he told Edward Kiersh of *Inside Sports,* "I've always had a desire to play, to be involved in the activity, even if it was just soccer in high school. I have to be involved actively. I can't just watch. I can't be on the sidelines."

When Kiersh asked Ripken what the streak symbolized, he said, "Dependability. I want to be there in the lineup for the team. I want to be counted on. I don't play the game just for myself."

One of the most significant and authoritative comments came from a man in Japan named Sachio Kinugasa. He was a catcher and third baseman in the Japan League and played in 2,215 straight games. He took an unselfish attitude toward Ripken and said, "I'm happy for Ripken. He's got a work ethic rare in the modern Major Leagues." Kinugasa said Ripken was a throwback to "the days before the free-agent system in American baseball, when players stuck around long enough to become the pride of their town."

One item of unfinished business remained—the ball that Ripken hit over the left field fence for a home run against the Angels' starting pitcher, Shawn Boskie. Bryan Johnson was sitting with his girlfriend in section 78, row K, when Ripken came to bat. As the long fly ball sailed off his bat and toward their seats, Johnson turned to his girlfriend and said, "Get ready to catch it, because I don't know if I can." She knew why—Johnson had a broken right hand and was wearing a cast on it.

Johnson told reporters later, "It bounced once. I grabbed it with my left hand. About eight other people started grabbing it. I held on for dear life." Then, like Secret Service agents guarding a president, members of the Orioles organization escorted him out of the stands and to the lower concourse. Reporters tried to ask questions. A fan offered $4,000 for the ball. Johnson refused, even after the man increased his offer to $5,000. Ushers spirited Johnson to the team's offices in the warehouse, as the fan called out, "Six thousand! . . . Seven!"

Johnson wouldn't yield. He said, "This is Cal's moment. It's a perfect moment."

One of the Orioles' representatives asked him, "What do you want for it?"

Johnson answered, "Just one thing. Just to meet Cal."

Johnson stood firm, and at 2:30 A.M. in the team's family room, Johnson was introduced to his hero. "I met Cal," he said. "I congratulated him. I gave him the ball. We had a nice little talk. He thanked me."

Ripken did more than that. He gave Johnson one of his bats and autographed it. Not just with his name, but with a personal message to go along with it: "Brian, thank you very much for the ball. It means a lot to me. We both share the same memory."

In 1939 shortly after the doctors at the Mayo Clinic diagnosed Lou Gehrig's illness, amyotrophic lateral sclerosis—known ever since as "Lou Gehrig's disease"—a fatal illness, his team honored him with a special day at Yankee Stadium on July 4. With his typical modesty and sincerity, Gehrig, knowing his days were numbered, leaned into the microphones at home plate and spoke the words that every baseball fan today can recite: "Today I consider myself the luckiest man on the face of the earth."

Fifty-six years later, a sign at Oriole Park on the night Cal Ripken broke Gehrig's streak said:

WE CONSIDER OURSELVES
THE LUCKIEST FANS ON THE FACE OF THE EARTH

The similarity to Gehrig's farewell words was both striking and fitting. Lou Gehrig and Cal Ripken were cut from the same mold and revered the same way by those fortunate enough to come into contact with them. When Ripken broke Gehrig's streak, the comparisons flowed freely.

Shirley Povich told his readers in *The Washington Post*, "Not by his super play alone, or by his work ethic, has Ripken renewed America's interest in baseball. The nation found a new interest in the man himself, who exemplifies the family values that politicos only talk about; who dedicated himself to making friends with the fans, so important to the game, a rebuke to overpaid colleagues who had no time for such; who, when the question was put to him point blank the other day, his modesty shined through and he said, 'Lou Gehrig was a better ballplayer than I am.' "

Ripken was being modest. Both men were respected all-stars, known for their fielding as well as their hitting. Ripken was a star with his glove, forcing a revision in the attitude that any man who was six four should play first base or in the outfield, but not shortstop. That was the domain of the smaller, quicker infielders—until Ripken came along. Gehrig, too, was a better than average fielder.

During the thirteen years leading up to the night Ripken broke Gehrig's record for playing in the most consecutive games, he had more extra base hits than anyone else in the Major Leagues—809. He was third in home runs during those years, second in runs batted in, fourth in runs scored, third in hits, and second in doubles. In those categories he was ranked with such hitting stars as Eddie Murray, Andre Dawson, Dave Winfield, Harold Baines, Rickey Henderson, Paul Molitor, Wade Boggs, Kirby Puckett, Don Mattingly, and George Brett.

Gehrig was such a feared hitter that he, not Babe Ruth, was the cleanup hitter in the Yankees' "Murderers Row." He achieved, and that's the right word for it, a lifetime batting average of .340 in seventeen major league seasons, including 493 home runs, and surely would have been a member of the prestigious "500 Home Run Club" if he had not been struck down by ALS in 1939 at the age of thirty-seven. He missed 500 by only 7 homers. He hit in the .370s three times and led the league with .363 in 1934. He also led the league in doubles twice, triples once, home runs three times, runs scored four times, and runs batted in five times, including 184 RBIs in 1931.

When it came to determination to be in the lineup every day, the two men were like twins. From 1982 to 1987, Ripken played in 8,243 straight innings, believed to be the major league record. During Ripken's streak of consecutive games, some 3,712 major league players were placed on the disabled list because of injuries, but never Ripken. He played through several injuries, including problems with his right ankle and knee.

Gehrig played with broken fingers, sprains, pulled muscles, torn tendons, lumbago, and high fevers. He was hit in his head by a pitched ball three times during his streak—in those days before batting helmets. When his streak finally ended, doctors X-rayed his hands and discovered seventeen fractures that had healed by themselves. Tommy Henrich, Gehrig's teammate in the last three years of his streak, said Gehrig broke every finger on both hands, some of them twice. Henrich said, "He never mentioned any of this to anyone."

The best commentary on Ripken's streak and on Cal came from Cal himself, when he stood at home plate that night and told the capacity crowd and the national television audience exactly what was going through his mind. Ever the professional, he had taken the time and the care to prepare a written text. He told the crowd and the viewers at home:

> When the game numbers on the warehouse changed during fifth innings over the past several weeks, the fans in this ballpark responded incredibly. I'm not sure that my reactions showed how I really felt. I just didn't know what to do. Tonight, I want to make sure you know how I feel.

Then he reminisced about growing up near Baltimore and his boyhood dream of being not just "a big league ballplayer, but also of being a Baltimore Oriole." He thanked the Baltimore fans and also remembered to thank baseball fans everywhere. "I've been cheered in ballparks all over the country," he said. "People not only showed me their kindness, but more importantly, they demonstrated their love of the game of baseball."

He made sure to thank "my Dad." He continued:

> He inspired me with his commitment to the Oriole tradition and made me understand the importance of it. He not only taught me the fundamentals of the game of baseball, but also he taught me to play it the right way, and to play it the Oriole way. From the very beginning, my Dad let me know how important it was to be there for your team and to be counted on by your teammates.
>
> My Mom—what can I say about my Mom? She is an unbelievable person. She let my Dad lead the way on the field, but she was there in every other way—leading and shaping the lives of our family off the field. She's the glue who held our lives together while we grew up, and she's always been my inspiration.

On the night he broke Lou Gehrig's record by playing in his 2,131st consecutive game, Cal Ripken credited Eddie Murray, his teammate of eight years, for showing Ripken "how to play this game, day in and day out." (John Cordes/National Baseball Hall of Fame Library, Cooperstown, N.Y.)

Ripken paid tribute to his friend and teammate of eight seasons, Eddie Murray, "who showed me how to play this game, day in and day out." Then he thanked his wife, Kelly, "for the advice, support and joy you have brought to me, and for always being there. You, Rachel and Ryan are my life."

Ripken saluted the man whose record he had just broken:

> Tonight I stand here, overwhelmed, as my name is linked with the great and courageous Lou Gehrig. I'm truly humbled to have our names spoken in the same breath.
>
> Some may think our strongest connection is because we both played many consecutive games. Yet I believe in my heart that our true link is a common motivation—a love of the game of

baseball, a passion for our team, and a desire to compete on the very highest level.

Then Ripken concluded with words that sounded like Lou Gehrig himself:

> I know that if Lou Gehrig is looking down on tonight's activities, he isn't concerned about someone playing one more consecutive game than he did. Instead he's viewing tonight as just another example of what is good and right about the great American game. Whether your name is Gehrig or Ripken, DiMaggio or Robinson, or that of some youngster who picks up his bat or puts on his glove, you are challenged by the game of baseball to do your very best day in and day out. And that's all I've ever tried to do.
> Thank you.

With his words and his career, Ripken made a prophet out of Thomas Boswell, the respected sports columnist of *The Washington Post*. Three years earlier, in a feature story in *The Washington Post Magazine,* Boswell had written:

> For the rest of the '90s, he may be good for more than baseball. He may remind us of the way we used to live.

And so he did.

But he did so much more than that by the simple timing of his feat. Columnist Hal Bodley wrote in *USA Today,* "Baseball was flickering like a candle in the breeze that enchanted September night when Cal Ripken saved the game. He didn't let the flame go out."

PART NINE
· · ·
1998

24

Expecting the Unexpected

The baseball world was buzzing with speculation by the mid-1990s that someone was going to break the record set by Roger Maris of the Yankees more than thirty years before, when he hit 61 home runs and broke the cherished record of 60 set by the universally popular Babe Ruth in 1927. Not only were more and more people becoming convinced that someone was going to top 61, they were also agreeing on who the most likely candidate was: Mark McGwire.

McGwire began fueling such speculation as early as 1992, when he hit 42 homers for the Oakland A's. On June 10 of that year, he hit a home run against Chris Bosio of the Milwaukee Brewers, the two hundredth homer of McGwire's career. He reached that level faster than all but four other of baseball's most famous and most feared sluggers: Ruth, Harmon Killebrew, Ralph Kiner, and Eddie Mathews.

By the start of the 1997 season, McGwire had stirred the imagination of baseball fans, the media, and his fellow players with seasons of 32, 33, 39 (twice), 42, 49, and 52 home runs. He wasn't simply hitting home runs, either. He was hitting tape-measure jobs. Early in 1997, he hit the longest home run in the history of the Seattle Kingdome—538 feet. Not only that, he hit it against his old college teammate from the University of Southern California, Randy Johnson, the six-foot ten-inch monster on the mound who threw fastballs that were hard to see and even harder to hit.

Then a new challenge developed. Midway through his twelfth season with the Oakland A's, the only big-league team he had played with, the

A's made a blockbuster deal by trading him to the St. Louis Cardinals of the National League for three pitchers on July 31, 1997. New speculation set in immediately: Would he be affected by the adjustment not just to a new team but to a new league, hitting against pitchers he hadn't seen before?

The answer was no. McGwire did more than simply adjust to his new environment. He tied Hank Greenberg and Jimmie Foxx as the three righthanded hitters who hit the most home runs in one season—58. In doing so, he became the only player except Ruth to hit fifty or more home runs in consecutive seasons. Twenty-four of his home runs came after he joined the Cardinals, in only two months. In September he finished strong with 15 home runs, breaking the team's record for the most home runs in one month and putting to rest any questions about adjusting to a new team and a new league.

The Cardinals' management was quick to recognize what McGwire was doing for the team. On September 16, the Cards gave McGwire a contract for $28 million over the next three years, including a signing bonus of $1 million. He could have signed for more with another team, but he wanted to stay with the Cardinals because he liked St. Louis and the fans there. He demonstrated his feelings by donating $1 million a year to a charitable foundation that he formed to help abused children in St. Louis and Southern California. At a news conference to announce the foundation, the big slugger cried and had to pause for thirty seconds at one point to compose himself. Then he looked into the cameras and said, "Let's just say children have a special place in my heart. I just really believe a guy in my position can really help out."

Recognition came from other sources as well. McGwire was chosen by *The Sporting News* as its Sportsman of the Year. His teammates chose him as their Man of the Year for his leadership and his commitment to the team both on and off the field.

By 1998, the talk that he might break the record of 61 homers in a season set by Roger Maris in 1961 was something more than a buzz. It became the subject of open conversation as baseball fans waited for the start of the season, agreeing that the man most likely to break the record was Mark McGwire.

Before the baseball world could start getting excited about McGwire and the beginning of the 1998 season, it had to deal with disheartening news. Harry Caray died.

Caray was one of the best known and best liked broadcasters in baseball, a man who loved good people, good times, and a good baseball game more than anyone else. He made no secret about his zest for fun, and even warned others not to miss the opportunity to have a good time: "I've always said that if you don't have fun while you're here, then it's your fault. You only get to do this once."

His son, Skip, followed his father into baseball broadcasting as the voice of the Atlanta Braves, and Harry's grandson, another Harry who goes by "Chip," is also a baseball broadcaster and was scheduled to join his grandfather in the booth when the senior Harry died. Skip confirmed his father's statement. "There's no person alive," he said, "who got his money's worth better than my old man."

Harry made it to the top the hard way, after becoming an orphan at age eight when his mother died. He never knew his father. He shined shoes to pick up whatever change he could and worked for forty cents a day selling newspapers on street corners. Later he went to work at WJOL, a small radio station in Joliet, Illinois. In 1945 he managed to talk himself into the job of broadcasting the games of the Cardinals in his hometown of St. Louis. The man who was described in later years by Bob Costas as "the sound track of summer" was being heard as far away as Minnesota, Texas, Alabama, Saskatchewan, and throughout the Midwest.

Caray became popular for his unabashed enthusiasm for baseball and became known all over America for starting his broadcasts with, "It's a bee-yoo-tiful day for baseball!" He described the suspense of the Cardinals' home runs with, "It might be—It could be—It IS—a home run!" When the Cubs were on a winning streak and won another one, he declared the victory official by shouting into his microphone, "Cubs win! Cubs win! Cubs win!"

He became known as the most famous singer of "Take Me Out to the Ball Game," performing it at the middle of the seventh inning during every Cubs home game at Wrigley Field. Harry, who changed his name from Harry Christopher Carabina before beginning his broadcasting career, got a kick out of asking people, "What Italian has sung to the most people?"

After they guessed Perry Como or Frank Sinatra or Dean Martin or others, Caray would say with delight, "Me! I sing to 40,000 people every day and countless more on TV and radio."

He was the voice of the Cardinals, the Chicago White Sox, and the Cubs and outdid both Lou Gehrig and Cal Ripken when it came to a consecutive games streak. He didn't miss a game from the start of his career in 1945 until 1987, when he suffered a stroke. Tim Wiles estimated in the Cooperstown *Freeman's Journal* that Caray broadcast 6,676 straight games.

His age was always the subject of uncertainty, another thing that amused him. When he died, estimates ran from seventy-eight to eighty-four. The venerable Satchel Paige, who also delighted in keeping his age a secret, once asked Harry, "How old would you be if you didn't know how old you were?"

In the 1960s, Caray was broadcasting the games of the Chicago White Sox when Bill Veeck was their owner. "There were years," Veeck said, "when Harry was the only star we had. They say guys in his business don't put people in the park. Caray drew more people than any player on the Sox or the opposition."

Curt Smith, author of the definitive book on baseball broadcasters, *Voices of The Game,* has written that proof of Caray's status as a gate attraction was found in his pay check. In 1971, Smith said, Caray earned attendance bonuses of $30,000 in addition to his base salary of $50,000, a handsome sum in those days.

In a magazine feature article about Caray, Smith described him as "the baseball balladeer who dwarfs conventional announcers—the booming presence whom Chicagoans call 'the Mayor of Rush Street,' locale of the Cubs' Wrigley Field. Unlike conventional announcers, he broadcasts from the bleachers from time to time, waves a fish net to snare foul balls and leads fans in a raspy rendition to "Take Me Out to the Ball Game" during every seventh-inning stretch."

Harry died, at a Valentine's Day dinner with his wife, Dutchie, at a restaurant in Rancho Mirage, California. Caray, who rejected all talk about retirement and said he hoped he would die "with my boots on," began to rise from his table to acknowledge several fans who had called out his name, and collapsed. He died five days later without regaining consciousness. It was February, the month when pitchers and catchers report for spring training.

In 1998, Mark McGwire wasted no time in fueling the fires about whether he would break Roger Maris's record. In the fourth inning on Opening Day, he blasted a grand slam against Ramon Martinez of the Dodgers at Busch Stadium in St. Louis. It was the first grand slam ever hit on Opening Day by a Cardinal and powered the Cards to a 6–0 victory. It wasn't even April yet—only March 31—and McGwire already had four runs batted in.

Mark McGwire seems to be measuring the dimensions of one of his 70 home runs in 1998. (Brian Spurlock/National Baseball Hall of Fame Library, Cooperstown, N.Y.)

McGwire didn't slow down. He hit four home runs in his first four games, tying the record set by Willie Mays. In the process he also passed Graig Nettles, the former Yankee third baseman, for the twenty-eighth spot on the all-time home run list with 391. He was due to pass several other players and milestones before the year was out. By the end of April, he had 11 home runs and 32 runs batted in. He hit another home run on May 1 and tied Al Kaline for twenty-sixth place on the all-time list with 399.

A week later, on May 8 at Shea Stadium in New York, McGwire hit his thirteenth home run of the season against the Mets' Rick Reed. It was more than that, however. It was the four hundredth home run of his career, a level that he reached faster than any other player in major league history. Meanwhile, Sammy Sosa, the right fielder for the Chicago Cubs, had seven homers.

For McGwire, the homers were coming at a dizzying pace and proving something to him after an injury-plagued career. "I'm a living example," he told Ronald Blum of the Associated Press, "that you can come back from really bad injuries and you can come back from a bad season."

On both counts, McGwire knew what he was talking about.

He had always hit home runs, starting with his first time at bat in the Little Leagues. But he could throw too, so his father, Dr. John McGwire, a dentist, who was his coach, made him a pitcher. While Mark was playing catch with Dad in their back yard, he broke his father's thumb.

The home runs kept coming, regardless of whether Mark was a pitcher or playing another position. By the time he was ten, young Mark had 18 home runs in thirty games. When he was a teenager, people were talking not only about how many homers he had but how far they were going. They were beginning to make him sound like a young Paul Bunyan. He actually hit one of his homers out of the county. While he was playing a game in Los Angeles County, Mark hit a long fly ball over a fence 350 feet from home plate. It kept right on going, cleared a cluster of trees and finally landed across the street in San Bernardino County.

Even after an attack of mononucleosis, Mark's high school baseball career was good enough that he was drafted by the Montreal Expos, but he turned down their offer of $8,500 so he could attend USC. As a nineteen-year-old sophomore pitcher, McGwire compiled a better record than his teammate Randy Johnson. He led the Trojans' staff with a 2.78 earned run average. He divided his time between the mound and first base and set a USC record by hitting 19 home runs in only fifty-three games. When baseball was made an Olympic sport in 1984, McGwire was chosen as the first baseman for the USA team, along with Will Clark, another home-run hitting first baseman headed for the Major Leagues. The Oakland A's drafted Mark for the 1985 season.

After an apprenticeship in the minors, McGwire led the American League in home runs in his first full season, 1987, with 49. As a twenty-three-year-old first baseman, he was six feet five inches tall, weighed 215 pounds, and had twenty-inch biceps that prompted other players to call him "Popeye."

When McGwire teamed up with Jose Canseco to become the formidable combination known as "the Bash Brothers," the A's won the American League pennant three years in a row, from 1988 through 1990. They swept the San Francisco Giants in four games in 1989 in a Series delayed for almost two weeks when a devastating earthquake struck San Francisco.

Those Series were painful experiences for McGwire. Even though he continued to have starring years during the regular season, his World Series performances were disappointing. In thirteen games, he hit only one home run and drove in only two runs. His combined batting average in forty-eight times at bat was .188. He had only nine hits—the homer, a double, and seven singles.

After the A's were swept by the Cincinnati Reds in the 1990 Series, while McGwire hit only .214 with three singles, no home runs, and no runs batted in, McGwire's career plunged to its low point in 1991. That was when he began to learn something about himself, and did something about it.

He hit only .201, a batting average so low for a star hitter that it is almost unimaginable. After hitting more than thirty home runs for four seasons in a row, he hit only 22 in 1991. After driving in 118, 99, 95, and 108 runs in those seasons, he drove in only 75 in 1991.

McGwire decided to seek counseling. Not with a hitting instructor but real counseling, with a psychiatrist. He was going through a painful divorce at the same time. During this same period, he began to spend more time with his three-year-old son, Matt. With the benefit of the counseling and his new closeness with Matt, McGwire's career took off again in 1992, even though injuries began to plague him again, as they had in the early years of his career. He missed twenty games in August with a strained muscle on the right side of his rib cage but still finished with 42 home runs, twenty above his 1991 figure, while raising his batting average 67 points to .268.

He also began to develop a new attitude to deal with the stress of his profession and his stardom. He began to remind himself, "What am I getting so stressed about? The Man Upstairs knows what's going to happen." He said later, "I totally believe that, and that takes the pressure off."

His comeback from that disastrous 1991 season was impressive enough that the fans elected him as the American League's starting first baseman in the All-Star Game for the fifth straight season. He thanked them in the pregame home run contest by knocking twelve pitches out of the ballpark in San Diego. At the end of the season, he finished fourth in the voting for the Most Valuable Player award, and UPI named him its Comeback Player of the Year.

Injuries bit him again in both 1993 and 1994. He injured his left heel, and his back started acting up, causing a sharp reduction in his playing time. Over those two seasons, he played in a total of only 74 games. In 1995, with the season shortened again by the strike that started the previous August, and with injuries still nagging at him, McGwire nevertheless managed to go on another streak. He hit 39 home runs in only 104 games and drove in ninety runs. The fans voted him to his seventh All-Star Game.

Injuries kept McGwire out of the game and landed him on the disabled list twice. He was hit by pitches eleven times, bruised a foot, and was still bothered by a sore lower back. After spending more time than he would have liked with the trainer and the doctor, McGwire hit the 269th home run of his career, breaking Reggie Jackson's team record for Oakland.

His homers continued to bring gasps of astonishment not only because of their number but because of their distance as well. One of them sailed over the roof at Tiger Stadium in Detroit. Another bounced on the railing of a stairway on Waveland Avenue beyond the Cubs' Wrigley Field. Still another landed in the players parking lot at Coors Field in Denver and was estimated at six hundred feet by Dave McKay. McKay had legitimate credentials for making his estimate. He was the Cardinals' batting practice pitcher, and he liked to tell people he had given up eight thousand pregame "home runs" to McGwire.

McGwire began the 1996 season by missing the first 18 games with a foot injury, but then he took off again, foot or no foot. He became the fourteenth player in history to hit fifty or more home runs, with 52, which was tops in both leagues. He led the A's in hitting with a .312 average, 60 points over his lifetime average, hit the three hundredth home run of his career, and launched one into the fifth deck of the Sky Dome in Toronto. Those who follow such things made a fascinating discovery at the end of the season: over one stretch of 162 games, the length of a regular season, going back to 1995, McGwire hit 70 home runs.

Then came his trade to the Cardinals during the 1997 season, his 58 home runs that made the whole baseball world sit up again, his new contract, his new charitable foundation, and his runaway start in '98 with 13 home runs by May 8. Four days later, he put on a show for the fans of the home team. Back in St. Louis, he hit his fourteenth homer against Paul Wagner of Milwaukee. The ball landed in the upper deck and was the longest in the history of Busch Stadium. Its distance was estimated at 527 feet, but the slugging star didn't give anyone much time to remember it. On May 16, he hit one 545 feet against Livan Hernandez of the Florida Marlins, the new Busch Stadium record and his second 500-foot home run in four days. It was also his fifth 500-footer of the season, and it was still only May 16.

The manager of the Marlins, Jim Leyland, said, "They disappear and get real small real quick. It's fortunate they only count as one run."

McGwire said, "It's the best ball I've ever hit. I don't think I can hit one better than that." But he didn't know how far it went until he was told after the game. "I was too worried about the game," which the Cardinals lost, 6–5, he said. "The game is more important than the distance of a home run."

David Wells reminded baseball fans the next day that pitching is still a part of the game, too. He pitched a perfect game, only the thirteenth in modern history, against the Minnesota Twins at Yankee Stadium.

The home runs kept exploding off McGwire's bat as May continued. In Philadelphia on May 19, he homered three times to lead the Cards to a 10–8 victory over the Phillies at Veterans Stadium. All three were 400-foot jobs, traveling 440, 471, and 451 feet. The last one won the game, prompting the Cardinals manager, Tony La Russa, to point out after the game that McGwire was not only hitting a lot of home runs but he was helping his team with them. "He's been clutch," La Russa said. "I think he's only hit one where the game wasn't close. He keeps hitting them in game situations."

The one-man fireworks display gave McGwire 407 home runs for his career, tying him with Duke Snider, the Hall of Fame star with the Brooklyn and Los Angeles Dodgers. One other statistic was attracting the most attention: McGwire, who tied Mickey Mantle's record for home runs in May with 16, was on course to hit seventy-five home runs for the season, fourteen more than the record held by Roger Maris for the past thirty-seven years. Someone asked him about that, and McGwire answered, "When somebody gets to fifty by September, then it's legitimate to talk about. Right now, I don't think it is."

Before the end of May, people were beginning to notice something else: Sammy Sosa was hitting home runs too. He hit two on May 25, his tenth and eleventh, against the Braves in Atlanta, followed by two more two days later against the Phillies at Wrigley Field. By the end of the month, McGwire had 27 home runs—and Sosa had 13.

That figure didn't last long. In the first eight days of June, Sosa hit seven home runs. Before the month was out, he was the one setting a record instead of McGwire.

25

"Like a Fairy Tale"

It wasn't as if McGwire and Sosa had to give Americans something to talk about. There was plenty of news in 1998 to fill our papers and the evening news on television. Kenneth Starr, the independent counsel appointed to investigate possible involvement of the Clintons in a real estate development in Arkansas called "Whitewater," was spending his time on a new subject as well: allegations that the president had carried on a sexual relationship with a White House intern whose name was becoming almost as famous as his—Monica Lewinsky.

But if that was bad news for Clinton, other news was much better for him, and for the country. On May 8, the labor department reported that the unemployment rate had dropped to 4.3 percent, the lowest level in twenty-eight years.

The most popular television show of the 1990s, *Seinfeld,* about four neurotic friends living in New York, was going off the air after making its debut on NBC in 1991. Its finale on May 14, just as McGwire and Sosa were starting to attract attention, was watched by seventy-six million viewers.

McGwire and Sosa weren't taking a back seat to the president of the United States, Seinfeld, or anyone else. They kept blasting home runs, and America kept talking about them. McGwire reached the halfway point in his pursuit of Roger Maris's record of 61 homers by hitting his thirty-first on June 12 in Phoenix off Andy Benes, another grand slam that helped the Cardinals defeat the Diamondbacks, 9–4. It was the team's sixty-fifth game. In 1961, Maris had had only 26 homers by that point. The homer was also McGwire's fifteenth in his last twenty games.

Buck Showalter, the Yankees manager, expressed the same enthusiasm as everyone else. "It's great for the game," he said, "great for the industry, and anyone who feels otherwise is pretty shallow." Then the manager in Showalter came out. "But," he added quickly, "you try to face him with nobody on base as much as possible."

As if McGwire weren't popular enough in St. Louis already, he became an even bigger hero to 47,549 fans when one of his home runs landed in Busch Stadium's "Big Mac Land," a spot advertising McDonald's restaurants. On the basis of his homer there, fans who were in the ballpark that day were able to get a free hamburger at McDonald's, compliments of the management—and McGwire.

Sosa's bat became even hotter than McGwire's in June. When the Cubs took the field in Chicago on June 15, McGwire was ten home runs ahead of Sosa, 31 to 21, but then Sosa found a friend. He hit three home runs in one game against Cal Eldred of the Milwaukee Brewers, a right-hander who was four inches taller than the six-foot Sosa and 50 pounds heavier at 235. All three blasts carried more than 400 feet—410, 415, and 420 feet—and cleared the fence in Wrigley Field at all three points of the outfield—left, center, and right fields.

Sosa's fireworks gave him fifteen home runs in his last sixteen games, and thirty-two runs batted in. Only seven homers separated the two baseball bombers.

Two days later, each man hit a home run. By then they were not only hitting home runs at a frantic pace, they were hitting them on the same days. Sosa was proving he could hit 400-footers with frequency too, like McGwire. When they each hit one on June 17, McGwire's went 347 feet in the Houston Astrodome. Sosa's went 430 feet at Wrigley Field.

The next day at the Astrodome, McGwire broke the major league record for the most home runs before the end of June with a 449-footer, only the eleventh upper deck home run in the history of the Astrodome. It was McGwire's thirty-third homer, passing Ken Griffey, Jr., who set the record only four years earlier. McGwire had eleven games left in June to add to his total. The two sluggers were packing them in wherever they played. When McGwire broke Griffey's record, there were 43,806 fans at the Astrodome, bringing the total attendance for the three-game series to 115,775.

But Sosa wouldn't let any daylight develop between the two. In the

Sammy Sosa of the Chicago Cubs was chasing both Mark McGwire and Roger Maris in 1998 and, like McGwire, broke Maris's record. He finished that incredible season with 66 home runs. (Courtesy of Photo File.)

same week his picture was on the cover of *Sports Illustrated*, he blasted out six more home runs in the next five days, including five in the first three days of that streak against the Phillies in Wrigley Field, followed by one in Detroit against the Tigers. The overdose gave Sosa 19 homers in June and broke the major league record set sixty-one years earlier by Rudy York for the most homers in one month. There were still ten days left in June.

Sosa set the record in the same ballpark where York had played for the

Tigers in the 1930s and '40s—Tiger Stadium, which was called Briggs Stadium when York set the record in 1937. The Tigers won, 6–4, and Sosa said later, "I'm still thinking about the game. It would have been much better if we had won."

By now fans were talking about Sosa as much as they were talking about McGwire, and it was baseball's great fortune that its two brightest stars of the moment were also two of the sport's best goodwill ambassadors. Each was the other's biggest cheerleader. Sosa told reporters frequently, "He's the man. He's my idol. No matter what people say, he's still my idol. I have a lot of respect for that guy. He's the guy everybody is looking for." As for himself, Sosa added, "I'm not going to go crazy . . . I have to stay patient and thank God for giving me so much opportunity. I have to continue to be the best player I can be."

For his part, McGwire said it "would be great if we tied" in home runs at the end of the season. McGwire captured the hearts of fans everywhere with his public devotion to Matt, by now a husky ten-year-old member of the team, wearing a Cardinals uniform and serving as their batboy. When his father would complete his trip around the bases on another of his homers, there was Matt at home plate to congratulate him, after which Dad would hoist him high into the air with great enthusiasm and a warm hug.

Sosa was not afraid to show his emotions either. His home runs were marked by kisses he blew to his mother back home in the Dominican Republic through the television camera and made cheery, smiling waves to the rest of the family and his friends in his home town of San Pedro de Macoris, a city of 178,000 about seventy miles from the capital of Santo Domingo.

Like McGwire, Sosa was enjoying the ride. "If I keep hitting home runs," he said, "maybe people will like me even more. I feel like I'm just lucky to be in the right place at the right time."

Tony Muser, the new manager of the Kansas City Royals and Sosa's hitting coach the year before, was not surprised that Sosa was on such a prolonged streak. "He's had periods throughout his career when he would get extremely hot," Muser said. "There were times when you couldn't get him out. He could hit any pitch at any time out of the ballpark."

Muser made his comments before his team met the Cubs in a three-game series at the end of June. He was asked how he hoped to handle Sosa despite his hot bat. "We do have a battle plan on how to approach

Sammy these next three games," he said. "But our pitchers have to carry out that battle plan. If we don't do that, Sammy may put some balls in the parking lot."

Whatever Muser's strategy was, it worked. Sosa went without a home run in the series against the Royals, but on the last day of the month, back home at Wrigley Field, he homered against Alan Embree of the Diamondbacks, his twentieth home run in one month. He was only four homers behind McGwire, who hit his thirty-seventh on the same day, also in his home ballpark, against Kansas City. It was another one of McGwire's long-distance shots, a 472-footer over the left field wall at Busch Stadium against Glendon Rusch.

The homer tied McGwire with Reggie Jackson for the most home runs before the All-Star Game, scheduled for six days later in Denver. McGwire was ahead of Jackson's pace. Reggie's homer came in his ninety-second game in 1969, Mark's in his eighty-first. McGwire had reason to hope he would stay ahead of Jackson's 1969 pace for the rest of the season. Jackson hit only ten more that year.

McGwire and Sosa were becoming one of the biggest running stories in America, but the Clinton-Lewinsky scandal was another. On the same day that McGwire tied Jackson with his thirty-seventh homer, Linda Tripp, a Pentagon public relations specialist and a close friend of Lewinsky, testified before a federal grand jury in Washington concerning twenty hours of tapes of conversations between the two women that Tripp had turned over to independent counsel Kenneth Starr. She delivered her testimony before three hundred reporters and photographers. Later her attorney, Anthony Zaccagnini, told the reporters his client found it "very easy" to answer questions before the jury.

By the All-Star break, McGwire had 37 home runs and the most votes of any National League player for the annual midsummer game. He was named by the fans on 3,377,145 ballots, the sixth time he was voted to the team. Sosa, with 32 homers and ahead of the record paces of both Maris and Ruth, was not elected by the fans to the starting team. He finished sixth in the voting for the three starting positions in the outfield. The National League's manager, Jim Leyland of the Florida Marlins, saved the fans from their own embarrassment and corrected their oversight by naming Sosa to the team as a substitute.

★   ★   ★

When play resumed after the All-Star break, moviegoers could see Jim Carrey in *The Truman Show* and Bruce Willis in *Armageddon,* or they could see the all-time classic *Gone With the Wind* or the feel-good movie about a veterinarian's love of animals, *Dr. Doolittle.*

But the attention of millions of Americans remained fixed on the McGwire-Sosa race. Only something like the shocking story in Washington on July 24 was enough to distract them. On that day, a man named Russell Weston slipped past guards at the Capitol building and shot two Capitol police officers to death. It was revealed later that Weston was a diagnosed schizophrenic and a former patient in a mental hospital.

McGwire began to feel the fatigue from the pressure and the long season. After playing in another eighteen straight games through most of the rest of July, he slipped into an 0-for-16 batting slump. He toyed with the idea of taking July 26 off but decided to play instead. The result was his forty-fourth home run of the season at Coors Field in Denver, a 452-foot blast to left field that set a Cardinals record for home runs. On the same day, Sosa hit his thirty-eighth homer, also a 400-footer, at Wrigley Field. There was this measure of just how close their two-man home run derby was: It was the twelfth time in the season that both men had homered on the same day.

Nobody gave the record-breaking ball back to McGwire. The fan who caught it decided to keep it because he'd had a dream that this would happen. McGwire didn't complain. "That's good enough for me," he said. "I'm into that stuff. I hope he has more dreams."

It was just past the midpoint of the season, and McGwire complained of feeling tired and said, "I'm not pressing at all. I'm tired. Period. Everybody goes through it." To emphasize his point, he said, "I'm not Cal Ripken. I'm not going to play every day. It's for me and for the better. I'm looking for myself to finish the year strong. I'm not going to burn myself out for anybody else. I've been doing it the last couple of years and playing a lot of games. Everybody talks about me staying healthy. This is a good way to stay healthy."

Sosa was going through the same kind of drop-off in production, at another time when the two men were duplicating each other's pace. After his record total of twenty home runs in June, Sosa cooled off considerably and hit only four more until the last week of July. Then he started making up for lost time with three in his next two games including two on July 27. His second homer that day in a 6–2 win by the Cubs over the

Diamondbacks in Phoenix was the first grand slam of his career, a 438-foot shot to center field. It marked the end of the longest streak of home runs without a grand slam from the start of a career in the history of the Major Leagues.

The next day Sosa hit another homer, and so did McGwire. Speculation heated up again about who would break the Maris record, or—amazingly enough—could it be that *both* men would?

By now McGwire had 45, Sosa had 41 and America was beginning to go slightly crazy. Sosa was sticking to his season-long belief. "I've said it all along," he reminded reporters. "McGwire is the man."

As the two-man chase continued, the questions from the reporters continued too, and, as sometimes happens when a drama is sustained over a long period of time, some of the questions were on the silly side. One of them came when McGwire was asked if he ever thought as a kid that he'd threaten to break the Maris record.

"No way," he answered emphatically. "How could a child sit back and say, 'I'm going to break Roger Maris's record?' "

But there they were, two men threatening not only to break the record for the most home runs in one season but threatening to do it with something to spare. The excitement level continued to rise, and the interest was coming from various quarters, not just from baseball fans and the baseball media. Art Taylor of Northeastern University's Center for the Study of Sports in Society said McGwire "seems to have this sense that he's on a mission and he's going to make everybody feel good when he does it. Now the fans are giving him the balls back and not wanting anything in return. It's like a fairy tale."

A sociologist at the University of California at Irvine, John Torpey, said, "An aura follows Michael Jordan wherever he goes. McGwire doesn't have the charisma of Jordan, but he also is viewed as a hero-like figure. We're living in a time where an otherwise popular president is in trouble. I think people are searching for heroes."

On July 31, McGwire had 45 home runs compared to 42 for Sosa. McGwire was on a pace to hit 67 for the season, six more than Maris hit in 1961.

The two challengers met head-to-head in Chicago on August 19, with the two tied at 47 homers each. Sosa took the lead for the first time all season with a home run in the fifth inning against Kent Bottenfield. As he trotted around the bases, the 39,689 fans in Wrigley Field gave him a standing ovation and chanted, "Sam-mee! Sam-mee!"

McGwire answered that three innings later with his forty-eighth homer and took the lead again with another shot in the tenth inning. Both McGwire homers traveled over four hundred feet. He was proving La Russa right about hitting his homers when they counted the most. His first homer of the game tied it, 6–6. His second won the game.

After the game Sosa said once more for emphasis, "That's why he's the man."

McGwire didn't wait for the game to end to show his admiration for his friendly rival. Sosa reached first base on a walk in the seventh inning. As he neared the bag, McGwire tapped his chest and kissed his fingers, duplicating Sosa's gestures to the people back in Dominican Republic, expressions that had become familiar around the National League and around the nation to the fans watching on television.

"Even though I'm on the other side and we're playing against him and I want to see our team win," McGwire said, "it's just awesome to see that kind of talent and the way he goes about his business. He's quite a player."

Tony La Russa was thankful that the pitchers on the other National League teams were not avoiding McGwire by issuing him too many walks. He asked, "How can he break the record if he only gets one swing a game? This is me talking, not Mark. Mark hasn't said a word. He wouldn't." The Cardinals' manager said he respected the way the Cubs' pitchers were willing to pitch to McGwire. "They challenged him all game today. We tried to do the same with Sammy."

The next day, McGwire caught up with one of his own rules, and vice versa. After telling reporters all season long that he wouldn't speculate on his chances to break the Maris record unless he had 50 home runs by September 1, he did it. He hit his fiftieth in New York, where Maris hit his sixty-first, on August 20 in the first game of a doubleheader at Shea Stadium against the Mets. With that blow, he became the first player to hit 50 home runs in three straight seasons. Then, in the second game of the doubleheader, he hit his fifty-first. Every home run now seemed to be some kind of a record or have some special significance attached to it. That fifty-first homer, for example, tied Babe Ruth for the most home runs in a three-year period—161.

Now he was ready to answer reporters' questions about his chances of passing Maris. "I'd have to say that I do have a shot," he said, "but I know it's going to be tough." He needed eleven more, with thirty-six games remaining. The question didn't seem to be whether he could do it, but by how much—and whether Sosa would do it, too.

McGwire was back in a home run groove with four in his last three games. "I'm getting my second wind," he said. "I've been feeling pretty decent at the plate, and it's just a matter of getting the pitches to hit."

Then, remembering the standing ovation he received from the 40,308 fans as he rounded the bases and pumped his fist after his record breaker, he told reporters in his postgame interview, "I have to thank the fans here in New York. It was tremendous. I mean, wow!—what a reception! They were rooting me on."

It was still a two-man race. The next day, Sosa hit a 430-foot home run to center field in Chicago as the Cubs defeated the San Francisco Giants and Orel Hershiser, 6–5. It was Sosa's forty-ninth homer.

Neither man would let up in this toe-to-toe match that became a running story in the morning paper and on the evening news. August 23 was an example of their continued duel. McGwire hit his 53rd homer that day in a 4–3 loss to the Pirates at Pittsburgh's Three Rivers Stadium. It was his 111th home run over the past two seasons, a record for a righthanded hitter in back-to-back years. On the same day, Sosa homered twice against Jose Lima as the Cubs lost a 13–3 game to the Astros at Wrigley Field. The first one traveled 440 feet and made Sosa the only Cub to hit 50 home runs in one season since Hack Wilson accomplished it with 56 in 1930.

The slugging match was still separated by only two home runs.

26

"Para Ti, Mami!"

In the Dominican Republic, Sosa's mother was following her son's heroics closely and proudly, and so was everyone else in the nation. Despite the excitement about her Sammy, Mireya Sosa remained philosophical. "My son will get as many home runs as God wants," she said, "not one more or one less"—but she admitted he could still pass McGwire and set a record. "What is happening this year to Samuel is because of the prayers that I say every day." She was literally living in the midst of Sammy's success, in a home forty miles east of Santo Domingo that he bought for her the year before as a Mother's Day present.

She was also living in the midst of the world's greatest breeding grounds for baseball. The publication *Total Baseball* reported that, on a per capita basis, more players in the Major Leagues came from San Pedro de Macoris than from any other city in the world. The Dominican Republic could boast of sixty-two players in the American big leagues, including eight from San Pedro alone.

When Sammy blew his kisses toward his mother via television after each of his home runs, he said something, and Dominicans knew what it was: *"Para ti, Mami!"*—"For you, Mommy." His mother said, "When he sends me those kisses, I really feel them personally."

Sammy had always done so many things for his mother, since his father died in 1975, when Sammy was only six years old. As soon as he was big enough, he began to earn money to help support his mother any way he could find. During the day, he shined shoes for fifteen cents and washed cars for sixty-five cents. At night he watched parked cars. It wasn't much, but the entire Dominican Republic was struggling. In a nation of eight million people, 30 percent of the workers were unemployed. Those who were lucky enough to have jobs at the sugar and oil refineries earned about $200 a month.

"Fortunately, thanks to God," Sammy's mother said, "we were never without bread. We didn't have luxuries, like good shoes or a new dress, but now we have those privileges."

At the age of sixteen, Sammy signed his first professional baseball contract in 1985 with the Texas Rangers for $3,500, a fortune to a boy who had to make his own baseballs from wadded-up socks so he could play the sport. At the airport, when his plane began boarding passengers and Sammy's time came to leave for America, his mother pleaded with him, "Don't go."

He answered, "I've got to."

She said, "If you go, we'll all die here." She knew that Sammy's money had helped to keep the family alive—herself, Sammy, and his four brothers and two sisters, eating one meal a day and living in a one-room apartment.

"I've got to go," the teenage boy said again, "but I'll be back. And I will help us all."

Young Sammy flew off to America to play in the Rangers' minor league system, then was traded to the Chicago White Sox and farmed out to Oklahoma City and Vancouver. As a fateful next step in his career, he was traded across Chicago to the Cubs at the start of the 1992 season, played in sixty-seven games, and then blossomed into a star. The next season, he earned the distinction of becoming a "30–30 man" with 33 home runs and 38 stolen bases, setting the entire Dominican Republic into a frenzy over their new national hero. His feat prompted the government to declare a two-day holiday.

He had 25 homers and 22 steals in 1994 and became a 30–30-man for the second time in three years in 1995 with 36 home runs and 34 stolen bases. He was becoming an even bigger name, but there was no way of knowing just how bright his star would shine in only three more years.

At the same time, Sosa was remembering his roots. After that second 30–30 season in 1995, Sosa became the highest-paid player on the Cubs with a salary of $8 million a year. He plowed some of it back into his homeland by paying for the construction of the Treinta-Treinta Plaza—Spanish for "30-30"—a three-story building housing a disco club, a bar, and a clothing boutique and hair salon operated by his sisters, Sonia and

Raquel. The grounds include a fountain with a statue of Sosa. Coins from the fountain are donated to the shoeshine boys of the city. When the Plaza was dedicated with a ribbon-cutting ceremony, the president of the Dominican Republic, Leonel Fernandez Reyan was there, along with the nation's most famous former player, Juan Marichal, the Hall of Fame pitcher who became known as "the Dominican Dandy" while winning 243 games, mostly for the San Francisco Giants, in the 1960s and 1970s.

San Pedro is a city marked by shanty houses and trash and garbage on the streets waiting to be burned. Its water supply is polluted, with sewage seeping into the drinking water. Swimming in the Caribbean Sea around San Pedro can be hazardous to your health. Manuel Puello, a worker for an electric company, told Tom Weir of *USA Today,* "Sammy has paid for wells so people can get water. The good thing about Sammy is that he helps old people and children. Hospitals, too. Sammy, he doesn't live here, but he can't do it all by himself."

McGwire hit another homer, his fifty-fourth, on August 26, a shot off Justin Speier of the Florida Marlins that went 509 feet over Busch Stadium's center field fence. It was McGwire's fourth homer of the year that went more than 500 feet. The manager of the San Francisco Giants, Dusty Baker, remained awed by McGwire's power with each new Bunyanesque blow. "For sheer, awesome distance, no one I know who has ever played the game has hit balls so far, so consistently," Baker said, and he should know. He played with Hank Aaron. "Big Mac has hit the longest balls in just about every park in the majors."

McGwire himself was candid on the subject. "Americans love power," he said. "Big cars. Big trucks. Big people. Baseball fans have always been drawn to the home run and the guy throwing close to 100 miles an hour. That's what they want to come and see."

Sosa hit a home run on the same day, and another two days later. Now only one homer separated the two men, with McGwire still out in front, 54 to 53. It was still only August 28 and they were within seven and eight home runs of the record.

McGwire hit numbers 56 and 57 in a game on September 1 against the Marlins in Miami's Pro Player Stadium, two tape-measure jobs that sailed 450 and 472 feet. With the second, he broke Hack Wilson's National League record for the most home runs in one season. The manager of the Marlins, Jim Leyland, said, "I've never seen anything like it. The guy is hitting balls out of Yellowstone Park."

McGwire and Sosa both admitted they were beginning to feel the effects of their heated duel. "It's a pretty awesome feat," McGwire said. "I'm totally excited." Sosa said, "Now it's getting a little bit exciting. Mark has 57, and that's a lot. Everybody knows that everybody is pulling for Mark, and I'm pulling for Mark, too. And I want him to break the record first."

The last part of that statement by Sosa was significant. Now he was admitting himself that he expected both of them to break the Maris record. Everyone else did, too.

A survey by *USA Today* showed that only 16 percent of 58,000 people surveyed wanted Sosa to break the record held by Maris, compared to 79 percent who said they were rooting for McGwire. When a reporter asked Sosa how he felt about that, he said, "That's why I say he's the man. The reason I say he's the man is because every time we're tied, he jumps out there right away. Yesterday I was tied for about six hours. After that—boom! He was back in charge."

Then a reporter asked Sosa how often he thinks about breaking the record, and Sammy got a laugh from the reporters when he said, "About 16 percent of the time."

McGwire reached the magic kingdom first. On September 5 the Cardinals were playing at home. Their highly popular Hall of Famer, Stan Musial, began the proceedings by playing "Take Me Out to the Ball Game" on his harmonica at home plate, and McGwire immediately took it from there. He hit his sixtieth home run of the season, a high line drive into the left field seats against Dennis Reyes of the Cincinnati Reds in a game won by the Cardinals, 7–0. The blow tied him with Babe Ruth's achievement of sixty home runs in one season, in 1927, and put McGwire in the exclusive class with Ruth and Maris as the only three men ever to hit sixty or more home runs in a single season. McGwire was the first righthanded hitter to do it.

It was a two-run homer in the first inning. As it headed toward the seats, Jack Buck, the veteran play-by-play announcer for the Cardinals, hollered into his microphone, "Wake up, Babe Ruth! There's company coming!" Fireworks exploded into the Missouri air over Busch Stadium close by the Mississippi River. The capacity crowd of 47,994 fans gave their hero a standing ovation. McGwire reciprocated with a curtain call and a salute.

McGwire was dazzled himself. "To be compared with Babe Ruth is just awesome," he said. "Until recently, I never thought anything like that could happen." There was plenty of time for still other things to happen, too. There were still twenty-one games left to beat Maris and maybe reach the unheard-of level of seventy home runs. While doing that, however, he would still have to do one other thing—beat Sosa. On the same day that McGwire hit his sixtieth homer, Sosa hit his fifty-eighth.

At the same time, the two slugging stars still had to share their prominence on America's front pages with President Clinton. In that same week, Clinton finally said what his advisers had been urging him to say: that he was sorry about his affair with Monica Lewinsky and about deceiving the American people. He made the admission one day after a fellow Democrat, Senator Joseph Lieberman of Connecticut, criticized the president's conduct. Speaking on the Senate floor, Lieberman called Clinton's conduct "immoral" and said Clinton deserved a "public rebuke."

At a photo session in Dublin with the prime minister of Ireland, Bertie Ahern, Clinton admitted that his actions were "wrong" and said he "regretted" them.

Attendance was up all over the National League as the fans continued to come back to baseball after the disastrous strike four years earlier. The public was in such a frenzy that McGwire was traveling with two security men protecting him. The Cardinal and the Cub were Page One news all over America, and in Europe and Japan as well.

Two days later, with the Roger Maris family in the stands at Busch Stadium, McGwire reached the magic number of 61. Again, he made quick work of things, connecting in the first inning on a fastball from Mike Morgan of the Cubs while Sosa witnessed the achievement from his position in right field, smiled and applauded. The home run was vintage McGwire—a 430-foot shot to left field that hit the front of the third deck at Busch Stadium and dropped into the crowd below.

Paul Newberry of the Associated Press pointed out that McGwire tied Maris on the same field where the late star played his last game, in 1968, as a member of the Cardinals. "McGwire's sense of timing was impeccable, as usual," Newberry wrote. "He had his son in the dugout, his father in the stands on his sixty-first birthday, his biggest rival applauding the moment from right field."

The two sluggers were acclaimed overseas as well. In Japan, the world's second most enthusiastic baseball country, where Babe Ruth is almost as popular as he is in this nation, its largest newspaper, *The Yomiuri,* told its readers, "All of America cheers the 'modern Ruth.' "

One Japanese man was especially gracious. Sadaharu Oh, who hit 868 home runs there, told the *Kyodo News,* "It's great for him to hit such a number. Congratulations. I express my respect for him, particularly for his power of concentration."

However, McGwire received mixed reviews on the other side of the world. In Europe, the London *Daily Telegraph* ran McGwire's picture on Page One. He was seen pumping his right fist into the air as he circled the bases. A headline next to the picture said:

AMERICA STOPS AS SPORTING HISTORY IS MADE

The story reported accurately that the superstar of the Cardinals "has all of America on the edge of its seat and the whole country gives the impression of supporting him." Then the paper added a negative note: "But his home run chase has not been without controversy, for he admits to taking a dietary supplement that contains steroids in order to maintain his muscle-bound bulk."

It had been known that McGwire was taking a drug called androstenedione, an over-the-counter dietary supplement. It was banned by the National Football League, the National Basketball Association, and the National Collegiate Athletic Association, but it was permitted by Major League Baseball. McGwire stopped using the drug in 1999. He told reporters, "I thought long and hard about it, and I don't like the way it was portrayed, like I was the endorser of the product, which I wasn't, but young kids take it because of me. I don't like that." Barry R. McCaffrey, the White House drug adviser, praised McGwire's decision.

Oddly enough, it remained for a London paper to describe the national acclaim for McGwire. One of the famous London tabloids, the *Daily Express,* published a full-page feature story by its tennis correspondent, who was in the United States to cover the U.S. Open. "America is totally transfixed," the article said, and no American would have disagreed with that statement. "Bill Clinton's bedroom indiscretions? No. Wall Street's latest roller-coaster ride? Wrong again. In a nation preoccupied with sports and statistics, the race to break the number of home runs in one baseball season merits top place in the public interest polls." A woman anchoring a British television newscast confessed that she had trouble understanding the fuss. "It's amazing," she said. "The ball is so small and the stadium is so big. How do they see anything?"

The leading sports newspaper in Italy, *Gazzetta Dello Sport,* ran updates every day for two weeks as the two stars slugged their way toward the Maris record. Another Italian publication, *Corriere Dello Sport,* told its readers that McGwire had become "entrenched in American history and given the same respect that is accorded Abraham Lincoln or Michael Jordan."

Then came *the* night.

Mark McGwire became baseball's single-season record holder when he hit his sixty-second home run of the season at 8:18 P.M. Central daylight time on September 8, 1998. With two outs in the fourth inning at Busch Stadium, he lined the first pitch he saw from Steve Trachsel of the Cubs, an eighty-eight-mile-an-hour fastball, over the left field fence. Ironically, the home run went 341 feet, his shortest of the year. He was so excited that he missed first base as he began his trip around the bases and had to go back and tag it. Every member of the Cubs infield shook his hand. At home plate, Catcher Scott Servais and McGwire embraced in a hug.

America's newest sports darling was mobbed at the plate by his teammates. He hoisted his batboy son, Matt, high over his head and each of them smiled from ear to ear as the capacity crowd and the national television audience took in the entire jubilation and smiled with the father and his son. In right field, Sammy Sosa applauded with his bare right hand against the fielder's glove on his left. He didn't limit it to that. He trotted into the crowd of rejoicers around home plate, gave McGwire a friendly hug, and exchanged high-fives with him.

Then the idol of St. Louis ran over to the box seats on the first base side of the infield and hugged the members of the Roger Maris family. With the crowd still standing, Mark stepped up to a microphone and told his fans, "To all my family, my son, the Cubs, Sammy Sosa, it's unbelievable. Thank you, St. Louis." Roger Maris, Jr., said, "I couldn't be happier for him."

No fan caught this historic ball. Instead, it was retrieved by a member of the ground crew, Tim Forneris, after it landed in a no-man's land under the left field stands, where no fan was able to get it. Forneris resisted the temptation to sell the ball at an auction, even though those who know about such things had been saying that whoever got the ball

Another home run explodes off the bat of Mark McGwire during his record-shattering season of 1998, when he broke Roger Maris's record of 61 homers in one season and became the first man to hit seventy. (© Rich Pilling/National Baseball Hall of Fame Library, Cooperstown, N.Y.)

would be able to sell it for $1 million, maybe more. Instead, Forneris walked in from the outfield and joined the crowd in the infield as various celebrities began to make speeches about McGwire's historic accomplishment.

Forneris kept it simple. Without fanfare he said, "Mr. McGwire, I think I have something that belongs to you." Then he handed him the ball. The celebration lasted eleven minutes, the biggest and longest during a baseball game since Cal Ripken broke Lou Gehrig's record for consecutive games in 1995.

No one in St. Louis had any way of knowing it at the time, but the same kind of celebrating was going on in ballparks all over the Major Leagues. The Phillies' manager, Terry Francona, said he could tell from the crowd noise at Veterans Stadium in Philadelphia that McGwire had broken Maris's record. "I heard the fans making noise," he said after the game, "and I thought it must have happened. I thought it was kind of neat that so many people had radios and that they cared about McGwire. It's just great for the game."

At Comiskey Park in Chicago, the players could sense things by the noise coming from the Bullpen Sports Bar behind the right field fence of the White Sox ballpark. "It gives you goose bumps," first baseman Frank Thomas said. "He's always been the best home run hitter I've ever seen. It couldn't happen to a better person." Thomas knew something about being cheered by the fans. He was the American League's Most Valuable Player while playing for the White Sox in 1993 and 1994.

The Oakland A's felt almost as happy about their former teammate's achievement as he did. Jason Giambi said, "That's the happiest he's ever been. We were in the clubhouse watching. It's exciting to be able to call Mac my friend." The Cards game was shown on the stadium video screen during batting practice before the Oakland-Minnesota game. Minnesota's Paul Molitor said, "Literally, chills went down the back of your neck and your spine. Almost everybody was fixated on the big screen."

Joe Carter, a home run hero himself when he won the 1993 World Series for the Toronto Blue Jays with a homer in the last game, expressed his admiration for McGwire. "You can get lucky one time, but not 62," he said. "I have no idea what that feels like to do that. To come through in a situation like that, every single day. Everything is scrutinized, every at-bat. I can't fathom what it felt like."

The Yankees and the Red Sox were playing at Fenway Park in Boston. David Cone of the Yankees said, "Just an amazing feat, right up there with Joe DiMaggio's hitting streak." Even though Cone was a pitcher himself, he was forgetting another record that may still be standing when all others have fallen, including DiMaggio's: Johnny Vander Meer's achievement of pitching two no-hit, no-run games in a row for the Cincinnati Reds in 1938. When we were talking a few years before his death, Vandie mentioned why he thought his record may outlast them all. "Because, to break my record," he said, "someone would have to pitch *three* no-hitters in a row, and I don't think that's going to happen."

When McGwire went home and tried to get some sleep, he couldn't. Still, he was in the lineup for the game the next day in Cincinnati, before another sellout crowd, after the Cardinals arrived at 4:30 A.M. When reporters wondered why he hadn't taken the day off to rest, McGwire told them, "When you've got fifty thousand fans out there, you've got to make some sort of showing."

On his first time up, the Cincinnati fans gave him a standing ovation that lasted more than a minute. He grounded out, then went out on a fly ball. As he left the field and headed toward the visitors' clubhouse, he tossed a ball and both batting gloves to the fans sitting behind the Cardinals' dugout.

The Reds' manager, Jack McKeon, said, "I think people want to see McGwire in person. If he hits one, fine. If he doesn't hit one, so what? They want to come out and see him. I'd love to see Babe Ruth play, even if he didn't hit one, just so I could say I saw Babe Ruth play. I think it's the same scenario here."

Sosa joined the exclusive sixty-homer club only one week after McGwire hit his sixtieth. He did it against Valerio De Los Santos of the Brewers in Chicago, and no one was any happier about it than Sosa himself. "I just have to say that I could never feel more happy than I do today," he said after the game, in which the Cubs outlasted the Brewers, 15–12, with five runs in the ninth inning. "Babe Ruth was one of the greatest guys to play baseball. He never really died. He's still alive. Everybody remembers him like it was yesterday. It's great to be tied with the Babe and be behind Roger Maris and Mark."

Sosa sent his homer to the front steps of a house across the street from Wrigley Field. "We had second and third and I didn't want to strike out," he said. "I came through. I hit sixty. I jumped up and said, 'Yes,' and that was about it. I didn't want to show the other team up."

The fans at Wrigley Field coaxed their hero out of the dugout three times for curtain calls and threw paper cups and other items onto the field while chanting the now-familiar, "Sam-mee! Sam-mee!"

Sosa, as always, took everything with his famous grace and unselfishness: "I have to say what I did is for the people of Chicago, for America, for my mother, for my wife, my kids and the people I have around me. My team. It was an emotional moment."

Baseball fans continued to marvel at the superhuman feats of the two strong men. The day after hitting his sixtieth home run, Sosa hit two more against the Brewers in Chicago and tied McGwire with sixty-two each. "I don't usually cry, but I cry inside," Sosa said after the game. "I was blowing kisses to my mother. I was crying a little bit."

McGwire was enjoying it, too. "It's awesome, outstanding," he said of Sosa's day. "I've been doing this for the last few years with Ken Griffey. We go back and forth." Then, speaking of his season-long duel with Sosa, McGwire said, "We've got until the 27th of September. I don't think you have to be a rocket scientist to figure out it's not over. I never once thought that was it."

McGwire called Sosa and congratulated him, and so did President Clinton. "The call from Bill Clinton," Sosa said, "that was something that makes me real proud of myself. He wants me to take the Cubs to the playoffs," Sosa said. "I said, 'I'll do my best.' "

He added, "The attention I've had is good enough for me. Mark was there first. I'm glad with what I've had. I have to say it's not only for me and Latin Americans. It's for the people in the United States who gave me this chance."

And, of course, he was happy, as always, for his mother. "Everything I do . . . every homer is for my mother. The way I can make her happy is to do good every day."

Two days later, on September 15, McGwire took the lead again by hitting his sixty-third homer, but Sosa caught him again the next day with a grand slam. For Sosa, the man who had never hit a grand slam before 1998, it was his third grand slam of the season. He hit a ninety-three-mile-an-hour fastball from San Diego's Brian Boehringer and sent it 434 feet into the upper deck at Qualcomm Stadium. The San Diego fans continued their applause until Sosa took a curtain call. They were still cheering when the inning ended. Sosa tipped his cap as he trotted out to his position in right field.

The tie lasted only two days until McGwire hit his sixty-fourth home run on September 18 in Milwaukee, followed by another one there on the 20th. That one made a prophet out of Matt McGwire. In spring training, he had predicted his dad would hit sixty-five home runs in 1998. McGwire said, "That's all I thought about when I was running around the bases."

27

"Get Up, Baby! Get Up! Get Up!"

Baseball news was made in another city that Sunday night, too—Baltimore—and it involved another favorite player, Cal Ripken. The glamour boy who was widely credited with saving the sport almost single-handedly in 1995 when he broke Lou Gehrig's record for playing in the most consecutive games ended The Streak. Ripken, by then thirty-eight years old, walked into Ray Miller's office at Oriole Park a half hour before the team's game with the Yankees and told the manager of the Orioles, "I think the time is right." The decision was his. He took himself out of the lineup after playing in 2,632 games in a row.

In the press box, the Orioles' public relations director, John Maroon, announced ten minutes before game time that there was a change in the Baltimore lineup, without specifying that Ripken would not be playing. Instead, he read the new lineup, which included a rookie, Ryan Minor, at third base and batting sixth, Ripken's spot.

At home plate a short time later, the two managers exchanged lineup cards, as usual. What wasn't usual was that the Yankees' manager, Joe Torre, was at home plate instead of Chris Chambliss, his hitting coach. Torre said he was suspecting something, so he decided to go to the plate himself for the pregame meeting with the other manager and the umpires.

When the managers returned to their dugouts for the start of the game, some of the Yankee players grabbed a look at the lineup card and spotted Ryan Minor's name at third base instead of Ripken's. New York's catcher, Joe Girardi, suggested that everyone in the dugout should step out of the dugout after the first out and tip his cap to Ripken.

At the start of the game, the fans were unsuspecting, even when young Minor trotted out to the third base spot for the Orioles. The Yankees' leadoff hitter, Chuck Knoblauch, grounded out to shortstop, and still there was no reaction from the crowd, but there was from the Yankees. Just as Girardi suggested, the entire team stepped out of the visitors' dugout on the third base side, and every player tipped his cap in the direction of Ripken across the infield. After the game, the Orioles' immortal said he was deeply touched by the gesture of respect and affection. Reporter Mark Maske of *The Washington Post* remembered what Kirby Puckett of the Minnesota Twins had said years earlier: "The players respect him more than anyone else they've ever seen in this game."

Then the fans recognized the momentous development occurring in front of them. They stood and thanked him with their applause and wouldn't stop cheering when Ripken bolted out of the dugout and waved for them to sit down again. The standing ovation continued as the fans kept cheering and the Yankees kept clapping. The next hitter for the Yankees, shortstop Derek Jeter, stood outside the batter's box. The Orioles' starting pitcher, Doug Johns, stood on the mound, content to wait until the cheering stopped.

Ripken emerged from the dugout again, acknowledged the cheers, which lasted three minutes, by facing each part of the ballpark and then motioned to Johns to throw the next pitch. Johns threw a pitch to Jeter, and an Orioles' game had started without Ripken in the lineup for the first time since May 29, 1982, when Ronald Reagan was less than halfway through his first term as president.

After the game, the future Hall of Famer told reporters at a news conference that he had called his parents earlier in the day to let them know what he had in mind, and both Mom and Dad expressed their support. He said it was "the answer I expected to hear." He didn't tell his teammates and instead went through his usual pregame stretching exercises and wind sprints across the outfield grass. At the time, Miller was filling out his lineup card in his office. Not knowing what Cal was planning, Miller penciled Ripken's name into the batting order, although, he said later, "I had a feeling" from an earlier conversation with Cal.

Ripken said at his news conference that he thought about ending his streak on the last day of the season, but the Orioles would be in Boston that day, and he wanted to end it in front of the Baltimore fans, at the Orioles' final game of the year at home. "I thought about it and decided, 'Let's end it in the same place it started,' " he said. "In my home state, in front of the best fans in the world."

Ripken added, "Baseball has always been a team game, and I've always thought the focus should be on the team, and there have been times during the streak that the focus was on the streak, and I never felt totally comfortable with that. It just reached a point where I firmly believed it was time to change the subject and restore the focus back where it should be."

Ripken stood above everyone else in consecutive games played—in any nation, including Japan, where Sachio Kinugasa played his 2,215 games in a row from 1970 to 1987. Ripken caught up with his Japanese counterpart on June 13, 1996, and passed him the next day. After Ripken took himself out of the lineup, the closest man to him in either league in consecutive games was Albert Belle of the Chicago White Sox, with 325 straight, 2,307 games behind Ripken.

After his one day off, Ripken was back in the Orioles' lineup. He sounded like someone who had just taken a whole year off, telling reporters, "It felt really good to be back playing again." He got two hits against the Toronto Blue Jays and moved past another star of Baltimore, Babe Ruth, into thirty-fourth place on baseball's all-time hit list.

The home run derby was making baseball fans all over again. A survey conducted that week by CNN/*USA Today* showed that 63 percent of 1,082 people surveyed said they were baseball fans to one degree or another, an increase of nineteen points since June. It was the highest figure since the poll began tracking the popularity of baseball in February 1993.

Not surprisingly, the sport reached its lowest point in the poll in April 1995, the month the Major League teams finally returned to action after the 1994 season was cut short in mid-August. Only 41 percent said they were baseball fans at the start of the 1995 season. The man most on the spot, Baseball Commissioner Bud Selig, was obviously delighted with the findings of the survey in September 1998. He said, "McGwire and Sosa are making history, and it's been nothing but good for baseball."

Three days later, Sosa hit two more homers, breaking an 0-for-21 slump with number 64 and then hitting number 65 to break Hank Greenberg's record in 1938 of eleven multi-homer games in one season.

The two giants were tied again. On September 25, a Friday night, much to everyone's surprise including his own, Sosa took the lead again—for forty-five minutes. He hit one into the third level of the Astrodome, a 462-foot drive. Now he had 66. But forty-five minutes later, McGwire caught up with him again, with a two-run shot in a 6–5 win by the Cards over the Montreal Expos in St. Louis.

A reporter told Sosa after the game about McGwire's home run and asked him if he was disappointed. Sosa responded immediately: "Disappointed for what, man? Mark is my friend, not my enemy."

There were two games left in the season.

Number 66 turned out to be Sosa's last home run of the season, but he could take consolation in the fact that his team was headed for the National League playoffs, which he had said all along was his goal for the season. McGwire, as things turned out, wasn't finished, but his season would end on Sunday. The Cardinals were going to miss the playoffs. For that reason, Tony La Russa said after the Friday night game, "As far as I'm concerned, Mark's home run chase is the most important thing for the next two days. We're pulling for him real, real, real hard."

McGwire rewarded his teammates and La Russa for their support with two home runs on Saturday at Busch Stadium against the Expos. Sosa was trailing McGwire, 66 home runs to 68, but he refused to concede. "It doesn't look good," he said, "but I still have a chance. I've always been saying Mark is going to finish ahead of me. He'll probably hit two more Sunday."

McGwire said he thought Sosa had "bigger things on his mind, helping the Cubs get into the playoffs."

The next day was Fan Appreciation Day in St. Louis, with another full house—46,110 fans. By the third inning, McGwire was on the verge of making Sosa look like a prophet. He hit a home run off a rookie, Mike Thurman. The fans gave him two curtain calls, and he responded by saluting them. The stage was set for the big finish: Would he be able to hit the magic number of 70 home runs in one season, a feat considered extremely unlikely if not impossible for any mere mortal? But then McGwire had been making people believe all season that he was no mere mortal—he was Superman.

In the seventh inning, against Carl Pavano, McGwire took what became his final swing of the 1998 season—and connected. On Pavano's first pitch, a fastball, McGwire hit a line drive toward the wall in left field. It was 3:19 P.M., Central daylight time. In the broadcasting booth,

the Cardinals announcer, Mike Shannon, their third baseman and outfielder for nine years in the 1960s and 1970s, said, "Swing and . . . " Then
he screamed in excitement:

*"Get up, baby! Get up! Get up! Get up! Home run! He's done it again!
Seventy home runs! Take a ride on that for history! They'll be shooting
at that one for years and years!"*

The home run was McGwire's fifth in three games over the weekend,
enabling him to conquer all the pressure sustained over most of the season and finish strong, the way champions do. As McGwire rounded the
bases for the seventieth time in one season, each of the Expos' infielders
shook his hand, just as the Cubs had done when he hit his sixty-second.
This celebration lasted for three minutes, through Brian Jordan's time at
bat.

After the game, McGwire couldn't believe what he had just achieved.
He told reporters surrounding him, "I can't believe I did that. It's ab-
solutely amazing. It blows my mind. I am almost speechless."

La Russa said, "It's stranger than fiction, what this man has done."

La Russa's opposite number, manager Felipe Alou of the Expos, said,
"I left it up to God and the kid on the mound. I didn't want to tamper
with history. Thank God the season's over, or he would hit 80."

When someone asked McGwire if he thought his record would last, he
said, "I think it will stand for a while. I know how grueling it is to do
what I've done this year. Will it be broken some day? It could be. Will I
be alive? Possibly. But if I'm not playing, I'll definitely be there."

The seventieth baseball hit out of the park that year by Mark Mc-
Gwire was recovered by Philip Ozersky of St. Louis, a twenty-six-year-
old research scientist making $30,000 a year, who was at the game with
one hundred fellow employees of his company. "I just went to see a baseball game," he said. "I'm a fan. I never dreamed of catching a home run
ball. I'd never caught one before, and I've been to many games."

Unlike some of the fans in the preceding weeks, he didn't give the ball
back. He sold it for $3 million at an auction at Madison Square Garden
in New York. Arlan Ettinger, the president of Guernsey's, the auction
house that handled the bidding, said, "It's an extraordinary accomplishment to reach $3 million. It's 23 times the world record for any baseball
ever sold and five to six times the record of any sports artifact."

The buyer was thirty-eight-year-old Todd McFarlane of Tempe,

Arizona, creator of a popular comic strip character named "Spawn" and the owner of McFarlane Toys, the fifth-largest action-figure manufacturer in the United States. He also owned eight other home run balls hit by McGwire and Sosa that season. "I made the biggest bet in the world that the record will not fall any time soon," he said. "If the record falls, I go from being a nut who paid $3 million for the crown jewel of sports memorabilia to an idiot who spent $3 million on a $5 ball."

Over the same weekend when McGwire hit his seventieth homer, Sosa's mind was on more than just home runs. A killer storm, Hurricane Georges, lashed across his hometown, killing more than two hundred persons and leaving twenty-three thousand others homeless. His countrymen knew Sammy would go to bat for them now, instead of for the Cubs, and he did. He obtained a contribution of $1 million from Major League Baseball. He flew back to the Dominican Republic soon after the baseball season ended to lend a hand himself, doing what he could to help the people in his hometown of Santo Domingo, the hardest hit area in the nation. He donated a sizable amount of money himself to the relief efforts, including some of his money from endorsements as well as other funds from his Sammy Sosa Charity Foundation.

After the season, the people of Dolgeville, New York, near the Baseball Hall of Fame in Cooperstown, also had reason to be grateful for the 1998 home run shootout, especially those who worked at the Rawlings Adirondack bat company. They had a record-setting year, too.

In November, the plant manager, Tim Socha, said, "Things have never looked better for this plant. The sales figures are many times more than what they were last year . . . and all because of Mark." The number of employees tripled from the year before. The plant was running three shifts a day, six days a week. Instead of the normal number of thirty employees for that time of year, the company had eighty-five and was hiring more people every day.

"Everyone is much more positive about baseball in general," Socha said. "Even kids are getting more interested in baseball after this summer."

Sosa's Cubs reached the National League playoffs, although they didn't survive, and McGwire set the record that looked as if it would last forever, unless he broke it himself or somebody like Ken Griffey, Jr., came along and broke it—or Barry Bonds.

Sosa and McGwire could look back on the most incredible two-man,

KEN GRIFFEY JR.

In any other season, Ken Griffey, Jr., of the Seattle Mariners would have received all the attention with his 56 home runs, but not in 1998, when Mark McGwire and Sammy Sosa monopolized the headlines. (National Baseball Hall of Fame Library, Cooperstown, N.Y.)

season-long home run performance in history. Their achievements were so overwhelming that they dwarfed anything accomplished by anyone else. One of their innocent victims was Griffey, the star hitter of the Seattle Mariners. He hit 56 home runs that year to lead the American League, but nobody knew it. In any other season, that accomplishment would have been on the front page of every sports section in the nation for the entire second half of the season as players, media, and fans alike speculated on his chances of beating the record set by Maris. On the contrary, Sosa and McGwire so overshadowed everyone else in both leagues that Griffey received what surely was the least amount of attention ever given to a man who hit 56 home runs in one season.

Sosa finished second to McGwire in home runs, but he found ample consolation in many other features of that season. He realized his hope of helping his team to reach the playoffs, hit 66 home runs, led the National League with 158 runs batted in and 134 runs scored, passed Roger Maris by the substantial margin of five homers, and was voted the National League's Most Valuable Player. McGwire needed to point to only one achievement: He beat Maris's supposedly insurmountable record by the unbelievable margin of nine home runs.

Almost as if to prove that 1998 was no fluke, both men reprised their acts in '99. Both of them hit more home runs than Maris's 61 in 1961— McGwire with 65 and Sosa with 63. Just as in '98, McGwire staged another big finish, closing the 1999 season with 6 home runs in his last seven games. His powerful ending to the season gave him 245 home runs in four years, an average of just over 61 a season, higher than Maris's onetime record.

When the season ended, Sandy Grady wrote in *USA Today*, "Just when we were sinking into a national funk, wallowing dismally under White House porn, tapes and impeachment gloom, along came two genuine heroes in a glitzy, gaudy spectacle that has made us laugh, argue and root.

"Thank you, Mac. Thank you, Sammy. Thank you, Abner Doubleday . . . Maybe in the summer of boom and gloom, Mac and Sammy saved our sanity."

PART TEN

. . .

2001

28

First Confusion, Then War

In America, the year 2001 began in a state of confusion and ended in a state of war.

It started after the nation had to wait more than a month to see who was going to be inaugurated president on January 20. It ended with the nation not knowing where its newest enemy was, how long the war on terrorism would last, or how and when we would know it was over.

The uncertainty over who would be president was caused by a razor-thin edge for Gov. George W. Bush of Texas in the voting, combined immediately with charges of voting irregularities in Florida. Supporters of the Democratic candidate, Vice President Al Gore of Tennessee, said the alleged irregularities swung Florida and the election itself into the Bush column. The controversy went all the way to the U.S. Supreme Court, whose members ruled in Bush's favor on a 5–4 vote on December 13. Only then, and after a concession speech by Vice President Gore, could Americans feel relatively certain about who their next president would be.

Finally, the headlines of the nation's newspapers were able to report the result of the election held more than a month before, as *The Washington Post* did in a clear, three-word banner headline across the top of Page One:

VICTORY FOR BUSH

After the ruling by the Supreme Court, the president-elect promised the American people that he would govern in a spirit of cooperation and would move beyond "the bitterness and partisanship" that had marked the five-week battle over the Florida vote so the nation could "seize the moment." He added, "I was not elected to serve one party, but to serve one nation. The president of the United States is the president of every single American, of every race and every background. Whether you voted for me or not, I will do my best to serve your interests and I will work to earn your respect."

Vice President Gore, speaking from the Old Executive Office Building next door to the White House, so near and yet so far from the office he sought, talked to the nation for seven minutes. He said, "While I strongly disagree with the court's decision, I accept it." He also told Americans, "In one of God's unforeseen paths, this belatedly broken impasse can point us all to a new common ground, for its very closeness can serve to remind us that we are one people with a shared history and a shared destiny."

While neither man could possibly imagine it, their calls for national unity would have dramatic application again only nine months later, on September 11, 2001.

Almost as a reminder of the uncertainty facing the world, the USS *Cole* limped into port at Pascagoula, Mississippi, on the same day that the Supreme Court voted. Built only five years earlier as a symbol of America's military might, she was carried into Pascagoula Bay aboard a heavy-lift vessel after being towed for six weeks from Yemen. She had been attacked there on October 12, 2000, in a bombing raid that killed seventeen U.S. sailors. She still had a gaping hole in her side that measured forty feet by forty feet.

Authorities said they viewed the attack as a suicide mission and arrested six suspects. Yemen's prime minister blamed the attack on "Afghan Arabs"—Islamic militants. Repairs were expected to take almost a year and cost up to $200 million.

Those baseball fans who were able to make it to the sports page after reading about the Supreme Court decision on the election learned that the commissioner of baseball, Bud Selig, had problems of his own. He expressed concern about the sport's economic problems and said, "The system has to be changed, and it will be changed."

Selig pointed to the signings of several free agents to large contracts only within the previous week. The biggest, and most shocking, was a deal signed by shortstop Alex Rodriguez with the Texas Rangers. His team agreed to pay "A-Rod" $252 million over ten years, an average of $25 million a season. Selig said, "The inequity in this system is now so apparent, the question is: How do we fix it and what do we do?"

Before the year was over, America would be facing critical new questions. Baseball, despite its economic problems, would rise to play a key role in the nation's ability and determination to recover. The man faced with the responsibility of leading the country through the suddenly perilous times was the first Little League baseball player to be elected president.

From the start, baseball seemed bound for one of its brightest seasons ever and was destined to be seen by more fans than ever. In the same week that the major league season began, the Census Bureau reported that the nation's population had risen to 281.4 million, the result of a jump of 32.7 million in the 1990s. It was the biggest population surge in American history, even bigger than the peak of the baby boomer years in the decade from 1950 to 1960.

With more people than ever to enjoy the sport, the highlights of the 2001 baseball season seemed to keep coming, right from the Opening Day in April until the end of what many qualified observers are still calling one of the greatest World Series ever played. Barry Bonds started it, and the Arizona Diamondbacks, an expansion team no less, finished it.

Bonds, the left fielder for the San Francisco Giants, was starting his sixteenth big-league season. A lefthanded hitter who stood six feet one inch tall and weighed 210 pounds, he was always a threat to set a home run record of one kind or another. Two reasons might have been his Godfather, Willie Mays, and his cousin, Reggie Jackson. Between the two of them, they had hit 1,223 home runs. The most important reason of all, however, might be that his father, Bobby Bonds, was a successful major league player for fourteen seasons, seven of them with the Giants, and hit 332 home runs of his own. Still another reason might be the son's eyesight—he has 20/15 vision.

Barry would turn thirty-seven years old on July 24. He went right to work. On Opening Day, April 2, he hit a home run in the fifth inning against San Diego's Woody Williams, to help the Giants win, 3–2, at Pacific Bell Park in San Francisco. It was the third time he hit a home run on Opening Day and it was the 495th homer of his career. Then, however, he went homerless for the next seven games, until connecting against the Padres again, on April 12 in San Diego off Adam Eaton.

That blow touched off a streak of ten home runs in sixteen games. He homered in three straight contests in the first week of May, then hit three in one game on May 19 at Atlanta against three different pitchers—Odalis Perez, Jose Cabrera, and Jason Marquis. He hit two more the next day, against John Burkett and Mike Remlinger. After his extended one-man fireworks display, Bonds had 22 home runs in forty-three games. By the All-Star Game, he had 39, a pace that had fans speculating for the second time in only four seasons that a supposedly unreachable home run record might be broken again.

In what was to be Cal Ripken's last season and his last All-Star Game, the living immortal of the Baltimore Orioles came to bat for the first time in the third inning and was saluted with a standing ovation. He stepped out of the batter's box and tipped his cap to the fans, then hit the first pitch he saw from Chan Ho Park into the bullpen in left center field in Seattle's Safeco Field, breaking a scoreless tie and starting the American League on the way to a 4–1 victory. It was the league's fifth straight win and its eleventh in the last fourteen games. Ripken, forty years and ten months old, became the oldest player to hit a home run in an All-Star Game. He was voted the game's Most Valuable Player and received several standing ovations from the appreciative Seattle fans. It was his second MVP award in an All-Star Game. In 1991 in Toronto, he won the award with a three-run homer and also won the annual treat for the fans, the Home Run Derby.

After the game, Park was both gracious and respectful in his comments about Ripken and his home run. "It was an amazing moment," Park said. "The first pitch I ever threw in an All-Star Game was the last home run for Mr. Ripken. It's a big gift for him. It made him MVP. That's pretty good."

Even in his twenty-first season in the big leagues, Ripken admitted he was pumped up when he came to bat for the first time in the 2001 game. Paul White reported in *USA Today* that Ripken said after the game, "I still had a shot of adrenaline or a long case of the goose bumps. I'm not sure what, but coming to the plate, I was excited . . . The ball went out of the ballpark and I felt I was flying around the bases . . . Then the curtain call after that. It was just a continuation of those goose bumps. I still have them right now thinking about it."

The game featured a unique tribute to Ripken from the American League players. Just before the first inning began, the league's starting shortstop, Alex Rodriguez, pushed Ripken off third, where the fans across the nation had voted him the starter, and shoved him toward shortstop, his old position for virtually all of his career. Ripken looked into the American League dugout, and manager Joe Torre was waving him over to short.

Rodriguez had suggested the salute in a phone call to Torre the week before the game. Ripken said later, "I must have been the only one on the whole planet that didn't know. I came out there and I thought, 'This isn't the time or the place to go back to short.' I haven't played it in so many years."

In that respect, Ripken wasn't any better off than Rodriguez, who had taken up the third base position, after never playing there in his professional career. The two returned to their elected positions after the first inning. In the sixth, Ripken received another honor, along with Tony Gwynn of the San Diego Padres. Both men were expected to retire after the season, so Commissioner Bud Selig surprised them by presenting each future member of the Hall of Fame with the Commissioner's Historic Achievement Award.

Gwynn said, "I knew something was up, because Bud was squirming all day. I had flashbacks of Boston, with Ted Williams and the All-Century team. The outpouring of love was amazing."

Bonds maintained his home run pace through July and August, and on September 6, he moved into historic home run territory. He homered against Albie Lopez of the Arizona Diamondbacks, his sixtieth of the season, becoming only the fifth player—along with Ruth, Maris, McGwire, and Sosa—to hit 60 home runs in one season. Three days later he had a three-homer game again, this time in Colorado against the Rockies, accomplishing something worth writing home about. He passed both Ruth and Maris and in the same game. He had 63 home runs for the season by the end of that game, and Mark McGwire's record of 70 homers in 1998 was within reach.

The media attention continued to increase, and so did the pressure that comes with it. Harmon Killebrew knows what that's like. He hit more home runs than any other righthanded hitter in the history of the American League—573—and was ahead of Babe Ruth's pace of 60 late in 1959. When we talked about that in New York a few years ago, Harmon said, "It's difficult, because when you get close to the record, the pitchers change it a little bit. They don't like to see you break any records, and they try to keep the ball away from you . . . The first year that I tied for the home run championship, in 1959 against Rocky Colavito, I was ahead of Ruth's pace for a long time, and then I had a long dry spell . . . The pitchers seeing me hit a number of home runs tried to keep the ball away from me. So that's the thing I think that the hitters run into."

Then the Hall of Fame slugger added, "And if the pitchers don't get you, the pressure from the news media will remind you every day of the record and the chase . . . Certainly the members of the media make you aware of it. If you're not thinking about it, they'll let you know about it. And I remember reporters talking about that record. I think then it starts to become not only a physical thing but a mental thing. You start to think about it, and sometimes the harder you try, the worse it gets and the more difficult it becomes."

Killebrew, who hit more than 40 home runs eight times and led the American League in homers six times while starring for the Washington Senators and the Minnesota Twins in the '50s, '60s, and '70s, admitted to being fascinated by Ruth's record while he chased Ruth. "There was something magical about hitting 60," he said. "Fifty-nine was a big number, but 60 was certainly a bigger one, and a magical type number. I remember Roger Maris, when he was going for that record, the tremendous media attention on him. The pressure that he had was almost unbearable for Roger. I remember him saying at the time that he almost wished he hadn't broken the record."

On September 9, Bonds hit his sixty-third homer against the Rockies in Colorado. Two days later, 8:46 A.M. on September 11, a clear and sunny day in New York City, a hijacked airliner crashed into the north tower of the World Trade Center. The plane was a Boeing 767, American Airlines Flight 11 from Boston to Los Angeles, carrying eighty-one passengers and a crew of eleven. Many people, including President Bush, at first thought it was a terrible accident. Seventeen minutes later, a second hijacked plane, United Flight 175 from Boston to Los Angeles carrying fifty-six passengers and nine crew members, crashed into the south tower. Accounts of the times vary, but the New York Police Department confirmed these times a year later, on the first anniversary of the attacks. Both buildings burst into flames at the moment of impact. Now almost everyone was saying the two collisions were an attack of terrorism.

Forty minutes after the second crash into the World Trade Center, a third hijacked plane, American Airlines Flight 77, a Boeing 757 with 58 passengers and a crew of six, from Washington to Los Angeles, crashed into the Pentagon in Virginia, the headquarters of the Defense Department, just across the Potomac River from the White House and downtown Washington. It was 9:37, according to the Department of Defense. One hundred and eighty-nine people were killed, 125 in the building and 64 on the plane, including five terrorists. The Pentagon was evacuated immediately. Two minutes later, the White House was also evacuated. At 9:57, President Bush left for Florida, then flew on to a secure location at Offutt Air Force Base in Omaha, Nebraska. Secret Service agents armed with automatic rifles were deployed to Lafayette Park across Pennsylvania Avenue from the White House.

At 10:10, a fourth hijacked airliner, United Airlines Flight 93 from Newark, New Jersey, to San Francisco, crashed into open land in Pennsylvania's Somerset County near Pittsburgh. At 10:22, the State Department, Justice Department, and World Bank buildings were evacuated, and twenty-three minutes later all federal office buildings in Washington were also evacuated. All flights inbound to the United States from across the Atlantic Ocean were diverted to Canada. The Federal Aviation Administration closed all U.S. airports until further notice.

New York's mayor, Rudolph Giuliani, appealed to his citizens to stay home. In Washington, city officials declared a state of emergency. When Mayor Giuliani was asked at a news conference how high the death toll at the World Trade Center might be, he said, "I don't think we want to speculate about that—more than any of us can bear."

On the first anniversary of the attacks, the New York Medical Examiner's office said its figures showed that 2,801 persons were killed in the attack on the World Trade Center. Only half of them—1,402—had been identified by September 11, 2002. Counting those killed at the Pentagon and in the open field in Pennsylvania, the death toll for America's latest day of infamy stood at more than three thousand.

On the day of the attacks, the Defense Department announced that five warships and two aircraft carriers, the USS *George Washington* and the USS *John F. Kennedy,* were being dispatched from the U.S. Naval Station in Norfolk, Virginia, to begin patrolling the East Coast as protection against further attacks.

America and the world changed immediately. People who are old enough to remember 1941 began calling the attacks another Pearl Harbor. Television networks preempted their daily programs and stayed on the story all day and evening. The newspapers reported the worst attack ever launched against the continental United States with headlines and front pages not seen since World War II. *The New York Times* displayed only two words in bold capital letters across the top of its front page:

U.S. ATTACKED

The Washington Post ran a three-line banner across the top of Page One:

TERRORISTS HIJACK 4 AIRLINERS, DESTROY WORLD TRADE CENTER, HIT PENTAGON; HUNDREDS DEAD

USA Today's front page displayed a color picture of the first tower exploding next to the doomed second tower. The picture ran across the full width of the page and down three-quarters of the page. Superimposed across the top of the two towers were words that sent chills down the spines of the paper's readers:

'Act of war'
Terrorists strike; death toll 'horrendous'

The New York *Daily News* needed only two words:

IT'S WAR

In an article on the second page of *USA Today*, reporter Mark Memmott wrote, "Americans who woke up Tuesday in peace went to bed at night convinced their nation is at war." He said a poll by *USA Today*, Gallup, and CNN showed that 86 percent of those surveyed considered the terrorist attacks to be "acts of war against the United States." Eighty-seven percent said the bulletins of the day before were the "most tragic news event" in their lives. On September 12, some 200,000 American flags were sold at Wal-Mart stores across the nation.

In Chicago, below the sign that says WRIGLEY FIELD, HOME OF THE CHICAGO CUBS, another sign said:

TONIGHT'S GAME CANCELLED

Fortunately, the game wasn't really canceled, only postponed. Commissioner Bud Selig postponed all games through the following Sunday, September 16, ninety-one games, the first time such an action had been taken during the regular season since D-Day in 1944. He said the games would be made up by extending the season one week.

Americans were reeling under the blows struck by the terrorists. Polls taken by various newspapers, magazines, and television networks reported that the people of the nation were badly shaken by the shocking attacks. In the most extensive poll, the National Opinion Research Center at the University of Chicago reported that more than half of the adults surveyed said they cried more, were experiencing difficulty sleeping, or felt dazed or nervous.

When the major league teams took the field again, the renewed spirit of patriotism that enveloped America was reflected at ballparks all over the country. The games began, as always, with the playing or singing of the National Anthem, but now they included something else in almost every ballpark—"God Bless America," before the game or during the seventh-inning stretch.

Fans entering the ballparks experienced something new for a baseball game—they had to pass through security checkpoints, just like at the nation's airports. On the field, the players wore American flags on their uniforms. Grounds crews painted red, white, and blue likenesses of ribbons on the outfield grass. The flags flying from the tops of America's ballparks weren't the only American flags anymore. Fans brought their own, waved them enthusiastically during the music and dressed in star-spangled shirts and hats as America became a red, white, and blue nation more than at any time since World War II and the bicentennial celebrations in 1976.

Baseball teams coming to New York visited what was being called "ground zero," where the World Trade Center's twin towers had stood. Players in various cities visited their firehouses. Members of the Mets and Yankees wore T-shirts and caps displaying the letters FDNY and NYPD.

Barry Bonds went homerless in his first two games after the terrorist attacks but connected for the distance against Houston's Wade Miller in San Francisco in the fifth inning on September 20 for his sixty-forth of the season, then hit two more in one game on September 23 in San Diego, both against Jason Middlebrook. When September ended, the Giants had played 156 games. Bonds had played in 147 of them and had 69 home runs. He needed two homers to break McGwire's record of 70, with six games left in the season.

After failing to spark public excitement anything like what McGwire and Sosa ignited in 1998, Bonds was now getting the attention and the headlines that his assault on the record deserved. Some four hundred newspaper reporters, broadcasters, producers, and other members of the media were following him around the league, although that figure was still only about half of the number who recorded McGwire's every move three years before.

As the home runs continued to soar off Bonds's bat all season long, other events also contributed to what people were saying—that 2001 would be a baseball season to remember. The purists who prefer good pitching over bombs-away hitting experienced excitement of their own. Despite all the attention being given to home runs, three pitchers made headlines by hurling no-hit, no-run games: Hideo Nomo of the Red Sox against the Orioles on April 4, A. J. Burnett of the Marlins against the Padres on May 12, and Bud Smith of the Cardinals, a rookie, on September 3, the second of the season against the Padres. Randy Johnson of the Diamondbacks struck out twenty hitters in nine innings on May 8, and Greg Maddux of the Braves pitched seventy and one-third innings without walking a batter.

Bonds wasn't the only one taking the minds of Americans off the events of September 11 and their aftermath. A whole team was doing it, too—the Seattle Mariners, under their manager, Lou Piniella. They were on their way to smashing the record for the most wins in one season, and Piniella might have been the most surprised person of all. In spring training, he sat behind his desk in Arizona trying to make out a lineup. It was only three weeks before the start of the season, and the Mariners' skipper, with fourteen years of experience as a major league manager behind him, couldn't figure out the makeup of his team for the 2001 season.

He said the new season wouldn't be the kind he prefers, when he can go with a set lineup. "This year isn't going to be like that," he said. "We don't have a set lineup with the players we have here."

Bret Boone, Seattle's new second baseman, disagreed because he was so impressed with the team's potential for scoring runs. "I look at what we have here," he told John Hickey of *Baseball Weekly*, "and I know we're going to have a good offense, a really good offense. Just wait. You'll see."

Boone helped to make his own prediction come true. He hit 37 home runs and drove in 141 runs. The Yankees had broken the American League record for most victories with 114 wins in 1998, topping the mark of 111, which had stood for forty-four years since the Cleveland Indians did it in 1954. The new standard set by the Yankees lasted only three years, like McGwire's record, also set in 1998.

The Mariners broke the Yankees' record with 116 victories, tying the major league record of the 1906 Chicago Cubs. They did it simply by out-performing their opponents in every category—pitching, hitting, running, and fielding—doing it at home and on the road. They won the American League West championship by fourteen games over the Oakland A's. The Mariners were in first place every day of the season, only the eighth time that a team has been able to do so. They clinched the pennant early, on September 19, when the A's lost a game to the Texas Rangers.

Seattle's biggest star came out of nowhere. To be more accurate, he came out of Japan. He was Ichiro Suzuki, the first non-pitcher from Japan to sign with a major league team. He was a star in the Japan Pacific League, where he won the batting championship seven times with the Orix Blue Wave. He started out in the United States by doing the same thing, winning the American League batting championship with a .350 average. He also led the league in stolen bases with 56, making himself the first player to lead his league in those two categories since Jackie Robinson had with the Brooklyn Dodgers in 1949.

Seattle's pitchers led the American League in earned run average, their hitters led the league in batting average and runs scored, their base runners led both leagues in stolen bases, and their fielders committed fewer errors than any other team in either league. They played eighteen teams and had a winning record against all of them, and they set a major league record by winning fifty-nine games on the road. How could a team that dominant miss?

With all that success, the Mariners still had something to prove: That they could win the World Series too. For that matter, could they even get *into* the Series? Or would the Yankees and the Diamonbacks be the two teams left standing to play for the right to represent their leagues in the playoffs?

29

Farewells

As the 2001 season neared its conclusion, baseball fans faced an adjustment of another kind: life without Mark McGwire, Cal Ripken, Tony Gwynn, and others– Paul O'Neill, Bret Saberhagen, Wally Joyner, and more. All of them were solid performers throughout their careers whose names were familiar to any fan of their sport. All were retiring after the 2001 season.

McGwire's manager, Tony La Russa, tried to talk his star out of it. "A couple of us did the best we could," he said. "He never wavered in his thinking, but I kept thinking that since he didn't announce it, he might change his mind. I mean, he has a lot of baseball left in him." McGwire finally got around to announcing his retirement after the season was over.

The cold statistics didn't agree with La Russa's assessment that McGwire could return to something approaching his old playing form. McGwire hit only .187 in 2001, the lowest batting average of his career, after off-season knee surgery. He played in only ninety-seven games and hit only 29 home runs.

In the ninth inning of one of the Cardinals games, La Russa lifted McGwire and put in a pinch hitter, Kerry Robinson, to lay down a bunt. After the game, the manager apologized, even though an apology wasn't necessary. "One of my lowest moments as a manager," La Russa said, "was pinch-hitting for Mark," which is also the lowest point for any one-time star. "But my heart was pure," La Russa continued. "I think I owe that to our club. I was just trying to win a game."

McGwire was walking away from a new two-year contract worth $30 million, but even that didn't influence him. "I don't play for numbers and I don't play for money," he said. He added that money "doesn't have any effect on me playing baseball."

Then he said, "As far as the numbers are concerned, whether you're the fifth all-time home run hitter or the tenth, there's no difference to me. You're in an elite group. And if things finish the way they are, I'm very proud about that."

Bob Nightengale quoted McGwire in *Baseball Weekly* on the question of whether he was tired of the game and simply didn't want to play it anymore. "It doesn't come down to *want*," McGwire answered. "It doesn't come down to playing. It comes down to what I can do physically. My body is pretty worn out. And my mind is definitely worn out."

The Cardinals second baseman, Fernando Vina, sounded like a kid when he talked about McGwire's departure, expressing the admiration that professional athletes have for the truly great ones. "It's sad, really," he said. "I miss him already . . . Just playing next to him was such an honor. I would be playing second base, look over at Mark at first, and think to myself, 'Wow, there's Mark McGwire.' "

One of McGwire's best friends and former teammates, Tom Lampkin, said he thought the star was becoming disenchanted with his sport. "He looked at the salaries and how they were influencing the game, and it made him sick," Lampkin said. "He thought there was too much emphasis placed on salaries instead of retaining the integrity of the game."

The Major League Baseball Players Association, the union for the players, released figures later that year that demonstrated the reasons for McGwire's concerns in dramatic figures. The Associated Press reported that the *average* salary in the Major Leagues had risen to $2,138,896, exceeding $2 million for the first time. It represented an increase of 12.8 percent over the previous year. For the third straight year, the Yankees had the highest average salary—$3,930,334. Babe Ruth, who drew criticism from some for making as much as $80,000 in one season, would have trouble believing that the *average* player on the Yankees was making almost $4 million a year. So, for that matter, would Joe DiMaggio, Mickey Mantle, Yogi Berra, Reggie Jackson, Dave Winfield, and a long line of others.

"It's like the home run record," Lampkin continued as he discussed McGwire's feelings about the sport. "The reason he loved breaking the record is because he thought it was good for the game of baseball."

When McGwire's body wouldn't allow him to perform up to his standards, and when he became upset with the emphasis on salaries of seven and even eight figures, he retired. With the $30 million that would still be coming to him if he played the next two seasons, Mark McGwire simply got up and walked away, because he thought it was the right thing to do.

Cal Ripken, forty-one years old, also walked off the field as a big-league baseball player for the last time on the last night of the 2001 season, October 6—21 years, 7,363 days and 3,001 games after it all began. Ripken was on deck as his teammate and best friend on the team, Brady Anderson, struck out to end the game, a 5–1 loss to the Boston Red Sox.

Seconds later, a microphone appeared at home plate, but words would not come easily to the hometown hero. He started and stopped several times, each time producing a cheer from the sellout crowd of 48,807 fans—Cal Ripken fans. Finally, he spoke. He mentioned his boyhood dream of growing up to be a big-league baseball player for the Orioles and thanked his family for helping him to achieve that dream. He thanked the fans and his teammates. He talked about "other dreams," including "pursuing my passion for baseball," which he has continued by establishing a baseball academy for youths in his hometown of Aberdeen, Maryland, and buying a minor league team.

Then he said, "One question I've been repeatedly asked these past few weeks is: How do I want to be remembered? My answer is simple. To be remembered at all is pretty special." He closed by saying, "I might also add that if, if I am remembered, I hope it's because by living my dream, I was able to make a difference."

His team and his fans expressed their appreciation with a variety of gifts including a portrait of his late father, a giant figure 8—his uniform number—made of bricks from the Orioles' former home, Memorial Stadium, where he began his big league career, a life-size statue to stand outside Oriole Park and a check from the team for $1 million for his youth baseball project. The mayor of Baltimore, Martin O'Malley, announced that a street near the ballpark would be renamed "Ripken Way."

Dave Sheinin wrote in *The Washington Post* that the tribute in Baltimore that day climaxed a nationwide farewell of three and a half months, starting with the announcement by Ripken that he would retire at the end of the season. He was hailed in every American League city. Sheinin wrote that the tributes at every stop along the way were "not so much a farewell tour as a moveable feast of love, the intensity of which surprised even Ripken."

After Anderson struck out, leaving Ripken stranded in the on-deck circle and denied the opportunity for one more time at the plate, one more chance to help his team with a game-winning hit, the crowd groaned in its disappointment. But Ripken still had another chance to show that he was a big leaguer in every sense, especially the most important ones. As Anderson walked past him with his head down in disappointment because he hadn't been able to get his pal one more time at bat, Ripken reached over and rubbed Anderson's batting helmet. He told him not to be upset.

"Perhaps," Sheinin, wrote, "it was better that way."

Right fielder Tony Gwynn of the San Diego Padres also called it a career at the end of the 2001 season after twenty seasons in the big leagues. That they retired after the same season is only one of the similarities between Gwynn and Ripken. They were born three months apart in 1960. Both played their entire careers with one team—the San Diego Padres in Gwynn's case. Both come from baseball families, with Gwynn's younger brother, Chris Gwynn, playing in the Major Leagues as an outfielder for ten years. And both Gwynn and Ripken are certain to be elected to baseball's Hall of Fame.

Gwynn won the National League batting championship eight times—while using the smallest bat in the Major Leagues—thirty-two and a half inches long and weighing only thirty-two ounces. Like Ted Williams, who said at the end of his career that he wished he had taken more batting practice, Gwynn did not achieve greatness with a bat simply because he was blessed with an abundance of natural talent. He outworked others, too, to develop that talent to its maximum degree of potential. He had his wife, Alicia, videotaped his every at bat so he could scrutinize his batting stroke every day.

Gwynn, a native of Los Angeles, starred in two sports from his earliest years. He learned baseball by playing with homemade balls, a pastime that produced rewards for three members of the Gwynn family. In addition to Tony and Chris, Charles, became a baseball star at Cal State–Los Angeles.

By the time Tony was thirteen, he was playing on an adult baseball team and was becoming even better in basketball. At San Diego State, he set the school's all-time basketball record for assists as a five-foot eleven-inch guard and was chosen by the San Diego Clippers in the tenth round of the 1981 player draft of the National Basketball Association on the same day he was drafted by the Padres in the baseball draft. Reasoning that a big-league baseball career would last longer than one in the NBA and that his chances for success were better, he signed with the Padres. Thirteen months later, he was playing in the Major Leagues.

Less than a half year later, however, he broke both wrists and was able to play in only 140 games over his first two seasons with the Padres. In his first full season, 1984, he won the league's batting championship with a .351 batting average and a league-leading total of 213 hits as he batted the Padres to the National League pennant.

In 1994, he duplicated George Brett's achievement of 1980 by threatening to become baseball's first .400 hitter since Williams in 1941. The disastrous strike caused a shortened season and canceled Gwynn's attempt to do what Brett or anyone else had not done since 1941. Instead, Gwynn had to content himself with a .394 batting average, four points higher than Brett's in 1980, great enough to win another batting championship and achieve his twelfth straight .300 season, which he extended to fourteen by 1996.

When he thought back over all the highlights of his career for Bob Nightengale of *Baseball Weekly,* Gwynn remembered his top thrill—his home run off David Wells of the Yankees in the first game of the 1998 World Series. "Hitting a home run at Yankee Stadium in a World Series," he said, "is something you dream of."

One senior citizen who didn't seem headed for retirement was Rickey Henderson, even though he was older than any of the new retirees, due to turn forty-four on Christmas Day 2001. On the contrary, rather than "hanging 'em up" as the ball players say about taking off the spikes for the final time, Henderson kept adding to his impressive credentials—and strengthening his case for membership in Cooperstown with McGwire, Ripken, and Bonds.

With two games left in the season, he stood on the verge of passing Ty Cobb with the most runs scored in history. He promised his teammates on the Padres before their game against the Los Angeles Dodgers he would slide into home plate if he scored another run and passed Cobb's record of 2,245 runs.

He kept his promise even though he broke the record with a home run off the top of the left field fence in San Diego on a ninety-three-mile-an-hour fastball from Luke Prokopec. Henderson slid home—feet first—then was mobbed by the rest of the team. He said he slid because the record meant more to him than his others. "It's not an individual record," he said. "You've got to have your teammates help you out. I've had some great teammates over the years. The slide home was a treat for my team-mates."

In the last game of the season, Henderson became the twenty-fifth member of big-league baseball's 3,000-hit club, with a double. The fact that it was a bloop hit did nothing to dampen Henderson's elation. "It's a great feeling, a feeling that you can't really describe," he said. "I thought I would never get there because I walk so much. If you continue to play as long as I've been playing, you get the opportunity to do it."

Henderson's double came on the first pitch he saw from John Thomson of the Colorado Rockies. Three Rockies—second baseman Terry Shumpert, right fielder Mario Encarnacion, and first baseman Todd Helton—ran toward the fly ball, but the ball dropped in among them in short right field about ten feet inside the foul line. Henderson's team-mates rushed onto the infield and he walked toward them with open arms.

Henderson's hit came in teammate Tony Gwynn's last game. "Man, what a sight," Gwynn said after the game—"Rickey cruising into second base and all his teammates running out there."

Henderson was making the 2001 season a memorable one for his own reasons. Before he entered the 3,000-hit club, he had already become baseball's all-time leader in runs scored and walks, after becoming the sport's all-time stolen base champion ten years earlier. He received a plaque to commemorate his milestone hit. He also received something that might mean even more to him. The Rockies' shortstop, Juan Uribe, who took the throw back into the infield on Henderson's hit, gave him the baseball.

All the talk about the aging veterans who were retiring overlooked something else about Barry Bonds in 2001—he wasn't getting any younger either. He turned thirty-seven in July, past the retirement age for most professional athletes, yet he was threatening to rewrite the history books with power hitting and a high batting average, the kind of once-in-a-career season usually achieved by younger players.

Bonds was still going strong even after passing Ruth, Maris, and Sosa in home runs—and hitting in the .320s. Gwynn, one of the best hitters in baseball throughout his career, said one reason for the success of Bonds was his batting stroke, something that Gwynn said never changed over Bonds's entire career. "The stroke is the same stroke," Gwynn said. "He's got the most efficient stroke in the game. It's short. It's to the ball."

Bonds was also still employing the techniques that he adopted when his father was in the big leagues from 1968 through 1981. Bobby used to bring real big-league bats home to Barry, and the son had to "choke up" on the bat handle because they were heavy for a child, gripping it about three-quarters of an inch above the bottom of the bat. Although Ty Cobb, with the highest lifetime average in the history of the sport, also choked up, as did many other hitters in earlier years, the trend over the past several decades has been for hitters to grip the bat all the way down at the bottom in an effort to hit more home runs. Barry was achieving that objective more successfully than anyone else in baseball, while still choking up on the bat, because choking up enables the hitter to generate more "bat speed," which in turn produces more power—and more home runs.

The grip wasn't the only explanation for the success of Bonds in 2001. Being a superb athlete was another key factor. In a profession full of star ball players, first baseman Jeff Bagwell of the Houston Astros said, "Barry might be the greatest player who ever played the game. I can't imagine any player being better than he is. I love baseball history, and I know people talk about Hank Aaron and Willie Mays, but I find it hard to believe anyone has ever been better than Barry."

Barry came by his baseball talent honestly. His father was blessed with the same rare combination of speed and power that he was able to pass on to his son. Dad Bobby hit 332 home runs, stole 461 bases and led the National League in runs scored twice, hit more than 30 home runs six times and stole more than 40 bases seven times.

When the talk during those long, cold winter nights turns to great father-son combinations in the big leagues, like three generations of the Boone family or the Cooper brothers in the 1940s, the Bonds family ranks at the top.

30

Shelters, Shadows, and Cheers

Barry Bonds remained stuck at 69 home runs for four games near the end of the 2001 season, hardly a cold spell by merely human standards, but by now baseball fans had come to consider Bonds *super*human. When the Giants and the Houston Astros began their game on Thursday night, October 4, at Houston's Enron Field, Bonds still had not caught up with McGwire, and time was running out. It was San Francisco's 159th game. There were only four games left. By the ninth inning, Bonds was still stuck at 69.

Worse yet, Houston's pitchers were not giving him a chance. They were ducking him by walking him. In the sixth inning, manager Larry Dierker of the Astros ordered Bonds to be walked intentionally even though Houston was losing, 8–1. It was the last of a three-game series in Houston. When Bonds came to bat in the ninth, he was 0-for-1 and had already been walked three times. The third walk of the night to Bonds gave the Astro pitchers a total of eight walks against him in those three games, seven of them on four pitches. Houston wasn't the only team afraid to pitch to Bonds. In the series before, San Diego's pitchers hit Bonds in two consecutive times at bat.

Before Bonds stepped into the batter's box in the ninth inning in front of 43,734 fans, Dierker called in a new pitcher, a flame-throwing rookie named Wilfredo Rodriguez. Houston was losing, 9–2. The first pitch from the rookie was clocked at ninety-five miles an hour on the radar guns used by big-league teams to determine the velocity of their pitchers. Bonds swung and missed. Then he took ball one, which was one

323

mile an hour faster at ninety-six. On the third pitch from Rodriguez, another fastball, this one ninety-three miles an hour, Bonds hit a fly ball of McGwire dimensions, sending the ball 454 feet into the second deck of the right field stands. He had tied McGwire's record of 70 home runs in one season almost before the ink about McGwire's achievement had a chance to dry in the record books. And the future looked just as bright for Bonds—three more games to break the record, all of them at home in San Francisco.

The home run did more than just tie Bonds with McGwire. It also added to his already sparkling array of achievements. It was the 564th home run of his career, putting him one ahead of cousin Reggie and making him the greatest lefthanded home run hitter in history except for Babe Ruth, who hit 714.

Better yet, the victory kept alive the Giants' hopes of making the playoffs. They were two games behind in two races—for the wild card or the championship of the National League West. Bonds, with no World Series experience in his career, had been insisting all season long that making the playoffs was his top priority.

Rodriguez offered no apologies for giving up the home run. "It was 9–2," he said. "I went up there to get him out."

The Giants returned to San Francisco for a Friday night game at Pacific Bell Park, where Bonds in April had become only the seventeenth player in history to hit five hundred home runs in his career. The Giants, having lost out in their bid to make the playoffs, were playing the Dodgers in their 160th game of the season and the 151st for Bonds. He ascended to the throne as baseball's all-time single-season home run king immediately. Against Chan Ho Park in the first inning, with the Dodgers already winning, 5–0, Bonds took the first pitch for ball one, then hit the next pitch for his seventy-first home run of the season. Again, his blow was of Ruthian and McGwire dimensions, this time 442 feet into the seats in right center field. His teammates rushed to home plate and set off a mob scene. As Bonds reached the plate, he raised his hands toward the sky as a way of expressing his thanks.

He embraced his eleven-year-old son, Nikolai. Fireworks exploded behind the fence in right field. The sellout crowd of 41,730 stood and cheered and began shouts of "Ba-ree! Ba-ree!" Bonds waved his appreciation and then went into the stands and hugged his wife, Liz. About the only people who were disappointed were the fans in the pleasure boats floating in "McCovey Cove," the inlet off San Francisco Bay where nine of Bonds's home run balls dropped during the season. Retrieving them from the water had become a favorite pastime of the fans in the boats.

Two innings later, as if for good measure, Bonds replayed his act. He hit his seventy-second home run, also against Park and also on a 1–0 pitch. It was the seventh home run of his career for Bonds against Park, the same pitcher who gave up Cal Ripken's home run in the All-Star Game three months earlier. The hit moved Bonds up to seventh on the all-time home run list behind only Hank Aaron, Ruth, Mays, Frank Robinson, Harmon Killebrew—all of them members of the Hall of Fame—and McGwire.

On the field after the game, a brief ceremony celebrated the achievement that still had people all over America shaking their heads in amazement. His teammates were standing behind him in the infield. One of them, Jeff Kent, held two-year-old Aisha Bonds. Bonds began to speak but then cupped his right hand over his mouth and cried.

After the postgame celebration, with the terrorist attacks of September 11 and the threat of more still on the minds of every American, Bonds told reporters, "I don't think that my role or any individual person has any effect on this. I think we did it together as a nation. It's nice to be on the field, to see people smile at all of us in one area and not feel afraid of being in that area."

William Gildea of *The Washington Post* said Bonds continued in that modest vein, saying, "We came together as a nation on our own. It didn't take baseball, football or any other sport to make that happen. It took the tragedy [of September 11] to make that happen."

In the same Saturday morning paper of October 6 that carried the quote by Bonds, readers of the *Post* learned the results of a poll to determine how much support there might be for a military response by the United States in retaliation for the terrorist attacks. The survey showed that 90 percent of those polled said they would support such action against groups or nations responsible for the attacks. The same poll showed that 45 percent would "strongly" support the military action even if it resulted in a long war with heavy casualties, while another 21 percent said they would "somewhat" support it. Only 26 percent said they would oppose military action leading to war.

★   ★   ★

Bonds arrived at the ballpark in San Francisco at 9:30 on Sunday morning on his motorcycle, two hours ahead of his teammates. America had just invaded Afghanistan in the new war against terrorism.

He owned the new home run record all right, but he paid a heavy price. Shortstop Shawon Dunston bet him in May that he would break McGwire's record. Bonds scoffed at the idea, but Dunston persisted, saying if Bonds did it, he wanted a new Mercedes, which carried a price tag of $100,000. Bonds, with no more than 49 home runs in any season, agreed. As he lounged in the dressing room before the last game of the season, the new record of 72 safely in his grasp, he laughed about the bet with Dunston. "Hey, man," he said, "I'll pay up. It was worth it. He'll have his car this week."

Bonds was making home run history with a new kind of bat, one made of maple wood from Canada, instead of the traditional ones made from ash wood. The maple bats are the product of Sam Holman, a Canadian carpenter who began manufacturing them in the late 1990s as a way to slow down the epidemic of cracked and broken bats. For a solution, he turned to maple wood, harder and denser than ash wood. He named his bat the "Rideau Crusher" after a canal that runs through Ottawa. Today somewhere between two hundred and three hundred major league players, depending on who is doing the estimating, are swinging "the Crusher," including Bonds. The maple bat has been called the first major advancement in bat manufacturing in a century.

Holman presented Bonds with a maple bat at the Giants' 1999 spring training camp in Scottsdale, Arizona. After Bonds tried it during batting practice, he told Holman the bat felt harder than his ash models and that the ball seemed to jump off the bat. However, Shawon Dunston was inclined to credit the man more than the bat for the record-shattering season by Bonds in 2001. "Even before maple bats came out," Dunston said, "he still hit 30 a year and was consistent. If Barry says it's the bats, it's the bats. But I say it's not. I say it's him. He's the best."

Bob Nightengale wrote in *Baseball Weekly* that Bonds, who was due to become a free agent in the off-season and would be able to sign with any team, was experiencing mixed emotions on that last morning of the season. "I don't know what I'm supposed to feel right now," he said. "I don't know what I'm supposed to think. I don't know if this is my last day in a Giants uniform. I don't know if I'll be here the rest of my career."

Instead, Nightengale said, Bonds was finding more pleasure in think-

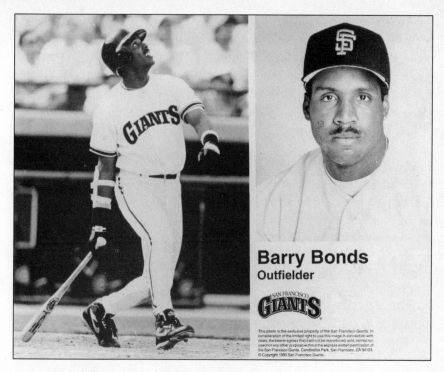

Barry Bonds
Outfielder

This photo is the exclusive property of the San Francisco Giants. In consideration of the limited right to use this image in connection with news, the bearer agrees that it will not be reproduced, sold, rented nor used for any other purpose without the express written permission of the San Francisco Giants, Candlestick Park, San Francisco, CA 94124. © Copyright 1993 San Francisco Giants.

Barry Bonds follows the flight of one of his 73 home runs in the 2001 season, a number that baseball experts and fans still find hard to believe. (National Baseball Hall of Fame Library, Cooperstown, N.Y.)

ing about a vacation with Liz after the season. "I owe her everything," he said. "She means the world to me. I've leaned on her so much, and she's always been there for me."

He talked about what the season meant to him personally: "I think this has changed everything. People aren't going to be throwing stones and flinging arrows at me. It's going to be different now."

His reasoning, he said, was that the Giants didn't make the playoffs, even with his historic season. "I just had the greatest season there ever was," he analyzed, "and it still wasn't good enough. We still didn't make the playoffs. It shows that one man doesn't make a team. And one man shouldn't be blamed when things go wrong."

As game time approached, Bonds learned he would be facing a knuckleball pitcher, the dread of every power hitter because the slow knuckleballs do not provide any power of their own—virtually all of it must come from the hitter. "Oh, man," he said, "just what I need. What next?"

At 1:51 on Sunday afternoon, October 7, Bonds stepped into the batter's box to face Dennis Springer, whose "butterfly pitches" were so slow they were barely registering on the radar gun. Bonds worked the count to three balls and two strikes. Then he saw another floater headed toward the plate at seventy-two miles an hour in this ninety-mile-an-hour era. He "double-clutched," as the players say, starting his swing, quickly checking it, then starting again just as quickly. The result was his seventy-third home run of the season, to right field. As he rounded the bases, he laughed and shrugged his shoulders.

He had reason to do both. The homer not only topped off the greatest season for power ever produced by any baseball player, it also gave him a set of numbers that were more than just sparkling statistics; they were historic achievements. His home run total became a record with his seventy-first when he passed McGwire, and he added two other records when he topped Babe Ruth in walks with 177 and slugging percentage with .863. The two marks had both endured for more than three-quarters of a century, since 1923 and 1920 respectively.

In 153 games, Bonds scored 129 runs, had 156 hits, drove in 137 runs, and was on base more than half the times he came to bat, with an on-base percentage of .515. Two more statistics illustrate just how great he was in 2001, and how much the other American League teams feared him: He was walked intentionally thirty-five times and hit by the pitch nine times.

When he crossed home plate after his seventy-third home run, he pointed his two index fingers to the sky again, still giving thanks. Meanwhile, two fans scrambled for the ball, and both claimed it was theirs. One sued the other, and the court case lasted fifteen days. On December 18, 2002, San Francisco judge Kevin McCarthy finally ruled that the ball, valued at a million dollars, belonged to both men and should be sold, with each man receiving half the purchase price.

Two members of baseball's Hall of Fame, Brooks Robinson and Bob Feller, talked in 2002 about the explosions of home runs in recent years and the reasons for them. In conversations for this book, they agreed that it was a combination of factors: bigger and stronger players, pitching diluted by expansion, the livelier ball, smaller ballparks, a reduced strike zone—and the maple bat.

Simple arithmetic supports the argument that the quality of pitching has changed because of expansion. With fourteen more teams in the big leagues than the original sixteen, and assuming a staff of 10 pitchers on each team, there were 140 pitchers in the big leagues in 2001 who would not have been there before the leagues began expanding in 1961.

Robinson said bluntly, "The pitching is as bad as you'll ever see it." Feller agreed. Feller, who hit eight home runs in his career even though pitchers are not expected to hit homers, said he would pitch against today's hitters the same way he pitched against the sluggers of his day—Ted Williams, Joe DiMaggio, Hank Greenberg, Jimmie Foxx, and others. "On the fists," he said, "and if they move away from the plate, you move your pitches in with them."

Will someone hit more than 73? Feller said, "Probably." He said it depends on the conditions, such as rules changes, equipment improvements, alterations in the strike zone, and other factors. "Eventually," he said, "someone probably will hit more than 73."

Robinson wasn't so sure. "I don't see it," he said. "It would be hard to do. I don't see it happening, but I didn't see 70 or 73 happening either."

On the day that Brooks was talking about home runs, Bonds hit two of them on the first day of the 2002 season, against the Dodgers in Los Angeles. Even after the long winter layoff, he didn't miss a beat, prompting his teammate J. T. Snow to say, "This guy's in another league. It doesn't surprise you. You almost come to expect it. I think the rest of us feel like we're Little Leaguers. We're fighting and scratching, and he's up there as relaxed as can be. He just does things others can't do."

For Bonds, the pressure was off after his seventy-third homer in 2001—or was it? The pressure has never seemed to be off where Barry Bonds is concerned. It was the same way with his father, and Barry remembers. Maybe that's why he seemed to many people—fans, media, teammates, opponents, and others—that he always had a chip on his shoulder. With all of his achievements, he never attained the popularity and hero worship that might be expected of a star athlete, especially a baseball player who hits a ton of home runs. Home run hitters are always among the most popular of sports heroes, but that widespread popularity—enjoyed first by Ruth and Gehrig and over the years by Aaron, Mays, Mantle, and so many others—always seemed to elude Bonds, or maybe Bonds eluded it.

His father was controversial, and so is the son. "No one gives my Dad credit for what he did," Barry said in an article by Hank Hersch in *Sports Illustrated* in 1990, when he was twenty-five years old and in his fifth season with the Pittsburgh Pirates "and they want to put me in the same category. He did 30–30 [30 home runs and 30 stolen bases in the same season] five times, and they say he never became the ballplayer he should have become. Ain't nobody else done 30–30 five times. Nobody. Zero. So I don't care whether they like me or they don't like me. I don't care."

Hersch describes the similarities between father and son: "Says the son: 'Tell me something I can't do, and I'll show you I can do it.' And the father: 'I would never say I was better than everybody else. But there was nothing on the field that *anybody* else could do that I couldn't.' "

Barry admits that he has a hidden motive behind his comments and attitude. "To me, when people say I have an attitude problem, it gives me an edge. It makes me mad, so I play better." He adds, "Since I was a kid, I've had a stamp on my neck: Barry Bonds has a bad attitude and only thinks of himself. Who else am I supposed to think about out there? I go out there to put up the best numbers to help us win. That's being part of the team."

Nine years later, after Bonds joined the San Francisco Giants as a free agent following the 1992 season, his team described some of his public service activities in the Bay Area in its 2001 *Press Guide*. By that time, he was a leader in the Barry Bonds Family Foundation, spearheading a three-year bone marrow campaign to raise $250,000 and register one thousand African Americans whose families are affected by leukemia or similar blood disorders. He also served as the spokesman for a summer reading program in 2000 and as a member of the board of San Francisco United Way. His image has appeared on billboards for a "Stop Youth Violence" campaign conducted by the California Police Activities League. After donating $100,000 to the Adopt-A-Special-Kid organization, he was honored at a special dinner in November 1996. The mayor of San Francisco, Willie Brown, proclaimed it "Barry Bonds Day" in San Francisco.

The Giants said Bonds purchased tickets for fifty bleacher seats per game for forty-two dates at Candlestick Park in June, July, and August for kids in the "Bonds Squad," members of the "Make-a-Family" program. He also pledged $10,000 a year to the Special Kids program plus $100 for each home run, stolen base, or run batted in. In 1993, he co-hosted a Thanksgiving TV special to raise funds for the victims of fires in Southern California and autographed baseballs and bats to be donated to the United Way for additional assistance to the victims. The *Press Guide* said Bonds was also honored by the Cardiac Arrhythmia Research and Education Foundation for his work with young athletes and his interest in combating sudden cardiac deaths.

The heading for that portion of the Bonds biography in the 2001 *Media Guide* was:

A Giant in the Community

As the baseball world prepared for the playoffs and the World Series, the rest of America prepared for the brave new world of life in an age of terrorist threats. That age was reflected in the rash of red, white, and blue across the country, the stories in the news media and conversations over lunch and dinner that dealt now with subjects of war and threats of war instead of the weather, politics, and the kids.

The new environment was evident in New York and Washington, the targets of September 11, and in every other city and town, large and small. One of those communities was the town of Northwood, New Hampshire. Northwood is the home of a company called Radius Defense and Engineering. The company makes shelters. In World War II, such facilities were called "bomb shelters." In the Cold War, with its atomic age, they were called "fallout shelters." Today they are "disaster shelters," built to protect their occupants from injury or death in the event of natural disasters such as hurricanes or tornadoes as well as nuclear attack, fallout, and biological warfare.

The company has been in business for twenty-six years. Since the terrorist attacks against New York and Washington, its volume of business has increased eightfold. The company's founder and president, Walton McCarthy, says he expanded his work force to five times its previous size after September 11, from fifteen to seventy-five. Sales tripled. The company received one hundred to five hundred E-mail messages every day requesting information on its egg-shaped fiberglass shelters. Every morning when Radius employees reported to work, there were ninety-nine messages on the company's answering machine. There would be more, but the machine can't hold any more. The company, which McCarthy says is the only manufacturer of disaster shelters in the world, used to produce one shelter a week. In only a few months after September 11, it was producing five a day.

The shelters were selling despite the cost involved, anywhere from $20,000 to $60,000. Individual customers were buying them, and so were businesses and government agencies, including the armed forces. They provide room for up to ten occupants and enough storage space to hold a food supply of anywhere from three months to a year, depending on the size of the shelter. A battery system operates an underground power plant.

The reawakened interest in shelters was in sharp contrast to the public opinion on the subject that existed for years. As the Cold War began to cool off with the Soviet Union's mounting internal problems in the 1970s and '80s, so did people's attitudes toward shelters and civil defense in general. After September 11, shelter sales were brisk at Radius. Mc-Carthy, who has a shelter of his own, offers an explanation: "The attacks changed the attitudes of a lot of people."

With the baseball season nearing its climax in October, a new and secret operation in our national government was starting to function, established by President Bush in the first hours following the terrorist attacks. Under a standing directive issued by President Dwight Eisenhower in the 1950s and in effect ever since, key executives of the federal agencies left Washington hastily and formed a "shadow government" at two undisclosed locations somewhere on the East Coast outside the nation's capital.

The "shadow government," with anywhere from 70 to 150 executives sheltered in bunkers to continue the functions of the national government in the event of a catastrophe, remained a secret until disclosed by *The Washington Post* on March 1, 2002. Staff writers Barton Gellman and Susan Schmidt reported that government officials "work underground 24 hours a day, away from their families," until relieved under a schedule of rotation.

The first officials assigned to the new operation were deployed "on the fly" on September 11, faced with the sobering responsibility of preventing the collapse of the federal government and the essential services that it provides to the American people. Some were airlifted out of Washington by helicopter to their secret locations. Others were transported speedily by buses. The arrangement has now become "an indefinite precaution," according to the *Post*, with every cabinet agency represented, along with several non-cabinet offices.

In the event of a major disaster in Washington that could cripple the functions of government, the responsibility of the shadow government would be to minimize disruptions to the distribution of food and water to the public, transportation, energy, and communications while continuing other functions necessary to protect the public's health and safety.

In the first days of the "shadow government," officials faced ninety days of "bunker duty" before being relieved and allowed to return to their families. Above ground, millions of Americans were turning their attention instead to baseball, seeking relief from the new concerns about war and peace.

For the Seattle Mariners and their fans, the smooth sailing continued. They won the championship of their division by defeating the Cleveland Indians, three games to two. The teams split the first two games but Cleveland overpowered Seattle in the third game, 17–2. The Mariners shook off the effects of that pounding and won the next two games and the division series by scores of 6–2 and 3–1.

The Yankees, meanwhile, were doing their part for a New York–Seattle shootout by winning their division series, three games to two, over the Oakland A's, even though the A's jumped off to a two-games-to-none advantage. They beat the Yankees, 5–3 and 2–0, but the Yankees came back to sweep the next three games, 1–0, 9–2, and 5–3, to qualify for a matchup against Seattle.

Meanwhile, the nation was learning of a new scare—letters laced with a bacterium that causes the infectious and often fatal disease, anthrax, which had arrived in the mail at the offices of NBC's Tom Brokaw in New York. On the day the Yankees won the division series over Oakland, a second anthrax letter arrived in the Washington offices of Senator Tom Daschle, the senate majority leader. Fears mounted that this was a new and deadly form of terrorism, one that could be spread rapidly through the mails by unknown terrorists. Americans began to exercise caution in opening their mail, and washing their hands after.

The baseball playoffs continued in the midst of this new development. The Yankees burst the Mariners' bubble in a hurry, winning the first two games, 4–2 and 3–2, their fourth and fifth straight playoff victories. Seattle stormed back with a vengeance in the third game, 14–3. The Yankees staged a comeback, too, winning the fourth game, 3–1, and then came up with a laugher of their own by winning the final game and the championship series, 12–3.

At the same time, Arizona, an expansion team only four years old, was also qualifying for the World Series, first by eliminating the St. Louis Cardinals, three games to two, for their division championship, then by defeating the Atlanta Braves in the National League's championship series, four games to one, after the Braves had won their tenth straight division title.

The Braves and the Diamondbacks split the first two games, but Arizona won the next three. Now the stage was set: The underdog expansion team against mighty New York, which was threatening to become the first team to win at least four World Series in a row since an earlier edition of the Yankees won five straight Series under Casey Stengel, from 1949 to 1953. Only one other team had won four Series in a row, the Yankees of Joe DiMaggio's rookie season, 1936 through 1939.

New York was in the enjoyable and enviable position of being both the betting favorite and the sentimental one. Fans who had rooted against the New York dynasty all their lives because the Yankees have been such a dominant team off and on starting with the Babe Ruth teams of the 1920s were suddenly rooting *for* New York because of September 11. People who used to say they rooted for "anybody but the Yankees" were hoping the city's baseball team would give its people something to smile about.

Even Lou Piniella, the manager of the losing Seattle team and a former Yankee star, expressed his feelings for the people of New York. "You know," he said after the Yankees had eliminated his Mariners at Yankee Stadium, "the amazing thing is that at about the eighth inning, when the fans were really reveling in the stands, the one thought that did come to my mind, strangely enough, is 'Boy, this city suffered a lot,' and tonight they let out a lot of emotions. And I felt for them in that way . . . I felt good for them. I really did."

Piniella's counterpart, manager Joe Torre of the Yankees, expressed a pride both in his city and his team. He said, "I wouldn't want to minimize what went on, but there's no question this club has taken on the adversity of September 11 and is working hard at showing the city its own form of unity. The city pulled together, and this team is showing that same competitive spirit."

Because of the Yankees' four-year streak of successes and the emotions behind them, the Diamondbacks were given little hope of winning the World Series. Columnist Mike Kahn, executive editor of Sports line.com, called New York's victory over Seattle "inevitable." After it became a fact, Kahn wrote, "The Yankees march on across the country to the Valley of the Sun against the Diamondbacks. Really, is there any doubt what's next?"

He wasn't the only one thinking or talking like that.

31

History's Partners, Again

America's "national pastime" and America herself became partners in history again in the fall of 2001. A World Series would be just what the doctor ordered, especially a down-to-the-wire, seven-game exciting duel, and that's exactly what America got. When it was over, players, fans, reporters, broadcasters, and owners were saying it was one of the greatest ever—and exactly the tonic the country needed.

The reminders of our new world were all around us, as would be expected in the historic, century-old connection between the nation and its sport. The Yankees held a morning workout the day before the first game of the Series, but Yankee Stadium was closed to the public. Before September 11, fans were free to walk around the stadium. Now, only members of the news media and team personnel were allowed inside.

A housewife from Long Island, Stephanie Johnson, expressed the attitude of most Americans, not just those in New York. She told Greg Boeck and Mel Antonen of *USA Today,* "The security is amazing, but I suppose there is nothing much else they can do. I guess you could say it is a constant reminder of what our city and country are going through."

In Phoenix, there were changes at Bank One Ballpark, too. Jets assigned to the Air National Guard were standing by. There would be no blimps flying overhead for those camera shots looking down at the ballpark. Fans would be watched closely not only by the security forces on hand but by others looking at more than one hundred video cameras. Bill Rathburn, former deputy chief of police for Los Angeles, who was in charge of security for the 1996 Olympic games in Atlanta, offered a sobering long-range view. "I think things only changed temporarily in the past," he said. "But this time, I think they'll stay changed."

Barry Bonds was on hand to throw out the first pitch—and to receive the Commissioner's Historic Achievement Award from Bud Selig. After Bonds thanked the record crowd of 49,646 fans for their support, Arizona's starting pitcher, six-foot five-inch righthander Curt Schilling, stood behind the mound and said a prayer. He also tucked a chain into his jersey. The chain was a gift from his late father, Cliff. That is only one part of Schilling's pregame ritual. He also leaves a ticket for his father when he is going to be pitching.

Then he went about the business of winning the first game of the World Series. He did it with a ninety-seven-mile-an-hour fastball, winning his fifth straight postseason start dating back to 1993. This one wasn't even close. The Diamondbacks beat the Yankees, 9–1. Schilling held New York to three hits over seven innings and struck out eight. The Yankees, winners of sixteen of their last seventeen World Series games, looked like anything but champions. Yankee errors and misplays that weren't scored as errors led to five unearned runs. Their starter, Mike Mussina, gave up a home run to Craig Counsell in the first inning and four more runs in the third, when David Justice contributed to New York's troubles by failing to catch a catchable fly ball hit by Steve Finley. Left fielder Luis Gonzalez, who hit 57 home runs during the regular season, hit a two-run homer in the inning. Gonzalez came out of the Arizona dugout for a curtain call, responding to a long round of applause from the fans, including Barry Bonds.

In only three innings Mussina threw 63 pitches. After the game, he said simply, "I was just awful." It was bad enough for the Yankees that they lost the first game, but there was more bad news concerning their immediate future: Arizona's pitcher for the second game would be Randy Johnson, the dominating, intimidating six-foot ten-inch left-hander called "The Big Unit," who was just as fast as Schilling—and five inches taller.

The news didn't get any better for the Yankees or their fans. The Diamondbacks won again, this time 4–0 on a three-hitter by Johnson. He struck out eleven hitters, walked only one and went the full nine innings. He didn't give up a hit until the fifth inning. Third baseman Matt Williams hit a three-run homer off Andy Pettitte that sealed Arizona's victory and gave the Diamondbacks a two-games-to-none lead over the world champions. Pettitte looked as invincible as Johnson for much of the time. At one point, he threw eighteen straight strikes.

Joe Torre gave Johnson high praise. "He was terrific," Torre said. "He lived up to what he's supposed to be. The axiom has never changed—good pitching stops good hitting."

Then the Series moved to New York for the next three games. That's when things became exciting.

The first pitcher in Yankee Stadium for the third game was President Bush. After giving the thumbs-up sign on the mound as the crowd applauded, he threw out the first ball, a strike most observers said, that even had what the players call "movement." It broke late, like a cut fastball, to the Yankees' backup catcher, Todd Greene. Arizona's manager, Bob Brenly, told the chief executive, "Very nice throw, Mr. President. Good stuff. Good stuff." He became the first president to throw out the first pitch at a World Series game since President Eisenhower, a former semipro player, performed the honors in 1956 at Brooklyn's Ebbets Field before a game between the Yankees and the Dodgers.

The President wasn't the only prominent Republican in the ballpark that night. Mayor Giuliani, dressed in a Yankee warm-up jacket, was there, sitting in his usual front-row seat next to the Yankees dugout. Senator John McCain of Arizona, who had campaigned against Mr. Bush for the Republican nomination for president the year before, sat next to Mayor Giuliani.

The President, wearing a New York Fire Department windbreaker, was not showing only his pitching skills out on the mound in the Bronx. He was showing his courage too. He was standing there in front of 55,820 people in Yankee Stadium, at a time of extreme concerns about security and terrorism, his nation at war, demonstrating to the world that he and his fellow Americans were not backing down, that life was going to continue in this country and he was going to lead the way. It may sound corny now, although it shouldn't, but at that time, it took leadership and just plain guts to stand out there, without a Secret Service agent or a police officer in sight to those millions who were watching all over the country on television.

He had more than the presidency among his qualifications for throwing out that first pitch. He headed the Texas Rangers as their managing general partner from 1989 to 1994. His baseball credentials extended all

President Bush gives the thumbs-up sign to the crowd at Yankee Stadium before throwing out the first pitch at the third game of the 2001 World Series, less than a month after the terrorist attacks on New York and Washington on September 11. (White House Photo by Eric Draper.)

the way to his boyhood, as a Little Leaguer in Texas. "I never dreamed about being president," he said. "I wanted to be Willie Mays." And no wonder. The current president is the third generation of Bush men to be involved in baseball. It is well known that his father, the first President Bush, played first base for Yale, but not so well known is that his grandfather did, too. Prescott Bush, who became a U.S. Senator from Connecticut, was Yale's first baseman around the time of America's entry into World War I.

Today's President Bush told reporters about one of the fringe benefits associated with his current job. In the White House one day, he said, "One of the great things about living here is that you don't have to sign up for a baseball fantasy camp to meet your heroes. It turns out they come here." When they do, the President knows what to ask of them. Even before his election, he was already the proud owner of more than 250 autographed baseballs.

First Lady Laura Bush testified to the President's love of baseball. At the Republican convention in the year 2000, she told others, "I sat by his side during some winning and many losing baseball seasons. But George never loses sight of home plate."

Somebody else who didn't lose sight of home plate was "Challenger," an American bald eagle who came gracefully swooping into the infield from center field before the start of each of the three games in New York.

The next pitcher to take the mound after President Bush was Roger Clemens of the Yankees, who had been warming up before the President delivered his opening pitch. "When President Bush came out," Clemens said after the game, "I stopped warming up. I wanted to take in that moment. There's a lot of things that went on this evening that I will remember for a long time."

Clemens, an all-star and a sure-shot future Hall of Famer, pitched like a man worthy of both of those honors, and he did it at a time when his team was on the brink of a full-scale crisis. The Yankees were 0–2, and no team had ever rallied from an 0–3 hole to win a World Series, or any other kind of postseason series. This was a game they simply *had* to win.

On a cold and windy night, the fans sat bundled up as Clemens won the game for the Yankees, 2–1, with relief help from the seemingly unhittable Mariano Rivera. The Yankees remained on the brink in a 1–1 tie until third baseman Scott Brosius came through in the clutch with a broken-bat single to left field with two outs in the sixth inning that scored Bernie Williams with what turned out to be the winning run. Clemens struck out nine Diamondbacks and limited them to three hits. Rivera pitched two perfect innings to save the win for New York and narrow the gap to two wins for Arizona and one for the Yankees.

The Yankees got some help from their opponents. Five of the members of Arizona's starting lineup had never played in Yankee Stadium before. Whether it was the jitters or not, the Diamondbacks, who led their league in fielding that year, committed three errors, and their pitchers threw three wild pitches.

The designated hitter for the Yankees, Chuck Knoblauch, noticed that the crowd wasn't quite as excited as you would expect in a World Series game, especially with the home team winning a must-win game. "I don't think it was that intense," Knoblauch said. "Maybe it's because the President was here and people are worried about the threats. Hopefully it will be different tomorrow."

Clemens, who pitched with a sore right hamstring muscle, said, "I knew it was a game that we had to have."

The defending World Series champions were a long way from being out of the woods. They were still behind in the Series, one win to two for Arizona, and their next opponent was the one who shut them down in the first game—Curt Schilling, who would be pitching with only three days of rest.

Manager Bob Brenly of the Diamondbacks told reporters, "He's the right guy." Torre told reporters Brenly was right. "It doesn't surprise me," he said.

When reporters asked Schilling his history of pitching on three days of rest, he replied, "Don't have one. Never done it before in the big leagues."

The tension level increased considerably in Game 4. The crowd was noisier and more enthusiastic, maybe reflecting the warmer temperatures and also sensing that their team needed their support to avoid another backs-to-the-wall situation. Schilling gave the Yankees and their fans cause for concern immediately, starting the game with ten straight strikes. Was it going to be another long night for the New Yorkers, and maybe an early exit from the Series after all?

The game unfolded as a nail-biter. The score was 1–1 entering the eighth inning, on home runs by Shane Spencer for the Yankees in the third and Mark Grace for the Diamondbacks in the fourth. With one out in the top of the eighth, Torre lifted his starter, Orlando Hernandez, in favor of Mike Stanton. The Diamondbacks proceeded to score two runs and take the lead on a single by Luis Gonzalez and a double by Erubiel Durazo. Later in the inning, pinch runner Midre Cummings scored on a grounder by Matt Williams, beating the throw from shortstop Derek Jeter to increase Arizona's lead to 3–1.

In the bottom half of the eighth, Brenly raised some eyebrows by lifting Schilling, even though he was pitching like a man who had enjoyed more than three days of rest between starts. After seven innings he had allowed only three hits and had thrown eighty-eight pitches. Despite Schilling's strong showing, Brenly called in Byung-Hyun Kim to pitch the eighth for the Diamondbacks.

Kim began to look like money in the bank by striking out the side. After the Diamondbacks failed to score in the top of the ninth, they took the field only three outs away from going ahead in the Series, three games to one.

Then, the fabled Yankee power seemed to come back to life, like ghosts rising from the graveyard on this Halloween night.

With one out and the bases empty, Kim gave up a single to Paul O'Neill, but seemed on his way to victory anyhow when he struck out Bernie Williams. But Tino Martinez, New York's first baseman, who had been hitless in nine at bats, sent a drive over the center field fence to tie the game, 3–3, and breathe new life into his team.

In the tenth inning, after the Diamondbacks again failed to score, Kim retired the first two New York hitters. He was one out away from extending the game to eleven innings and giving his team another chance to win and take that 3–1 advantage in the Series. The Yankees' hopes rested on Jeter, who was only 1-for-15 in the World Series.

Kim jumped ahead in the count, no balls and two strikes, and then Jeter fouled off three 0–2 pitches. Meanwhile, the clocked ticked to midnight. Now it was November 1. The scoreboard flashed a message never seen in the Major Leagues before:

WELCOME TO NOVEMBER BASEBALL

It was the first time a World Series game had been played in November. At 12:04 A.M., Jeter hit the next pitch for an opposite-field home run into the seats in right field. The first game-ending home run of Jeter's career won the game for the Yankees, 4–3, and pulled them even with the Diamondbacks in the World Series at two wins apiece. Some fans and reporters began calling him "Mr. November." Appropriately, one of those in the sellout crowd of 55,863 fans was Reggie Jackson—"Mr. October."

In the fifth game, history repeated itself to an extent that was hard to believe, and both teams and their fans realized that they were watching a special kind of World Series, one to remember. Some were already wondering if it might go on to become one of the greatest Series in history, ranking right up there with the '75 Series and a select few others.

Those feelings were strengthened by another cliff-hanger, the second extra-inning game in a row, as the Yankees defeated the Diamondbacks, 3–2, in twelve innings. The victim again, for the second time in twenty-four hours, was Arizona's relief pitcher Byung-Hyun Kim.

After Reggie Jackson and another former Yankee star, Don Mattingly, each threw out a "first" ball, the teams battled in a scoreless tie until the fifth inning, when home runs by Steve Finley and Catcher Rod Barajas gave Arizona a 2–0 lead. In the eighth, Bob Brenly made the same managerial decision he made the night before—lifting his starter, Miguel Batista in this case, even though he had a 2–0 lead. The Yankees had two outs and two men on base. Once again, the strategy worked at the beginning. Greg Swindell got Martinez on a fly ball, and the Diamondbacks still had their 2–0 lead going into the ninth.

The 56,018 fans began to mount a roar of support for the Yankees, which grew louder when they saw that Arizona was bringing in another pitcher—Kim. Yankees' catcher Jorge Posada made the Diamondbacks and their fans uneasy immediately by leading off the inning with a double. Kim got the next two hitters, Shane Spencer on a ground ball and Knoblauch on a strikeout. Now Kim was one out away from redeeming himself and putting his team only one win from a major upset victory in the World Series. All he had to do was get Scott Brosius.

Again, Yankee power, born in the Babe Ruth–Lou Gehrig era and immortalized over the decades by DiMaggio, Mantle, Maris, Jackson, and others, won for the Yankees. The team that became known for its "5 o'clock lightning" in the DiMaggio era, when the Yankees won so many games in the late innings with home runs, avoided disaster again. Brosius saved his team with a two-run home run off Kim to tie the game and send it into extra innings for the second straight night. On his way down the first base line, Brosius raised both fists into the air and his feet barely touched the ground as he began his triumphant tour of the bases. On the pitcher's mound, Kim hung his head, feeling fate's cruel sting for the second straight night.

The game rocked along until the twelfth inning. It was early the next morning when Chuck Knoblauch led off with his first hit of the Series and advanced to second on a sacrifice bunt by Brosius. Alfonso Soriano then singled off Albie Lopez, scoring Knoblauch ahead of the throw from Reggie Sanders in right field. The Yankees were come-from-behind, last-minute winners for the second night in a row. More than that, they found themselves ahead in the Series, three games to two, and only one win away from their fourth straight World Series championship.

The postgame comments expressed the disbelief felt by everyone, including the players. "No disrespect to the fans or the Diamondbacks," Knoblauch said, "but you have to sit back and kind of chuckle a little bit because it's so unbelievable."

Mike Mussina said, "You know they have to be thinking, 'I can't believe this is happening.' Not one night, but two nights in a row. I think we're all feeling the same emotions we were feeling twenty-four hours ago."

Brosius said, "It seemed like the whole situation was set again, and it happened again."

Joe Torre said, "I can't be surprised. It just happened the day before." He added significantly, "This is the most incredible couple of games I've ever managed."

Then the Series moved back to Arizona, where more surprises—even shocks—were waiting to unfold.

The first surprise was produced by the Diamondbacks. Back home in Bank One Ballpark, they unleashed Yankee-like power and clobbered New York, 15–2, with twenty-two hits, a World Series record. After six games, the Series was tied at three wins each. The teams had set the stage for what every baseball fan loves—a seventh game in the Series.

In that sixth game, Arizona jumped out in front with three runs in the second inning, two of them on a single by Tony Womack. Then, with Randy Johnson back on the mound, they cinched things against one of baseball's best lefthanders, Andy Pettitte, by knocking him out of the game in the third inning, after he had given up seven hits and six runs. In the third, the Diamondbacks rapped out nine hits and eight runs, off Pettitte and his successor, Jay Witasick. The game resulted in a strange combination of statistics: The home team had won all six games in the

Series, yet, with three wins by each team, the Diamondbacks had scored almost three times as many runs as the Yankees, 34–12.

The owner of the Yankees, George Steinbrenner, was at the game, after passing up the first two games at Arizona. Mayor Giuliani was there too, with twenty-five family members of rescue workers who were killed in the terrorist attacks against the World Trade Center.

The approach of a seventh game produced a strange touch of irony. The two starting pitchers, Roger Clemens for the Yankees and Curt Schilling for the Diamondbacks, would be crossing paths again. The two big, hard-throwing righthanders had met ten years earlier in Houston's Astrodome. Both men live in Houston and were working out as part of their off-season conditioning programs.

With that opportunity, Schilling introduced himself to Clemens, who had just won his third Cy Young Award with the Boston Red Sox as the best pitcher in the American League. Schilling was twenty-five years old and had only four victories after parts of four seasons in the big leagues, so he asked Clemens what he had to do to become a winner in the Major Leagues. Clemens answered bluntly by telling Schilling he had to apply himself more, both on and off the field, work harder and make himself into the pitching ace that he was capable of becoming. Schilling says today that the talk changed his life because it changed his attitude.

Now, ten years later, the two men were facing each other for the championship of the baseball world in a game watched by millions and at a time when the drama of the seventh game was accompanied by a different kind of drama, a new one, in the world itself.

"If the Lord had sat me down in January of this year," Schilling told columnist Hal Bodley of *USA Today*, "and asked me to script out a dream season, I couldn't have come up with this. Game 7 against Roger Clemens, with everything that's happened, the way the year has gone for my family, the way the year has gone for this team. What Roger did for me and has done for me throughout my career, I couldn't have dreamt this. I'm not that big of a dreamer."

With the arrival of the seventh game of this nail-biter, cliff-hanger World Series in Phoenix, baseball again took its position on America's center stage. It was Sunday night, November 4, the day the nation returned to standard time after the annual summer switch to daylight saving time. By the time the game was over, Mayor Giuliani echoed the feelings of baseball fans everywhere, whether they were rooting for the

Yankees or the Diamondbacks. "That," the Mayor said, "was the greatest Game 7 ever."

Alfonso Soriano moved the Yankees into a 2–1 lead in the eighth inning with a bases empty home run off Schilling. When Torre summoned Mariano Rivera into the game to pitch the bottom half of the inning, New York was making a strong threat to win the Series—with the score in its favor and the best relief pitcher in the sport on the mound. Rivera pumped even more confidence into his teammates by shutting out the Diamondbacks in their half of the eighth. It was his sixth straight scoreless inning in the Series. That the Yankees did not score in the ninth did nothing to lessen their confidence, not with Rivera going back to the mound for one more inning.

New York was threatening to win its fifth World Series in six years, prompting talk that this edition of the team was another Yankee dynasty. The Diamondbacks, if they could find two runs somewhere, were also threatening to score a memorable achievement: They could become a World Series champion faster than any expansion team in history. In 1997, the Florida Marlins, trailing the Cleveland Indians in the ninth inning of Game 7, pulled out the victory and won the World Series faster than any previous team, in only five years. Arizona could do it in four—if.

Mark Grace led off the Arizona ninth with a single. Then Rivera prompted a nationwide gasp by fielding Damian Miller's attempted sacrifice bunt and throwing the ball into center field, putting Arizona runners on first and second with no outs. Jay Bell bunted into a force play at third, but Tony Womack lined a double into the right field corner to tie the game, 2–2, as Miller scored from second.

The plot grew even thicker and tenser when Craig Counsell was hit by a pitch from Rivera to load the bases, still with only one out. That brought up Luis Gonzalez, and even the players were feeling the tension. Schilling said, "I wouldn't move on the bench. I wanted to get up and watch for the whole inning, but I was playing the luck seat." Johnson agreed. "It seemed pretty surreal to me," he said, "watching all this develop." Both men were aware of one of baseball's most attractive features: It's the only major team sport whose games are decided not by a clock but only after both teams have had the same number of chances to win.

With the Yankee infield drawn in, Gonzalez choked up on the handle of his bat, giving himself a better chance to make contact. Even after hitting those 57 home runs during the season, he was trying to maximize his chances of getting the hit to win the championship for his team. He knew he didn't need to grip the bat down at the bottom of the handle and hit a home run. He knew he needed only a hit—any kind, anywhere.

It worked. Gonzalez hit a bloop single to center field that scored Bell. Thirty-nine million fans saw it on Fox TV, the largest television audience for a baseball game in ten years and more than double the number of viewers who watched the Emmy Awards on CBS the same night.

The World Series was over. The underdog Diamondbacks had come from behind in the bottom half of the ninth inning in the last game of the World Series and upset the mighty Yankees, baseball's legendary power-house for most of the last eighty years. The crowd at Bank One Ballpark went crazy for more than an hour.

Randy Johnson, who had closed out the Yankees in the top of the ninth, was the winning pitcher, at age thirty-eight. Schilling did not get the win, but he and Johnson were voted the Most Valuable Players of the Series. Schilling got something else, praise from his boss. When Brenly lifted him after Soriano's home run in the eighth inning, he came to the mound and told Schilling, "You're my hero." He gave him words of as-surance as well. He said the homer "ain't going to beat us."

Schilling said the same kind of thing to Kim, the pitcher who surren-dered the two game-losing homers to the Yankees in Games 5 and 6. Moments after the Diamondbacks won the Series, in the midst of all the screaming and hollering, Schilling made it a point to find Kim in the in-field. He gave the twenty-two-year-old a long hug that expressed Schill-ing's loyalty and comfort for his teammate and fellow pitcher.

Greg Boeck of *USA Today* had a new explanation for the upset victory. He said the Diamondbacks "outmagicked" the Yankees. Steve Finley said the same thing. "That's what the World Series is all about," Ari-zona's center fielder said. "You have to create some magic."

Gonzalez said, "The way this Series played out, it could not have been scripted better for our ball club. The way we have battled fighting tooth and nail all year, up 2–0 in this series, go back down, 3–2, coming over here, two tough losses in Games 4 and 5, playing the way we did yester-day, and then Game 7, the way it ended. That was a storybook ending for our team, from front to back."

Then he expressed the feelings of millions when he said, "This is probably going to go down as one of the best World Series ever."

Seth Livingstone of *USA Today*'s *Baseball Weekly,* attached national significance to Arizona's victory and all that went into it. "Last night's

3–2 victory by the Diamondbacks," he wrote the next day, "was a master-piece to be viewed time and time again—another lesson in resiliency this country has seen repeatedly since September 11."

The 2001 World Series brought to mind words spoken by NBC's Bob Costas only four years earlier, in the moments after the 1997 World Series ended in an eleven-inning thriller. When he signed off at the end of the '97 telecast on the evening of October 26, Costas offered a commentary to his millions of viewers that perfectly described baseball's pluses and minuses at that point in its history. It was a description that still applies today, in this age of runaway salaries, labor disputes, and threats to move teams or even wipe them out. Speaking without notes or a script, Costas said:

> There is no denying that baseball as a game, and especially as an institution, has its share of problems. And this World Series emphasized some of those problems, no denying that.
>
> But this Series, especially game seven, reminded us why this can be the greatest game of all. Baseball, especially in the big games, has a capacity to generate a kind of sustained tension and drama that is both delicious and excruciating, and is all but un-matched in all of sports.
>
> This game takes its place in baseball history—a history that is the longest and richest of all the team sports, and it redeems a lot of what this 1997 baseball season has been about.
>
> Say what you want about the *institution* of baseball, the *game* of baseball can still be the best game on earth.

Costas was providing yet more proof of how baseball and the nation so often reflect each other. His description of the historic ability of America's national pastime to rise above its problems and achieve great-ness over the seasons could also be said of America herself.

Bibliography

Allen, Bob, with Bill Gilbert. *The 500 Home Run Club: Baseball's 15 Greatest Home Run Hitters, From Aaron to Williams.* Champaign, Ill.: Sports Publishing LLC., 1999.

Correll, John T. "The Decision That Launched the Enola Gay." Washington, D.C.: *Air Force Magazine,* 1994.

DiMaggio, Dom, with Bill Gilbert. *Real Grass, Real Heroes: Baseball's Historic 1941 Season.* New York: Zebra Books, 1990.

Feller, Bob, with Bill Gilbert. *Now Pitching: Bob Feller.* New York: Birch Lane Press, 1990.

Gilbert, Bill. *They Also Served: Baseball and the Home Front, 1941–1945.* New York: Crown Publishers, Inc., 1992.

Henrich, Tommy, with Bill Gilbert. *Five O'Clock Lightning.* New York: Birch Lane Press, 1992.

Kalinsky, George, and Jon Scher. *The New York Mets: A Photograph History.* New York: Macmillan Publishing USA, 1995.

McCullough, David. *Truman.* New York: Simon & Schuster, 1992.

Mead, William. *Baseball Goes to War (Even the Browns)*. Washington, D.C.: Farragut Publishing Company, 1985.

———. *The Explosive Sixties*. Alexandria, Va.: Redefinition, Inc., 1989.

Mead, William, and Paul Dickson. *Baseball: The Presidents' Game*. Washington, D.C.: Farragut Publishing Company, 1993.

Montella, Paul. *Home Run! The Year the Records Fell*. Champaign, Ill.: Sports Publishing Inc., 1998. (Compiled from the files of the Associated Press.)

Povich, Shirley, with Bill Gilbert. *All These Mornings*. New York: Prentice-Hall, 1969.

Snider, Duke, with Bill Gilbert. *The Duke of Flatbush*. New York: Zebra Books, 1988.

The 1976 World Book Year Book: A Review of the Events of 1975. Chicago: Field Enterprises Educational Corp, 1976.

The 1981 World Book Year Book: A Review of the Events of 1980—The Annual Supplement to the World Book Encyclopedia. Chicago: World Book—Childcraft International, Inc., 1981.

Index

• • •

Aaron, Hank, 47, 180, 219, 257
Abbott, Glenn, 218
Advertising, World War II and, 15–16
Afghanistan, 213, 222, 326
Agee, Tommie, 175, 182, 183
Agnew, Spiro, 197–98
Ahern, Bertie, 287
Aikens, Willie, 230
Air-conditioning, 95, 116, 118
Air Force Magazine, 34
Airlift, Berlin. *See* Berlin Airlift
Airplane (movie), 221
Air raid drills, 9
Alabama, USS, 39
Aldrin, Edwin ("Buzz"), 175–77
Alexander, Manny, 253
Alfred P. Murrah Federal Building terrorist
    bombing (1995), 240–41
All-American Girls Professional Baseball
    League, 202
Allen, Bob, 98, 150, 243
Allen, Dick, 224–25
Allen, Woody, 246
All-Star Games
    1945, 30, 241
    1961, 136
    1969, 173–74
    1980, 218–19
    1991, 249, 271
    1995, 241–42
    1998, 278
    2001, 308–9
All These Mornings (Povich), 127
Alou, Felipe, 180, 298
Al Qaeda, 306
Alston, Walter, 219
Altrock, Nick, 158
American Airlines Flight 77, 310–11
American in Paris, An (movie), 109
Anchors Aweigh (movie), 45
Anderson, Brady, 318, 319
Anderson, Dave, 209–10
Anderson, John, 222
Anderson, Sparky, 196, *196,* 197, 203, 206,
    219
Androstenedione, 288
Angell, Roger, 167
Angelos, Peter, 256
Angels California Angels, 125, 129
Anthrax, 333

Antonen, Mel, 335
Apollo 11, 175–77
Arena, Dominick, 177
Arizona Diamondbacks, 278, 333–34, 335–47
Armbrister, Ed, 203, 204
Armstrong, Louis, 185
Armstrong, Neil, 164, 175–77
Arroyo, Luis, 138
Astrodome, McGwire and, 275
Atlanta Braves, 180, 216, 217, 267, 333–34
Atlanta Hawks, 217
Atomic warfare, 34–36, 86, 88, 112, 140–41
Attendance, 49, 50, 160, 167, 287

Bagwell, Jeff, 322
Bailey, Pearl, 185, 186
Baker, Dusty, 285
Baltimore Orioles, 120, 160. *See also* Ripken,
    Cal, Jr.
    Ponson and, 208–9
    Throneberry and, 166
    1961, 151–52
    1969 World Series, 163, 180–87
    1975, 193
    1980, 217
Banks, Ernie, 175, 250
Banyard, Jim, 83
Barajas, Rod, 342
Barkley, Alben, 39
Barnett, Larry, 203, 204
Barry Bonds Family Foundation, 330
Barrymore, Ethel, 55
Baseball: The President's Game (Mead and
    Dickson), 171, 172
Baseball America, 114
Baseball Hall of Fame Library, 160
Baseball seasons
    1945, 3–49
    1948, 53–91
    1951, 95–121
    1961, 125–60
    1969, 163–87
    1975, 191–210
    1980, 213–34
    1995, 237–62
    1998, 265–301
    2001, 305–47
Baseball Weekly, 320
Bash Brothers, 270
Batista, Miguel, 342

Bauer, Hank, 243
Baxter, Frankie, 44
Beame, Abraham, 198
Bearden, Gene, 61–62, 66–67, 74–77, 83–84
Bee ball, Paige and, 64
Belanger, Mark, 181
Bell, Jay, 345
Belle, Albert, 296
Bench, Johnny, 194, 195–97
    1975 World Series, 202, 203, 204, 206
Bench, Ted, 195
Benes, Andy, 274
Bennett, Tony, 96
Bergman, Dave, 225
Berle, Milton, 54, 96
Berlin, Irving, 9, 89
Berlin Airlift, *57*, 57–58, 78, 85–91, *88*
Berlin Airlift Veterans Association, 91
Berlin Wall, 55–58, 85, 137, 138–41, 163
Berman, Chris, 254
Berra, Yogi, 61, 147, 168, 239
Betty Ford Center, 243–44
Bibliography, 349–50
Bicentennial (1976), 173–74
Billingham, Jack, 195
Binkowski, George ("Bingo Binks"), 28–29,
    41, 42
Black, Don, 70–71, 72, 77
Blackout curtains, World War II and, 9
Blair, Paul, 180, 182
Blitz, World War II and, 115
Bluege, Ossie, 29, 32, *37*, 40, 41–42, 43
Blum, Ronald, 269
Bodley, Hal, 262, 344
Boeck, Greg, 335, 346
Boehringer, Brian, 293
Boggs, Wade, 247
Bonds, Aisha, 325
Bonds, Barry, xii, 299, 321–22, 329–30, 336
    2001 season, 307–10, 313–15, 321–24, *327*
Bonds, Liz, 326–27
Bonds, Nikolai, 324
Bonds Squad, 330
Bonilla, Bobby, 240, 255
Boone, Bob, 228, 229–30, 233, 234
Boone, Bret, 314–15
Borbon, Pedro, 205
Borom, Eddie, 44
Borowy, Hank, 24, 46
Boskie, Shawn, 257
Boston Braves, 120
    1945, 12, 23
    1948, 54, 79
        World Series, 78–84
    1951, 103, 106
Boston Globe, 112
Boston Red Sox
    1945, 12, 18–19, 23
        vs. Senators, 31–32
    1946, 60
    1947, 60–61
    1948, 53–54, 60–61, 66, 72

    vs. Indians, 71–72, 74–77
    1961, 126, 153
        vs. Senators, 156–57
    1975, 192–94
        World Series, 197–98, 201–7
    1998, 291
Boswell, Thomas, 262
Bottenfield, Kent, 280
Boudreau, Lou, 12, 16, *73*
    1948 season, 61–62, 64, 66–67, 71–72,
        74–83
Bowa, Larry, 229, 230
Bracker, Milton, 107–8
Brainwashing, 116
Branca, Ralph, 109–11
Branch Davidians, 251
Brando, Marlon, 108
Breadon, Sam, 15
Breakfast at Tiffany's (movie), 145
Brecheen, Harry, 53
Brenly, Bob, 338, 340–42, 346
Brett, George, 220–21, 226, 320
    1980 World Series, 227, 228–29, 230–32,
        234
Bristol, Dave, 219
Brokaw, Tom, 333
Brooklyn Dodgers, xi, xii, 53, 120
    Robinson and, 19, 40
    1941, *vs.* Yankees, 48–49
    1945, 12, 21, 30–31
    1946, 53
    1947, 53, 61
    1951, 100, 101, 103–4, 114, 115, *115*
        vs. Giants, 106–14
Brosius, Scott, 339, 342–43, *343*
Brown, Jerry, 199
Brown, Warren, 46
Brown, Willie, 330
Brown vs. Board of Education, 131
Buck, Jack, 286
Budig, Gene, 254
Buendorf, Larry, 198–99
Buford, Don, 180–82
Bunning, Jim, 149
Burke, Joe, 158
Burkett, John, 308
Burleson, Rick, 205
Burris, Rick, 218
Bush, George H. W., 339
Bush, George W., 305–6
    baseball and, 338–39
    Ruth and, *69*, 69–70
    terrorism and, 310, 311, 332, 338
    2001 World Series, 337, *338*, 339
Bush, Laura, 339
Bush, Prescott, 339
Butterfly pitch, 13, 328
Byrnes, Jimmy, 16, 17, 18

Cabrera, Jose, 308
Caesar, Sid, 96
Cain, Bob, 105

Caldwell, Earl, 30
Camden Yards, 246, 318. *See also* Baltimore
  Orioles
Campanella, Roy, 110, 182
Canseco, Jose, 270
Cap, salary, 238–40
Caray, Harry, 266–68
Caray, Skip, 267
Carbo, Bernie, 203, 205–6
Cardenal, Jose, 232
CARE (Cooperative for American
  Remittances to Europe), 89
Carlton, Steve, 228, 232
Caron, Leslie, 109
Carrey, Jim, 279
Cars, 95, 96, 222
Carter, Jimmy, 200, 215, 216, 221–22, 234
Carter, Joe, 291
Carty, Rico, 180
Cash, Norm, 149
Castro, Fidel, 130
Catcher in the Rye (Salinger), 95–96
Catching, 196–97. *See also specific catchers*
Cavarretta, Phil, 24–25
Cepeda, Orlando, 180
Cerv, Bob, 144
Challenger, 251
Chambliss, Chris, 294
Chandler, Happy, 17, 18, 37, 107
Chandler, Spud, 61
Chapman, Sam, 41
Chappaquiddick Island, 177
Charles, Ed, 187
Chicago Cubs, 58–59, 202. *See also* Sosa,
  Sammy
  Maris and, 135
  1945, 12, 22, 24–25, 45–46, 46
  1969, 174–75, 177
    vs. Mets, 174, 177
  1998, *vs.* Cardinals, 288–91, *290*
Chicago White Sox, 12, 22, 160, 284
  1961, 126–27, 157
Christopher, Mel and Lou, 237
Chrysler Motors, 222
Churchill, Winston, 22, 35, 56
CIA (Central Intelligence Agency), 130
Cianfarra, Camille M., 108
Cincinnati Reds, 219
  1961, 138, 154–55
  1969, 166–67
  1975, 194–97
    World Series, 197–98, 201–7
  1980, 216
  1998, 286–87
Cincinnati Red Stockings, 173
Civil Defense, Office of, 140–41
Civil rights, 130–34. *See also* Integration
Clancy, Paul, 215
Clark, Allie, 76
Clark, Jack, 219
Clark, Tom, 39
Clark, Will, 270

Clay, Lucius D., 56
Clemens, Roger, 339–40, 344–45
Clemente, Roberto, 174, 249–50
Clendenon, Donn, 183, 185
Cleveland Buckeyes, 19
Cleveland Indians, 160
  Paige and, 62–65
  1945, 12, 39–40
  1947, 61, 66
  1948, 54, 58–67, 70–72, 78
    vs. Red Sox, 71–72, 74–77
    World Series, 78–84
  1975, 194
  2001, 333–34
Clift, Montgomery, 109
Clinton, Bill, 200, 238, 251–52, 256, 293
  Lewinsky and, 274, 278, 287
Clinton, Hillary Rodham, 251
Clooney, Rosemary, 96, 115
Closers, 218
CNN (Cable News Network), 217
Coal Miner's Daughter (movie), 221
Cobb, Ty, 64, 322
Coca, Imogene, 96
Cochrane, Mickey, 28, 101
Cohen, Herb, 113
Colavito, Rocky, 149, 310
Cole, Nat King, 54, 96, 115
Cole, USS, 306
Coleman, Choo-Choo, 165
College Park, Maryland, 13–14
College World Series (1947), 70
Collins, Michael, 175–77
Colorado Rockies, 309, 310
Comic strips, 96
Comiskey Park, 160. *See also* Chicago White
  Sox
Communism, 55–58, 118–19, 129–30, 138–41,
  191–92
Concepcion, Dave, 202, 203
Congress of Racial Equality (CORE), 130–33
Connor, Bull, 131
Connor, Tracy, 114
Constitution, U. S., 9, 131, 173
Cooperative for American Remittances to
  Europe (CARE), 89
Cooper, Cecil, 223–24
Cooper, Mort, 18
Cooper, Walker, 18
Copeland, Libby, 140
CORE (Congress of Racial Equality), 130–33
Corkins, Mike, 179
Correll, John T., 34
Corriere Dello Sport, 289
Cortisone, 55
Costas, Bob, 256, 267, 347
Costello, Al, 21
Counsell, Craig, 336, 345
Coyle, Harry, 207
Cramer, Doc, 32, 44
Credit cards, 96
Crime and violence, 198–200

Cronin, Joe, 159
Cronkite, Walter, 176
Crosby, Bing, 54, 115
Crosetti, Frank, 153
Crowley, Carolyn Hughes, 89
Cuba, 21, 129–30, 163
Cuellar, Mike, 181, 182
Cullen, Bill, 147

Dallas (TV show), 227
Daniels, Bennie, 138
Daniels, Dan, 158
Darcy, Pat, 195, 206–7
Dark, Alvin, 78
Daschle, Tom, 333
Dauer, Rich, 256
DeArmond, Mike, 220–21
Declaration of Independence, 9
Del Webb Construction Company, 128
Dempsey, Rick, 256
Denkinger, Don, 231
Dennis the Menace, 96
Derringer, Paul, 24
Desegregation, 18–19, 115
    Freedom Riders and, 130–33
Detroit News, 27
Detroit Tigers, xi, 27, 72, 238
    1945, 21–24, 27–29, 45–46
        vs. Browns, 43–45, 45, 46
        vs. Senators, 40–43
    1951, 104–5
    1961, 149
Dewey, Thomas E., 85
Dickson, Paul, 171
Dierker, Larry, 323–24
DiMaggio, Dom, 77, 98–99
    World War II and, 47–48
    1948 season, 53, 60–61
DiMaggio, Joe, 38, 61, 171, 243, 246
    Mantle and, 100
    Paige and, 64
    Ripken and, 252, 256
    World War II and, 6–7, 47
    1951 season, 114, 115, 115
Dior, Christian, 62
D. J. Kaufman (Washington, D.C.), 37
Doby, Larry, 62–63, 82, 84
Doerr, Bobby, 37
Doherty, Ed, 126, 157–58
Dominican Republic, 277, 281, 299
Donovan, Dick, 138, 156, 158
Doyle, Denny, 206
Draft, 56–57, 96, 100
    World War II deferments, 4, 6, 16–18, 39,
        48
Drago, Dick, 202
Drebinger, John, 83, 112
Dressen, Charlie, 103–4, 104, 110–11
Duck and cover drills, 141
Duke, Charles, 176
Duke of Flatbush (Snider), 109
Dulles, John Foster, 137

Dunston, Shawon, 326
Durante, Sal, 153–54
Durazo, Erubiel, 341
Durocher, Leo, 103, 106–7, 111, 114, 169,
    175, 179

Easley, Damion, 253
Eastern Airlines, 157
Eastman, Joseph B., 12
Eaton, Adam, 307
EBS warnings, 140
Education, 115, 116
Egypt, 176–77
Ehrhardt, Karl, 185, 186
Ehrlichman, John, 198
Eisenhower, David, 171
Eisenhower, Dwight D., 20, 22, 23–24, 85, 97,
    108, 128–29
Eldred, Cal, 275
Elliott, Bob, 78
Ellis, John, 238
Embree, Alan, 278
Encarnacion, Mario, 321
Enola Gay, 35
Erskine, Carl, 114
Eruzione, Mike, 213
Ettinger, Arlan, 298
Evans, Cliff, 171
Evans, Dwight, 203, 205, 206
Even the Browns (Mead), 17–18
Expansions, 120–21, 125, 165, 168
Explosive Sixties, The (Mead), 166

Falkenberg, Jinx, 89
Fallout, Cold War lingo and, 116
Fallout shelters, 140–41, 331
Falls, Joe, 27
Fame (movie), 221
Fankhauser, Henry, 13–14
Farmer, James, 130–33
Fehr, Donald, 239, 254
Feller, Bob, 64, 67, 328–29
    World War II and, 7, 39, 46–47, 48
    1945 season, 39–40
    1948 season, 58–60, 71–72, 74, 76, 80–83
Fenway Park, 197. See also Boston Red Sox
    1975 World Series, 202, 203–4
Ferrell, Rick, 13, 48
Fisher, Marc, 246
Filippelli, John, 207
Finley, Charles O., 208
Finley, Steve, 336, 342, 346
Firestone, Roy, 170
Fisher, Eddie, 115
Fisher, Jack, 152
Fisher, Marc, 246
Fisk, Carlton, 192–94, 195, 197
    1975 World Series, 203, 206–7, 209
Fitzgerald, John ("Honey Fitz"), 80
500 Home Run Club, 259
500 Home Run Club (Allen and Gilbert), 150,
    243
Flags, American, 8–9

Flanagan, Mike, 257
Florida Marlins, 272–73, 285
Flying saucers, 84
Folliard, Edward T., 128–29
Football, 192
Ford, Dan, 256
Ford, Gerald, 198–99, 202
Ford, Whitey, 154–55
Ford Motors, 222
Forneris, Tim, 289–90
Foster, George, 194, 204–5, 206
4-F, World War II and, 16–17, 29, 48
Foxx, Jimmie, 134, 266
Francona, Terry, 290–91
Franklin National Bank, 96
Frasier (TV show), 200
Free agent system, 208–9, 214, 306–7
Freedom Riders, 130–33, 163
Freedom 7, 132, *133*
Frey, Jim, 228, 230–31
Frick, Ford, 136
Fried, Davy, 113, 121
Frisch, Frankie, 103
Frishberg, Dave, 26
From Here to Eternity (Jones), 95–96
Fromme, Lynette ("Squeaky"), 198–200
Fuhrman, Mark, 252

Gaedel, Eddie, 104–5
Gagarin, Yuri, 134
Galehouse, Denny, 76
Gammons, Peter, 193, 254
Garfield, John, 45
Gasoline rationing, 8
Gassaway, Charlie, 23
Gaynor, Mitzi, 185
Gazzetta Dello Sport, 289
Gedeon, Elmer, 11
Gehrig, Lou, 258–60, 267–68
    Ripken and, 240, 245–46, 250, 251, 253,
    256, 258–59, 261–62
Gellman, Barton, 332
General Motors, 222
Gentry, Gary, 175, 180
George Washington, USS, 311
Gerard, Lou, 207
Geronimo, Cesar, 203, 205
Giambi, Jason, 208, 291
G. I. Bill of Rights, 116
Gilbert, Dave, 237–38
Gilbert, Katy Christopher, 237–38
Gildea, William, 325
Gillette Safety Razor Company, 80
Girardi, Joe, 295
Giuliani, Rudolph, 311, 338, 344–45
Glenn, John, 175–76
"God Bless America" (song), 9, 313
Golenbock, Peter, 146
Gone With the Wind (movie), 279
Gonzalez, Luis, 336, 341, 345–46
Gordon, Joe, 76
Gordon, Sam, 154

Gore, Al, 305–6
Gossage, Goose, 226
Grace, Mark, 340, 345
Grady, Sandy, 147, 301
Graham, Phil, 128–29
Grand Rapid Chicks, 202
Grant, Cary, 55, 185
Gray, Pete, 32–33
Grayson, Kathryn, 45
Great Caruso, The (movie), 109
Great Depression, 21, 201
Green, Dallas, 226, 232–33
Green, Gene, 137–38, 156
Greenberg, Hank, 22, 47, 134, 159, 266, 296
    1945 season, xi, 22–23, 39, 44–45, *45*
Greene, Todd, 338
"Green light letter," Roosevelt and, 4, *5*, 6, 48
Griffey, Ken, 194, 202, 218
    1975 World Series, 202, 204, 206
Griffey, Ken, Jr., 202, 275, 292, 299, 300, *300*
Griffith, Calvin, 127–28, 158, 159
Griffith, Clark, *4*, 6, 14–15, 20, 40, 127
Griffith Stadium, *5*, 6, 14, 127–28, 158. *See
    also* Washington Senators
1937 Opening Day, 3–4, *4*
1945, 20–21, 40–41
    Truman and, *37*, 38–39
1951 Opening Day, 96–98
1961 Opening Day, 125–27, 129
Grimm, Charlie, 46, 103
Gross, Greg, 229
Ground Zero (New York City), 313
Gullett, Don, 195
Gutenberg Bible, 9
Gutteridge, Don, 32
Gwynn, Chris, 319
Gwynn, Tony, 309, 319–20
    retirement of, 321–22

Hack, Stan, 24
Haefner, Mickey, 13, 17–18
Hagerty, Jim, 128
Haldeman, Robert, 198
Halvorsen, Gail ("Candy Bomber"), 87, 88,
    88, 89, *89*
Ham, Bus, 37
Hamey, Ray, 135
Harridge, Will, 74
Harris, Bucky, *4*, 61
Hawkins, Burt, 129
Haydock, Michael D., 116
Hayward, Susan, 108–9
Hearn, Jim, 107
Hearst, Patty, 200
Heath, Jeff, 78
Heaverlo, Dave, 216
Hegan, Jim, 67, 82
Helena, USS, 74–75
Helton, Todd, 321
Henderson, Myrtle, 186
Henderson, Rickey, 320–21
Hendricks, Ellie, 181, 182, 255

Henrich, Tommy, 48–49, 53, 61, 98–99, 260
Herman, Ken, 85–86, 88, 91
Hernandez, Livan, 272–73
Hernandez, Orlando, 340–41
Hershiser, Orel, 282
Hertz, Marguerite, 84
Hesitation pitch, Paige and, 64
Hickey, John, 315
Hickman, Jim, 175
Hinckley, John, 246
Hinton, Chuck, 156, 157
Hirohito, Emperor of Japan, 36
Hiroshima, 34, 35–36
Hockey, 192, 213–14
Hodges, Gil, 168–70, 178
  1969 World Series, 185, 186–87
Hodges, Joan, 185
Hodges, Russ, 111–12
Hoffa, Jimmy, 198
Holdsworth, Fred, 192
Holman, Sam, 326
Holmes, Tommy, 78, *81*, 81–82, 84
Home runs, 328–29
  Babe Ruth and, 134, 136, 144, 149, 150, 153
  Bonds (2001), 307–8, 309–10, 313–15,
    321–22, 323–34, *327*
  McGwire-Sosa dual (1998), 265–66,
    268–69, *269*, 274–82, 285–93, *290*,
    296–301
  Maris-Mantle dual (1961), 134–36, 143,
    144, 145, *148*
  Mays (1969), 178–80
Honda motorcycles, 55
Hoover, Herbert, 70, 96
Hoover, J. Edgar, 16
Hope, Bob, 89–90, 159
Horgan, Tim, 193
Hornsby, Bruce, 252
Hornsby, Roger, 64
Horwitz, Jack, 40
Hostetler, Chuck, 46
Houk, Ralph, 147, 149, 151
House Un-American Activities Committee
  (HUAC), 118–19
Houston Astros, 125, 222–23, 225–26, 323–24
Howard, Frank, 174
Howser, Dick, 217, 226
Hrbek, Kent, 247
Hubbard, Cal, 44
Humphrey, Hubert, 170
Hundley, Randy, 175
Hunter, Jim ("Catfish"), 208

Ilitch, Mike, 238
I Love Lucy (TV show), 114
Inflation, 55
Inside Sports, 257
Integration, 62
  Freedom Riders and, 130–33
  Paige and, 62–63
  of schools, 115, 131
Iran, 213, 214–15, 216, 222

Iron lungs, polio and, *142*, 142–3
Irvin, Monte, 107, 114
Israel, 54–55, 176–77
Italy, McGwire and, 289
I've Got a Secret (TV show), 147
Iwo Jima, 11, 20, 42

Jackson, Reggie, 223, 272, 278, 307
Jansen, Larry, 107, 114
Japan, baseball and, 241–42, 257, 287–88, 315
Jeep stunt, Price and, 60
Jenkins, Ferguson, 175
Jensen, Jackie, 70
Jeter, Derek, 295, 341–42
Jethroe, Sam, 19
John F. Kennedy, USS, 311
Johns, Doug, 295
Johnson, Bryan, 257–58
Johnson, Darrell, 204
Johnson, Davey, 181, 186
Johnson, Don, 24
Johnson, Lyndon, 134, 163–64
Johnson, Randy, 265, 270, 314
  2001 World Series, 336, 338, 343–44, 346
Johnson, Stephanie, 335
Johnson, Walter, 20, 128
Jones, Cleon, 174–75, 186–87
Jones, Harry, 75
Jones, James, 95
Jordan, Brian, 298
Judge, Joe, 41–42
Jump ball, Paige and, 64
Justice, David, 336

Kaese, Harold, 112
Kahn, Mike, 334
Kaiser, Robert G., 177
Kaline, Al, 149, 269
Kansas City Athletics, 120, 145, 146
Kansas City Monarchs, 19, 40, 64
Kansas City Royals, 168
  Brett and, 220–21
  1980, 217, 226
    World Series, 226, 227–34
  1998, 277–78
Kell, George, 16, 42
Keller, Charlie, 61, 98
Kelly, Gene, 45, 109
Keltner, Ken, 72, 76, 82
Kennedy, Bob, 84
Kennedy, Edward, 177
Kennedy, Jacqueline, 182
Kennedy, John F., 80, 125–26, 163, 170
  civil rights and, 131–33
  Cold War and, 139–40, 141
  Cuba and, 129–30
  space race and, 133–34
  1961 Opening Day, 125–27, 129
Kennedy, John F., Jr., 182
Kennedy, Robert, 131, 132, 164
Kennedy, Ted, 164
Kent, Jeff, 325

Keough, Matt, 218
Khomeini, Ayatollah, 214–15, 216
Khrushchev, Nikita, 137
Kiersh, Edward, 257
Killebrew, Harmon, 265, 309–10
Kim, Byung-Hyun, 341–43, 346
Kiner, Ralph, 265
King, Larry, xi–xii, 113, 121
King, Martin Luther, Jr., 130–34, 164, 199
Kinsey, Alfred C., 55
Kintetsu Buffaloes, 241
Kinugasa, Sachio, 257, 296
Kirby, Clay, 195
Kish, Ernie, 41–42
Klieman, Ed, 61
Knoblauch, Chuck, 295, 340, 342, 343
Knuckleballs, 13, 67
Koosman, Jerry, 175, 177–78, 180, 182, 186
Kopechne, Mary Jo, 177
Koppel, Ted, 215, 215
Korean War, 47, 90, 95–96, 97, 108, 114, 116, 201, 227
Koufax, Sandy, 171
Kranepool, Ed, 174
Kremenko, Barney, 101–2
Kubek, Tony, 147
Kuhel, Joe, 29
Kupcinet, Ira, 46
Kutyna, Marty, 138

Labor strike, 237–40, 245–46
Lachemann, Rene, 239
LaFollette, Robert, 39
Lampkin, Tom, 317
Landis, Kennesaw Mountain, 3–6, 7, 11–12, 18, 48
Langer, William, 16, 17, 18
Langford, Rick, 218
Lanza, Mario, 109
La Russa, Tony, 273, 281, 297–98, 316–17
Lary, Frank, 149
Latino players, World War II and, 21
Law, Rudy, 219
Lawrence, Bill, 112
Lawrence, Steve, 182
League of Their Own, A (movie), 202
Leahy, William, 39
Lee, Bill, 194, 202
Lee, Leron, 192
Leigh, Vivien, 108
Lemon, Bob, 61
Leonard, Dutch, 13, 17–18, 41
Lewinsky, Monica, 274, 278, 287
Lewis, Buddy, 29–30, 39
Leyland, Jim, 273, 278, 285
Lieberman, Joseph, 287
Lima, Jose, 282
Lindbergh, Charles, 97
Lindell, Johnny, 61
Lindsay, John, 182
Lingo, American, 115–16
Liska, Jerry, 46

Litwhiler, Danny, 18
Livingstone, Seth, 346–47
Lockman, Whitey, 107
Lodge, Henry Cabot, Jr., 134
Loh, Jules, 97
Lombardi, Joan, 169
Long ball, Paige and, 64
Long relievers, 218
Lopat, Eddie, 61
Lopez, Albie, 309
Los Angeles Dodgers, 120, 138, 167, 194
    1980, 222–23, 225–26
    2001, 324–25
Lou Gehrig Disease, 258
Lou Gehrig Memorial Award, 250
Louis, Joe, 55
Lovell, Bernard, 176
Lowrey, Peanuts, 24
LPs (long-playing records), 84
Lynn, Fred, 193–94, 204, 205, 205

MacArthur, Douglas, 37, 97, 98, 108
McBride, Bake, 227–28
McCaffrey, Barry R., 288
McCain, John, 338
McCarthy, Joe, 72, 75–76
McCarthy, Joseph (McCarthyism), 85–86, 118–19
McCarthy, Walton, 331, 332
McCormick, Mike, 78, 80–81
McCovey, Willie, 173, 218–20
McDonald, Ben, 239
McDonald, Richard and Maurice, 55
McDonald's, 55, 275
McFarlane, Todd, 298–99
McFarlane Toys, 299
McGowan, Bill, 30
McGraw, Tug, 178, 179, 187
    1980 World Series, 227–28, 229–30, 232–33, 234
McGullough, David, 35–36, 57–58
McGwire, John, 270
McGwire, Mark, xi–xii, 155, 265–301, 269, 290
    androstenedione and, 288
    background of, 270
    Bonds and, 314, 323–24
    injuries, 271–72
    retirement of, 316–18
    World Series and, 270–71
McGwire, Matt, 271, 277, 289
Mack, Connie, 4, 41
McKay, Dave, 272
McKeon, Jack, 292
MacLean, John, 158
MacLeish, Archibald, 9
McNally, Dave, 207–8
    1969 World Series, 181, 182, 185
McQuinn, George, 43, 70
McVeigh, Timothy, 240–41
Maddox, Garry, 226, 232
Maddux, Greg, 314

Madera, Doug, 197
Madison Square Garden, 159
Mae, Robert, 197
Maglie, Sal, 107
Magna Carta, 9
Major League Baseball Magazine (TV show), 78
Major League Baseball Players Association, 214, 238, 239, 317
Major league expansion, 120–21, 125, 165, 168
Managers, 169–70, 194. *See also specific managers*
Manpower shortage, in World War II, 15–19
Mansfield Independents, 173
Manson, Charles, 199
Mantle, Mickey, 98–101, 273
    death of, 155, 242–44
    1961 season, 125, 134–36, 143–55, *144, 148*
Mantle, Mutt, 101
Maple bats, 326
Marichal, Juan, 285
Maris, Pat, 149
Maris, Roger, 125, 155, 266, 310
    McGwire and, 273, 274–75, 280, 281, 287–88, 289–90
    1961 season, 134–36, 138, *144*, 143–55, *148*
Maris, Roger, Jr., 149, 289
Markward, Mary Stalcup, 118–19
Maroon, John, 294
Marquis, Jason, 308
Marsalis, Branford, 252
Martin, Billy, 169, 217–18
Martin, Whitney, 23
Martinez, Buck, 254
Martinez, Dennis, 249
Martinez, Ramon, 268
Martinez, Tino, 341, 342
M*A*S*H (TV show), 227
Masi, Phil, 80–81, 83, 84
Maske, Mark, 295
Mason-Dixon Line, 11
Masterson, Walter, 41–42
Mathews, Eddie, 265
Mattingly, Don, 243, 342
Mayo, Eddie, 44
Mays, Willie, 101–5, *102*, 112, 113, 179, 220, 269, 307
Mead, William, 17–18, 166, 171, 172
Meet the Press (TV show), 54
Memmott, Mark, 312
Memphis Chicks, 15, 32
Messersmith, Andy, 207–8
Metkovich, George, 31–32
Metzdorf, Bill, 237–38
Michaels, Al, 213
Middlebrook, Jason, 314
Middle men, 218
Middleton, Drew, 56, 83
Military uniforms, 37
Miller, Adam, 114
Miller, Bob, 166

Miller, Damian, 345
Miller, Jon, 256
Miller, Ray, 294–95
Miller, Stu, 136
Miller, Wade, 313–14
Milwaukee Braves, 120
Milwaukee Brewers, 249, 275, 292
Minnesota Twins, 125, 127, 158, 180
Minor, Ryan, 294–95
"Miracle of Googan's Bluff" (1951), xii, *102*, 111–12, 113–14
Mishkin, Vladimir, 213
Missouri, USS, 37
Mitchell, Dale, 61, 76
Mitchell, John, 198
Mize, Johnny, 7, 47
Molitor, Paul, 291
Monroe, Lucy, 10
Montreal Expos, 168, 177, 222, 270, 297–98
"Moon River" (song), 145
Moreland, Keith, 228, 232
Morgan, Henry, 147
Morgan, Joe, 194, 225
    1975 World Series, 201, 204, 206
Morgan, Mike, 287
Moses, Wally, 17–18
Mount Saint Helens eruption (1980), 216–17, 221
Movies, 45, 55, 108–9, 144–45, 221, 279
Moynihan, Daniel P., 200
Muchnick, Isadore, 18
Mungo, Van Lingle, 26–27
Munson, Thurman, 193
Murakami, Masanori, 241
Murray, Eddie, 261, *261*
Murray, Jim, 192, 209
Murray, Spud, 147
Murtaugh, Danny, 220
Muser, Tony, 277–78
Musial, Stan, 7, 53, 78, 286
Music, 54, 96, 115
Musicals, 45, 95, 144–45
Mussina, Mike, 336, 343

Nagasaki, 34, 36
NASA, *133*, 133–34, 164, 175–77, 251
National Anthem, 9, 10, 313
National Archives (Washington, D.C.), 9
National Baseball Hall of Fame Library, 160
"Nature Boy" (song), 54
NBC, 54, 96, 207
Negro Leagues, 18–19, 62, 63–64
Nessen, Ronald, 199
Nettles, Graig, 269
Newark Eagles, 62
Newberry, Paul, 287
Newcombe, Don, 109, *110*
New Frontier, Kennedy and, 125–26
Newhouser, Hal, 26–28, 40, 46, 67
New Jersey Turnpike, 96
Newsom, Buck, 28–29

Newsweek, 187
New York Daily News, 146, 171, 312
New York Giants, 120
  1945, 12, 22, 23
  1951, 101–3, *102*
    vs. Dodgers, 106–14
New York Mets, 125
  1962, 167–68
  1965, 168
  1968, 169
  1969, 165–70, 174–75, 177–87
    World Series, 163, 180–87
  2001, 313
New York Post, 145–46
New York Times, 10, 83, 107–8, 118, 171, 312
New York Yankees. *See also* Maris, Roger
  Mantle's death and, 242–44
  Stengel and, 165
  1941, 48–49
  1945, 12, 22, 23
    vs. Senators, 20–21
  1947, 53, 61
  1948, 60–61, 64–65, 66, 72, 74
  1951, 98–101
    World Series, 99, 113, 114, 115, *115*
  1961, 134–36
    vs. Senators, 137–38
    vs. Tigers, 149
    World Series, 154–55
  1980, 217, 226
  1998, 291, 294–95
  2001, 208, 313, 315, 333–34
    World Series, 335–47
Nichols, Terry, 241
Nicholson, Bill, 24
Niekro, Joe, 225
Niggeling, Johnny, 13
Nightengale, Bob, 317, 320, 326–27
Nightline (TV show), 215, *215*
9-11 terrorist attacks (2001), 310–13, 325–26,
  337
Nixon, Richard, 134, 141, 163, 170–72, 191,
  197–98, 209
Nixon, Russ, 154
Nolan, Gary, 195, 204
Noles, Dickie, 230–31
Nomo, Hideo, 241–42, 314
Nomura, Hideki, 242
Norman, Fred, 195
Norris, Mike, 218
Northey, Ron, 16–17
Now Pitching—Bob Feller, 74

Oakland A's, 193, 217–18, 265, 315
  McGwire and, 265–66, 270–71, 291
O'Connell, Danny, 157
ODonnell, Kenny, 126
Ogle, Jim, 136, 149
Oglivie, Ben, 223
Oklahoma City terrorist bombing (1995),
  240–41
Oklahoma Toad (Frishberg), 26

O'Malley, Martin, 318
O'Malley, Walter, 127
Onassis, Aristotle, 182
Onassis, Jackie Kennedy, 182
O'Neill, Harry, 11
O'Neill, Paul, 341
O'Neill, Steve, 43–44, 46
Operation Coronet, 35
Operation Olympic, 35
Orix Blue Wave, 315
Otis, Amos, 229
Ott, Mel, 22
Outlaw, Jimmy, 40
Owen, Mickey, 21
Ozersky, Philip, 298–99

Packwood, Bob, 252
Pafko, Andy, 24
Page, Joe, 53, 61
Paige, Leroy ("Satchel"), 62–65, *63,* 268
Palestine, 55
Palmeiro, Rafael, 255
Palmer, Jim, 180–82
Park, Chan Ho, 324–25
Parker, Dave, 223
Passeau, Claude, 24
Pastore, Frank, 216
Patkin, Max, 60
Patriotism, 313, 331
  World War II and, 8–10, 13, 15
Patterson, John, 131
Patterson, Robert, 14–15
Pavano, Carl, 297–98
Peanuts, 96
Pearl Harbor, 9, 47, 49, 311
Peck, Gregory, 55, 108–9
Pentagon terrorist attacks (2001), 310–13,
  325–26, 337
Perez, Odalis, 308
Perez, Tony, 194, 203
Pershing, John J., 23
Pesky, Johnny, 53, 60–61
Peterson, Gaylin, 199
Petrocelli, Rico, 205
Pettitte, Andy, 336, *336*–37, 343
Phi Delta Theta, 250
Philadelphia A's, 23, 41, 120
Philadelphia Phillies, 1980, 222–26
  1980 World Series, 227–34
Philadelphia Stars, 19
Pierce, Billy, 138
Pieretti, Marino, 42
Piersall, Jimmy, 166–67
Pignatano, Joe, 166
Pinch hitters, 232
Piniella, Lou, 314–15, 334
Pitching, 273, 314. *See also specific pitchers and
  pitches*
  Martin and, 217–18
  Paige and, 62–65
Pittsburgh Courier, 18
Pittsburgh Pirates, *99,* 167, 222, 223, 282

Polaroid Land cameras, 55
Polio epidemics, 8, *142,* 142–43
Pollet, Howie, 53
Polo Grounds, 107, 165–66, 167
Ponson, Sidney, 208–9
Posada, Jorge, 342
Postal Service, U.S., 114
Potsdam Declaration, 36
Potter, Charles E., 119
Potter, Nelson, 44, 82
Povich, Maury, 6
Povich, Shirley, 6, 42–43, 127–29, 201–2,
    239–40, 258–59
Powell, Boog, 150, 181, 183
Powers, Dave, 126
Powers, Francis Gary, 129–30
Prager, Joshua Harris, 114
Presidential election of 2001, 305–6
Presidential Unit Citation, 22
Pressley, Sue Anne, 240–41
Price, Jackie, 60
Price, Melvin, 17
Pride of the Marines (movie), 45
Prokopec, Luke, 321
Puckett, Kirby, 295
Puello, Manuel, 285
Purkey, Bob, 166–67

Qualls, Jimmy, 174
Quesada, Pete, 157–60
Quill, Michael J., 108
Quisenberry, Dan, 220, 228, 229, 232

Radio, 45, 140
Radio Peiping, 108
Radius Defense and Engineering, 331–32
Randolph, Willie, 226
Raschi, Vic, 67
Rathbun, Bill, 335–36
Rationing, in World War II, 7–8
Rawlings Adirondack, 299
Rayburn, Sam, 20–21
Reagan, Ronald, 222, 234, 246, 251
Reed, Rick, 269
Reed, Ron, 180, 228
Reese, Pee Wee, 37, 109–10
Regan, Phil, 253
Reid, T. R., 242
Remlinger, Mike, 308
Reserve clauses, 208–9
Reston, James, 191–92, 200
Reyan, Leonel Fernandez, 285
Reyes, Dennis, 286
Reynolds, Allie, 17–18, 61
RFK (Robert F. Kennedy) Stadium, 127–28,
    158, 170
Rice, Jim, 193–94
Richard, J. R., 222–23
Richards, Paul, 27, 152
Rickert, Marv, 80
Rickey, Branch, 40, 62, 81, 100, 107
Ride, Sally, 251

Rideau Crusher, 326
Ringle, Ken, 116
Ripken, Bill, 247–49, 253, 256
Ripken, Cal, Jr., 240, 245–62, *252,* 267–68
    ending of streak, 294–96
    last season (2001), 308–9, 318–19
Ripken, Cal, Sr., 247–49, 251, 260–61
Ripken, Fred, 248
Ripken, Kelly, 253, 255, 261
Ripken, Rachel, 253, 255, 261
Ripken, Ryan, 253, 255, 261
Rivera, Jim, 126
Rivera, Mariano, 339–40, 345–46
Rizzuto, Phil, 61, 64–65, 98, 153
Roberto Clemente Award, 249–50
Robinson, Brooks, 252, 256, 328–29
    1969 World Series, 183, *184,* 185
Robinson, Eddie, 76
Robinson, Frank, 180, 181, 183, 185, 194
Robinson, Jackie, 19, 40, 53, 62, 171
    1951 season, 106–7, 109–10
Robinson, Kerry, 316
Rockefeller, Nelson, 182
Rock 'n' roll, 115
Rodriguez, Alex, 306–7, 308–9
Rodriguez, Wilfredo, 323–24
Rommel, Eddie, 41
Roosevelt, Franklin Delano, 3–6, *4,* 20, 21
    "green light letter," 4, *5,* 6, 48
Rose, Pete, 174, 194, 224–25, 251
    1975 World Series, 204, 206, 209
    1980 World Series, 228, 229, 230–31, 233,
      234
Rosenberg, Julius and Ethel, 119
Ross, Charlie, 39
Rozelle, Pete, 192
RSO Shows, 89–90
Rusch, Glendon, 278
Ruth, George Herman ("Babe"), 259
    Bush and, *69,* 69–70
    death of, 55, *68,* 68–70, *71*
    home run record, 134, 136, 144, 149, 150,
      153
    McGwire and, 286–87
Ryan, Nolan, 175

Sabin, Albert, 143
Safe rooms, 331–32
Sain, Johnny, 78–80, *79,* 83
St. Louis Browns, 120
    Gray and, 32–33
    1941, *vs.* Senators, 37, 38, *38,* 39
    1943, 21
    1944, 21
    1945, 11–12, 17, 21, 23, 43
      vs. Tigers, 43–45, *45,* 46
    1948, 70–71
    1951, 104–5
St. Louis Cardinals, 15. *See also* McGwire,
    Mark
    1945, 11–12, 15, 18, 24
    1946, 53

1948, 54, 78
1969, 167
1997, 272–73
1998, *vs.* Cubs, 288–91, *290*
Salaries, 224, 238, 317–18
   cap on, 238–40
   free agency and, 208–9, 214, 306–7
Salinger, J. D., 95
Salk, Jonas, 143
Salkeld, Bill, 80
Salk vaccine, *142,* 142–43
Sammy Sosa Charity Foundation, 299
Sanders, Reggie, 343
San Diego Clippers, 320
San Diego Padres, 168, 293, 319–21
San Francisco Giants, 120, 167, 179, 218–19,
   285. *See also* Bonds, Barry
San Francisco United Way, 330
Santo, Ron, 175
Santos, Valerio de los, 292
Schilling, Curt, 336, 340–41, 344–45, 346
Schmidt, Mike, 223–24, 225, 226
   1980 World Series, 228, 229–30, 231–32
Schmidt, Susan, 332
School desegregation, 115, 131
School prayer, 55
Schwartz, Alan, 207
Scott, Everett, 249
Seasons
   1945, 3–49
   1948, 53–91
   1951, 95–121
   1961, 125–60
   1969, 163–87
   1975, 191–210
   1980, 213–34
   1995, 237–62
   1998, 265–301
   2001, 305–47
Seattle Mariners, 214–16, 238, 314–15,
   333–34
Seattle Pilots, 168
Seaver, Tom, *164,* 174, 175, 179–80
   1969 World Series, 180, 182–83, 186–87
Second World War. *See* World War II
Security, terrorism and, 313
Segregation, 18–19, 115. *See also* Integration
   Freedom Riders and, 130–33
Seinfeld (TV show), 274
Seitz, Peter, 207–8
Selective Service Act (1948), 56–57
Selig, Bud, 254, 296, 306–7, 309, 313, 336
Selkirk, George, 145, 169
Servais, Scott, 289
Servicemen's Readjustment Act (1944), 115,
   116
Sewell, Luke, *37,* 44
"Sexual Behavior in the Human Male"
   (Kinsey), 55
Shadow government, 332
Shalala, Donna, 251
Shannon, Mike, 298

Shea Stadium, 187. *See also* New York Mets
Shecter, Lenny, 145–46
Sheinin, Dave, 318–19
Shelters, 140–41, 331–32
Shepard, Alan, 132, *133, 134,* 175–77
Shepard, Bert, 14–15, 30–32
Shore, Dinah, 54, 115
Short, Bob, 159–60
Short, Joseph, 112
Short relievers, 218
Showalter, Buck, 242–43, 275
Shumpert, Terry, 321
Siebert, Dick, 42
Simpson, O.J., 251, 252
Sinatra, Frank, 45, 185
Singleton, Ken, 256
Sipple, Oliver, 199
Sisler, Dick, 102
60 Minutes (TV show), 227
Skelton, Red, 96
Slaughter, Enos, 48, 53
Smith, Bud, 314
Smith, Curt, 268
Smith, Dave, 225
Smith, Kate, 9
Smith, Ozzie, 256–57
Smith, Red, 171, 201–2
Smith, Wendell, 18–19
Snafu, 116
Snider, Duke, 109–12, 113, 114, 166–67, 273
Snow, J. T., 329
Soccer, 192
Socha, Tim, 299
Sophomore jinx, 247
Soriano, Alfonso, 343, 345, 346
Sosa, Mireya, 283, 284
Sosa, Sammy, 283–85, 314
   1998 season, 269, 273–93, *276,* 296–97,
      299–301
Southworth, Billy, 78, 80
Soviet Union, 112, 251
   Berlin and, 55–58, 83, 85–91, 137, 138–41
   Cuba and, 129–30
   Olympic hockey (1980) and, 213–14
   space race and, 133–34
Space exploration, 132, *133,* 133, *134,* 134,
   164, 175–77, 251
Spahn, Warren, 37, 78–80, *79,* 103
Speaker, Tris, 82
Speier, Justin, 285
Spence, Stan, 18
Spencer, Duncan, 215
Spencer, Shane, 340, 342
Sporting News, 15, 193, 266
Sports Illustrated, 276
Springer, Dennis, 328
Spring training, wartime restrictions on,
   11–13
Sputnik, 134
Stalin, Joseph, 58, 139
Stallard, Tracy, 153–54
Stanky, Eddie, 78, 81

Stanton, Mike, 341
Stargell, Willie, 223
Starr, Kenneth, 274, 278, 287
Star Wars (movie), 221
Steinbrenner, George, 217, 226, 344
Stengel, Casey, 98–101, *99*, 147, 163, 165–70, 186
Stennett, Rennie, 219
Stephens, Royce, 88
Stewart, Bill, 82, 83
Stoneham, Horace, 127
Stratton, Monty, 31
Streetcar Named Desire, A (movie), 108
Stuart, Dick, 220
Suez Canal, 176–77
Sullivan, Ed, 54, 185
Summer Olympics (1996), 335–36
Sutcliffe, Rick, 219
Suzuki, Ichiro, 315
Swift, Bob, 105
Swindell, Greg, 342
Swoboda, Ron, 177, 183, *184*, 185, 186
Symbionese Liberation Army (SLA), 200

Taft, Robert, 108
"Take Me Out to the Ball Game" (song), 267, 286
Tasby, Willie, 156
Taylor, Art, 280
Taylor, Elizabeth, 109
Taylor, Ron, 177–78, 182
Telecommunications, 119–20
Telephones, 95, 120
Television, 54, 95, 96, 114, 200, 207, 217, 227, 274
Terrorism, 306, 331–32, 335–36
    9-11 (2001), 310–13, 325–26, 337
    Oklahoma City (1995), 240–41
Texaco Star Theater (TV show), 54, 96
Texas Rangers, 159, 337, 339
    Nomo and, 241–42
    Rodriguez and, 306–7
    Sosa and, 284
Thomas, Frank, 291
Thompson, Hank, 107
Thomson, Bobby, 106, 107
    1951 home run, xii, *102*, 111–12, 113–14
Thomson, John, 321
Throneberry, Marv, 165, 166
Thurman, Mike, 297
Tiant, Luis, 194, 202, 203, 204–5
Tibbets, Paul W., Jr., 35
Tiger Stadium, 276–77. *See also* Detroit Tigers
Toledo Mud Hens, 15
Topping, Dan, 135
Torgeson, Earl, 78
Toronto Blue Jays, 214–16, 246
Torpey, John, 280
Torre, Joe, 294, 309, 334
    2001 World Series, 337, 340–41, 343, 345
Trachsel, Steve, 289

Transport Workers Union (TWU), 108
Travel restrictions, during World War II, 11–12
Travis, Cecil, 37, 38, 47, 48
Trillo, Manny, 225, 232
Trimble, Joe, 146
Tripp, Linda, 278
Trout, Paul "Dizzy," 27–28
Truman (McCullough), 35–36, 57–58
Truman, Bess, 37, 38, *38*, 39, 58
Truman, Harry, 20, 22, 23, 37–38, 96–97, 108, 120
    atomic bomb and, 34–36
    Cold War and, 56–58, 85, 86, 88, 90, 112
    Griffith Stadium, *37*, 38–39, 96–98
Truman, Margaret, 35, 58
Tully, Andrew F., 128
Turner, Ted, 217
Twombly, Wells, 209

Ullrich, Sandy, 21
Unemployment, 191, 198
United Airlines Flight 93, 311
United Flight 175, 310
UNIVAC, 120
University of Maryland, 13–14
Unser, Del, 226, 228, 232
Uribe, Juan, 321
USA Today, 286, 296, 312, 344

Vandenberg, Arthur, 39
Vander Meer, Johnny, 216, 291
Van Tien Dung, 191
Variety, 54
V-E Day (1945), 22, 37
Veeck, Bill, 58–60, *59*, 67, 104–5, 158–59, 214
    Paige and, 62–65
Vernon, Mickey, 60, 156, 157–58, 169
Veterans Stadium, 227. *See also* Philadelphia Phillies
Victory gardens, World War II, 8
Vietnam War, 90, 115, 163–64, 170, 177, 182–83, 191–92
Vina, Fernando, 317
Vinson, Fred, 39
Virdon, Bill, 226
Vitamin B12, 55
Voices of the Game (Smith), 268
Vukovich, John, 225

Wagner, Paul, 272
Wagner, Robert, 167, 185
Waitkus, Eddie, 106
Walker, Harry, 53
Walker, Hub, 43–44
Walker, Rube, 110–11
Wallace, George, 199
Walling, Denny, 225
Wall Street Journal, 114
War bonds, 9
War Mobilization and Reconstruction, 16
Warning track power, 33

War rationing, 7–8
War Relief Fund, 30
Warren, Earl, 132, 185
Washington Nationals, 6
Washington Post, 6, 21, 36, 85, 97, 128, 177, 241, 262, 305, 312
Washington Redskins, 14, 40, 127–28, 159
Washington Senators, 125, 159–60
    Hodges and, 169
    1941, *vs.* Browns, 37, *38,* 38–39
    1945, 20–21, 23, 28–30
        spring training, 12–15, 17–18
        vs. Dodgers, 30–31
        vs. Red Sox, 31–32
        vs. Tigers, 40–43
    1951 Opening Day, 96–98
    1961, 128–29, 156–60
        Opening Day, 125–27, 129
        vs. Yankees, 137–38
Washington Star, 129
Watergate scandal (1972), 171, 197–98
Weaver, Earl, 170, 246, 252
    1969 World Series, 180, *181,* 182
Webb, Del, 128, 129
Webb, Skeeter, 43–44
Weir, Tom, 285
Weis, Al, 185
Wells, David, 273, 320
Weston, Russell, 279
Westrum, Wes, 168, 169
What If? question, 46–47, 48
Wheeler, Earle, 176–77
White, Frank, 229, 231, 233, 234
White, Paul, 308
Wiles, Tim, 268
Wilhelm, Hoyt, 151–52
Wilks, Ted, 24
Will, George, 209
Williams, Bernie, 339–40
Williams, Billy, 175
Williams, Dick, 194
Williams, Eugene, 88–89
Williams, Marvin, 19
Williams, Matt, 336, 336–37, 341
Williams, Ted, 169–70, 171, 195, 220, 319
    World War II and, 6, 47, 48
    1948 season, 53, 60–61, 72, 74, 76
Williams, Woody, 307
Willis, Bruce, 279
Wills, Maury, 249
Wilson, Charles E., 108
Wilson, Hack, 285
Wilson, Willie, 229–30, 233–34
Winner Never Quits, A (movie), 33
Winnie, Ralph, 46–47, 48
Winsett, Tom, 26
Winter Olympics (1980), 213–14
Winters, Shelley, 109
Wise, Rick, 194
Witasick, Jay, 343–44

Wolff, Roger, 13
Womack, Tony, 343
Women in the workforce, 119
Woodling, Gene, 156
Woodstock (1969), 163
World Book Year Book (1976, ed.), 191, 192, 209
World Series
    McGwire and, 270–71
    1941, 48–49
    1945, 43–46
    1946, 53
    1947, 53, 61
    1948, 74, 77, 78, 80–83
    1951, 99, 114, 115, *115*
    1961, 154–55
    1969, 163, 180–87
    1975, 197–98, 200, 201–7, 209–10
    1980, 227–34
    1989, 270
    1990, 271
    1997, 347
    1998, 320
    2001, 333–34, 335–47
World Trade Center terrorist attacks (2001), 310–13, 325–26, 337
World War II, 3–10, 20–22, 34–35, 201, 241
    atomic bomb, 34–36
    baseball restrictions, 11–13
    desegregation, 18–19
    G. I. Bill and, 116
    Hodges and, 169
    lingo, 115–16
    manpower shortage, 15–19
    Roosevelt's "green light letter," 4, 5, 6, 48
    surrender, 36–39
    victory celebrations, 22, 23, 37
Wrigley, Phil, 202
Wyse, Hank, 24

Yale University, 69–70
Yankee Stadium, 335. *See also* New York Yankees
    Gehrig and, 258
    home runs and, 153
    Maris and, 135
    Ruth and, 68–69
    2001 World Series, *337,* 338–39
Yastrzemski, Carl, 153, 193, 206
"Yip, Yip, Yaphank" (musical), 9
York, Rudy, 135, 276–77
Yoshimura, Wendy, 200
You Can Negotiate Anything (Cohen), 113
Young, Dick, 112, 136, 171
Young, Don, 174
Young, Milton, 138

Zaccagnini, Anthony, 278
Zwerg, Jim, 131

BILL GILBERT is the author of twenty-one books, including the *New York Times* bestseller and Notable Book of the Year *The Duke of Flatbush*, with Duke Snider, *Real Grass, Real Heroes* with Dom DiMaggio and *How to Talk to Anyone, Anytime, Anywhere*, with Larry King. A former sportswriter and news reporter for *The Washington Post*, he lives in the suburbs of Washington, D.C.